SAT®
Practice Tests

ADVANCED
PRACTICE
SERIES

◇ For the Redesigned SAT

◇ Full Tests and Answer Explanations

◇ Created for Intensive Timed Practice

ies
TEST
PREP

Authors
Khalid Khashoggi, CEO IES
Arianna Astuni, President IES

Editorial
Patrick Kennedy, Executive Editor
Christopher Carbonell, Editorial Director
Marc Wallace, Mathematics Editor

Design
Kay Kang, www.kaygraphic.com

Contributors

Arianna Astuni	Chris Holliday
Danielle Barkley	Nathaniel Hunt
Victoria Brinson	Daniel Lee
Christopher Carbonell	Tallis Moore
Robert Collins	Joseph Miller
Patrick Kennedy	Rajvi Patel
Khalid Khashoggi	Marc Wallace
Philip Kowalski	Cassidy Yong
Nancy Hoffman	

Published by IES Publications
www.IESpublications.com
© IES Publications, 2016

ON BEHALF OF

Integrated Educational Services, Inc.
355 Main Street
Metuchen, NJ 08840
www.ies2400.com

We would like to thank the IES Publications team as well as the teachers and students at IES2400 who have contributed to the creation of this book. We would also like to thank our Chief Marketing Officer, Sonia Choi, for her invaluable input.

ISBN-10: 0-9964064-7-6

ISBN-13: 978-0-9964064-7-5

QUESTIONS OR COMMENTS? Visit us at ies2400.com

TABLE OF CONTENTS

Dear student,

When we started IES Publications, our mission was to translate the IES classroom experience into books that any student, anywhere, could use to his or her advantage. Thus, we created titles that target specific ACT and New SAT topic areas, much as we teach them at our IES campuses: each section, each question type, is singled out and given its own keen analysis. This approach led our students to perfect-2400 scores on the Old SAT, and is helping students secure New SAT scores in the 1500-1600 range even as you read these words.

Yet one crucial element of our approach had yet to make it into print. Our students have always valued the opportunity to try their skills on complete practice exams. A test-taker's strengths and weaknesses are perhaps never more apparent than on a full run of Reading, Writing, and Mathematics questions. And now, it is time to see your own test-taking abilities in their totality. You can use this Full Practice Test book to replicate the test-day experience, to figure out how to time each section, and to develop the right mentality for approaching the New SAT overall. Or you can use this volume in tandem with the rest of the Advanced Practice Series: discover where you need to make progress using our Reading and Grammar books, then open this volume and accelerate that progress.

How you make the most of these five practice tests is your decision. But however you decide, we can guarantee you that you will have both illuminating answer explanations and the resources of ies2400.com to back you up. We believe that you can take control of the test. Believe it yourself, turn to Test 1, and practice your way to your target score!

I wish you all the best in your test-taking endeavors.

Sincerely,

Arianna Astuni,
President, IES

TEST 1

Reading Test
65 MINUTES, 52 QUESTIONS

Turn to Section 1 of your answer sheet to answer the questions in this section.

Each passage or pair of passages below is followed by a number of questions. After reading each passage or pair, choose the best answer to each question based on what is stated or implied in the passage or passages and in any accompanying graphics (such as a table or graph).

Questions 1-10 are based on the following passage.

This passage is adapted from Charlotte Brontë, *Jane Eyre*, originally published in 1847. In this chapter, Jane, who works as a tutor and governess, describes a change in employment.

A new chapter in a novel is something like a new scene in a play, and when I draw up the curtain this time, reader, you must fancy you see a room in the George Inn at Millcote,
Line with such large figured papering on the walls as inn rooms
5 have; such a carpet, such furniture, such ornaments on the mantelpiece, such prints, including a portrait of George the Third, and another of the Prince of Wales, and a representation of the death of Wolfe. All this is visible to you by the light of an oil lamp hanging from the ceiling, and by that of an
10 excellent fire, near which I sit in my cloak and bonnet; my muff and umbrella lie on the table, and I am warming away the numbness and chill contracted by sixteen hours' exposure to the rawness of an October day: I left Lowton at four o'clock a.m., and the Millcote town clock is now just striking eight.
15 Reader, though I look comfortably accommodated, I am not very tranquil in my mind. I thought when the coach stopped here there would be some one to meet me; I looked anxiously round as I descended the wooden steps the "boots" placed for my convenience, expecting to hear my name
20 pronounced, and to see some description of carriage waiting to convey me to Thornfield. Nothing of the sort was visible, and when I asked a waiter if any one had been to inquire after a Miss Eyre, I was answered in the negative: so I had no resource but to request to be shown into a private room:
25 and here I am waiting, while all sorts of doubts and fears are troubling my thoughts.
It is a very strange sensation to inexperienced youth to feel itself quite alone in the world, cut adrift from every connection, uncertain whether the port to which it is bound
30 can be reached, and prevented by many impediments from

returning to that it has quitted. The charm of adventure sweetens that sensation, the glow of pride warms it; but then the throb of fear disturbs it; and fear with me became predominant when half-an-hour elapsed and still I was alone. I
35 bethought myself to ring the bell.
"Is there a place in this neighbourhood called Thornfield?" I asked of the waiter who answered the summons.
"Thornfield? I don't know, ma'am; I'll inquire at the bar."
40 He vanished, but reappeared instantly—
"Is your name Eyre, Miss?"
"Yes."
"Person here waiting for you."
I jumped up, took my muff and umbrella, and hastened
45 into the inn-passage: a man was standing by the open door, and in the lamp-lit street I dimly saw a one-horse conveyance.
"This will be your luggage, I suppose?" said the man rather abruptly when he saw me, pointing to my trunk in the passage.
50 "Yes." He hoisted it on to the vehicle, which was a sort of car, and then I got in; before he shut me up, I asked him how far it was to Thornfield.
"A matter of six miles."
"How long shall we be before we get there?"
55 "Happen an hour and a half."
He fastened the car door, climbed to his own seat outside, and we set off. Our progress was leisurely, and gave me ample time to reflect; I was content to be at length so near the end of my journey; and as I leaned back in the comfortable though
60 not elegant conveyance, I meditated much at my ease.
"I suppose," thought I, "judging from the plainness of the servant and carriage, my new employer is not a very dashing person: so much the better; I never lived amongst fine people but once, and I was very miserable with them. I wonder if
65 she lives alone except this little girl; if so, and if she is in any degree amiable, I shall surely be able to get on with her; I will do my best; it is a pity that doing one's best does not always answer."

CONTINUE →

1

Which choice best summarizes the passage?

A) A young woman reflects on a lifestyle that has ultimately left her unsatisfied.

B) A young woman feels anxieties over unknown conditions.

C) A young woman finds herself in comfortable surroundings soon after a series of disappointments.

D) A young woman yearns for the generosity that her employers have shown her in the past.

2

The passage most clearly indicates that Jane is

A) haughty.

B) saddened.

C) isolated.

D) embarrassed.

3

Which choice provides the best evidence for the answer to the previous question?

A) Lines 15-16 ("Reader, though . . . my mind")

B) Lines 27-31 ("It is a . . . quitted")

C) Lines 51-56 ("He hoisted . . . a half")

D) Lines 63-64 ("I never lived . . . with them")

4

In describing herself, Jane establishes a contrast between

A) emotion and outward appearance.

B) ambition and spiritual fulfillment.

C) education and practicality.

D) social position and individual talent.

5

As used in line 24, "resource" most nearly means

A) asset.

B) capability.

C) option.

D) advantage.

6

At the time of the events narrated in the passage, Jane is

A) reflecting on her literary and artistic ambitions.

B) recovering from a taxing day of travel.

C) desperately trying to forget recent events.

D) remembering a recent stroke of good fortune.

7

Which choice provides the best evidence for the answer to the previous question?

A) Lines 1-3 ("A new . . . Millcote")

B) Lines 10-14 ("my muff . . . striking eight")

C) Lines 33-35 ("then the throb . . . the bell")

D) Lines 57-58 ("Our progress . . . to reflect")

8

As used in line 31, "charm" nearly means

A) magic.

B) charisma.

C) uncertainty.

D) allure.

9

The dialogue in lines 47-55 ("This will be . . . a half") is primarily concerned with

A) the practical details of the final stage of Jane's journey.

B) the unusual nature of the vehicle that will transport Jane's luggage.

C) the differing social statuses of Jane and the carriage driver.

D) an unacknowledged grudge that Jane holds against the carriage driver.

10

The "doubts and fears" that Jane describes in line 25 can most accurately be attributed to

A) a new and challenging obligation.

B) a departure from familiar settings.

C) the loss of a dear friend.

D) the poor manners of the people at the inn.

CONTINUE

Questions 11-21 are based on the following passage and supplementary material.

Adapted from Victoria Brinson, "Genome Sequencing: Unlocking the Future."

In April 2013, actress Angelina Jolie underwent a double mastectomy in order to avoid future susceptibility to breast cancer. At the time she opted for the surgery, Jolie had not
Line actually been diagnosed with the disease. She made the decision
5 to undergo the procedure after genetic testing revealed that her DNA contained a gene mutation that put her at a relatively high risk of breast and ovarian cancers.

Jolie's situation was only the latest high-profile episode in the history of a much-publicized field of inquiry—genomics,
10 the study of fundamental genetic structure. Scientists had been working, often in the public eye, towards making genome testing a reality for decades. The Human Genome Project, whose goal was to map the complete sequence of human DNA, was begun in 1990 and took 13 years and $2.7 billion
15 to complete. Rapid scientific and technological advancements throughout the first decade of the 21st century transformed genome testing from a theoretical possibility into a very real option. In 2010 an individual could get his or her genome mapped for around $50,000. By 2013 the cost was $5000, and
20 by 2015 the $1000 genome test had finally arrived.

Several genetic mutations or variants have been linked to specific diseases. Scientists have found links to Alzheimer's, Parkinson's, various cancers, and a multitude of other medical disorders. They have also explored the field
25 of pharmacogenomics, which examines the different drug responses of specific genomes. Cancer treatments in particular have been transformed through these studies. As scientists learned to differentiate between the genomes of various cancerous tumors, treatments became targeted, paving the way
30 for blanket chemotherapy to become obsolete.

Many welcome these new studies as preludes to a medical revolution, although the science itself has stirred up controversy. One of the biggest issues at stake is personal privacy, an issue highlighted by the sequencing and subsequent
35 publication of the HeLa genome in 2013. The descendants of cancer patient Henrietta Lacks (1920-1951), individuals who provided the tissue from which the genome was taken, were not consulted before the results were published. Because no permission had been given by Lacks or her living relatives,
40 this was a pretty clear-cut case, but what happens when permission is given by the donor, to the detriment of that donor's relatives? Organizations have arisen and legislation has been passed to try to limit such ethical problems, but dangers persist. If a person's genetic predispositions become
45 public property, will discrimination result? Dangers here could range from individuals being turned down for health insurance or certain jobs to the stigmatization of entire ethnic or genetic groups.

Also of high concern is the impact that knowledge of
50 genetic predispositions might have on individuals. There were two conflicting opinions published on February 15, 2013, in a *Wall Street Journal* exchange on this issue. Dr. Atul J. Butte, founder of a company that offers genome interpretation, insists that genomic knowledge is inherently
55 beneficial. If people are aware of the diseases they are more likely to develop, they can become proactive and take charge of their health. He feels that genome sequencing offers a whole new set of tools that people and their doctors can utilize. Although misreading of genomes does in fact
60 occur, such occurrences are rare, perhaps one in hundreds of thousands.

Others contend that this type of knowledge can do more harm than good. Dr. Robert Green, a medical geneticist who responded to Dr. Butte, argued that the flaws were
65 simply too deep. He expressed worry about the undue stress that could be placed on the healthcare system as millions of relatively healthy patients insist on a barrage of tests that are, in the final analysis, unnecessary. In addition, he maintained that science has not come to the point where
70 it can infallibly predict what effect many gene mutations might have on individuals who are otherwise sound: "Soon, there may be evidence to support the benefits of screening healthy individuals. But not today."

For better or worse, or perhaps both, the Human
75 Genome Project changed the world. It unlocked mysteries hidden deep within humankind. Whether it is the key to a disease-free future or a Pandora's Box of trouble will be seen, but probably "not today."

CONTINUE

Gene Tests: Growth of Laboratory Directory

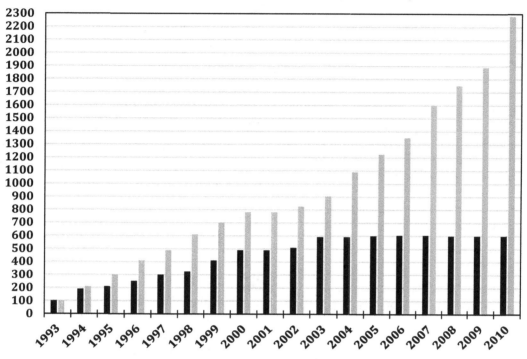

■ **Laboratories**   ▨ **Diseases for which testing is available**

11

Which choice best describes the developmental pattern of the passage?

A) A detailed account of a scientist's research on a particular treatment, followed by an explanation of the treatment's popularity.

B) A lighthearted anecdote taken from popular culture, followed by a more serious musing on the influence of a surgical operation.

C) An objective description of a revolutionary medical procedure, followed by an analytical consideration of the virtues and drawbacks of that procedure.

D) A summary of an organization's history and purpose followed by an impassioned argument against the ethics and practices of that organization.

12

In the first paragraph, the author mentions Angelina Jolie primarily in order to

A) quote a celebrity who has openly expressed doubt about the benefits of genome testing.

B) support the argument that widespread publicity and promotion have made genome testing more popular.

C) cite an example of a public figure who has undergone an apparently controversial procedure.

D) prove the author's point that everyone is susceptible to cancer and other life-changing diseases.

13

The passage indicates that genome testing

A) has become increasingly affordable and accessible to patients over the past few years.

B) has been met with much controversy regarding the accuracy and precision of a test's results.

C) has become popular mostly due to its endorsement by many celebrities and doctors.

D) has been found by researchers to produce more false diagnoses than real ones.

14

Which choice provides the best evidence for the answer to the previous question?

A) Lines 12-14 ("The Human . . . 1990")

B) Lines 18-20 ("In . . . arrived")

C) Lines 22-24 ("Scientists . . . disorders")

D) Lines 31-33 ("Many . . . controversy")

9

CONTINUE ➤

15

According to the passage, one advantage of genome testing is that it

A) helps patients to decide which treatments to take for their illnesses and prompts them to change their unhealthy lifestyles.

B) allows patients to understand the status of their health without having to worry about dangerous treatments and risky procedures.

C) accurately diagnoses and treats psychological as well as physical diseases while still being affordable and convenient.

D) eliminates the need for more general chemotherapy and allows doctors to administer treatments tailored to a specific tumor.

16

Critics of genome testing argue that the practice could

A) result in the marginalization of certain demographics.

B) leave otherwise healthy patients feeling a heightened sense of worry about their risk for illness.

C) gradually become more expensive because a person must test multiple times for different diseases.

D) lead to the publication of a person's medical and legal records without the patient's consent.

17

Which choice provides the best evidence for the answer to the previous question?

A) Lines 33-35 ("One of the . . . 2013")

B) Lines 44-48 ("If a person's . . . groups")

C) Lines 65-68 ("He expressed . . . unnecessary")

D) Lines 69-71 ("science has . . . sound")

18

As used in line 52, "exchange" most nearly means

A) trade.

B) debate.

C) deal.

D) quarrel.

19

As used in line 65, "deep" most nearly means

A) meaningful.

B) abstract.

C) catastrophic.

D) considerable.

20

According to the graph, between 1993 and 2010, the number of laboratories had increased by approximately

A) 500.

B) 600.

C) 1500.

D) 2250.

21

The author of the passage would most likely respond to the information in the graph with

A) approval, because the author had expressed admiration for scientists studying genome testing throughout the passage.

B) ambivalence, because the author has acknowledged that there are both benefits and drawbacks to genome testing that will not be fully realized in the present.

C) apathy, because the graph only concerns the growth of laboratories and not the spread of genome testing, which is the focus of the passage.

D) aversion, because the author is wary of the possible social and scientific consequences that genome testing could have.

CONTINUE

Questions 22-32 are based on the following passage and supplementary material.

Adapted from a recent article in an astrophysics magazine, this passage considers new technology in space exploration.

One of the reasons that space travel is so expensive is that, at present, to travel to and through space requires heavy single-use rockets. Heavy rockets require immense amounts
Line of fuel to generate thrust, so rockets are constructed in tank-
5 like sections that can detach as fuel is consumed. While this design increases rocket efficiency, it also makes travel or cargo shipment by rocket significantly more expensive than travel by airplane. A plane and a rocket of similar capacity cost about the same amount of money to build, but the cost per ton for a
10 given voyage is many orders of magnitude more expensive by rocket than by plane because the rocket can be deployed only once, whereas an airplane can complete many trips and thereby decrease the cost per ton over a longer lifetime.

Reusable rockets offer some promise for lowering the
15 cost per flight, and organizations like the American company SpaceX and the UK-based company Reaction Engines are developing rockets of just this sort. Rockets are not the only way to generate propulsion in space, however. Another type of engine sends charged particles called ions from a positively-
20 charged anode to a negatively-charged cathode; midway to the cathode, the ions form a plasma, or charged gas, and are trapped in a magnetic field where an electron beam neutralizes the ions and pushes them out of the engine, generating propulsion.

These ion engines, particularly engines of the type known
25 as Hall thrusters, have made over 200 flights to space in the past 45 years. The exhaust of the Hall thruster can reach a speed of 10 to 80 kilometers per second in order to push a spacecraft forward, but the engine itself only lasts about 10,000 hours because the ion flow degrades the wall of the engine.
30 An ion engine is extremely efficient compared to other means of propulsion—as many as 100 million times more

efficient than engines that propel vessels using chemical reactions—and such efficiency suits these engines to long missions. Unfortunately, with a limited lifespan for the
35 engine, a trip outside of Earth's orbit—for example, to Mars—would require multiple engines and more money.

Fortunately, the Electric Propulsion team at the French National Center for Scientific Research recently developed a solution to the degradation of the engine
40 wall: the team removed the wall so that the plasma would not interact with the engine at all. While this design increases the longevity of the engine, the rearrangement of the cathode and anode caused a decrease in thrust. As lead researcher Julien Vaudolon explains, "If the
45 magnetic field lines cross the anode, a large portion of hot electrons will be collected at the anode and won't take part in the ionization of the xenon atoms, resulting in high discharge current, low ionization degree, and consequently, low performance level."
50 In the next stage of experiments, the team moved the anode so that it was outside the magnetic field, an arrangement which retained the longevity benefits of the wall-less thruster without compromising thrust. The engine is not yet fully optimized, but with these
55 developments some of the limitations of the Hall thruster are no longer problematic.

There is a further benefit to the new wall-less thruster. Previously, because the deterioration of the wall was unpredictable, researchers faced considerable
60 challenges in creating computer models and simulations for their optimization studies. Now, according to Vaudolon, "The major difficulty in developing predictive simulations lies in modeling the interaction between plasma and wall." By removing the wall, the team also
65 removed the most unpredictable part of the system. The possibility of reliable computer modeling will allow researchers to develop more efficient Hall thrusters, and enable scientists better to study parts of the system that are less-understood, such as the behavior of the plasma.

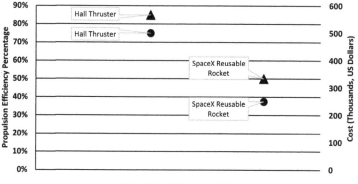

Cost and Propulsion Comparison of Rocket Engines

CONTINUE

22

This passage serves mainly to discuss

A) an interdisciplinary experiment that has helped to popularize reusable rockets.

B) a few ambitious space exploration goals that can be accomplished using Hall thrusters.

C) an approach to rocket design that has led to disputes among researchers.

D) a few of the virtues and drawbacks presented by a relatively new technology.

23

In the first paragraph, the author compares travel by rocket to travel by plane in order to

A) indicate why planes have not been used in space exploration.

B) show why typical rockets are less cost-efficient than planes.

C) establish the average lifespan of a reusable rocket.

D) suggest that commercial airlines and space exploration companies often collaborate.

24

The description in lines 18-23 ("Another . . . propulsion") serves mainly to explain

A) a technological breakthrough that made Space X and Reaction Engines famous.

B) how an ion engine functions.

C) why ion engines are so large.

D) why ion engines are especially cost-effective.

25

The experiments performed by Julien Vaudolon and his team were designed to address

A) a liability of the technology used in ion engines.

B) the exorbitant cost of creating ion engines.

C) whether ion engines can operate without forming plasma.

D) problems with rocket design that can only be understood using computer simulations.

26

Which choice provides the best evidence for the answer to the previous question?

A) Lines 14-17 ("Reusable rockets . . . this sort")

B) Lines 37-40 ("Fortunately, the . . . engine wall")

C) Lines 41-43 ("While this . . . in thrust")

D) Lines 65-69 ("The possibility . . . plasma")

27

As used in line 26, "reach" most nearly means

A) grasp.

B) extend.

C) attain.

D) accomplish.

28

Compared to earlier ion thrusters, Julien Vaudolon's thruster model is

A) more expensive.

B) more reliant on chemical reactions.

C) less unstable.

D) less durable.

29

Which choice provides the best evidence for the answer to the previous question?

A) Lines 30-34 ("An ion engine . . . missions")

B) Lines 44-49 ("If the magnetic . . . level")

C) Lines 54-56 ("The engine . . . problematic")

D) Lines 64-65 ("By removing . . . system")

30

As used in line 65, "system" most nearly means

A) computer program.

B) means of cooperation.

C) physical arrangement.

D) research methodology.

CONTINUE

31

The graph following the passage offers evidence that the Hall Thruster

A) is more cost-effective than the SpaceX Reusable Rocket.
B) can reach its top speed more efficiently than the SpaceX Reusable Rocket.
C) has better fuel efficiency than the SpaceX Reusable Rocket.
D) is less likely to to generate adequate propulsion for a mission to Mars.

32

The author would most likely attribute the differences in cost per flight between the Hall Thruster and SpaceX Reusable Rocket as represented in the graph to

A) engine lifespan.
B) magnetic fields.
C) cathode and anode locations.
D) fuel type.

Questions 33-42 are based on the following passages.

Passage 1 is an excerpt from *Walden* (1854) by Henry David Thoreau; Passage 2 is an excerpt from the speech "Americans and the English" (1872) delivered by Mark Twain.

Passage 1

　　　The nation itself, with all its so-called internal improvements, which, by the way are all external and superficial, is just such an unwieldy and overgrown
Line establishment, cluttered with furniture and tripped up by its
5　own traps, ruined by luxury and heedless expense, by want of calculation and a worthy aim, as the million households in the land; and the only cure for it, as for them, is in a rigid economy, a stern and more than Spartan simplicity of life and elevation of purpose. It lives too fast. Men think that it
10　is essential that the Nation have commerce, and export ice, and talk through a telegraph, and ride thirty miles an hour, without a doubt, whether they do or not; but whether we should live like baboons or like men, is a little uncertain. If we do not get out sleepers,[1] and forge rails, and devote days
15　and nights to the work, but go to tinkering upon our lives to improve them, who will build railroads? And if railroads are not built, how shall we get to heaven in season? But if we stay at home and mind our business, who will want railroads? We do not ride on the railroad; it rides upon us.
20　Did you ever think what those sleepers are that underlie the railroad? Each one is a man, an Irishman, or a Yankee man. The rails are laid on them, and they are covered with sand, and the cars run smoothly over them. They are sound sleepers, I assure you. And every few years a new lot is
25　laid down and run over; so that, if some have the pleasure of riding on a rail, others have the misfortune to be ridden upon. And when they run over a man that is walking in his sleep, a supernumerary sleeper in the wrong position, and wake him up, they suddenly stop the cars, and make a hue
30　and cry about it, as if this were an exception. . .
　　　Why should we live with such hurry and waste of life? We are determined to be starved before we are hungry. Men say that a stitch in time saves nine, and so they take a thousand stitches today to save nine tomorrow. As for *work*,
35　we haven't any of any consequence.

Passage 2

　　　This is an age of progress, and America is a progressive land. A great and glorious land, too—a land which has developed a Washington, a Franklin, a Wm. M. Tweed, a Longfellow, a Motley, a Jay Gould, a Samuel C. Pomeroy,[2]
40　a recent Congress which has never had its equal (in some respects), and a United States Army which conquered sixty Indians in eight months by tiring them out which is much

CONTINUE

better than uncivilized slaughter, of course. We have a criminal jury system which is superior to any in the world;
45 and its efficiency is only marred by the difficulty of finding twelve men every day who don't know anything and can't read. And I may observe that we have an insanity plea that would have saved Cain. I think I can say, and say with pride, that we have some legislatures that bring higher
50 prices than any in the world.

I refer with effusion to our railway system, which consents to let us live, though it might do the opposite, being our owners. It only destroyed three thousand and seventy lives last year by collisions, and twenty-seven
55 thousand two hundred and sixty by running over heedless and unnecessary people at crossings. The companies seriously regretted the killing of these thirty thousand people, and went so far as to pay for some of them—voluntarily, of course, for the meanest of us would not
60 claim that we possess a court treacherous enough to enforce a law against a railway company. But, thank Heaven, the railway companies are generally disposed to do the right and kindly thing without compulsion.

1: rectangular, traditionally wooden supports over which railway tracks are laid; Thoreau also mentions "sleepers" for the sake of wordplay
2: Twain here lists respected American politicians (Franklin, Washington) alongside notorious political bosses and businessmen (Tweed, Gould) from his own era.

33

According to the author of Passage 2, railway companies

A) build their railroads and trains cheaply by using unethical labor.

B) rarely have penalties imposed upon them by the authorities.

C) are charitable companies that offer money and aid to people in accidents.

D) have not imposed adequate safety rules, resulting in multiple collisions.

34

Both Passage 1 and Passage 2 call attention to which drawback of railroads?

A) The public protests that accompany the construction of railroads

B) The poverty of the people who build the railroads

C) The corruption of the courts that protect the railroads

D) The collisions and fatalities associated with railroads

35

The author of Passage 1 supports his position by

A) praising a group of rebels and freethinkers.

B) assessing the validity of a way of life.

C) explaining which nationalities are most oppressed by industry.

D) offering a personal account of misfortune.

36

Which choice provides the best evidence for the answer to the previous question?

A) Lines 7-9 ("the only cure . . . purpose")

B) Lines 20-22 ("Did you . . . man")

C) Lines 27-30 ("And when . . . exception")

D) Lines 33-35 ("Men say . . . tomorrow")

37

As used in line 7, "rigid" most nearly means

A) austere.

B) inflexible.

C) orthodox.

D) stable.

38

As used in line 37, "great" most nearly means

A) vast.

B) liberal.

C) distinguished.

D) wealthy.

CONTINUE

39

The author of Passage 2 suggests which of the following about the justice system in America?

A) Its courts are corrupt and allow the wealthy and powerful to walk free while doling out harsher punishments to the poor.

B) Its courts are unfairly favorable to the insane and grant them freedoms that would seem unreasonable if granted to other citizens.

C) Its courts rarely conduct criminal trials according to the law and instead rely on their own sentiments when making decisions.

D) Its courts regularly choose juries that are comprised of citizens who are uneducated and ignorant, making the judicial process unproductive.

40

Which choice provides the best evidence for the answer to the previous question?

A) Lines 43-47 ("We have . . . read")
B) Lines 47-50 ("And I may . . . world")
C) Lines 51-53 ("I refer . . . owners")
D) Lines 53-59 ("It only destroyed . . . of course")

41

Unlike the author of Passage 2, the author of Passage 1

A) explains why past government reforms have been ineffectual.
B) mentions a course of action that may alleviate some of America's problems.
C) sarcastically addresses words of praise to his opponents.
D) suggests that American progress is dubious and superficial.

42

In contrast to the "Men" mentioned in line 9, the author of Passage 1 is more

A) interested in pursuing agriculture.
B) determined to overturn existing laws.
C) optimistic about the influence of education.
D) skeptical of the value of industry.

Questions 43-52 are based on the following passage.

Adapted from Philip Kowalski, "How Humanity Learned to Walk."

In November 1974, in the Afar region of Ethiopia, paleoanthropologist Donald Johanson and his graduate student Tom Gray discovered the remains of an ancient human, or
Line hominid, with 40 percent of the skeleton preserved. Since the
5 sediment at the site was known to be at least 3.2 million years old, the fossilized remains were at the time thought to be the oldest example of a human ancestor. While digging, Johanson and his research assistant had been listening to the Beatles' album *Sgt. Pepper's Lonely Hearts Club Band*, which features
10 the song "Lucy in the Sky with Diamonds." Since the small size of the skeleton suggested that it was probably female, they decided to call it Lucy. An important discovery at the time, Lucy was ultimately assigned to a new species category called *Australopithecus afarensis*, though she was, in fact, not the first
15 of her species to be found.

In 1924, the anatomist Raymond Dart unearthed the skull of the so-called Taung Child, who had probably lived almost 3 million years ago; Dart identified this skull as a relic of *Australopithecus africanus*. Yet Dart's discovery was dismissed
20 as negligible by other anthropologists, who considered the skull nothing more than the fossilized remains of an ape. The significance of the Taung Child, however, is that Johanson was able to detect that Lucy, like the Taung Child, wasn't a knuckle dragger—she, in fact, walked as contemporary
25 human beings do. Her pelvis demonstrated that she had an upright gait, and the bone fragments of her knee and ankle also displayed evidence of bipedalism. According to Fred Spoor of the Max Planck Institute for Evolutionary Anthropology in Leipzig, Germany, Lucy's small size seems to indicate that
30 other members of her species were mostly male and perhaps polygamous, and that she may have been part of a "harem," a group of multiple females controlled by one dominant male.

Despite this seemingly revolutionary find, the famous paleoanthropologist Richard Leakey rejected the claim that
35 Lucy could even remotely figure as a direct ancestor of modern humans. But Johanson and others found fossil evidence that many other *Australopithecus afarensis* individuals did exist. Based upon the bone structure of these specimens, the researchers concluded that Lucy and the other members of her
40 species spent nearly as much time dwelling in trees as they did walking on the ground, and that they probably had established primitive social units that would be comparable to what we nowadays perceive as a kind of rudimentary family structure.

Since the discovery of Lucy in 1974, anthropologists
45 have of course continued digging and have found older and better preserved remains of early human ancestors, such as the 3.3 million year old *Australopithecus afarensis* baby

CONTINUE

named "Selam" as well as "Ardi," a 4.4 million year old
Ardipithecus ramidus that dislodged Lucy as the earliest
50 known skeleton of a human ancestor. But researchers
have also found remains of hominids that suggest that
contemporary humans had emerged as long ago as 7
million years. Despite these revelations that discount her
anthropological originality, Lucy captured the public's
55 imagination as the most interesting hominid fossil ever
found, certainly in 1974 and possibly even now. As
Johanson himself explained, she "showed us conclusively
that upright walking and bipedalism preceded all of the
other changes we'd normally consider being human" and
60 that "she gave us a glimpse of what older ancestors would
look like."

43

The main purpose of the passage is to

A) describe the process of uncovering and studying fossils
of early humans.

B) stress the importance of learning about the human
species' early ancestors.

C) inform the reader about various discoveries of early
humans and their significance.

D) argue that bipedalism was unnecessary in order for an
uncovered fossil to be considered that of a human.

44

The author would agree with which of the following
statements about Lucy?

A) Her uncovering was unprecedented and spurred a
revival of interest in early humans.

B) She was not the first fossil of her kind to be discovered.

C) She became less researched and influential as time went
by.

D) Her features were so unique as to require the creation of
a new species.

45

Which choice provides the best evidence for the answer to
the previous question?

A) Lines 13-15 ("Lucy . . . found")

B) Lines 19-21 ("Dart's . . . ape")

C) Lines 34-36 ("Richard . . . humans")

D) Lines 54-56 ("Lucy . . . found")

46

In the first paragraph, the author uses the words "thought
to be" and "suggested" primarily in order to

A) imply that at the time of her discovery, Lucy's traits
such as age and gender were inconclusive.

B) reflect the public's growing uncertainty concerning the
validity of Lucy's discovery.

C) indicate that facts about Lucy and other early humans
were not to be taken seriously.

D) hint at critics' skepticism and distrust of the uncovered
fossil's relation to humans.

47

As used in line 23, "detect" most nearly means

A) research.

B) monitor.

C) perceive.

D) inspect.

48

According to the passage, Dart's discovery of the Taung
Child was important because

A) interest in early humans had diminished greatly in the
years following Lucy's discovery, and the Taung Child
sparked an increase of research in the field.

B) the only discoveries of Lucy's species had been female,
and the Taung Child was the first in a series of male
early humans to be uncovered.

C) the Taung Child was believed to live nearly three
million years ago, therefore disproving the claim that
Lucy was the oldest early human ever found.

D) the fossil offered evidence that the Taung Child and
Lucy both had the ability to walk upright, a distinctive
characteristic of humans.

49

Which choice provides the best evidence for the answer to
the previous question?

A) Lines 16-19 ("In 1924 . . . *africanus*")

B) Lines 22-25 ("Johanson . . . do")

C) Lines 28-30 ("Lucy's . . . male")

D) Lines 44-48 ("Since . . . baby")

CONTINUE

50

In the final paragraph (lines 44-61), the author indicates that

A) since Lucy's discovery scientists have found fossils of even earlier hominids that are in superior condition.

B) Lucy is still remembered by scientists as the only fossilized human displaying traits of bipedalism.

C) other fossils have shown that Lucy is not an accurate model of what early humans would have looked like.

D) although older and better preserved human fossils have been found, Lucy is the only important hominid fossil known to the public.

51

As used in line 53, "discount" most nearly means

A) disregard.

B) overlook.

C) minimize.

D) disprove.

52

The author suggests that the public's interest in Lucy

A) has not diminished significantly since her initial discovery in 1974.

B) has decreased since the uncovering of older hominid fossils.

C) has dwindled as the result of a decline in science funding.

D) has been replaced by fascination with other types of archaeological remains.

STOP
If you finish before time is called, you may check your work on this section only.
Do not turn to any other section.

Writing Test
35 MINUTES, 44 QUESTIONS

Turn to Section 2 of your answer sheet to answer the questions in this section.

Each passage below is accompanied by a number of questions. For some questions, you will consider how the passage might be revised to improve the expression of ideas. For other questions, you will consider how the passage might be edited to correct errors in sentence structure, usage, or punctuation. A passage or a question may be accompanied by one or more graphics (such as a table or graph) that you will consider as you make revising and editing decisions.

Some questions will direct you to an underlined portion of a passage. Other questions will direct you to a location in a passage or ask you to think about the passage as a whole.

After reading each passage, choose the answer to each question that most effectively improves the quality of writing in the passage or that makes the passage conform to the conventions of standard written English. Many questions include a "NO CHANGE" option. Choose that option if you think the best choice is to leave the relevant portion of the passage as it is.

Questions 1-11 are based on the following passage.

Domfront: Where the Middle Ages Live

[1] It is hard to believe that way back, in the Middle Ages, the sleepy little town of Domfront was **1** of some importance to the region of Normandy where I live—and to France as a whole, too. [2] Kings fought each other here. [3] Domfront was alive and bustling and rich until the sixteenth century, **2** from where the old town declined into a sleepy state that has lasted for almost five hundred years. [4] Nobles squabbled over land and power. [5] Pilgrims on their way to Mont St. Michel rested from their journeys here. **3**

1
A) NO CHANGE
B) with some importance
C) by some importance
D) to some importance

2
A) NO CHANGE
B) when
C) which
D) how

3
To make this paragraph most logical, sentence 3 should be placed
A) where it is now.
B) after sentence 1.
C) after sentence 4.
D) after sentence 5.

CONTINUE

However, biennially, the dull and dusty sheets of history are thrown off and Domfront relives its glorious past. The oldest part of town, which lies near a few of the remaining medieval landmarks, **4** burst with banners and coats of arms. The distinctive rhythms of sackbuts and horns, shawms and pipes, timbrels and drums, rebecs and other stringed instruments **5** rebound from the ancient stone walls. White tented stalls fill the Place St. Julien, the original market square of Domfront. The stall-holders, dressed in the comfortable smocks and cloaks of the Middle Ages, sell hand-dyed clothes, leather belts and shoes, spices, candies, and **6** they make biscuits from recipes handed down through the generations. Elsewhere horses, draped and saddled, wait to be mounted by knights in armor for the jousting tournament. Archery butts are put in place, so that today's Robin Hoods can show their prowess. Wrestlers grapple and roll across the greensward. **7** These performers, as the residents of Domfront know, appear every year and never fail to astound.

4
A) NO CHANGE
B) bursts
C) which burst
D) bursting

5
A) NO CHANGE
B) rebuke
C) recover
D) reciprocate

6
A) NO CHANGE
B) biscuits, these are made from recipes
C) biscuits made from recipes
D) making biscuits from recipes

7
The writer wants to conclude this paragraph by mentioning a few additional spectacles that can be seen at the Domfront fair. Which choice best accomplishes this goal?
A) NO CHANGE
B) Flag throwers, jugglers, and tumblers draw gasps from the engaged onlookers.
C) Once you are done watching these feats, you can stroll through town and appreciate the aura of history that surrounds you.
D) It doesn't even matter whether wrestling was popular centuries ago: the spirit of festivity is overwhelming.

CONTINUE

This is the weekend of Le Mediaeval, a festival that takes place during the first weekend of August. The events begin on Friday afternoon, when all the parking places in the old town are cleared of vehicles and **8 replaced by** tented stalls. That evening there is a banquet for the inhabitants of the town, provided that they have paid for their tickets and that they arrive in medieval garb.

The next morning Le Mediaeval officially begins with a parade of the market stallholders, led by mounted knights and halberdiers in costume. The mayor welcomes the procession with a speech **9 and, to great fanfare declares** the opening of the celebrations. There is a crowd of locals and tourists, many of them dressed in period costume, **10 and they swell** as the weekend proceeds. The old city is alive again, as it was in days long past. By Sunday afternoon the streets are packed and noisy.

The festival officially ends at 6:00 p.m. on Sunday. By early Monday morning, the old town has returned to normal. No flags, no music, no stalls remain. Domfront sleeps for **11 another two years, failing to wake up.** Until then, the past is another country only glimpsed in dreams.

8
A) NO CHANGE
B) replacing
C) it replaces
D) they replace

9
A) NO CHANGE
B) and to great fanfare, declares
C) and, to great fanfare, declares
D) and to great fanfare; declares

10
A) NO CHANGE
B) and it swells
C) and the costumes swell
D) and the attendance swells

11
A) NO CHANGE
B) another two years, never to awaken.
C) another two years.
D) two years all over.

CONTINUE

Questions 12-22 are based on the following passage.

Beyond Rosie the Riveter: Women and World War II

World War II was the most extensive military effort in U.S. history. As a result, more men were drafted into the military [12] than any previous war. As more and more men were deployed overseas, the soldiers' stateside positions in the military and their prior jobs outside of the military became vacant. Without enough men to fill these positions, the government allowed women to assume roles previously restricted to men. [13] More than one million women moved to Washington D.C. to work for the civil service, and by 1944 approximately one out of three civil service workers [14] are female. Across the country, more than six million women accepted [15] a production job in wartime factories; hundreds of thousands of women served in the military itself.

For most of the war, women were not permitted to participate directly in missions and campaigns, [16] however in 1942 Congress passed a law allowing women to serve in the Army, Navy, and Coast Guard. The following year, women were allowed into the Marines as well. Women were not placed in combat roles, so many instead worked as nurses in military hospitals, though some women served as pilots and engineers. In addition to those in paid positions, more than three million women served as Red Cross volunteers and many more volunteered with other aid and relief organizations.

12
A) NO CHANGE
B) than in any previous war.
C) as any previous war.
D) as in any previous war.

13
At this point the writer is considering adding the following sentence:

> Indeed, many women were offered government employment to compensate for the dearth of available men.

Should the writer make this addition?
A) Yes, because the sentence explains the reason why women were initially allowed to take on government jobs.
B) Yes, because the sentence adds details that expand upon a previous point.
C) No, because the sentence merely repeats information previously presented in the passage.
D) No, because the sentence fails to explain which government jobs women were permitted to take.

14
A) NO CHANGE
B) is
C) was
D) were

15
A) NO CHANGE
B) a production job in one of the wartime factories
C) jobs in production at factories during wartime
D) production jobs in wartime factories

16
A) NO CHANGE
B) because
C) and
D) yet

CONTINUE

[17] <u>During this time of great change, women also began to take on other jobs historically reserved for men.</u> The now iconic "We Can Do It!" motivational poster of a female production worker, [18] <u>popular known</u> as Rosie the Riveter, was produced by the U.S. government and distributed in an effort to inspire more women to take on factory jobs. These jobs were extremely important to the American war effort because the U.S. military needed thousands of planes, tanks, ships, munitions packages, tools, and other supplies on an ongoing basis. The demand was so great [19] <u>so</u> women in military factories worked six days per week, often for extended hours and with very few holidays.

For many women, working in U.S. factories constituted the first time that their employment was appreciated by society. Traditionally, jobs seen as [20] <u>"women's work"—such</u> as domestic labor, teaching, and sewing—were not highly regarded. With new employment opportunities came greater economic freedom and respect.

17

Which answer choice best sets up the paragraph?
A) NO CHANGE
B) Suddenly, women found themselves able to advance very quickly within their chosen fields.
C) Still, some women preferred to keep their jobs as full-time homemakers.
D) The government, however, prioritized a wholly different women's role.

18

A) NO CHANGE
B) know to be popular
C) known popularly
D) known in popularity

19

A) NO CHANGE
B) that
C) for
D) DELETE the underlined word.

20

A) NO CHANGE
B) "women's work," such
C) "women's work" (such
D) "women's work" such

CONTINUE

Unfortunately for the female workers, such new and invigorating employment disappeared [21] when the war ended in 1945, the soldiers returned home. Men returning from war were entitled to return to their pre-war jobs, and so most female workers were quickly laid off. [22] On the contrary, women were generally expected to return to their pre-war domestic lives, though many would have preferred to continue on empowering career paths.

21
A) NO CHANGE
B) when the war ended in 1945 and the soldiers returned home.
C) when the war ended in 1945 and the soldiers returning home.
D) when the war ended in 1945, it prompted the return home of the soldiers.

22
A) NO CHANGE
B) As a result
C) Instead
D) Despite this

CONTINUE

Questions 23-33 are based on the following passage and supplementary material.

Being Grateful for Gratitude

It is sometimes said that a grateful heart is a happy heart; now, psychological research is available to support [23] it. Gratitude often leads people to spend more time thinking about positive things, about the exact events and people for which they are grateful. This focus on the positive can lead to greater optimism about future events and a greater appreciation [24] to people who have been helpful.

Examining just these notions, psychologists Robert A. Emmons and Michael E. McCullough conducted an experiment [25] in which they asked three groups of participants to write a few sentences per week for 10 weeks. Participants in the first group [26] was instructed to write about something for which they were grateful; participants in the second group were instructed to write about something that they found annoying; and participants in the third group were instructed to write about events that had had an impact (either positive or negative) on them. At the end of the study, people who wrote about gratitude exhibited higher life satisfaction and optimism than [27] participants in either of the other two groups. [28] Moreover, the participants who wrote about gratitude exercised more and had fewer medical appointments than did those who wrote about irritation.

23

A) NO CHANGE
B) that being true.
C) them.
D) this notion.

24

A) NO CHANGE
B) about
C) around
D) of

25

A) NO CHANGE
B) where
C) that
D) when

26

A) NO CHANGE
B) were
C) is
D) are

27

A) NO CHANGE
B) did participants in either of the other two groups.
C) either of the other groups of participants.
D) the participants of either of the other groups exhibited life satisfaction.

28

The author is considering deleting the underlined sentence. Should the writer make this deletion?

A) Yes, because the information in this sentence contradicts the argument advanced in the paragraph.
B) Yes, because this sentence is unrelated to the main subject of the passage.
C) No, because this sentence introduces a concept integral to the passage's main point.
D) No, because this sentence provides information in support of the passage's argument.

CONTINUE

It may not be surprising that focusing on gratitude is a more effective path to happiness than focusing on irritation or some combination of positive and negative events, but how does gratitude compare to other positive psychological factors? Psychologist Martin E. P. Seligman designed an experiment to compare various positive techniques to each other, [29] he assigned one positive psychology technique to each of 411 participants. The gratitude assignment was to write a letter of gratitude to someone and then personally deliver the letter to that person. Participants who were given the gratitude assignment experienced a [30] great increase in happiness than participants who were given any other positive psychology assignment did.

Gratitude not only increases one's own happiness [31] but also, if one is a business executive, boosts the productivity of one's subordinates. In a University of Pennsylvania experiment, the director of annual giving told one group of university fundraisers how grateful she was for their work. Another group of fundraisers did not receive this speech. During the following week, those who received the director's speech of gratitude made [32] 10 more fundraising calls than those in the control group did. It may, in fact, literally pay to be grateful.

[29]
A) NO CHANGE
B) by assigning
C) assigning
D) being assigned

[30]
A) NO CHANGE
B) more great
C) greater
D) greatest

[31]
A) NO CHANGE
B) and also
C) also
D) but also it

[32]
Which of the following most accurately interprets the data from the graph?
A) NO CHANGE
B) 40
C) 50
D) 80

CONTINUE

Effect of Gratitude Speech on Fundraising Productivity

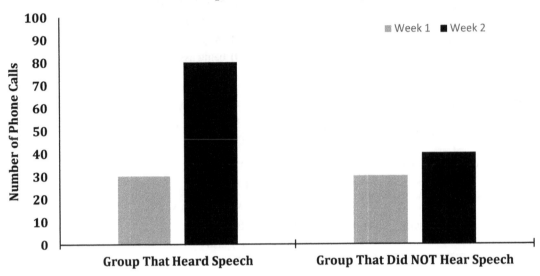

There are still unanswered questions about gratitude: after all, gratitude *correlates* to positives, but does it *cause* [33] theirs? However, given that all these studies randomly divided their participants into groups rather than comparing broad, vague personality types, the results strongly suggest a causative relationship between expressing gratitude and reaping clear benefits.

33

A) NO CHANGE
B) them
C) it
D) its

CONTINUE

Questions 34-44 are based on the following passage.

The Good Graces of Seawater Greenhouses

One of today's humanitarian dilemmas **34** are over-population. Scientists are predicting that by 2050 the global food output will need to increase beyond current levels by 60 percent in order to meet demand. This rise in agricultural production is expected to put an additional strain on the world's already precarious freshwater supply. Nowhere is this resource crisis more apparent **35** as desert countries with poor environments for food production.

Many desert countries, like **36** those in the Horn of Africa, must rely on other nations for their food needs. This is troubling on multiple **37** counts but the prices of imported foods are generally too high for the already-disadvantaged desert populations, and governments must consequently subsidize the imported food in order to prevent mass starvation. For the economies of such nations, strain and instability result. In addition, countries that rely on food imports can never be self-sufficient; long-term, their potential for economic growth suffers.

34
A) NO CHANGE
B) is
C) was
D) were

35
A) NO CHANGE
B) as in desert counties
C) than desert countries
D) than in desert countries

36
A) NO CHANGE
B) that of
C) the ones you can find in
D) in

37
A) NO CHANGE
B) counts: the
C) counts, the
D) counts, because, the

CONTINUE

In the early 1990s, British inventor Charles Paton began working on a greenhouse design that he felt could break this cycle of deprivation. First assembled in 1994, **38** he fashioned a greenhouse prototype that was the product of principles that seem somewhat counterintuitive. Instead of heating a plant environment in order to grow food, as traditional greenhouses do, Paton's greenhouse was designed to cool and humidify the air. The idea proved transformational because **39** more cooler and humid conditions are exactly what many countries need in order to begin producing their own food.

40 [1] These greenhouses were designed to work in desert areas that are in close proximity to oceans. [2] Notable side benefits include the salt-laden greenhouse atmosphere (which combats pests and parasites) and the condensed seawater (which provides nutrients that can be extracted and fed to the plants). [3] Paton's structures use seawater **41** to filter the sunlight and to cool and humidify the air. [4] Then, they use solar power to condense that seawater into freshwater.

38

A) NO CHANGE
B) he employed principles that seemed somewhat counterintuitive to fashion his greenhouse prototype.
C) the greenhouse prototype he fashioned was the product of principles that seem somewhat counterintuitive.
D) his greenhouse prototype he fashioned was resulting from the product of principles that seem somewhat counterintuitive.

39

A) NO CHANGE
B) more humid and also cooler
C) more cooler, more humid
D) cooler, more humid

40

To improve the logic of the paragraph, sentence 2 would best be placed
A) where it is now.
B) before sentence 1.
C) before sentence 4.
D) after sentence 4.

41

A) NO CHANGE
B) to filter the sunlight, to cool the air, and to humidify them.
C) to filter the sunlight, to cool and humidifying the air.
D) to filter, to cool, and to humidify the sunlight and air.

CONTINUE

These greenhouses have been tested in desert nations including the Canary Islands, the United Arab Emirates, Australia, and Oman. [42] Additionally, some of these countries are seriously considering supplementing their greenhouse programs with certain newly developed irrigation techniques, some of which may prove to be more cost-effective solutions. One of the largest initiatives to incorporate seawater greenhouses is the Sahara Forest Project in Jordan. There, seawater greenhouse engineering has been combined with other innovations, including concentrated solar power. The scientists responsible for each of these greenhouses have been [43] cautious optimistic about the outcomes.

Aware of the promise of seawater greenhouses, more countries are beginning to express an interest in building their own. Universities based in Europe and the United States have even begun working with African governments to develop pilot projects. Whether or not seawater saves the world remains to be seen, [44] but these greenhouses have already given many a reason for hope.

42

The writer is considering deleting the underlined sentence. Should the writer make this deletion?

A) Yes, because the underlined sentence is entirely unrelated to the subject matter of the passage.
B) Yes, because the underlined sentence distracts from the author's discussion of the passage's main point.
C) No, because the underlined sentence lends support to the passage's main point.
D) No, because the underlined sentence provides an important rebuttal to the arguments set forth by the author.

43

A) NO CHANGE
B) cautious optimistically
C) cautiously optimistic
D) cautious as optimistic

44

The author would like to conclude by reiterating the passage's main point. Which answer choice best accomplishes this goal?

A) NO CHANGE
B) and drastic steps must be taken to ensure the agricultural self-sufficiency of numerous ailing nations.
C) and perhaps we will never fully understand how to best utilize this exceedingly abundant resource.
D) but the answer is ultimately of little consequence to affected nations.

STOP
If you finish before time is called, you may check your work on this section only.
Do not turn to any other section.

Math Test - No Calculator
25 MINUTES, 20 QUESTIONS

DIRECTIONS

For each question from 1-15, choose the best answer choice provided in the multiple choice bank and fill in the appropriate circle in the provided answer key. Alternatively, for questions **16-20**, answer the problem and enter your answer in the grid-in section of the answer key. Refer to the directions given before question 16 as to how to enter your answers for the grid-in questions. You may complete scratch work in any empty space in your test booklet.

NOTES

A. Calculator usage **is not allowed** in this section.
B. Variables, constants, and coefficients used represent real numbers unless indicated otherwise.
C. All figures are created to appropriate scale unless the question states otherwise.
D. All figures are two-dimensional unless the question states otherwise.
E. The domain of any given function is all real numbers x for which the function, $f(x)$, is a real number unless the question states otherwise.

REFERENCE

$$A = \pi r^2$$
$$C = 2\pi r$$

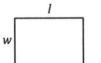
$$A = lw$$

$$A = \frac{1}{2}bh$$

$$c^2 = a^2 + b^2$$

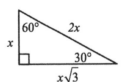
Special Right Triangle

Special Right Triangle

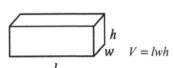
$$V = lwh$$

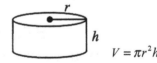
$$V = \pi r^2 h$$

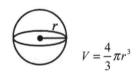
$$V = \frac{4}{3}\pi r^3$$

$$V = \frac{1}{3}\pi r^2 h$$

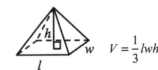
$$V = \frac{1}{3}lwh$$

There are $360°$ in a circle.
There are 2π radians in a circle.
There are $180°$ in a triangle.

CONTINUE

1

$$4x = 2y + 10$$
$$2x - 2y = 7$$

If (x, y) is the solution to the system of equations above, what is the value of y?

A) -2

B) -1

C) $-\dfrac{1}{2}$

D) $\dfrac{1}{2}$

2

$$\frac{3(2x+5)}{(6x+5)(6x+15)}$$

Given $x \neq -\dfrac{5}{2}$ and $x \neq -\dfrac{5}{6}$, which of the following is an equivalent form of the expression above?

A) $\dfrac{1}{3x+1}$

B) $\dfrac{1}{2x+5}$

C) $\dfrac{1}{6x+15}$

D) $\dfrac{1}{6x+5}$

3

Billy has been spending a half of an hour each night using a cell phone app to help keep his brain stimulated. In the app, he is presented with 100 words with which he must correctly identify the definition from four answer choices. When the round is done, Billy's score is calculated by the number of incorrect definitions that he chose. The goal is to get a score of zero. Billy had a score of 64 on his third night and a score of 48 on his seventh night. If Billy's score reduces by the same amount each night, on which of the following nights will Billy receive a perfect score of 0?

A) The 4th night

B) The 10th night

C) The 19th night

D) The 20th night

4

Which of the following expressions is nonpositive for all values of x?

A) $1 - x^2$

B) $1 - |x - 1|$

C) $(-|x|)^3$

D) $-(-|x|)^3$

CONTINUE

5

In the function $f(x) = Kx^2 + 1$, K is a constant. If $f(8) = 33$, what is the value of $f(4)$?

A) 3

B) 9

C) 17

D) 33

6

$$f(x) = 3x + 5$$

Given the function above, which of the following is equal to $\frac{1}{3}x + 5$ for all values of x?

A) $f(\frac{1}{27}x)$

B) $f(\frac{1}{9}x)$

C) $f(\frac{1}{3}x)$

D) $f(-3x)$

7

$$\frac{a(b+a)}{2a} = 5$$

If the equation above is true, which of the following must also be true?

A) $\frac{b}{2} + a^2 = 5$

B) $b + \frac{a}{2} = 5$

C) $b = a - 10$

D) $a = 10 - b$

8

Which of the following systems of linear equations represent two lines that are perpendicular to each other?

A) $y + 2x = 4$
   $y - 2x = 6$

B) $2y + 2x = 13$
   $-2y - 2x = 3$

C) $3y + 6x = 12$
   $-6y + 3x = 9$

D) $8y + 4x = 20$
   $4y + 8x = 20$

CONTINUE

9

The function $f(x) = x^2 + 7$ passes through the points $(a, 16)$ and $(b, 16)$, where the sum of a and b is 0. What is the value of $|a - b|$?

A) 0

B) 3

C) 6

D) 8

10

$$x - 2 = \sqrt{x}$$

When solved as a quadratic equation, which of the following values of x is an extraneous solution to the equation above?

A) -1

B) 1

C) 2

D) 4

11

$$\frac{4m}{m + \dfrac{1}{24}} = 8$$

What is the value of m in the equation above?

A) $-\dfrac{4}{3}$

B) $-\dfrac{3}{4}$

C) $-\dfrac{1}{12}$

D) $-\dfrac{1}{96}$

12

A package of 4 muffins is priced at x dollars and a package of 8 muffins is priced at $x + 3$ dollars. Angela purchased one package of 4 muffins at 50% off the marked price and Rachel purchased one package of 8 muffins at 50% off the marked price. If Rachel, Angela, and 10 of their friends decided to split the overall price of the 12 muffins evenly, which of the following expressions represents the amount, in dollars, each of them paid in terms of x?

(Assume that there is no sales tax.)

A) $x + \dfrac{3}{2}$

B) $2x + 3$

C) $\dfrac{2x + 3}{12}$

D) $\dfrac{2x + 3}{24}$

CONTINUE

13

In the quadratic equation $x^2 - a^2 = ax$, a is a constant. What are the solutions for x?

A) $a \pm a\sqrt{5}$

B) $\dfrac{a \pm a\sqrt{5}}{2}$

C) $a \pm \sqrt{-3a}$

D) $\dfrac{a \pm a\sqrt{-3}}{2}$

14

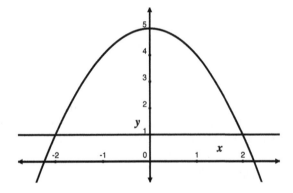

The relations $y = 1$ and $y = 5 - x^2$ are graphed in the xy-plane above. How many ordered pairs (x, y), where both x and y have integer values, would satisfy the system of inequalities defined by $y > 1$ and $y < 5 - x^2$?

A) 7

B) 8

C) 14

D) 15

15

$$\frac{(16+3i)(1+4i)}{i}$$

If the expression above is rewritten in the form $a - bi$, where a and b are positive integer constants, what is the remainder when a is divided by b?

A) 3

B) 4

C) 5

D) 6

CONTINUE

DIRECTIONS

For each question from 16-20, solve and enter your answer in the grid-in section of your answer sheet as described below.

A. Write out your answers in the boxes at the top of each column in order to help you fill in the circles accurately. Remember, you will only receive credit for the circles that are filled in correctly, not for the written answer at the top of the columns.

B. Mark only a single circle in each column.

C. There are no negative answers.

D. If the problem has more than one correct answer, grid only one of the correct answers.

E. When your answer is a **mixed number**, such as $1\frac{1}{2}$, it should be entered as 1.5 or $3/2$. You cannot enter a mixed number because there is no room to fill in a circle that represents a space.

F. If you enter a **decimal answer** with more digits then the grid can handle, the answer may be rounded or truncated, but it absolutely must fill the entire grid.

Answer: $\frac{8}{21}$

Answer: 6.4

Written answer →

Decimal point →

← Fraction line

Answer: 102 - both positions are correct

REMEMBER: You can begin writing your answers in any column as long as there is enough space. Leave unused columns blank.

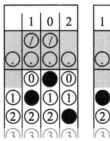

The ways to correctly grid $\frac{7}{9}$ are:

CONTINUE →

16

In the triangle above, the cosine of $y°$ is $\dfrac{12}{13}$. What is the cosine of $x°$?

17

$$Ax + 2y = 12$$
$$8x + 32y = 144$$

For what value of A will the system of equations above have no solutions?

18

Truck A leaves a loading dock and averages 40 miles per hour until it makes a stop in Dover County. Truck B leaves the same loading dock two hours after Truck A and averages 60 miles per hour until it makes a stop in Dover County as well. If both trucks arrive in Dover County at the same time, how many miles is Dover County from the loading dock?

19

$$x^3 - 2x^2 - 9x + 18 = (x - a)(x - b)(x + c)$$

If the equation above is true for all values of x and a, b, and c are all positive constants, what is the value of abc?

CONTINUE

20

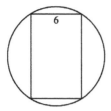

A rectangle that has one side measuring 6 inches is inscribed in a circle with an area of 25π square inches. What is the area of the rectangle in square inches?

STOP
If you finish before time is called, you may check your work on this section only.
Do not turn to any other section.
37

Math Test - Calculator

55 MINUTES, 38 QUESTIONS

DIRECTIONS

For each question from 1-30, choose the best answer choice provided in the multiple choice bank and fill in the appropriate circle in the provided answer key. Alternatively, for questions **31-38**, answer the problem and enter your answer in the grid-in section of the answer key. Refer to the directions given before question 31 as to how to enter your answers for the grid-in questions. You may complete scratch work in any empty space in your test booklet.

NOTES

A. Calculator usage **is allowed**.
B. Variables, constants, and coefficients used represent real numbers unless indicated otherwise.
C. All figures are created to appropriate scale unless the question states otherwise.
D. All figures are two-dimensional unless the question states otherwise.
E. The domain of any given function is all real numbers x for which the function, $f(x)$, is a real number unless the question states otherwise.

REFERENCE

$A = \pi r^2$
$C = 2\pi r$

$A = lw$

$A = \frac{1}{2}bh$

$c^2 = a^2 + b^2$

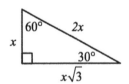
Special Right Triangle

Special Right Triangle

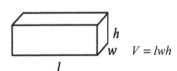
$V = lwh$

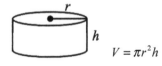
$V = \pi r^2 h$

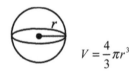
$V = \frac{4}{3}\pi r^3$

$V = \frac{1}{3}\pi r^2 h$

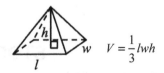
$V = \frac{1}{3}lwh$

There are $360°$ in a circle.
There are 2π radians in a circle.
There are $180°$ in a triangle.

38

CONTINUE →

1

Melvin created a daily spending budget for the vacation that he is taking in Florida. Melvin plans to spend no more than $85 each day that he is on vacation. If Melvin has $600 in his vacation account, which of the following expressions represents the remaining amount of money in his vacation account d days from the beginning of his vacation given that Melvin spends his maximum daily spending budget each day?

A) $600 + 85d$

B) $600 - 85d$

C) $85 + 600d$

D) $85 - 600d$

2

In a population of 20,000 Americans, 4,000 prefer to park their cars inside of a garage. If a random sample of 100 Americans from this population were selected, how many people in the sample could one expect to prefer parking inside of a garage?

A) 2

B) 4

C) 10

D) 20

3

Juan and Amelia raised a total of $2,800 for cystic fibrosis research. If Juan raised $100 more than half of the amount that Amelia raised, how much money did Amelia raise for cystic fibrosis research?

A) $900

B) $1,000

C) $1,800

D) $1,900

4

Line k in the xy-plane only has points in Quadrants I and II. Which of the following is not true?

A) Line k has a slope of 0.

B) Line k has a positive y-intercept.

C) Line k has a positive x-intercept.

D) Line k is parallel to the x-axis.

39

CONTINUE

5

Brandon pays $36 for a yearly membership to a digital music streaming service. If Brandon would like to purchase a song, it costs an additional $0.98. If Brandon's total annual payment for the music service was $71.28, on average, how many songs did Brandon purchase per month?

A) 2

B) 3

C) 12

D) 36

6

Six yards of rope were divided evenly among 9 people. How many inches of rope did each person receive?

(1 yard = 36 inches)

A) 2

B) 4

C) 24

D) 48

7

If pressure, measured in pascals, is equal to the force of an object in newtons divided by the contact area in square meters, which of the following combinations of force and area creates closest to 10,000 pascals of pressure?

A) 200,000 N and 20,000 m^2

B) 20,000 N and 10,000 m^2

C) 5,000 N and 5 m^2

D) 2,000 N and 0.2 m^2

8

Camera and Cell Phone Sales in 2010

Sales Period	Camera Sales	Cell Phone Sales	TOTAL
Jan.-Mar.	20	120	140
Apr.-June	28	120	148
July-Sept.	30	94	124
Oct.-Dec.	42	66	108
TOTAL	120	400	520

In the table above, cell phone sales from January to June account for what proportion of the total sales?

A) $\frac{3}{13}$

B) $\frac{6}{13}$

C) $\frac{3}{5}$

D) $\frac{5}{6}$

CONTINUE

9

In the xy-plane, the graph of a function has only one x-intercept and one negative y-intercept. Which of the following could be the function?

A) $y = -x^2$

B) $y = x^2 - 1$

C) $y = x^2 - 2x + 1$

D) $y = -x^2 - 4x - 4$

---- ▼ ----

Questions 10 and 11 refer to the following information.

Hours of Sleep versus Hours of Study

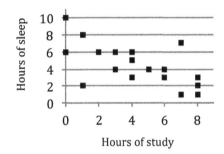

A recent sleep study was conducted on high-school seniors to determine if there is an association between the number of hours of sleep and the number of hours of study that each student averages per weeknight. The collected data for a random sample of 18 students is presented in the scatterplot above.

10

The student with the highest ratio of hours of study to hours of sleep had how many hours of sleep?

A) 1

B) 6

C) 8

D) 10

11

Which of the following linear functions using h for hours of study could most reasonably estimate $f(h)$, the number of hours of sleep?

A) $f(h) = \dfrac{1}{4}h + 6$

B) $f(h) = \dfrac{3}{4}h + 8$

C) $f(h) = -\dfrac{3}{4}h + 8$

D) $f(h) = -\dfrac{5}{3}h + 10$

---- ▲ ----

12

Motorcycle's Value versus Time

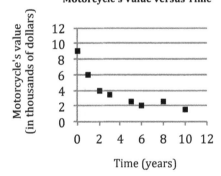

The value of a motorcycle was assessed periodically over the first 10 years of its existence. Which of the following models would best represent the relationship between time and the motorcycle's estimated value?

A) A linear growth model

B) A linear decay model

C) An exponential decay model

D) An inverted quadratic model

41

CONTINUE ➡

13

$$S(x) = I(1 + \frac{r}{100})^x$$

The equation above can be used to determine the overall account balance, $S(x)$, of a savings account x years from the opening of the account given an initial account balance, I, and an annual interest rate of r %. Which of the following gives r in terms of $S(x)$, I, and x?

A) $r = 100\sqrt[x]{\dfrac{S(x)}{I}} - 100$

B) $r = 100\sqrt[x]{\dfrac{S(x)}{I}} - 1$

C) $r = 100\sqrt[x]{I}\sqrt[x]{S(x)} - 100$

D) $r = 100\sqrt[x]{I}\sqrt[x]{S(x)} - 1$

14

Ankit has a block of ice in the shape of a cube that has a volume of $27\,ft^3$. Ankit plans to cut the ice block into small ice cubes that measure 2 inches in all directions. How many such ice cubes can Ankit create? (Note: There are 1728 cubic inches in $1\,ft^3$.)

A) 5,832

B) 11,664

C) 23,328

D) 46,656

15

Which of the following scatterplots would best be modeled by an equation in the form $y = mx + b$, where b is a positive constant and m is a negative fractional constant?

A)
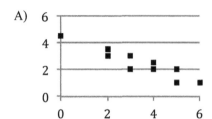

B)
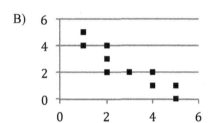

C)
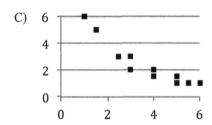

D)
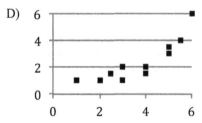

CONTINUE

Questions 16 and 17 refer to the following information.

$$C_1(h) = 640 + 12mh$$
$$C_2(h) = 400 + 15mh$$

Mrs. Jamerson is having all of the rooms on the first floor of her house painted. She has received the two quotes shown above where $C_1(h)$ represents the total cost for having the job completed with Company 1, $C_2(h)$ represents the total cost for having the job completed with Company 2, m represents the number of men on the job, and h is the estimated number of hours to complete the job.

16

If one extra man is needed for the job than initially quoted, which of the following is true?

A) The hourly cost for Company 1 will increase by more than the hourly cost for Company 2.
B) The hourly cost for Company 2 will increase by more than the hourly cost for Company 1.
C) The hourly cost for the two companies will increase equally.
D) The increase in hourly cost for each company cannot be determined.

17

If it is determined by both companies that ten men are necessary to complete the job, what is the least integer number of hours, h, where the total cost to have the house painted by Company 1 would be less than the total cost to have the house painted by Company 2?

A) 8
B) 9
C) 35
D) 80

18

$$6m \le 2$$

If the equation above is true, what is the greatest possible value for $2m + 1$?

A) $\dfrac{1}{3}$

B) $\dfrac{2}{3}$

C) 1

D) $\dfrac{5}{3}$

19

A clear jar is filled with black, red, and green marbles. There are 6 black marbles and each marble is uniquely marked with a number 1 through 6. There are also six red marbles and six green marbles numbered the same way. Given that a black or a red marble is randomly selected, what is the probability that it is marked with a number greater than 4?

A) $\dfrac{1}{9}$

B) $\dfrac{1}{3}$

C) $\dfrac{4}{9}$

D) $\dfrac{2}{3}$

CONTINUE

Questions 20 and 21 refer to the following information.

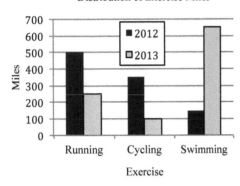

Distribution of Exercise Miles

Jackson exercises regularly and attempts to accumulate 1000 miles of cardiovascular exercise each year by means of running, cycling, and swimming. The bar graph above shows how Jackson's 1000 miles of exercise were distributed in the years 2012 and 2013.

20

Which of the following forms of exercise had the greatest percentage decrease in miles from 2012 to 2013?

A) Running

B) Cycling

C) Swimming

D) Running and Cycling equally

21

What percentage of Jackson's total miles of exercise for 2012 and 2013 was accounted for by swimming?

A) 22.5

B) 37.5

C) 40

D) 65

22

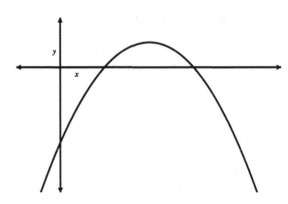

Which of the following equations could represent the parabola graphed in the xy-plane above?

A) $y = -x^2 - 4$

B) $y = -x^2 + 4x - 3$

C) $y = -x^2 - 4x - 3$

D) $y = x^2 - 4x + 3$

23

$$0 = x^3 - 4x^2 - 9x + 36$$

Which of the following values of x is *not* a solution to the equation above?

A) −4

B) −3

C) 3

D) 4

CONTINUE

24

If a and b are numbers such that $|a-b| > 10$, which of the following must be true?

    I. $a-b > 0$

    II. $|a+b| > 10$

    III. $ab > 0$

A) None

B) I only

C) II only

D) I and III only

25

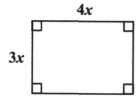

The perimeter of the rectangle shown above is 56 inches. What is the length of a diagonal of the rectangle in inches?

A) 10

B) 12

C) 16

D) 20

26

$$G(x) = 10 + 0.55x$$

In the equation above, $G(x)$ represents the increased value of a renovated home in thousands of dollars, given x, the amount of money spent on renovations by the homeowner in thousands of dollars. Which of the following best describes the value of the constant 0.55 in the context of the equation?

A) The value of a home will increase by $5,500 dollars for every $1,000 the homeowner invests into renovations.

B) The value of a home will increase by $550 dollars for every $10,000 the homeowner invests into renovations.

C) The value of a home will increase by 55 cents for every dollar the homeowner invests into renovations.

D) The total value of a home will be equivalent to 55% of the money that the homeowner invests into renovations.

27

The average weight of four bags of concrete is 85 pounds. If two additional bags of concrete are added, the average weight of all of the bags increases to 92 pounds. What is the average weight in pounds of the two additional bags of concrete that were added to the original four bags of concrete?

A) 3.5

B) 7

C) 99

D) 106

CONTINUE

28

The polynomial function f follows the form $x^2 + bx + c$, and has two roots at $(-1,0)$ and $(2,0)$. Which of the following is an equivalent form of the polynomial in which the coordinates of the vertex appear as constants in the equation?

A) $f(x) = (x - \frac{1}{2})^2 - \frac{9}{4}$

B) $f(x) = (x - \frac{1}{2})^2 - 2$

C) $f(x) = (x - 1)^2 - 2$

D) $f(x) = (x - \frac{3}{2})^2 - 5$

29

$$f(x) = 1 - x^3$$
$$f(x) = mx + b$$

Line h follows the form $f(x) = mx + b$. If line h and the function $f(x) = 1 - x^3$ are to be graphed in the xy-plane, what is the greatest integer value of m for which the system of equations will have 3 distinct solutions?

A) -4

B) -1

C) 0

D) 1

30

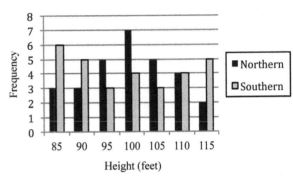

Distribution of Pine Tree Heights

The bar graph above gives the distribution of the heights of pine trees for 30 randomly selected trees in the northern part of a county and 30 randomly selected trees in the southern part of the county. Which of the following is true about the data presented in the bar graph?

A) The standard deviation of pine tree heights in the northern part of the county is less than the standard deviation of pine tree heights in the southern part of the county.

B) The standard deviation of pine tree heights in the northern part of the county is greater than the standard deviation of pine tree heights in the southern part of the county.

C) The standard deviation of pine tree heights in the northern part of the county is approximately the same as the standard deviation of pine tree heights in the southern part of the county.

D) The standard deviations of the heights of pine trees cannot be calculated with the given data. Therefore, a comparison between the standard deviations of pine tree heights in the northern and southern parts of the county cannot be determined.

CONTINUE

DIRECTIONS

For each question from 31-38, solve and enter your answer in the grid-in section of your answer sheet as described below.

A. Write out your answers in the boxes at the top of each column in order to help you fill in the circles accurately. Remember, you will only receive credit for the circles that are filled in correctly, not for the written answer at the top of the columns.

B. Mark only a single circle in each column.

C. There are no negative answers.

D. If the problem has more than one correct answer, grid only one of the correct answers.

E. When your answer is a **mixed number**, such as $1\frac{1}{2}$, it should be entered as 1.5 or $3/2$. You cannot enter a mixed number because there is no room to fill in a circle that represents a space.

F. If you enter a **decimal answer** with more digits then the grid can handle, the answer may be rounded or truncated, but it absolutely must fill the entire grid.

Answer: $\frac{8}{21}$

Written answer →
Decimal point →
← Fraction line

Answer: 6.4

The ways to correctly grid $\frac{7}{9}$ are:

Answer: 102 - both positions are correct

REMEMBER: You can begin writing your answers in any column as long as there is enough space. Leave unused columns blank.

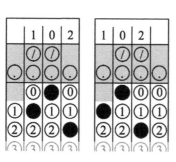

CONTINUE ➡

31

$$T_{HR} = (220 - Age)(Intensity)$$

A person can calculate his or her target heart rate, T_{HR}, in beats per minute, using the equation above, where intensity is a percentage in decimal form. According to the model, at an intensity of 60%, a 5-year increase in age would correspond to a decrease in the target heart rate of how many beats per minute?

32

Jonathan is using an international shipping service to ship a box of medical supplies. The company requires that the package have a volume of less than 120 cubic centimeters. If Jonathan's box of supplies has a base that measures 3 inches by 4 inches, what is the greatest height that the box can measure, rounded to the nearest tenth of an inch?

(1 inch = 2.54 centimeters)

33

Nadia is having some friends over to eat a pizza and to watch a movie. She invited 8 friends, but only expects half to attend. Nadia plans to cut the pizza into a number of slices that is equal to the number of friends that arrive. If 6 of Nadia's friends attend, the central angle that defines each slice will be how many degrees fewer than the number of degrees she expected for each slice?

34

A Koi fish pond that holds 2200 quarts of water was just completed. If one hose can fill the pond at 30 quarts per minute and a second hose can fill the pond at 20 quarts per minute, how long will it take to fill the pond, in minutes, if both hoses are running the entire time?

CONTINUE

35

A bowl is filled with a total of 140 red and green candies. If $\frac{4}{7}$ of the candies are red, how many green candies must be removed from the bowl such that $\frac{2}{3}$ of the remaining candies are red?

36

$$PV = nRT$$

The Ideal Gas Law is shown above where the four gas variables are: pressure (P), volume (V), number of moles of gas (n), and temperature (T). The final variable, R, is the gas constant. If pressure remains constant and both the number of moles of gas and the temperature are reduced by half, by what percent will the volume be reduced?

49

CONTINUE

---▼---

Questions 37-38 refer to the following information.

$$A_{Value} = I(1+\frac{r}{100})^t$$

A savings account follows the model above where the account's current value, A_{Value}, can be calculated at any time based on the initial account value, I, the percentage growth rate, r, and the number of years that have passed since the opening of the account, t.

37

If the initial deposit in the account was $1,000 and in the first year the account's value increased by $5, what is the correct value for r?

38

Let K represent the account's value after 4 years have passed using the percentage growth rate, r, calculated in problem 37 and the initial account value of $1,000. To the nearest dollar, what amount of money should have been initially deposited into the account to attain an account value of K after only one year?

---▲---

STOP

If you finish before time is called, you may check your work on this section only.

Do not turn to any other section.

Answer Key: TEST 1

SECTION 1—READING

1.	B	11.	C	22.	D	33.	B	43.	C
2.	C	12.	C	23.	B	34.	D	44.	B
3.	B	13.	A	24.	B	35.	B	45.	A
4.	A	14.	B	25.	A	36.	D	46.	A
5.	C	15.	D	26.	B	37.	A	47.	C
6.	B	16.	A	27.	C	38.	C	48.	D
7.	B	17.	B	28.	C	39.	D	49.	B
8.	D	18.	B	29.	D	40.	A	50.	A
9.	A	19.	D	30.	C	41.	B	51.	D
10.	B	20.	A	31.	C	42.	D	52.	A
		21.	B	32.	A				

SECTION 2—WRITING

1.	A	12.	B	23.	D	34.	B
2.	B	13.	B	24.	D	35.	D
3.	D	14.	C	25.	A	36.	A
4.	B	15.	D	26.	B	37.	B
5.	A	16.	D	27.	B	38.	C
6.	C	17.	A	28.	D	39.	D
7.	B	18.	C	29.	C	40.	D
8.	A	19.	B	30.	C	41.	A
9.	C	20.	A	31.	A	42.	B
10.	D	21.	B	32.	B	43.	C
11.	C	22.	B	33.	B	44.	A

SECTION 3—MATH

1.	A
2.	D
3.	C
4.	C
5.	B
6.	B
7.	D
8.	C
9.	C
10.	B
11.	C
12.	D
13.	B
14.	A
15.	A

Fill-Ins:

16.	.384, .385, or 5/13
17.	.5 or 1/2
18.	240
19.	18
20.	48

SECTION 4—MATH

1.	B	13.	A	24.	A
2.	D	14.	A	25.	D
3.	C	15.	A	26.	C
4.	C	16.	B	27.	D
5.	B	17.	B	28.	A
6.	C	18.	D	29.	B
7.	D	19.	B	30.	A
8.	B	20.	B		
9.	D	21.	C		
10.	A	22.	B		
11.	C	23.	A		
12.	C				

Fill-Ins:

31.	3
32.	.6 or 3/5
33.	30
34.	44
35.	20
36.	75
37.	.5 or 1/2
38.	1015

Answer Explanations

SAT Practice Test #1

Section 1: Reading

QUESTION 1.

Choice B is correct. While the early segments of the passage establish that Jane is facing new conditions and traveling to "Thornfield" (line 21), the passage goes on to establish that Jane is experiencing "doubts and fears" (line 25) and that she does not know exactly what her assignment at Thornfield entails. (In lines 61-68, for instance, Jane offers a few speculations about the family that will employ her.) This combined anxiety and uncertainty justifies B and eliminates A (since little is known of Jane's earlier "lifestyle") and C (since no "disappointments" are mentioned). D can also be eliminated because it involves the wrong emphasis: the passage is concerned mostly with Jane's present and future, NOT her backstory.

QUESTION 2.

Choice C is correct. In lines 27-31, the passage establishes that Jane is "quite alone in the world", thus justifying C. The passage contradicts other negatives: Jane was in fact miserable with "fine people" (line 63, eliminating A), is confused and anxious but not truly sad (eliminating B), and seems awkward and unsure in lines 36-55 but does not voice embarrassment about her conduct (eliminating D).

QUESTION 3.

Choice B is correct. See above for the explanation of the correct answer. A explains that Jane is anxious, C records a conversation and alludes to some of Jane's uncertainties, and D explains Jane's PAST attitudes of dissatisfaction. Only B aligns with a previous answer choice, though emotions that are not named CAN be gleaned from the other references.

QUESTION 4.

Choice A is correct. In lines 15-16, Jane explains that she is "comfortably accommodated" in her new surroundings but not "very tranquil" in her mind. This contrast lines up directly with A and is expanded upon in Jane's descriptions of the inn and of her emotions. Jane never describes her education or specific talents at any length (eliminating C and D, respectively), and DOES accept the only real ambition mentioned in the passage: entering her new position. B thus misinterprets the content as a contrast.

QUESTION 5.

Choice C is correct. The word "resource" refers to the possibility of being "shown into a private room" (line 24), or to an "option" that Jane would have. C is the best answer, while A, B, and D are all strong positives that would refer to TALENTS or VIRTUES, not to a simple, everyday CHOICE that could be made.

QUESTION 6.

Choice B is correct. As explained in lines 10-14, Jane has endured "sixteen hours" of harsh outdoor conditions since leaving Lowton: she is now warming herself and recovering from this travel. This content justifies B and can be used to eliminate C (too thoroughly negative) and D (not negative at all). Make sure not to confuse the discussion of "A new chapter" (line 1) or "a play" (line 2) as a justification for A: these are IMAGES that Jane uses, not direct indications that she has AMBITIONS to create art or literature.

QUESTION 7.

Choice B is correct. See above for the explanation of the correct answer. A uses imagery to set up Jane's narrative, C indicates that Jane is anxious, and D describes the later stages of the journey in a positive manner. Be careful of wrongly aligning the negative C with Question 6 C and the positive D with Question 6 D: forgetting and good fortune are not among this passage's actual themes.

QUESTION 8.

Choice D is correct. The word charm refers to "adventure", which Jane finds attractive or alluring in certain respects. Choose D and eliminate A (which refers too literally to mystical charms), B (which means enthusiasm and can only refer to people) and C (which wrongly introduces a strong negative tone).

QUESTION 9.

Choice A is correct. The conversation involves the placement of Jane's luggage, the distance that she will travel, and the time it will take to cover this distance: these "practical details" make A an excellent description. The "vehicle" is only mentioned in line 50 and is not described at any length (eliminating B); furthermore, no information, other than the fact that he speaks abruptly, is offered about the carriage driver. This small piece of information does not justify inferences about social status (eliminating C) or grudges (since Jane has only met the driver and does not reflect on his conduct at any length, eliminating D).

QUESTION 10.

Choice B is correct. In the paragraph that follows the line reference, Jane describes the sensation of being "cut adrift from every connection" (lines 28-29): this sensation is linked to her own "doubts and fears" since she is on her own at the inn. This information supports B. Jane never explains EXACTLY what her new duties will be (eliminating A), never mentions a specific "friend" (only general connections, eliminating C), and reflects on HERSELF, not on the people AROUND her (eliminating D).

QUESTION 11.

Choice C is correct. The passage begins by explaining the field of "genomics" (line 9) and a few of the recent events that surround it; the author then goes on to describe the forms of "controversy" (line 33) and debate that surround genomics. This information supports C and eliminates A (which assumes that the passage becomes entirely positive) and D (which assumes that the passage becomes entirely negative). While B rightly seems to allude to Angelina Jolie's "double mastectomy" (lines 1-2), this "surgical procedure" is almost entirely disregarded in the later stages of the passage, so that this answer mistakes a small detail for an overall explanation of the developmental pattern.

54

QUESTION 12.

Choice C is correct. In the first paragraph, the author links celebrity Angelina Jolie's "double mastectomy" (lines 1-2) to "genetic testing" (line 5), a testing method that is revealed as hotly debated in later paragraphs. This information supports C. Eliminate A because Jolie is only described (NOT quoted herself); eliminate B because it is not clear that Jolie has PROMOTED genome testing, only that she has UNDERGONE genome testing. D is too broad: it avoids direct reference to Jolie and raises an issue ("everyone is susceptible") that is at best tangential to the author's record of the genome testing debate.

QUESTION 13.

Choice A is correct. In lines 18-20, the author explains that genome mapping costs dropped by a factor of 50 between 2010 and 2015: this information supports the idea that such testing is more "affordable and accessible". The other answers distort the author's discussion of current genomics debates: while tests are accurate (eliminating B), the USEFULNESS and IMPLICATIONS of these tests remain problematic issues. C misrepresents the information about Angelina Jolie in the first paragraph (who simply underwent genome testing) and wrongly assumes that other celebrities have been visibly involved; D wrongly assumes that lines 62-73 ("Others contend . . . today") which describe a HYPOTHETICAL problem, describe an ACTUAL problem.

QUESTION 14.

Choice B is correct. See above for the explanation of the correct answer. A explains the costs and objectives of the Human Genome Project, C explains the effectiveness and accuracy of genetic testing, and D indicates that genetic testing is controversial, but not WHY. In fact, the positive answer C can be used to eliminate Question 13 B and D, which wrongly assume that testing PROCEDURES are badly flawed.

QUESTION 15.

Choice D is correct. In lines 26-30, the author explains that genome testing can allow greater precision in the treatment of cancer and perhaps eliminate "blanket chemotherapy" (line 30). This information supports D. Cancer is the only disease that the author discusses at length in terms of genetic testing: the article never mentions everyday lifestyle choices (eliminating A) or psychological ailments (eliminating C). B is out of scope: even an accurate cancer or disease diagnosis based on genetic testing MAY involve high-risk procedures for successful elimination.

QUESTION 16.

Choice A is correct. In lines 44-48, the author calls attention to the possible "stigmatization of entire ethnic or genetic groups" (lines 47-48) as a result of genetic testing. This information supports A, while the record of DECREASING costs in lines 18-20 indicates that C is a faulty answer. B and D both rely on unjustified extrapolations from the passage: in lines 62-73, problems with testing healthy people are noted, but never the "worry" or other psychological costs; in line 35, the "publication of the HeLa genome" is mentioned, but the publication of "medical and legal records" for a large number of people is not linked to this event.

QUESTION 17.

Choice B is correct. See above for the explanation of the correct answer. A introduces the HeLa genome controversy, C notes the excessive activity and pressure that genome testing could place on the healthcare system, and D notes the difficulty of predicting the effects of gene mutations. None of these answers align with an answer to the previous question, though be careful of pairing A with Question 16 D and C with 16 B or C.

QUESTION 18.

Choice B is correct. The word "exchange" is used to describe the "conflicting opinions" (line 51) of two experts on genomics: these opinions were published in the *Wall Street Journal*. A "debate" would be an appropriate wording, while A refers to goods (not ideas), C falsely assumes that a reconciliation was reached, and D indicates that the conversation was hostile or trifling (when in fact it was analytic in nature and featured in a newspaper).

QUESTION 19.

Choice D is correct. The word "deep" refers to the flaws that Robert Green cited in his discussion of genetic testing. These flaws would be evident or "considerable", since Green argues that such testing can cause stress on the medical industry and may not be especially useful. A is wrongly positive, while B wrongly indicates that the flaws are DIFFICULT to explain or pin down (even though Green has just explained and emphasized the severity of the flaws) and C wrongly indicates that the flaws would lead to disasters (when the most that they would do is put additional stress on the healthcare system).

QUESTION 20.

Choice A is correct. As indicated by the dark bar, there were 100 laboratories in 1993 and 600 laboratories in 2010: in other words, the number of laboratories increased by 500. Do not forget to subtract the figure from the year 1993 (an error which would result in B, 600), and do not use the light gray bars at all (an error which would result in C or D, which both introduce figures above 600).

QUESTION 21.

Choice B is correct. Throughout the passage, the author has noted the possible advantages and drawbacks of the growth of genetic testing, ultimately concluding that it is not clear whether genomics research has changed the world "For better or worse, or perhaps both" (line 74). This information establishes the author's "ambivalence" or spirit of divided uncertainty about the growth of genomics, a phenomenon that the chart records by showing the growing number of labs and of diseases tested. B is appropriate, while A is too positive, D is too negative, and C wrongly indicates that the author is "apathetic" about or uninterested in the growth of genomics. In contrast, the author is engaged, but has not arrived at a single set opinion about the virtues of genetic testing.

QUESTION 22.

Choice D is correct. The passage introduces the technology surrounding "Reusable rockets" (15), then describes an experiment that created promising ion engines that, nonetheless, are "not yet fully optimized" (line 54). D refers appropriately to this "relatively new" technology and refers appropriately to both positives and negatives. A ("popularize") assumes that the results have been wholly positive, while C ("disputes") wrongly emphasizes negatives. B focuses on the "goals" of the rockets, not on the EXPLANATION of the rockets themselves and of their development that takes up much of the passage.

QUESTION 23.

Choice B is correct. In this paragraph, the author introduces the "cost-per-ton" (line 9) of plane travel and rocket travel: planes are more cost-efficient because they can "complete many trips" (line 12). This information supports B, while other answers refer to outside factors: it is clear why rockets have not been used in transit (but NOT why planes have not been used in space exploration, eliminating A); it is clear that reusable rockets have relatively short lifespans (but NOT what the average lifespan is, eliminating C); it is not clear that airlines and space exploration companies collaborate at all (since these two industries are simply COMPARED, eliminating D).

QUESTION 24.

Choice B is correct. The line reference describes how "Another type of engine" uses the movement and interaction of ions to create propulsion. This information justifies B, while the size of an ion engine is not mentioned here at all (eliminating C) and cost effectiveness is mentioned primarily in the first paragraph (eliminating D). A is a trap answer: although SpaceX and Reaction Engines are DEVELOPING ion engines, it is not clear that ion engines explain why these companies are FAMOUS.

QUESTION 25.

Choice A is correct. In lines 37-40, the team headed by Vaudolon is mentioned as trying to address the "degradation of the engine wall" in ion engines. This information on a technological flaw supports A: the cost-efficiency of the engines has already been established in the earlier, broader stages of the passage and was not a motivation for the experiment (eliminating B), Vaudolon's engines still form "plasma" (line 40, eliminating C), and computer simulation is only mentioned explicitly in the FINAL paragraph as a late stage of the experiment (eliminating D).

QUESTION 26.

Choice B is correct. See above for the explanation of the correct answer. A explains the cost efficiency of reusable rockets generally, C describes a trade-off that resulted from Vaudolon's design, and D describes a later stage of Vaudolon's research. None of these answers, as demanded above, deals with the main objective that the research was "designed to address".

QUESTION 27.

Choice C is correct. The word "reach" refers to the speed of Hall Thruster exhaust: this speed would be registered as a measure or "attained". A refers to physical GESTURES (not a MEASUREMENT), B wrongly assumes that the speed is a physical thing that is increasing in size, and D would be best for a HUMAN accomplishing a goal, not inanimate EXHAUST.

QUESTION 28.

Choice C is correct. As explained in lines 64-65, Vaudolon's design removes "the most unpredictable" element of ion thruster design: his team's design is thus more stable, or less unstable. This information supports C and eliminates D. Expense is considered primarily in the opening paragraphs and is not explicitly mentioned in the discussion of Vaudolon's thruster (eliminating A), while Vaudolon's thruster REARRANGES engineering elements but still relies heavily on chemical reactions (eliminating B).

QUESTION 29.

Choice D is correct. See above for the explanation of the correct answer. A indicates the efficiency of ion engines in general, B explains how Vaudolon manipulated the ion engine configuration, and C explains that the engine developed by Vaudolon is promising but not ideal. Though all relevant to the overall topic of ion engines, none of these answers clearly COMPARES Vaudolon's engine to other engines.

QUESTION 30.

Choice C is correct. The "system" referred to in the passage is Vaudolon's ion engine setup. C properly describes a physical object built by scientists: B refers to the actions of PEOPLE rather than to created OBJECTS, while A and D both refer to topics from the passage but do NOT directly fit the word "system" as used to describe the engine configuration.

QUESTION 31.

Choice C is correct. While the Hall Thruster has a propulsion efficiency of roughly 85%, the SpaceX Reusable Rocket has a propulsion efficiency of roughly 50%, a difference that supports C as a statement of the Hall Thruster's superior fuel efficiency. While the chart indicates that the Hall Thruster is MORE expensive and thus less cost-effective than a similar reusable rocket (eliminating A), the chart does not explicitly consider either acceleration rates (eliminating B) or the requirements for a Mars mission (eliminating D).

QUESTION 32.

Choice A is correct. The author notes that reusable rockets offer "some promise for lowering the cost per flight" because single-use rockets have short lifespans and cites SpaceX as a company that is developing such rockets. However, while SpaceX Reusable Rockets are cost efficient but have limited propulsion capabilities, Hall Thrusters are more powerful and thus relatively expensive, requiring "multiple engines and more money" (line 36) for substantial trips. A appropriately paraphrases this reasoning to explain the low costs of the SpaceX Reusable Rocket recorded in the graph. B, C, and D all refer to aspects of how ion engines are ENGINEERED, not to the central FACTOR (reusability that increases engine lifespan) that makes the Space X Reusable Rocket more cost-effective.

QUESTION 33.

Choice B is correct. In the final paragraph of Passage 2, it is explained that railway companies have been linked to fatalities yet that there is no "court treacherous enough to enforce a law against a railway company" (lines 60-61). This cynical description supports B, while the overall negative, sarcastic tone taken toward the railway companies eliminates C. However, Passage 2 does not explain HOW the railroads are built or WHY so many fatalities occur: thus, eliminate A and D, respectively.

QUESTION 34.

Choice D is correct. While Passage 1 describes how the railroads can "run over a man" (line 27), Passage 2 mentions the "three thousand and seventy lives" (lines 53-54) destroyed by railroad collisions. This information supports D. Only Passage 1 calls attention to the people who build the railroads (eliminating B), only Passage 2 deals with the legal corruption that protects the railroads (eliminating C), and NEITHER Passage 1 nor Passage 2 cites public protests (eliminating D), even though both AUTHORS criticize the railroads.

QUESTION 35.

Choice B is correct. In lines 33-35, the author of Passage 1 addresses what "Men say" commonly and takes issue with a certain line of conduct: this information supports B. Other answers distort the passage's content: the author is HIMSELF a rebel or freethinker, but does not praise a larger group (eliminating A); the author refers to nationalities linked to industry in lines 21-22, but does not say that these are the nationalities MOST oppressed by industry (eliminating C); the author describes misfortune in lines 27-30, but is not speaking about a PERSONAL experience (eliminating D).

QUESTION 36.

Choice D is correct. See above for the explanation of the correct answer. A explains a desirable lifestyle, B links a few demographic groups to the railroad, and C describes a man who encounters misfortune. None of these aligns effectively with an answer to the previous question, though be careful not to pair A with Question 35 A, B with Question 35 C, or C with Question 35 D.

QUESTION 37.

Choice A is correct. The word "rigid" refers to an "economy" (line 8) or lifestyle that is notable for being stern and simplified: the word "austere" effectively characterizes exactly such a lifestyle. B and D both wrongly assume that the lifestyle cannot CHANGE at all (when in fact it may remain austere but change in other ways), while C means "observing traditional beliefs" and is thus a poor fit for Thoreau's recommendation for a new, better lifestyle.

QUESTION 38.

Choice C is correct. Although used in a sarcastic manner, the word "great" is paired with the word "glorious" and indicates the reasons why America is well-known. C, "distinguished", is an appropriate fit. A wrongly refers to physical size, B is concerned with either political ideology or personal generosity (topics that are secondary at best here), and D discusses material wealth (while Twain is more interested in basic matters of reputation and never directly mentions wealth at this point).

QUESTION 39.

Choice D is correct. In lines 43-47, the author of Passage 2 sarcastically calls America's legal system "superior" and notes that it relies in large part on men who "don't know anything and can't read". This information supports A, while B, C, and D all raise topics that are tangential to the passage: only the penalties on the railroads (not on the poor and wealthy generally) are discussed, an "insanity plea" (line 47) is mentioned but not compared to the rules for "other citizens", and HOW people make trial decisions ("sentiments") is never explained.

QUESTION 40.

Choice A is correct. See above for the explanation of the correct answer. B describes the insanity plea in America and the power of money in politics, C notes that the railroads are oppressive, and D describes railroad fatalities and how the railroads responded. None of these answers characterize the justice system in a way that fulfills the demands of the previous question, though be cautious of taking B as evidence for Question 39 A or B.

QUESTION 41.

Choice B is correct. While Passage 1 indicates that a "Spartan simplicity of life" (line 4) can solve some of America's problems, Passage 2 does not call attention to any such solution. (At most, the author of Passage 2 speaks cynically of the good intentions of the railroad ownership.) This information supports B, while A is relevant ONLY to Passage 2, since Passage 1 is concerned mostly with railroads and individuals, not the government. C and D describe features of BOTH passages and must be eliminated.

QUESTION 42.

Choice D is correct. While the "Men" are interested in new projects and pursuits, the author of Passage 1 argues that such pursuits have "tripped up" (line 4) the nation and that, despite all the activity, there is not any work "of any consequence" (line 35). This information supports D and contradicts C, since the author is considerably PESSIMISTIC about the influences in the nation. A ("agriculture") and B (overturning "laws") refer to interests that are never EXPLICITLY attributed to the author and must thus be eliminated.

QUESTION 43.

Choice C is correct. The passage begins by explaining the famous fossilized skeleton known as Lucy, then asserts that she was "not the first of her species to be found" (lines 14-15) and describes other findings such as the Taung Child, Selam, and Ardi. These various discoveries help to explain how humans might have developed: C is thus the best answer. A focuses too much on the process of finding these fossils (not on their SIGNIFICANCE), B wrongly treats the passage as PERSUASIVE rather than INFORMATIVE, and D calls attention to a detail (bipedalism) but neglects the author's larger emphasis on a RANGE of fossils.

QUESTION 44.

Choice B is correct. In lines 13-15, the author explains that Lucy was "not the first of her species to be found" despite her importance. This information supports B and eliminates both A and D, which both indicate that Lucy was NOT the first of her species. Although the author notes that other fossils are important, the passage does not argue that Lucy has fallen in stature: in fact, lines 55-56 suggest that she is the "most interesting hominid fossil ever found" both years ago and "possibly even now". This information thus contradicts answer C.

QUESTION 45.

Choice A is correct. See above for the explanation of the correct answer. B describes a discovery OTHER than Lucy (the Taung Child), C summarizes one of Richard Leakey's arguments (NOT one of the author's), and D indicates Lucy's high level of recognition. Make sure not to wrongly take D as a justification for a positive answer such as Question 44 A or D.

QUESTION 46.

Choice A is correct. The words in the question prompt express uncertainty and refer (respectively) to Lucy's status as "the oldest example of a human ancestor" (lines 6-7) and her "female" gender (line 11). These pieces of evidence refer to factors that interested the researchers who found Lucy and support A. B, C, and D all refer to Lucy's RECEPTION rather than her DISCOVERY, and C and D both introduce negatives that have no relation to the tone of this informative paragraph.

QUESTION 47.

Choice C is correct. The word "detect" refers to a single observation made by an anthropologist, that Lucy "wasn't a knuckle-dragger" (lines 23-24). In other words, this statement would be an observation or perception, so that C, "perceive", is an effective answer. Both B and D refer to observation that occurs OVER TIME, not to a SINGLE observation. Trap answer A relates to the overall topic of the passage, but it is not clear that Lucy's posture was an ONGOING research topic, only that Johanson offered a SINGLE perception related to Lucy.

QUESTION 48.

Choice D is correct. In lines 22-25, the author indicates a similarity between Lucy and the Taung Child: both, instead of dragging their knuckles over the ground, walked upright "as contemporary human beings do". This information supports D. Other answers are contradicted by the content of the passage: the Taung Child was discovered BEFORE Lucy (eliminating A), the Taung Child's likely gender is never specified (eliminating B), and while Lucy was "at least 3.2 million years old" (lines 5-6), the Taung Child probably lived "3 million years ago" (line 18, contradicting D, which indicates that the Taung Child is OLDER than Lucy).

QUESTION 49.

Choice B is correct. See above for the explanation of the correct answer. A explains the discovery and dating of the Taung Child (but NOT the discovery's importance), C explains the structure of Lucy's society (NOT the Taung Child in particular), and D explains that fossils older than Lucy have been found (but does NOT mention the Taung Child). Be careful not to take C as evidence for Question 48 B, which raises the issue of gender.

QUESTION 50.

Choice A is correct. In the final paragraph, the author states that anthropologists have found human ancestor remains that are "older and better preserved" (lines 45-46) than Lucy, then returns to the topic of Lucy's significance. This information supports A, while only Lucy's "originality" (line 54) is called into question: other fossils such as the Taung Child have displayed bipedalism (eliminating B) and Lucy is described as an accurate "human ancestor" (line 50, eliminating C). D is a trap answer: although Lucy is in fact better known than other fossils, she is not the ONLY hominid fossil known to the public.

QUESTION 51.

Choice D is correct. The word "discount" refers to "revelations" (line 53) that Lucy is NOT the first human ancestor of her kind. In other words, an idea has been definitively negated or disproven, so that D is the best answer. A and B are negative but do not offer the needed content: the ideas about Lucy would REQUIRE attention to be negated and could not be simply "disregarded" or "overlooked". C is too weak, and would describe an idea that has DECREASED in popularity, not been COMPLETELY disregarded.

QUESTION 52.

Choice A is correct. In lines 55-56, the author describes Lucy as "the most interesting hominid fossil ever found, certainly in 1974 and possibly even now". This information supports A, while B, C, and D are all inappropriate negatives; C and D also introduce the topics of "science funding" and "archaeological remains" unlike Lucy (respectively), topics that are not considerations of this passage.

Section 2: Writing
Passage 1, Domfront: Where the Middle Ages Live

QUESTION 1.

Choice A is correct. This question requires you to determine the correct idiomatic expression: "of some importance" is the standard English phrase for describing the "little town of Domfront." (The same accepted usage occurs in phrases such as "idea of some importance" and "person of some importance.") B, C, and D all use prepositions that do not fit the standard idiom.

QUESTION 2.

Choice B is correct. The underlined portion must describe the "sixteenth century," which is a time period and thus takes "when" as the best reference. A refers to a place, C refers to a thing, and D refers to a means or a procedure.

QUESTION 3.

Choice D is correct. Sentence 3 begins by describing the energy of Domfront, then points out the "sleepy state" of the town, an idea discussed at length in the next paragraph. It would thus be best to use this sentence to transition to the next paragraph, justifying D as the best answer. Both A and C would interrupt the series of examples of activity in old Domfront that takes up much of the paragraph, while B would wrongly introduce these examples with a reference to the town's "sleepy state," which is traced to a different time period.

QUESTION 4.

Choice B is correct. The paragraph as a whole describes Domfront in the present tense, so the present "bursts" is the best verb for the subject "the old part." A is a past tense form (or may be read as a noun), while C and D both create sentence fragments rather than proper subject-verb combinations.

QUESTION 5.

Choice A is correct. The verb must describe the "rhythms" or sounds of the instruments mentioned in the sentence: "rebound" would properly refer to how a sound bounces off "stone walls." Of the false answers, A refers to a reprimand, C refers to the act of getting better, and D refers to the act of complementing or giving in return, so that all of these answers assume incorrect contexts.

QUESTION 6.

Choice C is correct. The underlined portion should provide the final noun in a list of items available at the Domfront festival: thus, look for parallelism. C rightly refers to "biscuits", while A ("they make") and D ("making") both break the parallelism and B ("these are made") introduces a comma splice.

QUESTION 7.

Choice B is correct. This question requires a reference to "additional spectacles": "Flag throwers, jugglers, and tumblers" have not been mentioned earlier, so that B is an excellent answer. A ("performers"), C ("feats"), and D ("wrestling") all refer to spectacles that have ALREADY been mentioned, not to ADDITIONAL spectacles as demanded by the prompt.

QUESTION 8.

Choice A is correct. The underlined phrase should be in parallel with "cleared of": "replaced by" offers the correct, past tense verb form. B breaks parallelism by introducing an -ing verb form, while C and D both disrupt the parallelism by introducing superfluous pronouns.

QUESTION 9.

Choice C is correct. In the relevant sentence, the non-essential phrase "to great fanfare" should describe how the mayor "declares" the opening of the celebration: it is best to offset this phrase using two commas. A, B, and D all wrongly divide the subject "mayor" from the verb "declares" using a single unit of punctuation.

QUESTION 10.

Choice D is correct. For this question, find a phrasing that is logical in the context of the passage: at a festival that energizes the otherwise inactive town of Domfront, "attendance" would naturally "swell." Trap answer A wrongly assumes that the people in attendance would INDIVIDUALLY swell or grow larger, B introduces an ambiguous pronoun, and C wrongly assumes that the costumes would swell.

QUESTION 11.

Choice C is correct. The best answer for this question will be consistent with the style and logic of the passage. A and B should be eliminated because these choices simultaneously indicate that the Domfront festival both happens EVERY two years and will NEVER happen again, while D is much too colloquial in phrasing. C is thus the most sensible and concise answer.

Passage 2, Beyond Rosie the Riveter: Women and World War II

QUESTION 12.

Choice B is correct. In the original phrasing, "the military" is wrongly compared to "any previous war". Eliminate A and choose B, which rightly indicates that the situation in World War II was different from the situation "in any previous war". C and D construct the comparison using "as" instead of "than", which is idiomatically incorrect in the relevant sentence.

QUESTION 13.

Choice B is correct. Earlier in the passage, the writer explains that jobs once worked by men "became vacant" and that "the government allowed women to assume roles previously restricted to men": one such role involved direct employment by the government, as specified in the new sentence. Choose B and eliminate A (since the sentence states a FACT, rather than arguing a REASON). C is incorrect because it is not firmly established earlier that women were given direct government jobs, while D uses flawed reasoning: even though the sentence does not pinpoint specific government jobs, it does effectively anticipate the discussion that follows.

QUESTION 14.

Choice C is correct. The subject of the underlined verb "are" is "one" (since the phrase "out of every three civil service workers" is an interrupting phrase that must be factored out. Eliminate the plural answers A and D. Because the sentence describes a situation in the 1940s, the underlined verb must also be in past tense: eliminate B and choose C as the best answer.

QUESTION 15.

Choice D is correct. The underlined portion must effectively refer back to the plural noun "women", who would accept plural "jobs". Eliminate A and B (which both refer to a single "job" for multiple women"), then choose D over the wordy and awkward C.

QUESTION 16.

Choice D is correct. This sentence presents a contrast between how women were "not permitted to participate" and the eventual measures that allowed women to "serve in the Army, Navy, and Coast Guard". B and C do not articulate contrasts, while A ("however") cannot connect two independent clauses in the way that a conjunction such as "but" or "yet" can. Thus, D is the best answer.

QUESTION 17.

Choice A is correct. While the previous paragraph discusses how women contributed to medical work and combat missions, this paragraph focuses on women's jobs in factories and on production lines. The best replacement will emphasize that the author is continuing to discuss new women's roles, as A effectively does. B is more closely related to ideas in the next paragraph, C distracts from the discussion of women's employment by discussing women as homemakers, and D returns to the topic of "government" (which was an emphasis only earlier in the passage).

QUESTION 18.

Choice C is correct. The phrase should describe HOW "Rosie the Riveter" was known, so that "popularly known" is the best construction. A wrongly treats both underlined words as adjectives (while "popularly" should MODIFY "known"), and B and D are awkward expressions that are not as concise as C.

QUESTION 19.

Choice B is correct. The underlined word should be part of a standard phrase introduced by "so" and describing degree or extent: "so . . . that" is the proper English usage. A and C both distort this common expression, while D turns the sentence into two independent clauses ("demand was", "women . . . worked") that are not effectively linked.

QUESTION 20.

Choice A is correct. The descriptive phrase "such as domestic labor, teaching, and sewing" must be offset by two dashes, as accomplished by A. In B, C, and D, the subject "jobs" is improperly separated from the verb "were" by a single dash.

QUESTION 21.

Choice B is correct. For this question, eliminate choices that introduce structural errors at the underlined portion: A and D both create comma splices. While B and C both avoid this error, C introduces faulty parallelism ("the war ended", "soldiers returning"), while B properly puts two full subject-verb ("the war ended", "the soldiers returned") combinations in parallel.

QUESTION 22.

Choice B is correct. The previous sentence explains that female workers were "quickly laid off", while the sentence introduced by the underlined portion explains what was "generally expected" of women as a result of this shift. Thus, look for an answer that creates a cause-and-effect relationship between the sentences: B does so, while A, C, and D all wrongly introduce contrast relationships.

Passage 3, Being Grateful for Gratitude

QUESTION 23.

Choice D is correct. The underlined pronoun should refer to an IDEA supported by research on gratitude, particularly the idea that "a grateful heart is a happy heart". D properly references an idea or notion, while A (an ambiguous "it"), B (an ambiguous "that"), and C ("them", which does not refer to any noun directly) do not clarify the content of the sentence as needed.

QUESTION 24.

Choice D is correct. Look for the correct idiomatic phrase: "appreciation of" is standard English usage, as in "appreciation of one's advantages" and "appreciation of one's family". A, B, and C all distort this phrase by introducing incorrect prepositions.

QUESTION 25.

Choice A is correct. The underlined phrase must refer directly to the noun "experiment", which is a THING and will naturally take "which" as the proper pronoun in any descriptive phrase. B can only describe a LOCATION, C creates an awkward construction and is best used to introduce a THOUGHT or IDEA, and D must refer to a TIME.

QUESTION 26.

Choice B is correct. The subject of the underlined verb is the plural "Participants", since the interrupting phrase "in the first group" must be factored out. Eliminate A and C, which involve singular verbs; then note that the sentence describes an experiment which was performed in the past. Thus, eliminate the present-tense D and choose the past-tense B as the best answer.

QUESTION 27.

Choice B is correct. The correct version of this sentence should compare the actions of "people who wrote about gratitude" to the actions of other "participants". While A wrongly compares the actions of the "people" directly to the "participants", and C wrongly compares the actions to "either of the other groups", B rightly compares the actions of the "people" to what the participants "did". Thus, choose B over the unnecessarily wordy D.

QUESTION 28.

Choice D is correct. Because the underlined sentence introduces a new point about gratitude that advances the writer's argument, it should be kept: eliminate A and B, but also eliminate C, since the sentence BUILDS OFF a point ("Moreover") rather than INTRODUCING a concept. Thus, D is the best answer.

QUESTION 29.

Choice C is correct. The underlined portion must both logically refer to the action taken by Seligman and obey correct grammar. While A involves a comma splice, B wrongly assumes that Seligman designed the experiment by assigning (not that he designed the experiment, THEN assigned the techniques) and D wrongly indicates that Seligman HIMSELF was "being assigned" a technique. Only C properly refers back to how Seligman performed his research by "assigning" techniques.

QUESTION 30.

Choice C is correct. As indicated by the word "than", the sentence should entail a comparison. A ("great . . . than") does not properly compare increases in happiness as the sentence demands. D would only be appropriate to a comparison involving more than two groups, while B ("more great") is closer in meaning to "more impressive" than "larger". The concise C is the best answer.

QUESTION 31.

Choice A is correct. The sentence relevant to this question involves the standard phrase "not only . . . but also", so that A is the best answer. B, C, and D all disrupt this standard pairing with different second conjunctions.

QUESTION 32.

Choice B is correct. According to the graph, the group that heard the speech made 80 phone calls in the second week, while the group that did not made 40 phone calls. B properly records the difference at 40 phone calls, while A records the increase within the group that didn't hear the speech, C records the increase within the group that did hear the speech, and D records the second-week number of phone calls for the group that did hear the speech.

QUESTION 33.

Choice B is correct. The underlined portion must properly refer back to the noun "positives", so that the plural "them" is the best pronoun. While C is singular, A and D are both possessive pronouns that indicate ownership, NOT pronouns that would refer directly to factors such as "positives".

Passage 4, The Good Graces of Seawater Greenhouses

QUESTION 34.

Choice B is correct. The underlined verb takes the subject "One" (since "of today's humanitarian dilemmas" is an interrupting phrase that most be temporarily disregarded). Eliminate plural choices A and D; then, consider that the "One" is present "today" and must be described in the present tense. Thus, eliminate C and choose B.

QUESTION 35.

Choice D is correct. The relevant sentence should involve the standard comparison phrase "more . . . than", so that A and B must be eliminated. Be cautious of trap answer C, which involves a faulty comparison: the sentence is meant to explain the situation "in desert countries", not to indicate that the "crisis is more apparent than desert countries", since the crisis is NOT a country. Thus, D is the best answer.

QUESTION 36.

Choice A is correct. The underlined portion must refer back to "desert countries" using an effective pronoun. B wrongly uses a singular pronoun, C is excessively wordy, and D awkwardly omits any pronoun whatsoever. A, which is concise and grammatically correct, is the best answer.

QUESTION 37.

Choice B is correct. The sentence refers to the "troubling" situation involving food needs in Africa, then explains problems that surround the high food prices and "already disadvantaged desert populations". Thus, the sentence follows an idea-and-illustration structure, so that B is the best answer. A wrongly introduces a contrast, C introduces a comma splice, and D uses faulty punctuation, since "because" cannot be fully separated from an independent phrase by a comma.

QUESTION 38.

Choice C is correct. The phrase "First assembled in 1994" should logically refer to Paton's greenhouse prototype, NOT to Paton. A and B thus involve misplaced modifiers, while D introduces redundancy with the phrase "resulting from the product of", since "result" and "product" are interchangeable ideas. C is thus the most concise and effective answer.

QUESTION 39.

Choice D is correct. To create the proper comparison in this sentence, prioritize both concision and grammar. Both A and C use the grammatically incorrect phrase "more cooler", while B is needlessly wordy. (It is also not clear whether or not the "more" in B is meant to modify "cooler", and it is best to eliminate confusion of this sort.) D is thus the best answer.

QUESTION 40.

Choice D is correct. While sentence 1 introduces the topic of how the greenhouses were "designed to work", sentences 3 and 4 explain exactly how the greenhouses work and sentence 2 mentions the "side benefits" of greenhouses. It would be most logical to place the discussion of benefits AFTER the full explanation of the greenhouses and how they operate: thus, D is the best answer. A and C would continue to wrongly split up the explanation of how the greenhouses operate, while B would turn sentence 2 into a problematic and ambiguous topic sentence, since this sentence does not mention the "greenhouses" as directly as sentence 1.

QUESTION 41.

Choice A is correct. Because multiple verbs occur in series in this sentence, try for effective parallelism. While A creates parallelism between "to filter" and "to cool and humidify", C wrongly introduces "humidifying" into this structure. B wrongly introduces an ambiguous pronoun ("them"), while D distorts the meaning of the original sentence so that all the verbs illogically refer to all of the nouns involved.

QUESTION 42.

Choice B is correct. At this point in the passage, the author is discussing the use of seawater greenhouses: a consideration of "irrigation techniques" only interrupts this analysis. Choose B and eliminate C and D, since the example of irrigation is IRRELEVANT rather than supporting or contradictory. Although the sentence should be deleted, it is not "entirely unrelated" to the passage's discussion of desert countries, which are in fact mentioned: thus, eliminate A on the basis of its faulty logic.

QUESTION 43.

Choice C is correct. In the underlined phrase, "cautious" should describe HOW "optimistic" the scientists are and should be replaced with the adverb "cautiously". Thus, eliminate A and B and choose C; trap answer D COMPARES the words "cautious" and "optimistic" rather than relating them in terms of DEGREE.

QUESTION 44.

Choice A is correct. Throughout the passage, the author has pointed to seawater greenhouses as a promising solution that has not yet been universally accepted: the correct answer should refer to the greenhouses using a positive tone. A fits all of these requirements, while B omits any reference to the author's position on the greenhouses and C and D wrongly assume that the author's tone is primarily negative.

Section 3: Math Test - No Calculator

QUESTION 1.

Choice A is correct. The first equation can be rewritten as $4x - 2y = 10$. If the second equation is then multiplied by -2, the second equation gives $-4x + 4y = -14$. Then, if both equations are added together, the x variable is eliminated leaving $2y = -4$, or $y = -2$.

Choices B, C, and D are incorrect and may have resulted from errors in computation or conceptual understanding of when solving the linear system.

QUESTION 2.

Choice D is correct. Distributing the 3 in the numerator will yield the expression $6x + 15$ which also appears in the denominator. Simplifying the overall expression by canceling the $6x + 15$ in the numerator and the denominator gives the expression $\dfrac{1}{6x + 5}$.

Choices A is incorrect and may result from attempting to simplify the $2x$ in the numerator with the pair of $6x$'s in the denominator and likewise, the 5 with the 5 and 15 in the denominator. Choice B is incorrect and may result from accidentally cancelling the $2x + 5$ with the $6x + 5$. Choice C is incorrect and may be the result of only distributing the 3 in the numerator to the $2x$ and not the 5, which would then cancel with the $6x + 5$ in the denominator.

QUESTION 3.

Choice C is correct. Billy's score on the 3rd night was 64 and his score on the 7th night was 48. Billy's score was reduced by 16 over the course of 4 nights. Since Billy's score reduces by the same amount each night, the change in score, 16, divided by the change in days, 4, gives a reduction of 4 points each night. To get from 48 to zero, it will take $\dfrac{48}{4}$, or 12 nights to achieve a score of zero. 12 nights from the 7th night is the 19th night.

Choice A is incorrect because Billy's score was 48 on the 7th night which is already past the 4th night. Choices B and D are incorrect because neither of those days allows for a linear decrease with a score of 64 on the 3rd night and a score of 48 on the 7th night.

QUESTION 4.

Choice C is correct. In the expression $(-|x|)^3$, besides 0 which is the greatest possible solution, every number is the cube of a non-zero negative value, which is negative.

Choices A and B are incorrect because if you enter a value of 0 for x in both cases you will get a positive value of 1. Choice D is incorrect because it makes every value in Choice C the opposite. So, in Choice D, 0 is the lowest value and every non-zero value of x yields a positive solution.

QUESTION 5.

Choice B is correct. Since $f(x) = Kx^2 + 1$ and $f(8) = 33$, substituting 6 for x and 33 for $f(x)$ gives $33 = K(8)^2 + 1$. Then, solving the equation for K gives $32 = 64K$ which makes $K = \dfrac{1}{2}$. Substituting this value for K and evaluating $f(4)$ by substituting 4 for x gives $f(4) = \dfrac{1}{2}(4)^2 + 1$, or $f(4) = \dfrac{1}{2}(16) + 1$. Thus, $f(4) = 8 + 1 = 9$.

Choice A is incorrect because it is the answer if the 4 is input, but not squared. Choice C is incorrect because it assumes the constant K is 1. Choice D is incorrect because it assumes the constant K is 2.

QUESTION 6.

Choice B is correct. If one evaluates $f(\dfrac{1}{9}x)$ using $f(x) = 3x + 5$ by substituting $\dfrac{1}{9}x$ for every instance of x, the equation yields $f(\dfrac{1}{9}x) = 3(\dfrac{1}{9}x) + 5$, which simplifies to $\dfrac{1}{3}x + 5$.

Choices A, C, and D are incorrect because none will produce a coefficient of $\dfrac{1}{3}$ when substituted appropriately.

QUESTION 7.

Choice D is correct. The equation $\dfrac{a(b+a)}{2a} = 5$ can be rewritten as $\dfrac{b+a}{2} = 5$. It follows that $b + a = 10$, or $a = 10 - b$.

Choices A, B, and C are incorrect and most likely result from miscalculations when rewriting the original equation $\dfrac{a(b+a)}{2a} = 5$. For example, choice A may be the result of a distribution error in which the a is distributed and reduced properly with the first term, but distributed and not reduced with the second term.

QUESTION 8.

Choice C is correct. In order for two lines to be perpendicular when in the form $y = mx + b$, their slopes, m, must have opposite reciprocal values. In choice C, if $3y + 6x = 12$ is rewritten in the form $y = mx + b$, it yields $y = -2x + 4$. Likewise, if $-6y + 3x = 9$ is rewritten in the form $y = mx + b$, it yields $y = \dfrac{1}{2}x - \dfrac{3}{2}$. In this form it is easy to see that -2 and $\dfrac{1}{2}$ are opposite reciprocals.

Choices A, B, and D are incorrect and may be the result of confusing perpendicular slopes with parallel slopes or of other potential miscalculations, such as a missed sign.

QUESTION 9.

Choice C is correct. One can see that the two solutions $(a,16)$ and $(b,16)$ share a common y-value of 16. If this value is substituted for $f(x)$ in the quadratic equation $f(x) = x^2 + 7$, the equation yields $16 = x^2 + 7$, or $9 = x^2$. Thus the solutions $x = \pm 3$. Substituting the two x-values into the expression $|a - b|$ yields a value of 6 regardless of which value you substitute for a or b.

Choices A, C, and D are incorrect and may be the result of calculation errors in solving for a and b. For example, choice A may be the result of mistaking $|a - b|$ for $|a + b|$.

QUESTION 10.

Choice B is correct. To solve for x, square each side of the equation, which gives $(x - 2)^2 = (\sqrt{x})^2$, or $(x - 2)^2 = x$. Then by expanding the left side $(x - 2)^2$ the equation becomes $x^2 - 4x + 4 = x$, or $x^2 - 5x + 4 = 0$. From here, factoring the left hand side gives $(x - 4)(x - 1) = 0$, and so $x = 1$ or $x = 4$. Substituting 1 for x in the original equation gives $1 - 2 = \sqrt{1}$, which yields $-1 = 1$, which is an extraneous solution.

Choices A and C are incorrect because -1 and 2 could only arise as solutions from calculation errors. Choice D is incorrect because if 4 is substituted into the original equation, $4 - 2 = \sqrt{4}$, or $2 = 2$, which is true and not extraneous.

QUESTION 11.

Choice C is correct. Multiplying each side of the equation $\dfrac{4m}{m + \frac{1}{24}} = 8$ by $m + \dfrac{1}{24}$ gives $4m = 8(m + \dfrac{1}{24})$. Distributing 8 over the parentheses gives the equation $4m = 8m + \dfrac{1}{3}$, or $-4m = \dfrac{1}{3}$. Solving for m, one gets $m = -\dfrac{1}{12}$.

Choices A, B, and D are incorrect and may be the result of calculation errors or improper use of the distributive property.

QUESTION 12.

Choice D is correct. The price of Rachel's package was x dollars and the price of Angela's package was $x + 3$ dollars. Thus, the total price of all muffins without discount was $2x + 3$ dollars. However, since both purchases were made at 50% off the marked prices, the actual price was $0.5(2x + 3)$, or $x + \dfrac{3}{2}$. Since the cost was split evenly among Rachel, Angela, and 10 other friends, we must divide this total by 12, yielding $\dfrac{x + \frac{3}{2}}{12}$, or $\dfrac{2x + 3}{24}$.

Choice A is incorrect because the total price was not divided evenly among the 12 friends. Choices B and C are incorrect because neither expression accounts for the 50% discount on the final purchase price.

QUESTION 13.

Choice B is correct. The equation $x^2 - a^2 = ax$ can be rewritten in the form

$x^2 - ax - a^2 = 0$. Applying the quadratic formula, $\dfrac{-b \pm \sqrt{b^2 - 4ac}}{2a}$, to this equation with

$a = 1$, $b = -a$, and $c = -a^2$ gives $\dfrac{-(-a) \pm \sqrt{(-a)^2 - 4(1)(-a^2)}}{2(1)}$, or $\dfrac{a \pm a\sqrt{5}}{2}$.

Choices A, C, and D are incorrect and may be the result of applying the quadratic formula inappropriately.

QUESTION 14.

Choice A is correct. In the graph, $y > 1$ represents the region strictly above the horizontal line at 1. $y < 5 - x^2$ represents the region strictly below the parabola. Plotting every coordinate point with integer coordinates that falls in this region yields the following 7 points: $(-1, 2)$, $(0, 2)$, $(1, 2)$, $(-1, 3)$, $(0, 3)$, $(1, 3)$, and $(0, 4)$.

Choices B, C, and D are incorrect and may be the result of misinterpreting the constraints of the inequalities. For example, Choice D is incorrect because 15 would be the correct number of coordinate points with integer coordinates that satisfy the system of inclusive inequalities defined by $y \geq 1$ and $y \leq 5 - x^2$.

QUESTION 15.

Choice A is correct. To rewrite $\dfrac{(16 + 3i)(1 + 4i)}{i}$ in the form $a - bi$, one must first

expand the numerator which gives $\dfrac{16 + 64i + 3i + 12i^2}{i}$, or $\dfrac{4 + 67i}{i}$. Multiplying the

numerator and the denominator by i gives $\dfrac{4 + 67i}{i} \cdot \dfrac{i}{i} = \dfrac{4i + 67i^2}{i^2}$. Since $i^2 = -1$, this

expression is equivalent to $\dfrac{4i - 67}{-1}$, or $67 - 4i$. Since the question asks for the remainder

when a is divided by b, if one divides 67 by 4, one is left with a remainder of 3.

Choices B, C, and D are incorrect and may be the result of errors in expanding the numerator or errors in converting to the form $a - bi$.

QUESTION 16.

The correct answer is .384, .385, or $\dfrac{5}{13}$. The cosine of $y°$ is $\dfrac{12}{13}$ the ratio of the side

adjacent to the $y°$ angle and the hypotenuse is $\dfrac{12}{13}$. One can use this ratio in the right

triangle to recognize the pythagorean triple 5-12-13. Then, it follows that the ratio of

adjacent to hypotenuse for the $x°$ angle would be $\dfrac{5}{13}$.

QUESTION 17.

The correct answer is .5 or $\frac{1}{2}$. In order for a system of linear equations to have no solutions using the elimination method, both variables must be eliminated. Multiplying the first equation $Ax + 2y = 12$ by 16 gives $16(Ax + 2y = 12)$, or $16Ax + 32y = 192$. This makes the y-coefficient in both equations the same. In order for the system to have no solutions, the x-coefficient must be the same in both equations. Setting $16A = 8$ gives $A = \frac{1}{2}$.

QUESTION 18.

The correct answer is 240. Knowing $D = rt$, Truck A's trip can be represented by the equation $D = 40t_1$, where D represents the distance between the loading dock and Dover County and t_1 represents the time that Truck A spent traveling to Dover County. Truck B's trip can be represented by the equation $D = 60(t_1 - 2)$, where D represents the same distance between the loading dock and Dover County that Truck A had traveled and $t_1 - 2$ represents the two hours less that Truck B traveled to get to Dover County. Setting the equations equal to each other yields $40t_1 = 60(t_1 - 2)$. Distributing the 60 gives $40t_1 = 60t_1 - 120$ and through solving yields $-20t_1 = -120$, or $t_1 = 6$. Substituting 6 for time in Truck A's equation gives $D = 40(6) = 240$.

QUESTION 19.

The correct answer is 18. The polynomial on the left-hand side can be factored by grouping into the form on the right-hand side of the equation. On the left-hand side of $x^3 - 2x^2 - 9x + 18 = (x - a)(x - b)(x + c)$, one can group the first two terms together and the last two terms together and factor both groups which yields the expression $x^2(x - 2) - 9(x - 2)$, which can be further simplified to $(x^2 - 9)(x - 2)$. Factoring the binomial $x^2 - 9$ and rearranging the order of the factors yields $(x - 2)(x - 3)(x + 3) = (x - a)(x - b)(x + c)$. Since a, b, and c are positive constants, $a = 2$, $b = 3$, and $c = 3$. Therefore, $abc = (2)(3)(3) = 18$.

QUESTION 20.

The correct answer is 48. When a rectangle is inscribed in a circle, the connection between the circle and the rectangle is that the diameter of the circle is the diagonal of the rectangle. If the area of the circle is 25π and the formula for finding the area of a circle is πr^2, solving $\pi r^2 = 25\pi$ yields $r^2 = 25$, or $r = 5$. It follows that the diameter is 10 inches. Since the diagonal of a rectangle splits the rectangle into two right triangles and these triangles each have one side length measuring 6 inches and a hypotenuse measuring 10 inches, recognizing the Pythagorean triple 6-8-10 gives us the length of the rectangle, 8 inches. Using the area formula for a rectangle $A = lw$, $A = (8)(6) = 48$ square inches.

Section 4: Math Test - Calculator

QUESTION 1.

Choice B is correct. Melvin will spend the budgeted $85 each day for d days. Therefore, Melvin will spend a total of $85d$ dollars. Because his vacation account had $600 to start and Melvin has spent $85d$ dollars, Melvin will have $600 - 85d$ dollars left in his account.

Choices A and C are incorrect because both expressions indicate that his account will be growing in size which cannot happen because he is spending money. Choice D is incorrect because it indicates that his vacation account started with $85 and that he would be spending $600 each day.

QUESTION 2.

Choice D is correct. Since the population data is known, it is reasonable to estimate that a random sample from that population will follow the same proportion as the population. 4,000 out of 20,000 people prefer to park inside of a garage, or 20%. So, it follows that 20% of the random sample of 100 people from that population, or $100(.20) = 20$, should prefer parking in a garage.

Choices A, B, and C are incorrect and may be the result of miscalculating the appropriate percent of the sample.

QUESTION 3.

Choice C is correct. Let x be the amount of money, in dollars, that Amelia raised for cystic fibrosis research. Since Juan raised $100 more than half of the amount of money that Amelia raised, Juan raised $\frac{1}{2}x + 100$ dollars. Since they raised a combined total of $2,800, the equation $x + \frac{1}{2}x + 100 = 2800$ must be true. Simplifying, $\frac{3}{2}x + 100 = 2800$ yields $\frac{3}{2}x = 2700$, or $x = 1800$. Therefore, Amelia raised $1,800 for cystic fibrosis research.

Choice A is incorrect because $900 is half of the amount of money Amelia raised, but not $100 more than half. Choice B is incorrect because it is the amount of money that Juan raised for cystic fibrosis research. Choice D is incorrect and may be the result of incorrectly adding 100 when solving for Amelia's total.

QUESTION 4.

Choice C is correct. Quadrants I and II together are defined to be the area above the x-axis. If Line k only has solutions above the x-axis, it must be a horizontal line, which by definition has a slope of 0. In order to be in quadrants I and II, it must be above the x-axis as defined above. This means that Line k must have a positive y-intercept. Therefore, if Line k has a slope of 0 and a positive y-intercept, it will have no x-intercept.

Choice A is incorrect because Line k <u>does</u> have a slope of 0. Choice B is incorrect because Line k <u>does</u> have a positive y-intercept. Choice D is incorrect because Line k has a slope of 0 and the x-axis has a slope of 0, which <u>does</u> make them parallel.

QUESTION 5.

Choice B is correct. Let s represent the number of songs that Brandon purchased in a year. Since the annual membership fee for the digital music streaming service is $36 and each song purchase costs $0.98, the total of the annual membership fee and all of the song purchases in a year can be represented by the expression $36 + 0.98s$. Since Brandon's annual dues were $71.28, the equation $36 + 0.98s = 71.28$ must be true. Therefore, $0.98s = 35.28$, or $s = 36$. If Brandon purchased 36 songs in one year, then his average monthly song purchases are $36 \div 12$, or 3.

Choices A and C are incorrect and may be the result of errors in solving the appropriate equation. Choice D is incorrect because it gives the total number of song downloads for the year, not the monthly average.

QUESTION 6.

Choice C is correct. Because there are 36 inches in 1 yard, 6 yards of rope have a measure of $6(36) = 216$ inches. If these 216 inches are distributed evenly to 9 people, each person will receive $216 \div 9 = 24$ inches of rope.

Choices A, B, and D are incorrect and are most likely the result of errors in properly applying the unit conversion and dividing.

QUESTION 7.

Choice D is correct. Pressure is equivalent to force divided by the area of an object that makes contact with another surface. This can be expressed as $Pressure = \dfrac{Force}{Area}$.

Substituting 2,000 newtons of force and a contact area of $0.2\ m^2$, $Pressure = \dfrac{2,000N}{0.2m^2}$ which yields a pressure of 10,000 pascals of pressure.

Choices A, B, and C are incorrect because when force is divided by area in each case, the result is well below 10,000 pascals of pressure.

QUESTION 8.

Choice B is correct. According to the table, of the 520 total sales, 120 are cell phone sales from January to March and another 120 are cell phone sales from April through June. Therefore, there were a total of 240 cell phone sales from January through June. This leaves the proportion of total sales that were cell phone sales between January and June as $\dfrac{240}{520}$, or $\dfrac{6}{13}$.

Choice A is incorrect because $\dfrac{3}{13} = \dfrac{120}{520}$, which is the proportion of total sales that were

from cell phone sales in January through March or April through June, but not both.

Choice C is incorrect because $\dfrac{3}{5} = \dfrac{240}{400}$, which is the proportion of all cell phone sales

that took place in the period from January to June. Choice D is incorrect because

$\dfrac{5}{6} = \dfrac{240}{288}$, which is the proportion of total sales in the period from January to June that

were cell phone sales.

QUESTION 9.

Choice D is correct. All of the answer choices are quadratic equations and in order for a quadratic equation to have only one x-intercept, it must be the square of a single factor and that x-intercept must be a maximum or a minimum of the function. Further, if the function has a negative y-intercept, the function must be an inverted parabola and the x-intercept must be a maximum. Since $y = -x^2 - 4x - 4$ is the only solution that is an inverted parabola that can be written as the square of a single factor, $y = -(x+2)^2$, it is the only function that fits the required criteria.

Choice A is incorrect because it has a y-intercept of 0, which is not negative. Choices B and C are incorrect because they are parabolas that are concave upward, a form which does not allow for a single root and a negative y-intercept.

QUESTION 10.

Choice A is correct. In order to have the highest ratio of hours of study to hours of sleep, one looks for the student that had the highest number of hours of study and the lowest number of hours of sleep. This student, who had studied for 8 hours, had 1 hour of sleep.

Choices B and D are incorrect because 6 hours and 10 hours of sleep were attained by the students with the *lowest* ratio of hours of study to hours of sleep. Choice C is incorrect because 8 hours is the number of hours studied by the student with the highest ratio of hours of study to hours of sleep, not the number of hours slept.

QUESTION 11.

Choice C is correct. If one removes the student who studied for one hour and slept for 2 hours and removes the student who studied for 7 hours and slept for 7 hours, a general trend is present in the data points. The number of hours of sleep ranges from 6 to 10 when hours of study is at 0 and falls to 0 to 3 hours of sleep when the study hours reach 8. Using these ranges, we can see that the y-intercept should be at approximately 8 and the number of hours of sleep falls by approximately 6 hours over the course of the 8

hours of study. This gives a slope of $-\dfrac{6}{8}$, or $-\dfrac{3}{4}$.

Choices A and B are incorrect because the slopes are positive. Choice C is incorrect and may result from an error in calculating the *y*-intercept, which is too high.

QUESTION 12.

Choice C is correct. The value of the motorcycle starts at \$9,000 and drops quickly to \$4,000 over the course of two years. The value of the motorcycle then drops by approximately \$2,000 over the next 8 years. This non-linear decay follows an exponential decay model in the form $y = 9,000(r)^t$, where *r* is a fractional constant that is greater than 0 but less than 1.

Choices A and B are incorrect due to the fact that the scatterplot clearly does not follow a linear model. Choice D is incorrect because in an inverted quadratic model, the value of the motorcycle would decay slowly at first and decay more rapidly as time went on.

QUESTION 13.

Choice A is correct. Solving $S(x) = I(1 + \frac{r}{100})^x$ for *r* first yields $\frac{S(x)}{I} = (1 + \frac{r}{100})^x$,

or $\sqrt[x]{\frac{S(x)}{I}} = 1 + \frac{r}{100}$. By subtracting 1 from both sides and multiplying by 100,

$r = 100\sqrt[x]{\frac{S(x)}{I}} - 100$.

Choices B, C, and D are incorrect and may be the result of errors in isolating the appropriate variable.

QUESTION 14.

Choice A is correct. Since $1728\ in^3$ are equivalent to $1\ ft^3$ and Ankit has a cube of ice

with a volume of $27\ ft^3$, multiplying gives $(\frac{1728 in^3}{1 ft^3})(27\ ft^3) = 46,656 in^3$. Each cube

Ankit cuts will measure 2 inches X 2 inches X 2 inches. Since the volume of a cube is given by s^3, we know that the volume of a single smaller cube is $(2)^3$, or $8\ in^3$. Then, by dividing the volume of the larger cube by the volume of a single smaller cube, one gets

$\frac{46,656 in^3}{8 in^3} = 5,832$ cubes.

Choices B, C, and D are incorrect and may result from calculation errors when dividing up the volume of the large cube. For example, choice D is incorrect because carving 46,656 cubes from a single cube whose volume is $46,656\ in^3$ would make the volume of each smaller cube $1\ in^3$, not $8\ in^3$.

QUESTION 15.

Choice A is correct. An equation in the form $y = mx + b$ where *b* is a positive constant and *m* is a negative fractional constant, has a positive *y*-intercept and a slope that gently

78

decreases from left to right. The scatterplot shown in answer choice A is the only one that would best be modeled by this equation.

Choice B is incorrect because it would best be modeled by a linear model with a slope of exactly -1. Choices C and D are incorrect because they would best be modeled by exponential decay and growth models, respectively.

QUESTION 16.

Choice B is correct. Given that one extra man is needed to complete the job and assuming that the initially quoted hours stay the same, if m is increased by 1 in the equation for Company 1, $C_1(h)$ will increase by one multiple of $12h$. In the equation for Company 2, if m is increased by 1, $C_2(h)$ will increase by one multiple of $15h$. Given that h is the same in both equations, the quote for Company 2 will increase by more.

Choices A and C are incorrect and may result from misinterpreting the coefficients and the slope of each linear equation. Choice D is incorrect since h occurs in both equation and nothing implies that h has a different value for both equations. Therefore, if h is the same in both quotes, hourly cost can be calculated from the number of men on the job, m.

QUESTION 17.

Choice B is correct. Given that both jobs require ten men, the least number of hours, h, where the total cost to have the house painted by Company 1 would be less than the total cost to have the house painted by Company 2 can be calculated by solving $640 + 12(10)h < 400 + 15(10)h$. Simplifying the equation gives $640 + 120h < 400 + 150h$ and after combining like terms the equation simplifies to $240 < 30h$. Therefore, $8 < h$. So, the least value for h is 9.

Choice A is incorrect and may result from misreading and trying to determine when the two companies will cost the same. Choices C is incorrect and may result from a calculation error while solving. Choice D is incorrect and may result from substituting one man in each equation rather than 10 men.

QUESTION 18.

Choice D is correct. Dividing both sides of the inequality $6m \leq 2$ by 3 gives $2m \leq \dfrac{2}{3}$.

Adding 1 to both sides of $2m \leq \dfrac{2}{3}$ yields $2m + 1 \leq \dfrac{2}{3} + 1$, or $2m + 1 \leq \dfrac{5}{3}$. Therefore, the greatest possible value of $2m + 1$ is $\dfrac{5}{3}$.

Choice A is incorrect because it gives the greatest possible value of m, not of $2m + 1$. Choice B is incorrect because it gives the greatest possible value of $2m$, not of $2m + 1$. Choice C is incorrect because it gives the greatest *integer* value of $2m + 1$, which was not required by the question.

QUESTION 19.

Choice B is correct. There are a total of 18 marbles in the jar. However, the question dictates that a black or a red marble will be selected at random. This reduces the total to 12. There are two black marbles marked with a number greater than 4 and two red marbles marked with a number greater than 4. This is a total of 4 marbles. So, the probability of randomly selecting a marble with a number greater than 4 given that the marble is black or red is $\frac{4}{12}$, or $\frac{1}{3}$.

Choice A is incorrect and may result from multiplying the probability of randomly selecting a black marble with a number greater than 4, $\frac{1}{3}$, with the probability of randomly selecting a red marble with a number greater than 4, $\frac{1}{3}$. $\frac{1}{3} \times \frac{1}{3} = \frac{1}{9}$. Choices C and D are incorrect and may result from errors in calculating the proability of selecting numbers that are 4 or less.

QUESTION 20.

Choice B is correct. One must calculate by what percent of its original value each form of exercise was reduced. This can be calculated by taking the initial value and multiplying by a decay factor $(1-x)$, where x is percent decrease in decimal form, which results in a final value. In the case of Cycling, the initial value in 2012 is 350 miles which gets multiplied by a decay factor and results in a value of 100 miles in 2013. So, the equation $350(1-x)=100$ yields $1-x=0.285$. Simplifying further gives $x=0.714$, or a 71.4% decrease which is the largest decrease of the 3 exercise types.

Choices A and C are incorrect and may be the result of a conceptual error in understand the concept of percent decrease. Choice D is incorrect and may result from finding the decrease in mileage, not the *percentage* decrease in mileage.

QUESTION 21.

Choice C is correct. Jackson's total miles of exercise for 2012 and 2013 is 2,000 miles; 1,000 miles for each year. Adding the number of miles he swam each year, 150 and 650, gives 800 miles. Finding the percentage of his overall miles for 2012 and 2013 accounted for by swimming can be calculated by dividing the miles swum by the total miles: $\frac{800 miles}{2,000 miles} = 0.40$, or 40%.

Choices A, B, and D are incorrect and may be the result of errors in calculating the percentage or misinterpreting the question. For example, choice D is incorrect because 65% is the percentage of Jackson's total miles accounted for by swimming in 2013 only.

QUESTION 22.

Choice B is correct. Since the graph shows an inverted parabola with a negative *y*-intercept and a two positive *x*-intercepts, the function whose graph is shown must have those characteristics. Factoring $y=-x^2+4x-3$ gives $y=-(x-3)(x-1)$, a function whose graph is an inverted parabola with a negative y-intercept and two positive x-intercepts.

Choice A is incorrect because it has *no* x-intercepts. Choices C is incorrect because it has two *negative* x-intercepts. Choice D is incorrect because its graph is *not* an inverted parabola and the function has a *positive* y-intercept.

QUESTION 23.

Choice A is correct. The polynomial, with four terms, can be factored by grouping the first two terms together and grouping the second two terms together. $0 = x^3 - 4x^2 - 9x + 36$ becomes $0 = (x^3 - 4x^2) + (-9x + 36)$ which factors to $0 = x^2(x-4) - 9(x-4)$. Factoring out the $(x-4)$ gives $0 = (x-4)(x^2 - 9)$ which can ultimately be fully factored to $0 = (x-4)(x-3)(x+3)$. In this form, it is clear that the solutions are 4, 3, and -3. The only answer that is not a solution to the equation is -4.

Choices B, C, and D are incorrect because they are all solutions to the equation and the question asked for the answer that is *not* a solution.

QUESTION 24.

Choice A is correct. If a and b are numbers such that $|a - b| > 10$, absolute value rules state that a and b are more than 10 apart. This however does not dictate whether these numbers are positive or negative. A counterexample to statement I could have $a = -12$ and $b = 1$. Substituting these values gives $a - b = (-11) - (1) = -12$ which is *not* greater than 0. A counterexample to statement II could have $a = -6$ and $b = 6$. Substituting these values gives $|(-6) + (6)| = 0$ which is *not* greater than 10. A counterexample for statement III could use the same values for a and b used in the counterexample for statement II. Substituting these values gives $(-6)(6) = -36$ which is *not* greater than 0. The three counterexamples prove that *none* of the statements are true.

Choices B, C, and D are incorrect and may result from errors in generating counterexamples that disprove some of the statements.

QUESTION 25.

Choice D is correct. The perimeter can be represented by the equation $3x + 4x + 3x + 4x = 56$ which can be simplified to $14x = 56$, or $x = 4$. Since $x = 4$, the length of the rectangle is $3(4) = 12$ and the width of the rectangle is $4(4) = 16$. In the diagram, the diagonal forms a pythagorean triple with the length and the width, $3x : 4x : 5x$. So, the diagonal, or hypotenuse in the pythagorean triple, is equal to $5(4) = 20$.

Choice A is incorrect and may result from miscalculating the value of x. Choices B and C are incorrect and may result from misreading the question and solving for the length or width of the rectangle, respectively.

QUESTION 26.

Choice C is correct. In order to interpret the value of the coefficient 0.55 in the equation, one must first understand the context of the equation. The equation gives the increase in value of a home based on the amount of money that the homeowner invests in renovations. Since the equation is linear, $10 + 0.55x$, the y-intercept may represent the increased value of the home regardless of home improvements. This may be due to an improvement in the housing market. The slope, 0.55, is directly attached to x, the amount of money in thousands of dollars that the homeowner invests in home improvements. The coefficient 0.55 can be considered as a percentage, 55% to be exact. So, in the context of the question, any money invested in home improvements by the homeowner will return 55% of the investment. In choice C, 55 cents is returned on every dollar spent, which is 55%.

Choices A, B, and D are incorrect because they do not represent a 55% return for each dollar that is invested by the homeowner toward home improvements.

QUESTION 27.

Choice D is correct. Since average can be calculated by dividing the sum of a set of numbers by the number of numbers, the sum of four bags of concrete divided by 4 must equal 85, $\dfrac{a+b+c+d}{4} = 85$. Multiplying by 4 on both sides gives the sum of the four bags, $a+b+c+d = 340$. When two additional bags are added, the average increases to 92, which gives the equation $\dfrac{a+b+c+d+(e+f)}{6} = 92$, which produces the sum $a+b+c+d+(e+f) = 552$. In order to calculate the average of the two additional bags, one must find the sum of the two additional bags and divide by 2. Substituting $a+b+c+d$ with 340 in the equation $a+b+c+d+(e+f) = 552$ gives $340+(e+f) = 552$ which gives the sum $(e+f) = 212$. Finally, dividing by 2 gives the average weight of the two additional bags, $\dfrac{(e+f)}{2} = 106$.

Choices A, B, and C are incorrect and may be the result of a misinterpretation of the question or a conceptual error in understanding the concept of averages

QUESTION 28.

Choice A is correct. The coordinates of the vertex appear as constants in a quadratic equation when it is written in vertex form. Using the given roots $(-1,0)$ and $(2,0)$, one can expand the multiplied binomial factors $(x+1)(x-2)$ and get the equation in standard form, $f(x) = x^2 - x - 2$. The quadratic equation in standard form can be rewritten in vertex form by completing the square:

$$f(x) = x^2 - x - 2 = (x^2 - x + \frac{1}{4}) - \frac{1}{4} - 2 = (x - \frac{1}{2})^2 - \frac{9}{4}$$

In the form above, the quadratic equation displays the vertex, $(\frac{1}{2}, \frac{9}{4})$, as coefficients.

Choices B, C, and D are incorrect and may result from errors in completing the square to convert from the standard form of a quadratic function to vertex form.

QUESTION 29.

Choice B is correct. Since the question asks about the slope of a line that intersects the function $f(x) = 1 - x^3$, it may be easier to look at the function $f(x) = -x^3$, since the y-intercept has no bearing on the slope of a line. Looking at the graph of $f(x) = -x^3$, one can see that the only way to attain 3 points of intersection with the cubic function and the line is if the line has a negative slope. Since the question asks for the greatest *integer* value of the slope and the greatest negative integer is -1, one should try the linear equation with a slope of -1, $y = -x$. Using the substitution method to solve the system of equations yields $-x = -x^3$, or $x^3 - x = 0$. Completely factoring the binomial gives $x(x+1)(x-1) = 0$ which displays three distinct roots 0, -1, and 1. Since -1 is the greatest negative integer possible, it is the greatest slope for which the system has three distinct solutions.

Choices A is incorrect because, although it intersects $f(x) = 1 - x^3$ three times, it is not the greatest integer slope that does. Choices C and D are incorrect because the graphs of the linear equations with slopes of 0 and 1, respectively, do not intersect the function $f(x) = 1 - x^3$ three times.

QUESTION 30.

Choice A is correct. The standard deviation is a measure of the spread of a distribution and can be thought of as the average distance from the mean. If a distribution has a low standard deviation, the average distance from the mean is low. This is a scenario where more data is collected closer to the mean, or closer to the center of the distribution. On the other hand, if a distribution has a high standard deviation, the averge distance to the mean is high. This is a scenario where data is more spread out or appears farther from the center of the distribution. A normal distribution, or a typical bell curve, would generally have a lower standard deviation than a distribution that is flat across or even higher on the outer edges because it has more data closer to the center which is closer to the mean of the distribution. Looking at the distributions of trees from the northern and southern parts of the county, it appears that the trees from the northern part of the county follow a normal distribution, or bell-curved shape, whereas the trees from the southern part of the county seem more spread out. This implies that the standard deviation of pine tree heights in the northern part of the county is less than the standard deviation of pine tree heights in the southern part of the county.

Choices B, C, and D are incorrect and may result from a misunderstanding of the visual attributes of the standard deviations of distributions presented in bar graphs.

QUESTION 31.

The correct answer is 3. Substituting .60 for *intensity* the equation yields $T_{HR} = (220 - Age)(.60)$ and by distributing the .60, the equation becomes $T_{HR} = 132 - .60(Age)$. This equation follows a linear model with a slope of $-.60$. This signifies a reduction of .60 beats per minute for every age increase of one year. So, an increase of 5 years would yield $-.60(5) = -3$, or a reduction of 3 beats per minute.

QUESTION 32.

The correct answer is .6 or $\frac{3}{5}$**.** First, one must convert the units so that they all match. Since the question is asking for an answer in inches, one should first convert 120 cubic centimeters into cubic inches. One cubic inch measures $1in. \times 1in. \times 1in.$ which is equivalent to $2.54cm \times 2.54cm \times 2.54cm$, or $16.387cm^3$. Dividing 120 by 16.387 gives $7.32in^3$. The volume of a rectangular solid is calculated using the formula $V = lwh$. Substituting 3 for length, 4 for width, and 7.32 for volume, gives the equation $(3)(4)h = (7.32)$ which simplifies to $12h = 7.32$, or $h = 0.61$. 0.61 rounded to the nearest tenth is .6. Either the fraction $\frac{3}{5}$ or its decimal equivalent, .6, may be gridded as the answer.

QUESTION 33.

The correct answer is 30. Since Nadia expects 4 people to attend, she plans to cut the pizza into 4 slices. Since a full pizza is $360°$, dividing by 4 yields $\frac{360°}{4} = 90°$. Nadia expected the central angle that defines each slice to be $90°$. Since 6 people actually attend, the pizza will be cut into six slices which gives $\frac{360°}{6} = 60°$. The difference between the central angle she expected and the central angle that actually occured is $90° - 60° = 30°$.

QUESTION 34.

The correct answer is 44. If one hose can fill the pond at 30 quarts per minute and the other hose can fill the pond at 20 quarts per minute, if both hoses are filling the pond for m minutes, the equation $30m + 20m = 2200$ can be solved to find m, the number of minutes that the hoses take to fill the pond together. Simplifying, one gets $50m = 2200$, or $m = 44$.

QUESTION 35.

The correct answer is 20. If there are 140 red and green candies in a bowl and $\frac{4}{7}$ of the candies are red, one can calculate the number of red candies, $\frac{4}{7}(140) = 80$, and the number of green candies, $\frac{3}{7}(140) = 60$. Since only green candies will be removed, the 80 red candies will remain untouched. To achieve a red to total ratio of $\frac{2}{3}$, the proportion $\frac{2}{3} = \frac{80}{total}$ can be solved to find the total number of candies that must remain in the bowl. Cross-multiplying gives $2total = 240$, or $total = 120$. In order to have the total reduced from 140 to 120, 20 green candies must be removed.

QUESTION 36.

The correct answer is 75. In the equation $PV = nRT$, if pressure remains constant and the number of moles of gas and the temperature are reduced to half, one can substitute $\frac{1}{2}n$ for n and $\frac{1}{2}T$ for T which yields the equation $PV_1 = (\frac{1}{2}n)R(\frac{1}{2}T)$, which simplifies to $PV_1 = \frac{1}{4}nRT$. Substituting PV for nRT yields $PV_1 = \frac{1}{4}PV$, or $V_1 = \frac{1}{4}V$. The new volume, V_1, must become $\frac{1}{4}$ of the old volume. Reducing to $\frac{1}{4}$ of the old volume is equivalent to a reduction of 75%.

QUESTION 37.

The correct answer is .5 or $\frac{1}{2}$. Since the account value increased by \$5 in the first year, the account value at the end of one year is $\$1,000 + \$5 = \$1,005$. Substituting 1,005 for the account value after 1 year, 1,000 for the initial account value, and 1 for the number of years into the equation $A_{Value} = I(1 + \frac{r}{100})^t$ yields the equation $1,005 = 1,000(1 + \frac{r}{100})^1$.

Dividing by 1,000 yields $1.005 = 1 + \frac{r}{100}$ and subtracting 1 gives $.005 = \frac{r}{100}$. Solving for r gives $r = .5$. Either the fraction $\frac{1}{2}$ or its decimal equivalent , .5, may be gridded as the answer.

QUESTION 38.

The correct answer is 1015. Calculating the account value after 4 years have passed, K, using an initial value of \$1,000 and a growth rate of .5% yields $K = 1,000(1 + \frac{.5}{100})^4$ which is equivalent to $K = 1,000(1.005)^4$. Raising 1.005 to the fourth power and multiplying by 1,000 gives $K = 1,000(1.02) = 1,020$. Then, substituting 1,020 for the account value, .5 for r, and 1 for t yields $1,020 = I(1 + \frac{.5}{100})^1$ which can be simplified to $1,020 = I(1.005)$, or $I = 1,014.93$. Rounding to the nearest dollar gives \$1,015. An initial account value of \$1,015 will yield the same account value after one year as a \$1,000 initial account value will yield after four years at the same growth rate. Disregard the comma when gridding your answer.

TEST 2

Reading Test
65 MINUTES, 52 QUESTIONS

Turn to Section 1 of your answer sheet to answer the questions in this section.

DIRECTIONS

Each passage or pair of passages below is followed by a number of questions. After reading each passage or pair, choose the best answer to each question based on what is stated or implied in the passage or passages and in any accompanying graphics (such as a table or graph).

Questions 1-10 are based on the following passage.

The following is an excerpt from a novella published in 2015. Klaus, the main character, is a man in his late 30s who has spent several years working on agricultural projects in Africa.

The taxi pulled away, and the silence of the early, Bavarian, November morning surged back. Klaus glanced across the road. The land descended quite sharply to a terrace
Line flanked by council houses, each one silent and gray. No lights
5 were lit. No whiff of smoke ascended from the chimneys. These dwellings could have been abandoned, he thought, they were so impassive. Beyond them, he could just make out the deserted fields that lay along the banks of the small river, itself hidden by a sullen mist.
10 He thought of the noises and the colors of early morning in the Ethiopian town he had left so urgently, just three days before. At this time of the day, the road in front of his house in Africa surged with women in brightly-patterned scarves, with babies strapped to their backs, balancing on their heads straw
15 baskets filled with vivid fruits. Scrawny children in torn shorts and vests ran ahead, behind, dodging through the chattering women—kicking up the red earth in clouds of laughter.
Klaus turned to face the cottage. He pushed the little wooden gate hard. It opened stiffly, grating across the narrow
20 concrete path. The last time he had been here, he had promised that he would replace the supporting hinges, but—what with one thing and another—he had forgotten to carry out his promise. He would do it tomorrow. He put the small case down on the front doorstep and fumbled in his pocket for the key to
25 the door.
Inside, on the floor of the porch, was a small pile of letters. Automatically, Klaus picked the letters up. The envelopes all had little windows through which the addresses could be seen. Nothing but bills and demands. He sighed and placed
30 everything on the little shelf beside the door, on a pile of

similar, unopened communications that lay there. He pushed open the inner door to the living room, only to be faced with an exhibition of exhausted debris.
The room was cold and silent. In the fireplace were the
35 remains of a deadened fire, ashes spilling onto the grubby tiled hearth. The old television set stood in the corner, its back blocking much of the light that filtered through the latticed windows. Facing it, on the sagging sofa, lay a crumpled dressing-gown, an abandoned novel, a few
40 squashed cushions, and the faded carpet. A stained coffee table supported a mug half-filled with cold and congealed coffee, a battered pair of spectacles, and a small folder from which several photos spilled across the table. Dust was everywhere. He glanced at the clock on the wall: it had
45 stopped.
There was a tap on the front door. He turned. It was the young woman who lived next door. She looked at Klaus, timidly.
"I heard the taxi." She spoke quietly. "I thought you
50 might like a cup of tea."
"Thank you, but I'm fine as I am. Good to see you again. It has been quite a journey."
"Yes, it must have been difficult." She paused. "Your mother just stepped out."
55 "Meaning she'll be back several hours from now. I can wait."
"I'm sorry. You know she's never been easy."
"Yes, I know. All my life."
The young woman looked around the room, then
60 returned her eyes to Klaus. "But she was always very proud of you. She is always telling us about what you are doing, out in Africa."
"I didn't write that often."
"She told us how busy you were." The young woman
65 paused. "She hasn't been herself recently. But I think that having you here will do her a lot of good."
"Yes," said Klaus, wearily. "I suppose it will."

CONTINUE

1

Which choice best summarizes the passage?

A) A man reflects on his past as the result of a catastrophe.

B) A man makes a new acquaintance and arrives at a meaningful understanding.

C) A man revisits familiar settings and comments on one of his relationships.

D) A man precisely and affectionately observes the condition of his mother's home.

2

As used in line 19, "stiffly" most nearly means

A) uncomfortably.

B) pretentiously.

C) without ease.

D) with great power.

3

It can be inferred from the passage that Klaus is

A) well aware of his mother's habits and personality.

B) uncomfortable about the independence his mother displays.

C) eager to help his mother adapt to new circumstances.

D) unsure whether his mother reads his letters.

4

As used in line 31, "communications" most nearly means

A) exchanges.

B) messages.

C) confessions.

D) disclosures.

5

Between the first and the second paragraph, the narrator's focus shifts from

A) Klaus's cynical observations to his plans for an enjoyable future.

B) Klaus's immediate surroundings to the area where he normally resides.

C) Klaus's memories of his childhood to a remarkable occurrence from his adulthood.

D) the poor state of Klaus's hometown to Klaus's interest in an array of cultures.

6

The descriptions in the passage indicate that Klaus's mother

A) has neglected the upkeep of her home.

B) has little knowledge of her son's activities.

C) is on poor terms with her neighbors.

D) is eager to leave her community and travel abroad.

7

Which choice provides the best evidence for the answer to the previous question?

A) Lines 5-7 ("No whiff . . . impassive")

B) Lines 27-29 ("The envelopes . . . demands")

C) Lines 40-45 ("A stained . . . stopped")

D) Lines 64-66 ("She told . . . of good")

8

The "promise" in line 23 is best understood to refer to

A) a burden that Klaus has found elaborate reasons to avoid.

B) a simple household task that Klaus has not yet fulfilled.

C) the potential for reconciliation between Klaus and his mother.

D) Klaus's ability to understand different ways of life.

9

The "young woman" (line 47) who interacts with Klaus can best be described as

A) awestruck.

B) pompous.

C) idiosyncratic.

D) attentive.

10

Which choice provides the best evidence for the answer to the previous question?

A) Lines 46-48 ("There was . . . timidly")

B) Lines 49-50 ("I heard . . . of tea")

C) Lines 53-54 ("Yes, it . . . out")

D) Lines 59-62 ("The young . . . Africa")

CONTINUE

Questions 11-21 are based on the following passage and supplementary material.

The following is adapted from Philip Kowalski's "In Search of a Global Language."

Esperanto is a constructed language invented by the Polish linguist L. L. Zamenhof and introduced at large in 1887 with the publication of his book Unua Libro. His intent was to
Line design a universal language that could unite disparate cultures
5 and contribute to mutual, global identification in an effort to promote peace and discourage warfare as a means of addressing international conflicts. Esperanto was not conceived to replace all native languages; rather, it was created as an alternative second language to allow diverse populations to communicate
10 without obliterating speakers' indigenous cultures. According to the non-profit educational association Esperanto USA, the language is much easier to learn than many others, and it lacks a political bias, thus minimizing ideological and denominational differences among Esperanto speakers around the world.
15 Although many critics view Esperanto as the antiquated work of a crank linguist, it is still taken seriously today, as the presence of worldwide Esperanto associations attests. Its continual linguistic viability can be accounted for by its attractiveness as an alternative to English as an unofficial
20 global language, since Esperanto evades the prejudice and suspicion against Westerners that individuals in Russia and the Middle East feel. (Historical conflicts have led some in these countries to see the use of English as a "universal" language as oppressive and imperialistic.) But despite its claims to
25 universality, Esperanto partakes of much of the vocabulary, grammar, and syntax of the Romance languages of French, Italian, Portuguese, Spanish, and Romanisch, often bypassing non-European language structures entirely.
A short and simple sample translation of an English
30 sentence into Esperanto perhaps provides the best sense of what the language is like:

Learning Esperanto can be a benefit to those
who wish to engage with a fascinating community
of others interested in global progress.
35 *Lernante Esperanton povas esti profito por tiuj kiuj*
deziras engaĝiĝi kun fascina komunumo de aliaj
interesita tutmonda progreso.

As this translation demonstrates, those familiar with Romance languages can immediately recognize linguistic
40 similarities. For example, "tout le monde" from the French and "todo el mundo" from Spanish can be discerned in the Esperanto word "tutmonda." All of these phrases are usually rendered as "everyone" but can be literally translated as "all the

world" or, in the case of this sentence, "global."
45 But the fact that Esperanto appears to partake so fluidly of European Romance languages has been leveled as a criticism against its implementation, especially among native English speakers and within business communities where English is already the common language of
50 expediency. While English is a hybrid of a form of German called Anglo-Saxon and a form of French called Anglo-Norman, many English speakers not acquainted with any modern Continental European languages find Esperanto baffling. Additionally, as the linguist Ted Alper claims,
55 Esperanto is difficult to learn, is not in fact politically neutral or gender neutral, and is also neither beautiful nor useful.
In our globalized yet discordant twenty-first century, it seems unlikely that Esperanto will ever achieve linguistic
60 ascendancy. Yet it is also worth noting that the idealism that motivated Esperanto's original construction as a measure for securing world peace in late nineteenth century Europe—soon to be ravaged by the destructive political forces that would fuel both World War I and World War
65 II—has not entirely waned: even today, Zamehof's idealism reminds speakers of any language that, while universal verbal identification may not be possible, language can be a medium of cultural appreciation and peaceful agreement. Given the contemporary political and ideological chaos
70 of the present, an effort to employ Esperanto as a binding linguistic force may seem quaint and naïve to many, but to a small, inspired minority it is still a way—however small—to unite far-flung factions in some sort of mutual understanding.

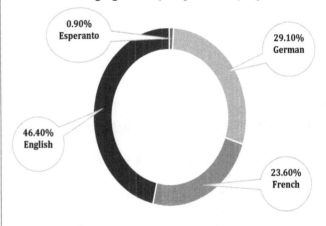

Second Languages of EU (European Union) Population

0.90% Esperanto

29.10% German

46.40% English

23.60% French

CONTINUE

11

In the context of the whole passage, the first paragraph serves mainly to

A) summarize the author's thesis about Esperanto and other constructed languages.

B) provide a brief summary of the purpose and theoretical advantages of a constructed language.

C) introduce a constructed language that the author will promote later in the passage.

D) give an overview of the history of constructed languages and list a few prominent examples.

12

Which choice best describes the developmental pattern of the passage?

A) An intricate biography of an idealistic linguist

B) A detached description of an ancient language

C) An earnest promotion of a philosophy

D) A detailed analysis of the value of a language

13

The author would most likely respond to Esperanto USA's claim about the political neutrality of Esperanto (lines 11-14) with

A) the argument that the political neutrality of Esperanto has not made it appealing to any particular country.

B) the addition that Esperanto also lacks gender-specific pronouns to avoid displaying bias towards a gender.

C) the statement that Esperanto is heavily influenced by Romance languages and ignores non-European ones.

D) the assertion that many countries have rejected Esperanto because they believe it erases their culture.

14

Which choice provides the best evidence for the answer to the previous question?

A) Lines 20-22 ("Esperanto . . . feel")

B) Lines 25-28 ("Esperanto . . . entirely")

C) Lines 38-40 ("those . . . similarities")

D) Lines 65-68 ("Zamehof's . . . agreement")

15

The passage indicates that some critics of Esperanto

A) question the usefulness of Esperanto in a world where English is considered a universal language and learning any other language would be unnecessary.

B) agree that the creation of a universal language would promote world peace but state that Esperanto has not been developed enough to be a valid candidate.

C) dismiss the language as unsophisticated and outdated and characterize its speakers as stubborn and pretentious.

D) argue that Esperanto is difficult for native English speakers to learn because of its many connections to Continental European languages.

16

Which choice provides the best evidence for the answer to the previous question?

A) Lines 15-17 ("Although . . . attests")

B) Lines 42-44 ("All of . . . global")

C) Lines 52-54 ("many . . . baffling")

D) Lines 58-60 ("In our . . . ascendancy")

17

As used in lines 45-46, "partake so fluidly of" most nearly means

A) divide completely between.

B) receive generously from.

C) engage directly with.

D) sample freely from.

18

As used in line 49, "common" most nearly means

A) prevalent.

B) basic.

C) approved.

D) crude.

CONTINUE

19

Over the course of the final paragraph (lines 58-74) the focus shifts from

A) the doubtfulness of Esperanto becoming a widely used language to a description of Esperanto's application of Zamenhof's original ideas.

B) an acknowledgment of a potential counterargument regarding the practicality of Esperanto to a rebuttal asserting that Esperanto is too impractical to be used.

C) the various purposes of Esperanto when it was first developed to its increased use after it gained media exposure.

D) the history of the study of language development to the implications of learning a language such as Esperanto in school.

20

The author of the passage would most likely characterize the percentage of Esperanto speakers shown in the graph as

A) educated businessmen.

B) socially conscious adolescents.

C) idealistic scholars.

D) people in positions of power.

21

The data in the graph most directly provide support for which idea in the passage?

A) The rate of people learning Esperanto is rising as the language becomes more popular outside the U.S.

B) Esperanto speakers primarily consist of intellectual and inspired youth who believe in world peace.

C) The number of people who speak Esperanto has slowly decreased over the past decade.

D) Esperanto has only been learned by a small population compared to languages such as English.

Questions 22-32 are based on the following passage and supplementary material.

This passage is adapted from a recent article that surveys new developments in the search for extraterrestrial life.

Long an object of myth and legend, Mars has occupied a special place in the hearts and minds of humanity. The Red Planet beckons us with its mystery—on the one hand showing us a mirror of Earth, and on the other hand showing us its
5 opposite. Evidence indicates that Mars used to be a lush, warm planet which may have supported life. While life could theoretically evolve in dry conditions, most life requires water, and finding water on the Red Planet would have staggering implications for astronomy, anthropology, and biology. To date,
10 no life has been discovered on Mars, yet NASA has uncovered evidence of liquid water on the surface of the famed Red Planet.

Mars has a red surface due to the high iron content of its rocks. It is a planet of extremes: it has the tallest mountain on any planet in the Solar System, Olympus Mons, as well as the
15 deepest and longest valley, the Valles Marineris (named for the Mariner 9 probe which made the discovery). Mars is quite a bit farther away from the sun than the Earth is, so temperatures are often very low: they can drop to -125C. During Mars's summer, highs can reach 20C in regions near the equator. Mars is also
20 the site of the largest dust storms in the solar system, which can cover the entire planet for months at a time.

Humans have long known that water, in the form of ice, can be found on the varied and tumultuous surface of Mars. In 2001, the Mars Odyssey probe discovered vast sheets of ice that
25 hide beneath the Martian terrain. Scientists quickly found out, even more astonishingly, that Mars has massive polar ice caps that have an average thickness of more than 2 miles. If the ice caps were to melt, all of Mars would be flooded with water to a depth of more than 20 feet.
30 Indeed, it is liquid water that's chiefly of interest for scientists and for hypothetical forms of Martian life alike: the search for liquid water has gone on for decades, with few hopeful signs and much disappointment. In 2011, however, scientists uncovered new evidence that water flows on the
35 Martian surface during the warmer summer months. Integral to the new research were the dark lines that appear on certain steep slopes every year. These lines, called recurring slope lineae (RSL), were first discovered by Lujendra Ojha, now at the Georgia Institute of Technology in Atlanta.
40 Ojha was cautious at first, downplaying his discovery of the RSL and trying to emphasize that they didn't prove that Mars has liquid water. That all changed, however, in 2015, when he and his team discovered evidence of hydrated salts, called perchlorates, which appear in areas where the dark
45 lines also appear. This is definitive evidence that liquid water

CONTINUE

does exist on Mars in some form. "The presence of hydrated salts in these flows means that the streaks are forming due to contemporary water," Ojha said.

50   This monumental discovery has fueled plans for new Mars missions—which might even culminate in a possible manned mission to Mars. Yet Ojha's findings should fuel caution, not haste. With liquid water comes a very real possibility that life could exist on Mars. This life would probably be some form of microorganism, and these tiny creatures pose a huge
55 contamination risk. Humans simply have no idea what could happen if a Martian microorganism were to somehow make its way to Earth as an unplanned stowaway.

    We must also be wary of contamination in the opposite direction. It's hard enough to make sure that robots are sterile
60 enough to explore the Martian surface—let alone people in space suits. A microorganism hitching a ride on a robot, or on a human explorer, could potentially take root in the water on Mars and contaminate the planet irreversibly. If that were to happen, it could extinguish any other life which may or may
65 not exist on the Red Planet. Finding liquid water on Mars has given a new impetus to the human imagination, and to the need—unimaginative as it sounds—for the most meticulous science possible.

This graph shows variation in the amount and the depth of water detected beneath NASA's Mars rover Curiosity by use of the rover's Dynamic Albedo of Neutrons (DAN) instrument at different points along the distance the rover has driven.

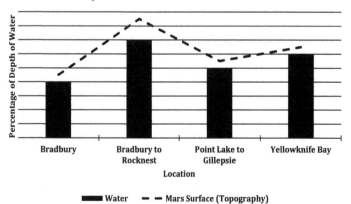

Depth of Water Relative to Surface of Mars

Percentage of Depth of Water

Bradbury   Bradbury to Rocknest   Point Lake to Gillepsie   Yellowknife Bay

Location

■■■ Water   ‐ ‐ Mars Surface (Topography)

22

Which of the following best describes the passage?

A) A synopsis of the history of human presence on a planet.

B) A description of a scientific discovery and an explanation of its influence.

C) An earnest appeal against experimentation on a particular subject.

D) An objective analysis of two opposing views on a controversial study.

23

The author indicates that Mars

A) cannot harbor life because of its fluctuating temperatures and constant dust storms.

B) could hypothetically support life regardless of a paucity of water.

C) is covered with massive ice caps that contain life beneath their surfaces.

D) is a home for many interesting but lethal microorganisms.

24

Which choice provides the best evidence for the answer to the previous question?

A) Lines 6-7 ("life could . . . conditions")

B) Lines 19-20 ("Mars . . . system")

C) Lines 26-27 ("Mars . . . miles")

D) Lines 45-46 ("liquid . . . form")

25

As used in line 45, "definitive" most nearly means

A) conclusive.

B) precise.

C) official.

D) specific.

CONTINUE ➡

26

According to the passage, the search for liquid water on Mars

A) culminated in a 2001 discovery of polar ice caps and ice sheets beneath the planet's surface up to two miles thick.

B) has not been undertaken for years because scientists have concluded that Mars's climate is much too hostile to sustain life.

C) had been unsuccessful for decades until a breakthrough in 2011 when scientists found evidence of water flowing on Mars's surface.

D) seemed to be futile until the invention of hydrated salts that were used as tools to detect the presence of water on Mars.

27

Which choice provides the best evidence for the answer to the previous question?

A) Lines 7-10 ("most life . . . Mars")

B) Lines 22-25 ("Humans . . . terrain")

C) Lines 32-35 ("the search . . . months")

D) Lines 42-45 ("That all . . . appear")

28

The passage states that recurring slope lineae

A) were caused directly by the perchlorates which had formed as water flowed down Mars's steep slopes every summer.

B) harbored various species of microorganisms that had been ignored for decades by researchers focusing on water beneath Mars's surface.

C) caught the attention of scientists when they were detected on polar ice caps but not anywhere else on Mars's surface.

D) were clear evidence of the presence of liquid water on the surface of Mars when they appeared along with hydrated salts.

29

The author suggests that interaction between life on Earth and life on Mars could potentially

A) inspire a new generation of writers and artists who now have the ability to visit Mars and other planets.

B) become dangerous for Mars's climate if humans settle and build cities on its surface.

C) accelerate the progression of technology and space travel to planets outside the solar system.

D) lead to microorganisms becoming invasive species and causing harm to life on both planets.

30

As used in line 67, "meticulous" most nearly means

A) accurate.

B) creative.

C) cautious.

D) ethical.

31

According to the graph, DAN detected the greatest percentage of the depth of water

A) in Bradbury.

B) in between Bradbury and Rocknest.

C) in between Point Lake and Gillespie.

D) in Yellowknife Bay.

32

Do the data in the graph support the information in the passage?

A) Yes, because the graph shows that water is prevalent on Mars's surface and that it is most common along steep slopes and mountains.

B) Yes, because the graph shows that there is water beneath Mars's surface, which is consistent with the information in the passage.

C) No, because the graph states that water can be found beneath Mars's surface, while the passage argues that it is only found above ground.

D) No, because the graph displays the percentage of water found in Mars's subsurface, while the passage focuses on water on Mars's surface.

CONTINUE

Questions 33-42 are based on the following passage.

This passage is taken from the opening chapter of Revolution and Counter-Revolution (1851) by Karl Marx. In the paragraphs that follow, Marx describes revolutionary activity within France and Germany and the counter-measures taken by the governments of those countries.

The first act of the revolutionary drama on the continent of Europe has closed. The "powers that were" before the hurricane of 1848 are again the "powers that be," and the more
Line or less popular rulers of a day, provisional governors, triumvirs,
5 dictators, with their tail of representatives, civil commissioners, military commissioners, prefects, judges, generals, officers, and soldiers, are thrown upon foreign shores, and "transported beyond the seas" to England or America, there to form new governments in *partibus infidelium*, European committees,
10 central committees, national committees, and to announce their advent with proclamations quite as solemn as those of any less imaginary potentates.
A more signal defeat than that undergone by the continental revolutionary party—or rather parties—upon all
15 points of the line of battle, cannot be imagined. But what of that? Has not the struggle of the British middle classes for their social and political supremacy embraced forty-eight, that of the French middle classes forty years of unexampled struggles? And was their triumph ever nearer than at the very moment
20 when restored monarchy thought itself more firmly settled than ever? The times of that superstition which attributed revolutions to the ill-will of a few agitators have long passed away. Everyone knows nowadays that wherever there is a revolutionary convulsion, there must be some social want in
25 the background, which is prevented, by outworn institutions, from satisfying itself. The want may not yet be felt as strongly, as generally, as might ensure immediate success; but every attempt at forcible repression will only bring it forth stronger and stronger, until it bursts its fetters. If, then, we have been
30 beaten, we have nothing else to do but to begin again from the beginning. And, fortunately, the probably very short interval of rest which is allowed us between the close of the first and the beginning of the second act of the movement, gives us time for a very necessary piece of work: the study of the causes
35 that necessitated both the late outbreak and its defeat; causes that are not to be sought for in the accidental efforts, talents, faults, errors, or treacheries of some of the leaders, but in the general social state and conditions of existence of each of the convulsed nations. That the sudden movements of February
40 and March, 1848, were not the work of single individuals, but spontaneous, irresistible manifestations of national wants and necessities, more or less clearly understood, but very distinctly felt by numerous classes in every country, is a fact recognized

everywhere; but when you inquire into the causes of the
45 counter-revolutionary successes, there you are met on every hand with the ready reply that it was Mr. This or Citizen That who "betrayed" the people. Which reply may be very true or not, according to circumstances, but under no circumstances does it explain anything—not
50 even show how it came to pass that the "people" allowed themselves to be thus betrayed. And what a poor chance stands a political party whose entire stock-in-trade consists in a knowledge of the solitary fact that Citizen So-and-so is not to be trusted.
55 The inquiry into, and the exposition of, the causes, both of the revolutionary convulsion and its suppression, are, besides, of paramount importance from a historical point of view. All these petty, personal quarrels and recriminations—all these contradictory assertions that it
60 was Marrast, or Ledru Rollin, or Louis Blanc, or any other member of the Provisional Government, or the whole of them, that steered the Revolution amidst the rocks upon which it foundered—of what interest can they be, what light can they afford, to the American or Englishman who
65 observed all these various movements from a distance too great to allow of his distinguishing any of the details of operations? No man in his senses will ever believe that eleven men, mostly of very indifferent capacity either for good or evil, were able in three months to ruin a nation of
70 thirty-six millions, unless those thirty-six millions saw as little of their way before them as the eleven did.

33

Over the course of the passage, the focus shifts from

A) an objective report of the political state in Europe following a rebellion to a pessimistic questioning of that rebellion's true objective.

B) a somber depiction of the life of an English revolutionary to an incensed plea for change and economic equality.

C) an appreciative description of the nature of revolution to a call for the understanding of the causes of its rise and suppression.

D) a discussion of the advantages and disadvantages of a political ideology to an admiring promotion of the philosophy.

34

As used in line 41, "irresistible" most nearly means

A) inevitable.
B) tempting.
C) fascinating.
D) powerful.

CONTINUE

35

It can be reasonably inferred from the passage that revolution

A) was previously considered to be perpetrated by a few malevolent individuals.

B) is a foolish and idealistic concept that can never truly achieve lasting change.

C) often causes more disruption and chaos than order and peace.

D) is confusing and difficult to understand for someone who has never experienced it.

36

Which choice provides the best evidence for the answer to the previous question?

A) Lines 1-3 ("The first . . . be")

B) Lines 21-23 ("The times . . . away")

C) Lines 47-49 ("Which . . . anything")

D) Lines 63-65 ("of what . . . Englishman")

37

Marx uses the phrase "bursts its fetters" (line 29) mainly to highlight that

A) the events of 1848 have created a state of affairs in which strict and tyrannical rulers have stifled any voices of reason.

B) the willpower of people who are united for a cause will be enough to overpower attempts to suppress an uprising.

C) in order to cause any significant social reform there must be a change in the mentality of lower and middle class individuals.

D) the efforts of citizens to gain more rights and equality have not been enough to liberate them from the cruelty of an authoritarian regime.

38

The second paragraph (lines 13-53) is primarily concerned with establishing a contrast between

A) the hard work of revolutionaries and the minimal effort it takes to dismantle a rebellion.

B) the ardent attempt of citizens to create an uprising and the futile attempts of those in power to repress it.

C) the collective endeavors of revolutions and the seemingly singular causes of their downfalls.

D) the fanciful and optimistic mindset of young rebels and the grim realities of their situations.

39

As used in line 64, "light" most nearly means

A) aid.

B) opinion.

C) context.

D) advice.

40

Marx mentions "Marrast, or Ledru Rollin, or Louis Blanc" (line 60) in order to

A) cite examples of people who have been unfairly depicted as the sole causes of a revolution's failure.

B) emphasize the corruption and abuse of power rampant within the French Provisional Government.

C) express his gratitude for the individuals who had the courage to stand up against the tyrannical authority.

D) describe individuals who were initially contributors to revolutions but maliciously sabotaged them.

41

Marx contends that it is most important to

A) act immediately and efficiently to replace corrupt officials and create political reform.

B) study and analyze the true influences behind an uprising and its subsequent downfall.

C) unite poor and middle-class citizens with a common cause and teach them the values of socialism.

D) cause social and economic change through legislation and election of more effective politicians.

42

Which choice provides the best evidence for the answer to the previous question?

A) Lines 13-16 ("A more . . . that")

B) Lines 26-29 ("The want . . . fetters")

C) Lines 51-54 ("And what . . . trusted")

D) Lines 55-58 ("The inquiry . . . view")

CONTINUE

Questions 43-52 are based on the following passages.

These articles were written by two science journalists as part of a recent series on issues in developmental psychology and cognitive science.

Passage 1

Although it is tempting and even trendy to assume that listening to music improves cognitive functioning, attempts to address this issue through scientific experimentation have not
Line yet arrived at particularly conclusive results. In 1993, a study
5 conducted at the University of California explored whether exposure to music immediately prior to completing a task involving analysis led to improved cognitive performance. Three dozen college-aged students listened to a ten-minute excerpt from a sonata composed by Mozart, then completed a
10 spatial reasoning test; the same students also completed similar tests after sitting in silence for ten minutes and after listening to someone read in a monotone voice for ten minutes. Scores showed that the students performed better after listening to the Mozart composition, indicating a possible connection between
15 exposure to music and improved cognitive functioning. The study, however, as later researchers would note, relied on a fairly small sample size, tested only one particular age group, and measured only very short-term changes in cognitive ability.

While the initial results of the study were modest in
20 scope, the notion that music could make someone smarter captured the public's imagination. Dubbed the "Mozart Effect," an inflated version of the study's main finding began to circulate, propagating the belief that exposure to classical music, especially during infancy and childhood, could
25 improve cognitive ability, academic performance, and scores on standardized tests. The Mozart Effect was an effective marketing tool for recordings, tapes, and music-producing toys. In 1998, the Governor of Georgia even provided hospitals with copies of Mozart CDs to distribute to the parents of newborns.
30 In the two decades since the University of California study's publication, scientists have conducted numerous experiments in order to gauge the Mozart Effect. A 2010 meta-analysis compiling the results of 39 studies concluded that "evidence in favor of or against the Mozart Effect seemed to be
35 published roughly in equal parts, thus rendering primary studies powerless to resolve the issue whether or not the effect exists."

Passage 2

Proponents of the Mozart Effect have been aggressively questioned on the grounds of methodology and experimental procedure in recent years. But the question that should really
40 make us re-evaluate the Mozart Effect isn't necessarily a matter of science: what if Mozart Effect researchers had used a musician less lofty than Mozart to arrive at their conclusions? What, for instance, if they had discovered the effect using a pop song? A lot of us would have trouble taking the Green
45 Day Effect, the Taylor Swift Effect, or the Lil' Jon Effect seriously, and a lot of the parents who avidly buy their toddlers Mozart CDs would be horrified at the idea that punk songs or rap music could make anyone—much less their children—think more effectively. The problem is
50 that this idea isn't particularly far from the truth.

After all, why should classical music be the only form of sound that generates the Mozart Effect, or something like it? Gordon Shaw and Frances Rauscher, the University of California at Irvine researchers who
55 were the earliest investigators and promulgators of the Mozart Effect, found that "there are patterns of neurons that fire in sequences, and that there appear to be pre-existing sites in the brain that respond to specific frequencies." There is no reason why those frequencies
60 are associated exclusively with Mozart or with classical music in general; what Shaw and Rauscher have formulated is in fact a phenomenon that we see every day. Athletes will listen to heavy metal or stadium songs to get energized before they compete, while anyone who
65 has ever come home from a hard day of work should know the soothing effect of soft rock, the right hip hop, the music of a sitar, or indeed Mozart's own symphonies.

The Mozart Effect is a reality, but a reality that has been formulated simplistically and festooned with
70 elitism. How we think is a product of the music we hear, but precious little of that music is Mozart.

43

Which choice best describes the relationship between the two passages?

A) Passage 1 openly condemns a controversial phenomenon that Passage 2 views as scientifically inaccurate but harmless.

B) Passage 1 questions the reasoning behind a popular practice that Passage 2 earnestly advocates.

C) Passage 1 expresses doubts about the validity of the results of an influential experiment that Passage 2 views with some legitimacy.

D) Passage 1 criticizes the public's acceptance of a widespread viewpoint while Passage 2 examines the rationale behind the viewpoint.

CONTINUE

44

On which of the following points would the authors of both passages most likely agree?

A) Because the brain is plastic and changing, it is likely that music would enhance intellectual ability.

B) The Mozart Effect is based on unsubstantiated and unproven assumptions about cognitive functions.

C) Although the Mozart Effect may have some accuracy, research on the phenomenon is incomplete.

D) The Mozart Effect can be expanded on to include musical genres besides classical that have cognitive benefits.

45

According to Passage 1, the 1993 study conducted at the University of California

A) had manipulated data to make it appear that classical music was responsible for improved intelligence.

B) was based on incomplete and unreliable research that used outdated technology to record its results

C) yielded results that were only dependent on specific circumstances determined by the experiment.

D) was inaccurate since it did not take factors like age and long-term cognitive change into consideration.

46

Which choice provides the best evidence for the answer to the previous question?

A) Lines 12-14 ("Scores . . . composition")

B) Lines 15-18 ("The study . . . ability")

C) Lines 19-21 ("While . . . imagination")

D) Lines 26-29 ("The Mozart . . . newborns")

47

As used in line 19, "modest" most nearly means

A) basic.

B) humble.

C) insignificant.

D) limited.

48

The author of Passage 2 mentions "the Green Day Effect, the Taylor Swift Effect, or the Lil' Jon Effect" (lines 44-45) primarily in order to

A) compare the results of a spatial reasoning test after listening to pop music and to classical music.

B) introduce the author's hypothesis that listening to other genres of music could also have benefits.

C) point out the absurdity of improving cognitive ability through listening to music.

D) provide a lighthearted digression in an otherwise pessimistic discussion.

49

As used in line 62, "formulated" most nearly means

A) conveyed.

B) created.

C) developed.

D) prepared.

50

The author of Passage 1 would most likely respond to the views of the Mozart Effect presented by the author of Passage 2 with

A) open agreement, because the Mozart Effect can be applied to other genres of music besides classical.

B) grudging acceptance, because there is no other explanation for improved cognitive functioning.

C) guarded skepticism, because studies have been inconclusive about the phenomenon's existence.

D) complete disagreement, because the Mozart Effect was proven to be a fabricated hoax.

51

Which choice provides the best evidence for the answer to the previous question?

A) Lines 2-4 ("attempts . . . results")

B) Lines 26-27 ("The Mozart . . . toys")

C) Lines 30-32 ("In the two . . . Effect")

D) Lines 34-35 ("evidence . . . parts")

CONTINUE

52

As used in line 42, "less lofty" most nearly means

A) less towering.

B) more humble.

C) less resilient.

D) overly modest.

STOP

If you finish before time is called, you may check your work on this section only.

Do not turn to any other section.

Writing Test
35 MINUTES, 44 QUESTIONS

Turn to Section 2 of your answer sheet to answer the questions in this section.

DIRECTIONS

Each passage below is accompanied by a number of questions. For some questions, you will consider how the passage might be revised to improve the expression of ideas. For other questions, you will consider how the passage might be edited to correct errors in sentence structure, usage, or punctuation. A passage or a question may be accompanied by one or more graphics (such as a table or graph) that you will consider as you make revising and editing decisions.

Some questions will direct you to an underlined portion of a passage. Other questions will direct you to a location in a passage or ask you to think about the passage as a whole.

After reading each passage, choose the answer to each question that most effectively improves the quality of writing in the passage or that makes the passage conform to the conventions of standard written English. Many questions include a "NO CHANGE" option. Choose that option if you think the best choice is to leave the relevant portion of the passage as it is.

Questions 1-11 are based on the following passage.

Restaurant Woes

Late in the summer of 2015, a New York restaurant once thought to hold great promise served **1** its' last meal. Alder, a much-publicized tavern-style eatery, seemed to have all the right ingredients. As concocted by celebrity chef Wylie Dufresne, the Alder menu featured experimental twists on classic pub fare, while Alder itself **2** occupied a prime piece of East Village real estate. The restaurant's disappearance after only two and a half years of operation shocked its devotees, and may have even been a disappointment to more skeptical diners: **3** *New York Times* food critic Pete Wells, who gave Alder a very mixed review on his first and only visit, nonetheless stated that Alder and its cuisine "belongs to anybody who wants to see things differently."

1
A) NO CHANGE
B) it's
C) its
D) their

2
A) NO CHANGE
B) oppressed
C) was preoccupied with
D) overran

3
The writer is considering deleting the underlined portion of the sentence. Should the writer make this deletion?
A) Yes, because the *New York Times* is not mentioned anywhere else in the passage.
B) Yes, because the author ultimately argues against Pete Wells's ideas about Alder.
C) No, because the author argues elsewhere that Alder was criticized in major newspapers.
D) No, because it provides important context for understanding Pete Wells's position.

100

CONTINUE ➤

Outsiders may be shocked, but restaurant industry insiders know that they are working within a **4** notoriously unstable and volatile industry. Restaurants have always been tricky businesses to run: a successful restaurant requires an almost perfect balance of publicity, innovation, atmosphere, and efficiency. In fact, such a lack of balance may have been part of what doomed Alder. Customer complaints frequently centered on the noisy and uncomfortable main dining room, **5** because serving portions were quite possibly too small to encourage group dinners and repeat visits.

6 Not all celebrity chefs have Dufresne's bad luck. While it is unlikely that a massive chain such as McDonald's or Chipotle will go under, the success of these companies keeps small restaurants from rising. Prospering chains have an advantage when it comes to buying prime real estate, and buying a lot of it. Smaller eateries may thus be squeezed out of those urban areas with the greatest **7** amount of prospective customers. Even in different settings—for instance, a suburban town with few chain restaurants and several independent restaurants—a new restaurant may fight an uphill battle to secure loyal customers.

4
A) NO CHANGE
B) notorious, unstable, and volatile
C) notoriously unstable
D) notorious and unstable

5
A) NO CHANGE
B) while
C) until
D) unless

6
Which choice most effectively introduces the discussion that follows?
A) NO CHANGE
B) In fact, some food critics despised Alder from the outset.
C) Actually, few restaurant owners have the talent to turn their passion projects into business empires.
D) There are other clear reasons why restaurants fail.

7
A) NO CHANGE
B) amounts
C) number
D) numbers

CONTINUE

Moreover, the problems that afflict major restaurant chains can spell the death of small restaurants. An *E. coli* outbreak in the autumn of 2015 sent Chipotle's stock price tumbling; in the case of a smaller restaurant, a similar outbreak would completely interrupt business and **8** halted cash flow. Few small restaurants could survive negative publicity comparable to **9** the multimillion-dollar Chipotle.

[1] Perhaps the key to running a successful restaurant is anticipating such liabilities before they become realities—and then anticipating liabilities beyond even these. [2] Indeed, Wylie Dufresne's own weak point isn't cuisine or atmosphere. [3] In 2014, he was forced to close his restaurant WD-50 because the building that housed it was **10** slated for demolition; there is speculation that zoning strictures were also responsible for Adler's demise. [4] It's real estate. [5] Good business is a matter of foresight: not even the most engaging restaurant is exempt from this rule. **11**

8
A) NO CHANGE
B) halts cash flow.
C) halt cash flow.
D) be halting cash flow.

9
A) NO CHANGE
B) restaurants like the multimillion-dollar Chipotle.
C) that which met the multimillion-dollar Chipotle.
D) those which met the multimillion-dollar Chipotle.

10
A) NO CHANGE
B) slated with
C) slated from
D) slated against

11
To make this paragraph most logical, sentence 4 should be placed
A) where it is now.
B) after sentence 1.
C) after sentence 2.
D) after sentence 5.

Questions 12-22 are based on the following passage.

How Shakespeare Works

If Shakespeare [12] were alive, well, and talented today, he would not be writing for the theater. It seems clear—from what we know of his meteoric rise through seventeenth-century society—that he had a sharp nose to sniff out money. He wouldn't be writing short-run plays [13] today, instead he would be at the top of modern show business. We would know a 21st-century Shakespeare from his appearances on the covers of news magazines, his stints on late night talk shows, and [14] his remarks about his latest album or movie. We would read about the number of times he has been seen with members of European Royal families or has been invited [15] at the White House.

Yet we would not have *The Complete Works of William Shakespeare*. It seems clear that, were Shakespeare living today, [16] we would have precious little time to send a Tweet, let alone write plays for posterity.

12
A) NO CHANGE
B) was
C) is
D) would be

13
A) NO CHANGE
B) today; instead, he
C) today, and he
D) today; but he

14
A) NO CHANGE
B) remarking
C) when people remark
D) he also remarks

15
A) NO CHANGE
B) for the White House.
C) from the White House.
D) to the White House.

16
A) NO CHANGE
B) he would have
C) we have
D) he has

CONTINUE

Fortunately, we do have *The Complete Works*. However, it should be noted that we would not have access to them had it not been for the enthusiasm of Hemminge and Condell, a couple of seventeenth-century character actors whose role in the preservation of Shakespeare's writing [17] is still not understood by contemporary scholars: although publishing was well-established by the seventeenth century, plays were ephemeral, meant to be performed, seen, and discarded. The only dramatist to have his plays printed was Ben Jonson, and he personally oversaw the printing process to ensure that what he [18] had written was issued in accurate versions.

[19] Although Hemminge and Condell decided to publish Shakespeare's works, they undertook an act of homage to the memory of a fellow member of the theatrical profession. It was not an easy task, that's for sure. They had to try to find the original, hand-written scripts that had been literally dashed off by Shakespeare in the urgency of achieving his deadlines, each document full of changes of mind and crossing-outs and notes scribbled in the margins. Where these were not available, then the individual actors' scripts had to be [20] exhumed—and these would have to be pieced together laboriously, for an actor never received a full version of the play, only the pages containing his lines and cues. Sometimes, there were no originals to be found and Hemminge and Condell had to rely on the often-unreliable memories of the surviving members of their theater company.

[17]

Which choice is most relevant to the writer's topic and argument in this paragraph?
A) NO CHANGE
B) has been underestimated because they were not writers themselves
C) is made all the more significant by the challenges they faced
D) was not motivated solely by money

[18]

A) NO CHANGE
B) had wrote
C) has written
D) has wrote

[19]

A) NO CHANGE
B) When Hemminge and Condell
C) Surprisingly, Hemminge and Condell
D) Hemminge and Condell

[20]

A) NO CHANGE
B) gotten from somewhere
C) unearthed
D) unburied

Thus it was that the great Shakespeare [21] Industry, which was an industry based on cut-and-paste recollections of verses—was set in motion by two of Shakespeare's greatest fans. Yet this worldwide industry generates [22] millions of dollars a year all round the world. The money-minded Shakespeare would probably have approved.

21

A) NO CHANGE
B) Industry, as
C) Industry—
D) Industry,

22

A) NO CHANGE
B) every year millions of dollars all over the globe.
C) millions of dollars a year on an annual basis.
D) millions of dollars annually.

CONTINUE

Questions 23-33 are based on the following passage and supplementary material.

Somebody's Got a Date . . . with Carbon

[1] Carbon dating is the process by which radioactive elements, such as carbon-14, are used to give estimates of how old something is. [2] While carbon dating was pioneered by Willard Libby in 1960, carbon dating practices have been refined over time. [3] The **23** predictably behaving of radioactive isotopes can give us insight into the timeline of Earth's history—whether we want to inspect a fossil, a rock, or organic material. [4] No method of dating is entirely precise, yet because carbon dating is combined with other methods **24** they can give us a reasonably accurate estimate of the true age of a sample. [5] "The methodologies and instruments for radiometric dating have been expanded and fine-tuned in the half-century since, and very accurate dating is now possible," according to the Smithsonian Institute. **25**

23

A) NO CHANGE
B) predictable behavior
C) predictably behavior
D) predictable behaving

24

A) NO CHANGE
B) he or she
C) it
D we

25

To improve the logic of the paragraph, sentence 4 is best placed
A) where it is now.
B) before sentence 1.
C) before sentence 2.
D) before sentence 3.

The term "carbon dating," [26] therefore, is something of a misnomer, since carbon is just one of the radioactive elements that can be used to estimate age. The entire process is referred to as "radiometric dating." Of the 18 or so elements that are used to measure dates under this method, carbon-14 [27] is one of these elements with some significant limitations. For example, carbon-14 cannot be used to date something that is inorganic, including rocks and even fossils (which themselves are minerals in the shape of long-gone organic matter). Nevertheless, radiometric dating is often called "carbon dating" in non-academic contexts.

[28] So, how often do researchers use carbon dating? The entire setup relies on the predictable half-lives of radioactive elements, including carbon. "Half-life" is a measure of how [29] much atom decay into stable, non-radioactive forms. For carbon-14, the half-life is approximately 5730 years (plus or minus 40 years). That means that after 5730 years, we can expect half of the carbon in a given sample to have decayed into a non-radioactive form. Of course, this relatively short timeline means that carbon is more useful for estimating the ages of samples that are [30] of any age.

26
A) NO CHANGE
B) however
C) regardless
D) furthermore

27
A) NO CHANGE
B) is just one element
C) is one element
D) is one

28
Which choice best sets up the paragraph?
A) NO CHANGE
B) So, how applicable is carbon dating?
C) So, what sorts of objects does carbon dating work on?
D) So, why is carbon dating important?

29
A) NO CHANGE
B) much atoms
C) many atom
D) many atoms

30
The information in the chart best supports which of the following choices?
A) NO CHANGE
B) thousands, not millions, of years old.
C) millions and billions of years old.
D) trillions of years old.

Isotopes	Half Life (in years)
Carbon-14	5730
Iron-60	2.6 Million
Uranium-238	4.5 Billion
Samarium-147	106 Billion

CONTINUE

Fortunately, scientists don't need to rely on carbon alone. Other common elements used in radiocarbon dating include Uranium-238, with a half-life of 4.5 billion years, and Samarium-147, **31** which has exactly the same half-life. Of course, **32** dating samples based only on radiometric measurements are less reliable than using multiple complementary methods. Luckily, dendrochronology—time measurement based on the predictable tree ring patterns of certain tree species, especially bristlecone pines—can be used to check and "correct" radiometric dating.

When these and other methods of dating are carefully used together, we can form a reasonably confident estimate of the age of a sample. **33** Date determination always holds some uncertainty, but procedural tweaks can give scientists the workable estimates they need.

31

Which of the following is an accurate interpretation of the information in the chart?
A) NO CHANGE
B) which has a longer half-life.
C) which has a shorter half-life.
D) which has an immeasurable half-life.

32

A) NO CHANGE
B) using dating samples based only on radiometric measurements are less reliable than using multiple complementary methods.
C) data sampling based only on radiometric measurements is less reliable than multiple complementary methods.
D) data samples based only on radiometric measurements is less reliable than multiple complementary methods.

33

The writer would like to conclude by restating the passage's main point. Which answer choice best accomplishes this?
A) NO CHANGE
B) While we colloquially refer to the process as "carbon dating," scientists often examine different atoms to determine how old something is.
C) While current radiocarbon dating techniques are relatively reliable, researchers are constantly looking for even more accurate ways to date artifacts.
D) The process of carbon dating has revolutionized research methods in various scientific fields of study.

Questions 34-44 are based on the following passage and supplementary material.

Whose Business Is Social Media?

It has only been a few decades since the customary way for prospective employers to check on a potential hire 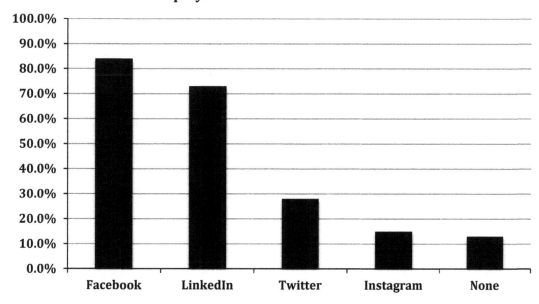34 was to interview neighbors and family members. The advent of social media has changed that dramatically. As employers have learned to navigate and utilize social media, they have found that social media platforms can be deployed to do everything from researching 35 respective employees to keeping top hires satisfied down the road.

34
A) NO CHANGE
B) is
C) had been
D) has been

35
A) NO CHANGE
B) perspective
C) perceptive
D) prospective

Employers' Use of Social Media Sites

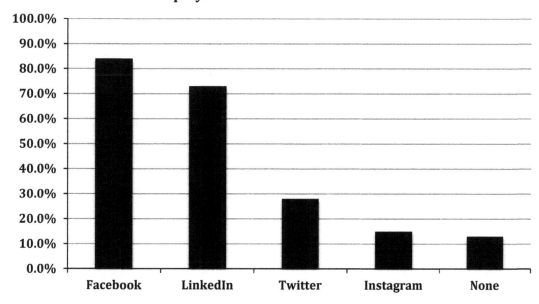

CONTINUE

Various social media [36] makes it easy for employers to verify potential employees' résumés and to find out a lot more about prospective hires. According to a 2014 poll, many employers use social media in their hiring processes and [37] some even use more than one type to pre-screen potential candidates. Furthermore, the results indicate a preference among respondents for [38] Twitter over the more professionally-oriented LinkedIn. By scanning social media accounts, [39] applicants' professionalism, qualifications, and compatibility with a company's culture can be gauged by human resources representatives.

[36]

A) NO CHANGE
B) making
C) make
D) is making

[37]

Which choice best represents the information presented in the graph?

A) NO CHANGE
B) many employers used more than four social media sites to pre-screen potential candidates.
C) the percentage of social media use increases based on the employer location.
D) no employers use background checks to pre-screen potential candidates.

[38]

Which of the following is an accurate interpretation of the graph?

A) NO CHANGE
B) Instagram
C) Facebook
D) both Facebook and Twitter

[39]

A) NO CHANGE
B) human resources representatives can gauge professionalism, qualifications, and compatibility with a company's culture of the applicant.
C) human resources representatives can gauge applicants' professionalism, qualifications, and compatibility with a company's culture.
D) it is possible for human resources representatives to gauge applicant's professionalism, qualifications, and compatibility with a company's culture.

[40] Hiring offices can employ a few new tactics to gain access to potential employees' social media pages. Most notably, some companies began requesting Facebook login passwords during the hiring process. The move was a foolish one for [41] much reasons: it immediately put the applicant supplying the password on the defensive; such applicants quickly adapted by creating false Facebook profiles. [42] Additionally, this practice also made companies vulnerable to anti-discrimination lawsuits.

Most companies soon realized that being this invasive was not the right approach. They became less openly aggressive, although they continued to seek ways to utilize social media. Many companies now use apps to search the Internet for information about potential employees. They have also found other ways—[43] many of which are not the least bit intrusive— to connect with prospective employees online.

40

Which of the following is the best topic sentence for the paragraph?
A) NO CHANGE
B) Not all social media platforms are created equal.
C) In the beginning, mistakes were made.
D) Some employers are more social media savvy than others.

41

A) NO CHANGE
B) many
C) much of
D) many of

42

A) NO CHANGE
B) Additionally, this practice made companies vulnerable to anti-discrimination lawsuits as well.
C) This practice also made companies vulnerable to anti-discrimination lawsuits.
D) This practice also made companies vulnerable to anti-discrimination lawsuits, too.

43

Which choice best provides an example of one of the "other ways" suggested by the author?
A) NO CHANGE
B) which sometimes can be as simple as a Facebook friend request
C) although some employers strongly prefer avoiding Internet research
D) since some social media sites go so far as to facilitate specific employee search methods

CONTINUE

In fact, some companies now actively encourage social media usage. Unisys, Sprint, and HP, among others, have developed social media training programs to help their employees understand the right and wrong ways to approach popular sites. The thinking here is that, when approached correctly, social media can become a valuable business tool by helping employees to be more productive. Outlook Amusements, a technology company, uses social media to build rapport among its employees. The company site allows employees to interact with the HR department, a feature that has helped to reduce employee turnover. Sabre Holdings has also created its own social media page, "Sabre Town," in order to promote communication and collaboration among its workers.

Already an integral part of many **44** people's personal lives, daily use of social media is becoming more and more important in their professional lives as well. Although there is potential for abuse, there are also many benefits to be gleaned from sites and apps as informal as Tumblr, Instagram, Facebook, and more, as savvy companies have learned.

44
A) NO CHANGE
B) peoples
C) peoples's
D) person's

STOP
If you finish before time is called, you may check your work on this section only.
Do not turn to any other section.

Math Test - No Calculator

25 MINUTES, 20 QUESTIONS

DIRECTIONS

For each question from 1-15, choose the best answer choice provided in the multiple choice bank and fill in the appropriate circle in the provided answer key. Alternatively, for questions **16-20**, answer the problem and enter your answer in the grid-in section of the answer key. Refer to the directions given before question 16 as to how to enter your answers for the grid-in questions. You may complete scratch work in any empty space in your test booklet.

NOTES

A. Calculator usage **is not allowed** in this section.
B. Variables, constants, and coefficients used represent real numbers unless indicated otherwise.
C. All figures are created to appropriate scale unless the question states otherwise.
D. All figures are two-dimensional unless the question states otherwise.
E. The domain of any given function is all real numbers x for which the function, $f(x)$, is a real number unless the question states otherwise.

REFERENCE

$A = \pi r^2$
$C = 2\pi r$

$A = lw$

$A = \frac{1}{2}bh$

$c^2 = a^2 + b^2$

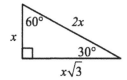
Special Right Triangle

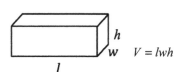
Special Right Triangle

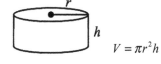
$V = lwh$

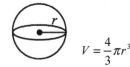
$V = \pi r^2 h$

$V = \frac{4}{3}\pi r^3$

$V = \frac{1}{3}\pi r^2 h$

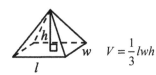
$V = \frac{1}{3}lwh$

There are $360°$ in a circle.
There are 2π radians in a circle.
There are $180°$ in a triangle.

CONTINUE ➡

1

If $4x = 12$, what is the value of $2x - 1$?

A) 5

B) 7

C) 23

D) 25

2

$$f(v) = 75 - 12.50v$$

The balance on a gift certificate for a gym, $f(v)$, is given by the equation above. If v represents the number of visits to the gym, which of the following is the best interpretation of the number 75 in the equation?

A) The gym charges $75 per visit.

B) The gym charges $75 per day.

C) The gift certificate allows for 8 total visits to the gym.

D) The gift certificate had an initial value of $75.

3

Line k is perpendicular to the line $y = -4x + 2$ and goes through the points $(0, -2)$ and $(20, m)$. What is the value of m?

A) 1

B) 3

C) 38

D) 78

4

$$\frac{\theta}{360}(2\pi r)$$

The expression above is used to calculate the length of an arc given θ, the measure of the central angle that defines the arc in degrees, and r, the measure of the circle's radius in inches. If an arc measures 22π inches and its central angle measures at most $45°$, what is the shortest possible measure of the circle's radius in inches?

A) $\dfrac{11}{2}$

B) 11

C) 88

D) 176

CONTINUE

5

$$6x - 2y = 10$$
$$-3x + y = -10$$

How many ordered pairs (x, y) satisfy the system of equations above?

A) 0

B) 1

C) 2

D) Infinitely many

7

In the equation $(x-3)^2 = h$, if $h = 25$ and $x > 0$, what is the value of x?

A) -2

B) 2

C) 5

D) 8

6

$$(3a + 3b)(a - b)$$

Which of the following is equivalent to the expression shown above?

A) $3a^2 + 6ab - 3b^2$

B) $3a^2 - 6ab + 3b^2$

C) $3a^2 + 3b^2$

D) $3a^2 - 3b^2$

8

$$f(x) = \frac{x^a x^b}{x^3}$$

If $a + b = 12$, what is the value of $f(2)$?

A) 16

B) 128

C) 512

D) 1,024

115

CONTINUE

9

Which of the following equations has solutions in all four quadrants of the xy-plane?

A) $f(x) = x^2 + 1$

B) $f(x) = x^3$

C) $f(x) = 2 - |x - 1|$

D) $f(x) = -|x - 3| - 7$

10

$$P = \frac{2(s - c)}{5}$$

A craftsman's net pay, P, is calculated using the equation above given the sale price of the item that is sold, s, and c, the cost to produce the item. Which of the following gives the cost to produce an item, c, in terms of P and s?

A) $c = s - \dfrac{2P}{5}$

B) $c = s - \dfrac{5P}{2}$

C) $c = \dfrac{2(s - P)}{5}$

D) $c = \dfrac{5(s - P)}{2}$

11

Line k contains the points $(-4, 0)$ and $(3, 2)$. Line m contains the points $(-3, 2)$ and $(4, 0)$. If line k is written in the form $y = m_1 x + b_1$ and line m is written in the form $y = m_2 x + b_2$, what is the value of $m_1 b_2 + m_2 b_1$?

A) $-\dfrac{2}{7}$

B) 0

C) $\dfrac{2}{7}$

D) $\dfrac{4}{7}$

12

$$i(3 + 2i)(12 - 8i)$$

Which of the following complex numbers is equivalent to the expression above? (Note: $i = \sqrt{-1}$)

A) $16 + 36i$

B) $36 + 16i$

C) $20i$

D) $52i$

CONTINUE

13

A 55 kilogram fallen tree branch decays at a rate of 25% per year. Which of the following equations could be used to determine $f(t)$, the remaining mass of the tree branch t years after it has fallen?

A) $f(t) = 55(0.25)^t$

B) $f(t) = 55(0.75)^t$

C) $f(t) = 55 - 0.25t$

D) $f(t) = 55 - 0.75t$

14

$$\frac{x^3 - 2x^2 + 4x + 6}{x - 4}$$

If the expression above is written in the form

$ax^2 + bx + c + \dfrac{k}{x-4}$, where a, b, and c are nonzero

constants, what is the value of k?

A) −22

B) −10

C) 54

D) 66

15

What is the product of all of the solutions of the equation $2x^2 + 10x + 1 = 0$?

A) $\dfrac{1}{2}$

B) $\dfrac{1}{8}$

C) $\dfrac{1}{16}$

D) $-\dfrac{5}{2}$

CONTINUE

DIRECTIONS

For each question from 16-20, solve and enter your answer in the grid-in section of your answer sheet as described below.

A. Write out your answers in the boxes at the top of each column in order to help you fill in the circles accurately. Remember, you will only receive credit for the circles that are filled in correctly, not for the written answer at the top of the columns.

B. Mark only a single circle in each column.

C. There are no negative answers.

D. If the problem has more than one correct answer, grid only one of the correct answers.

E. When your answer is a **mixed number**, such as $1\frac{1}{2}$, it should be entered as 1.5 or $3/2$. You cannot enter a mixed number because there is no room to fill in a circle that represents a space.

F. If you enter a **decimal answer** with more digits then the grid can handle, the answer may be rounded or truncated, but it absolutely must fill the entire grid.

Answer: $\frac{8}{21}$

Answer: 6.4

Written answer →

Decimal point →

← Fraction line

Answer: 102 - both positions are correct

REMEMBER:
You can begin writing your answers in any column as long as there is enough space. Leave unused columns blank.

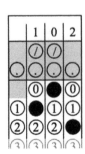

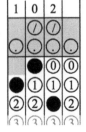

The ways to correctly grid $\frac{7}{9}$ are:

CONTINUE →

16

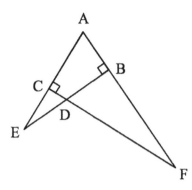

In the figure above, if $\overline{AB}$ measures 4 and $\overline{AC}$ measures 6, what is the measure of $\overline{BE}$ if $\overline{CF}$ measures 15?

17

At a large family birthday party, there were mini pumpkin pies and blocks of chocolate fudge for dessert. Each mini pumpkin pie could feed four people and each block of fudge could feed two people. If 16 people ate dessert at the party and at least one pie and one block of fudge were eaten, what is the greatest number of mini pumpkin pies that could have been consumed if no partial pies were eaten?

18

$$(ax - c)(bx + c) = 5x^2 - 49$$

If the equation above is true for all values of x and a, b, and c are all positive constants, what is the value of abc?

19

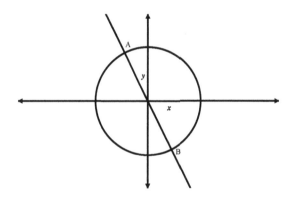

If the equation of the above circle is given in the form $x^2 + y^2 = D$ and the length of $\overline{AB}$ is $10\sqrt{5}$ inches, what is the value of D?

CONTINUE

20

$$K^2 x + 8y = 30$$

$$\frac{K}{2}x + 4y = 5$$

In the system of equations above, both K and x are positive integers. What is a value of K^2 that makes the system of equations true?

STOP

If you finish before time is called, you may check your work on this section only.

Do not turn to any other section.

Math Test - Calculator

55 MINUTES, 38 QUESTIONS

DIRECTIONS

For each question from 1-30, choose the best answer choice provided in the multiple choice bank and fill in the appropriate circle in the provided answer key. Alternatively, for questions **31-38**, answer the problem and enter your answer in the grid-in section of the answer key. Refer to the directions given before question 31 as to how to enter your answers for the grid-in questions. You may complete scratch work in any empty space in your test booklet.

NOTES

A. Calculator usage **is allowed**.
B. Variables, constants, and coefficients used represent real numbers unless indicated otherwise.
C. All figures are created to appropriate scale unless the question states otherwise.
D. All figures are two-dimensional unless the question states otherwise.
E. The domain of any given function is all real numbers x for which the function, $f(x)$, is a real number unless the question states otherwise.

REFERENCE

$A = \pi r^2$
$C = 2\pi r$

$A = lw$

$A = \frac{1}{2}bh$

$c^2 = a^2 + b^2$

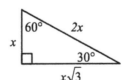
Special Right Triangle

Special Right Triangle

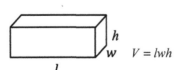
$V = lwh$

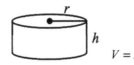
$V = \pi r^2 h$

$V = \frac{4}{3}\pi r^3$

$V = \frac{1}{3}\pi r^2 h$

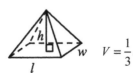
$V = \frac{1}{3}lwh$

There are $360°$ in a circle.
There are 2π radians in a circle.
There are $180°$ in a triangle.

CONTINUE

1

A Goodwill store donates 5 of every 120 donated articles of clothing that it receives to a local shelter. If the Goodwill store donated 24 articles of clothing to the shelter this past month, how many articles of clothing were donated to the Goodwill store?

A) 1

B) 10

C) 576

D) 600

2

If $6x + 2 = 8$, what is the value of $6x - 2$?

A) -1

B) 1

C) 4

D) 12

Questions 3 and 4 refer to the following information.

18 people are stranded at sea on a lifeboat. The number of days of emergency food rations aboard the lifeboat is inversely proportional to the number of passengers on board. There is currently enough food for the 18 passengers to eat for 4 days.

3

If 6 more stranded people were helped onto the lifeboat, how many days worth of food would be available for all passengers?

A) $\dfrac{4}{3}$

B) 2

C) 3

D) 12

4

If the number of rations of food that remained with the initial 18 passengers was only 25% of all of the rations that were initially packed on the lifeboat, how many additional days could the 18 passengers have survived if all of the initial food rations were still intact?

A) 16

B) 12

C) 4

D) 3

CONTINUE

5

A tailor is paid $8 for each shirt that he repairs, $10 for each pair of pants that he repairs, and $22.50 for each suit that he modifies. Which of the following equations represents M, the amount of money in dollars that the tailor receives for repairing s shirts and modifying u suits?

A) $M = 8s + 22.5u$

B) $M = 10s + 22.5u$

C) $M = 8s + 10u$

D) $M = 8s + 10p + 22.5u$

6

$$P(h, v) = 28h + .0001v$$

A webmaster is paid based on the equation above. The webmaster is paid $28 for each hour that he works and receives a stipend of $0.0001 for each time someone visits the website. Which of the following is closest to the number of hours that the webmaster worked in a week in which his total paycheck was $860 and the website had 200,000 visitors?

A) 24

B) 30

C) 31

D) 38

7

During a fitness test in gym class, a gym teacher gives every student 5 points for every minute of continuous physical activity and 1 point for every jumping-jack that the student completes. If a student's final score was 95 and the student completed 80 jumping-jacks, for how many minutes did the student perform continuous physical activity?

A) 2

B) 3

C) 10

D) 15

8

$$f(x) = x - g(x)$$
$$g(x) = x - 1$$

Given the system of equations above, what is the value of $f(g(x))$?

A) -1

B) 0

C) 1

D) $2x - 3$

CONTINUE

9

Which of the following equivalent forms of the linear equation $y = 2x - 1$ gives both coordinates of a point that lies on the line as coefficients or constants in the equation?

A) $y - 2x = -1$

B) $y + 1 = 2x$

C) $y + 1 = 2(x+1)$

D) $y - 1 = 2(x-1)$

10

$$a + b \le 200$$
$$15a + 10b \le 2500$$

A custodial worker at a high-rise apartment complex is using a service elevator to transport 15-pound boxes of toilet paper and 10-pound boxes of paper towels to the upper levels of the building. The elevator is large enough to transport 200 total boxes or a maximum of 2500 pounds. Given the system of inequalities above, which of the following is true?

A) The elevator can transport a total of 250 boxes of paper towels in a single trip.

B) The elevator can transport a total of 200 boxes of toilet paper in a single trip.

C) The elevator can be filled to capacity and transport an equal number of boxes of toilet paper and boxes of paper towels.

D) The elevator must always transport more boxes of paper towels than boxes of toilet paper.

11

	Daily Hours of Driving	Days of Driving per Week	Average Speed (mph)
Meryl	6	5	50
Dana	8	4	40
Randy	10	3	60

Given the table above, how many more miles does Meryl drive in a week than Dana?

A) 220

B) 300

C) 1280

D) 1500

12

A research study was conducted during the holiday season to determine whether people in a large metropolitan area preferred to shop for holiday gifts online or in person at a store. Two hundred randomly selected customers exiting a mall in the metropolitan area were asked whether they preferred to shop in person or online and only 24 responded that they preferred to shop online. Which of the following statements can best be inferred from this research study?

A) 12% of all people living in the metropolitan area prefer to shop for holiday gifts online.

B) 12% of all people living in the metropolitan area prefer to shop for holiday gifts in person.

C) Nothing reliable can be inferred. The location of the survey made the results biased.

D) The study's results are unreliable due to a sample size that is too small.

CONTINUE

13

The moon is approximately 240,000 miles from Earth. If a rocket leaves Earth and takes one day to reach the Moon, which of the following is the closest to the average speed of the rocket in kilometers per hour?

(1 mile ≈ 1.609 kilometers)

A) 622

B) 1,610

C) 6,215

D) 16,100

14

The largest domesticated breed of cat is the Maine Coon. An adult male Maine Coon is 125% larger than its female counterpart. If an adult female Maine Coon weighs 12 pounds, the weight in pounds of an adult male Maine Coon is most likely which of the following?

A) 5.3

B) 9.6

C) 15

D) 27

15

$$p(x) = -x^2 + 12x - 20$$

In the function above, $p(x)$ represents a company's profits x years after 1980. For how many years did the company break even or return a positive profit?

A) 0

B) 2

C) 8

D) 10

16

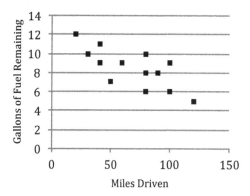

Gallons of Fuel Remaining as Compared to Miles Driven

A line of best fit is calculated from the data in the scatterplot above to estimate the number of remaining gallons of fuel based on the number of miles driven. The line of best fit that models the data has the equation $G(x) = 13.8 - 0.06x$, where x represents the number of miles driven and $G(x)$ is the estimated number of gallons remaining. Based on the model, which of the following would be the best estimate for the number of remaining gallons of fuel given that 150 miles were driven?

A) 4

B) 5

C) 6

D) 7

CONTINUE

Questions 17 and 18 refer to the following information.

Distribution of Family Vacations

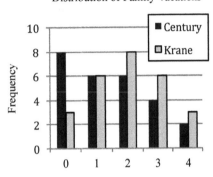

A random sample of 26 students from both Century High School and Krane High School were asked about the number of family vacations they take during a given school year. The results are displayed in the bar chart above. There are a total of 1,820 students in Century High School and 2,600 students in Krane High School.

17

What is the average number of family vacations taken by all of the randomly selected students?

A) 1.46
B) 1.73
C) 2.00
D) 2.12

18

Estimating from the data collected in the bar chart, how many more students are expected to take 1 vacation in Krane High School than in Century High School?

A) Approximately 180 more students are expected to take 1 family vacation in Krane High School than in Century High School.

B) Approximately 600 more students are expected to take 1 family vacation in Krane High School than in Century High School.

C) The number of students taking 1 family vacation in Krane High School is the same as the number of students taking 1 family vacation in Century High School.

D) The number of students taking 1 family vacation in Krane High School is less than the number of students taking 1 family vacation in Century High School.

19

	Blue Tint	Red Tint
pH of 1-4	2	8
pH of 5-10	4	4
pH of 11-14	9	1

A group of science students are classifying sample solutions by the color of the liquid and the pH level of the liquid. The data is collected in the table above. If a solution with a pH level of 1-4 is randomly selected, what is the probability that the solution has a blue tint?

A) $\frac{1}{4}$

B) $\frac{1}{5}$

C) $\frac{2}{15}$

D) $\frac{1}{14}$

CONTINUE

Questions 20 and 21 refer to the following information.

$$A_p = (2\pi r + 2)(h + 2)$$

A print company uses the formula above to calculate the necessary print area, including bleed margins, for printing labels for cylindrical cans based on r, the radius of the can, and h, the height of the can.

20

If the company wanted to calculate the height of a can from a given radius, r, and print area, A_p, which of the following equations would be used?

A) $h = \dfrac{A_p}{2\pi r + 2} - 2$

B) $h = 2 - \dfrac{A_p}{2\pi r + 2}$

C) $h = \dfrac{A_p - 2}{2\pi r + 2}$

D) $h = A_p(2\pi r + 2) - 2$

21

Cylinder A has a height of 4 inches and a radius of 1 inch. Cylinder B has a height of 8 inches and the same radius as Cylinder A. The print area required for Cylinder A is what percent smaller than the print area required for Cylinder B?

A) 40

B) 60

C) 200

D) 250

22

When advertising job opportunities, a large corporation opted to list the median salary for all of its employees rather than advertise the average salary. In recent hiring cycles, the company discovered through internal surveys that newly hired employees were under the impression that their starting salaries would be higher given the average salaries they read about in former employment ads. The corporation most likely chose to list the median salary instead of the average salary for which of the following reasons?

A) A few employee salaries are much lower than the rest of the employee salaries, which skews the average salary downward.

B) A few employee salaries are much higher than the rest of the employee salaries, which skews the average salary upward.

C) The salaries of the empolyees are extremely scattered and spread out.

D) The salaries of the employees are very close together with very little difference from employee to employee.

23

A cereal manufacturer is selling large boxes of cereal. The manufacturer would like to keep the target weight of each box between 17.5 ounces and 19.5 ounces. Which of the following inequalities could be used to determine whether the weight of a randomly selected box of cereal, x, meets the target weight requirement set forth by the manufacturer?

A) $|x - 18.5| < 1$

B) $|x + 18.5| \le 1$

C) $|x - 1| < 18.5$

D) $|x - 1| \le 18.5$

CONTINUE

24

The graph of a quadratic function f has x-intercepts at $(d,0)$ and $(e,0)$, where d is greater than e. The x-coordinate of the vertex of the parabola is equivalent to $2e+d$. If d and e are integers, which of the following could be the equation of f?

A) $f(x) = x^2 - 4x + 2$

B) $f(x) = x^2 - 4x - 12$

C) $f(x) = -x^2 + 8x - 12$

D) $f(x) = -x^2 + 6x - 9$

25

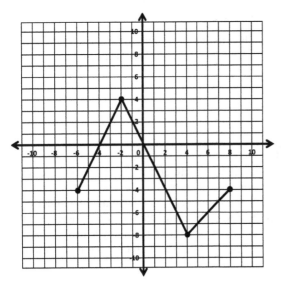

The complete graph of the function f is shown in the xy-plane above. Which of the following values is not equal to $f(-6)$?

A) $-f(-2)$

B) $f(2)$

C) $f(4) + 2$

D) $f(8)$

26

$$x^2 + y^2 - 8y = 9$$

The equation above is of a circle in the xy-plane that has an area of what?

A) 9π

B) 16π

C) 25π

D) 81π

27

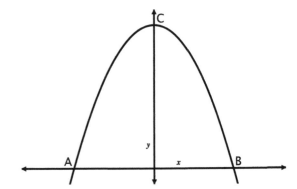

The graph of the function $y = -2x^2 + 18$ is shown above. The function intercepts the x-axis at the points A and B. The function intercepts the y-axis at the point C. If point D lies on the x-axis and is one-fourth of the distance from A to B, what is the slope of the line that goes through points C and D?

A) -27

B) 6

C) 12

D) 27

CONTINUE

28

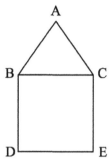

If $\triangle ABC$ is equilateral and has an area of $16\sqrt{3}$, what is the area of the pentagon $ACEDB$?

A) 64

B) $80\sqrt{3}$

C) $16+16\sqrt{3}$

D) $64+16\sqrt{3}$

29

$$(x^2 + bx) + c(x + d) = x^2 + 5x + 12$$

If the equation above is true for all values of x and b, c, and d are all positive integer constants, which of the following cannot be the value of d?

A) 2

B) 3

C) 4

D) 6

30

Moped's Value: $V_1(t) = 10,000 - 1,000t$

Dirt Bike's Value: $V_2(t) = 10,000(0.9)^t$

The value of a moped t years after its purchase follows the linear decay model defined above. The value of a similarly priced dirt bike t years after its purchase follows the exponential decay model defined above. Within which of the following intervals is the value of the moped greater than the value of the dirt bike?

A) 0 to 1 years

B) 1 to 2 years

C) 2 to 3 years

D) The value of the moped is never higher than the value of the dirt bike.

CONTINUE

DIRECTIONS

For each question from 31-38, solve and enter your answer in the grid-in section of your answer sheet as described below.

A. Write out your answers in the boxes at the top of each column in order to help you fill in the circles accurately. Remember, you will only receive credit for the circles that are filled in correctly, not for the written answer at the top of the columns.

B. Mark only a single circle in each column.

C. There are no negative answers.

D. If the problem has more than one correct answer, grid only one of the correct answers.

E. When your answer is a **mixed number**, such as $1\frac{1}{2}$, it should be entered as 1.5 or $3/2$. You cannot enter a mixed number because there is no room to fill in a circle that represents a space.

F. If you enter a **decimal answer** with more digits then the grid can handle, the answer may be rounded or truncated, but it absolutely must fill the entire grid.

Answer: $\frac{8}{21}$ Answer: 6.4

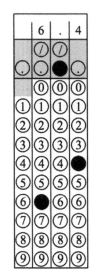

The ways to correctly grid $\frac{7}{9}$ are:

Answer: 102 - both positions are correct

REMEMBER:
You can begin writing your answers in any column as long as there is enough space. Leave unused columns blank.

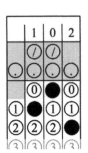
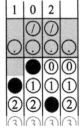

CONTINUE ➡

31

A man stands 77 inches tall and states that he is, "*F* feet *I* inches tall," where *I* is less than 12. What is the value of $F + I$?

32

Enrique and Sadie took a total of 122 photos while they were on vacation. If Enrique had 20 more than half the number of photos on his cell phone than Sadie had on her cell phone, how many photos were on Sadie's cell phone?

33

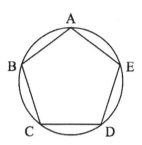

A regular pentagon is inscribed in a circle with an area of 121π. If the length of arc $\overset{\frown}{ABC}$ is written in the form $D\pi$, what is the value of *D*?

34

A college professor has noted that his freshman environmental design class has steadily grown to a size of 122 students. If the class size was only 54 students when he started teaching the course 17 years ago, the course enrollment has had an average increase of how many students per year?

CONTINUE

35

Line k crosses the x-axis at 5 and is parallel to the line with equation $5y - 12x = 5$. What is the distance between the x-intercept and the y-intercept of Line k?

36

$$B = 3{,}520(0.8)^m$$

Polly is spending a semester studying abroad in Spain. The equation above models the remaining balance in euros of Polly's spending account after m months have passed. By what percent does Polly's spending account balance decrease over the course of three months?

CONTINUE

---▼---

Questions 37-38 refer to the following information.

$$A_{Current} = 1.05(\frac{P_{Current}}{P_{Last}})(A_{Last})$$

A small manufacturer and supplier of bookshelf audio systems spent $5,200 last year on advertising. The manufacturer calculates its current advertising budget in dollars each year, $A_{Current}$, using the formula above where $P_{Current}$ represents the net profit from the current year's sales, P_{Last} is the net profit from last year's sales, and A_{Last} is the advertising budget from last year in dollars.

37

If the company were to have a current net profit that was 20% larger than last year's, how many dollars could the company expect to spend on advertising in the current year?

38

If the company's current net profit were actually $142,500 and the current advertising budget had to be reduced to $5,187, how much larger was last year's net profit than this year's net profit?

---▲---

STOP

If you finish before time is called, you may check your work on this section only.
Do not turn to any other section.

Answer Key: TEST 2

SECTION 1—READING

1.	C	11.	B	22.	B	33.	C	43.	C
2.	C	12.	D	23.	B	34.	A	44.	C
3.	A	13.	C	24.	A	35.	A	45.	D
4.	B	14.	B	25.	A	36.	B	46.	B
5.	B	15.	D	26.	C	37.	B	47.	D
6.	A	16.	C	27.	C	38.	C	48.	B
7.	C	17.	D	28.	D	39.	C	49.	A
8.	B	18.	A	29.	D	40.	A	50.	C
9.	D	19.	A	30.	C	41.	B	51.	A
10.	B	20.	C	31.	B	42.	D	52.	B
		21.	D	32.	D				

SECTION 2—WRITING

1.	C	12.	A	23.	B	34.	A
2.	A	13.	B	24.	C	35.	D
3.	D	14.	A	25.	A	36.	C
4.	C	15.	D	26.	B	37.	A
5.	B	16.	B	27.	D	38.	C
6.	D	17.	C	28.	B	39.	C
7.	D	18.	A	29.	D	40.	C
8.	C	19.	B	30.	B	41.	B
9.	C	20.	C	31.	B	42.	C
10.	A	21.	C	32.	C	43.	B
11.	C	22.	D	33.	A	44.	A

SECTION 3—MATH

1.	A	12.	D
2.	D	13.	B
3.	B	14.	C
4.	C	15.	A
5.	A		
6.	D	**Fill-Ins:**	
7.	D	16.	10
8.	C	17.	3
9.	C	18.	35
10.	B	19.	125
11.	B	20.	25 or 4

SECTION 4—MATH

1.	C	13.	D	24.	B	**Fill-Ins:**	
2.	C	14.	D	25.	C	31.	11
3.	C	15.	C	26.	C	32.	68
4.	B	16.	B	27.	C	33.	44/5 or 8.8
5.	A	17.	B	28.	D	34.	4
6.	B	18.	A	29.	A	35.	13
7.	B	19.	B	30.	A	36.	48.8
8.	C	20.	A			37.	6552
9.	D	21.	A			38.	7500
10.	C	22.	B				
11.	A	23.	A				
12.	C						

Answer Explanations

SAT Practice Test #2

Section 1: Reading

QUESTION 1.

Choice C is correct. The passage describes how Klaus revisits his mother's "cottage" (line 18) in the early stages: later, Klaus talks with the "young woman who lived next door" (line 47) about his relationship with his mother. This information supports C. A states that the passage describes a "catastrophe" (yet such a negative occurrence never arises) and D states that Klaus observes the cottage "affectionately" (yet many of his remarks are in fact critical). Because the young woman is already familiar to Klaus, B, which wrongly specifies a "new acquaintance", must also be eliminated.

QUESTION 2.

Choice C is correct. The word "stiffly" describes how a gate "opened": the gate required a hard push and grated along the ground. This information supports C and contradicts D. A refers to a personal REACTION while B refers to an ATTITUDE: neither is an effective description of a resistant "gate".

QUESTION 3.

Choice A is correct. In lines 55-58, Klaus refers to his mother's tendency to stay away from home and voices his awareness that she has a difficult personality. He is thus familiar with her, justifying A. Klaus observes her independence but does not voice discomfort (eliminating B), responds to his mother's new circumstances not eagerly but "wearily" (line 67, eliminating C), and observes a lapse in his WRITING, not in his mother's READING (line 63, eliminating D).

QUESTION 4.

Choice B is correct. In context, Klaus is sorting out documents, first "bills and demands" (line 29), then "communications" which his mother has disregarded. These discarded documents would contain "messages" to her, making B an effective answer. A wrongly assumes that the mother has been PART of an exchange, when in fact she neglects the "communications"; C and D both assume that the subjects of the "communications" are personal and emotional, yet there is no context for this assumption.

QUESTION 5.

Choice B is correct. In the first paragraph, Klaus observes an "early, Bavarian, November morning" (lines 1-2) in the town where he has just arrived; the second paragraph presents a memory of "the Ethiopian town he had left so urgently" (line 11) but where he has a house. This information supports B and eliminates A, which assumes that the second paragraph describes the FUTURE rather than the past. C wrongly discusses Klaus's "childhood" rather than his present, while D refers to an "array of cultures" rather than the SINGLE Ethiopian culture that interests Klaus.

137

QUESTION 6.

Choice A is correct. In lines 40-45, the author describes some of the unappealing sights in the home of Klaus's mother and observes that "dust was everywhere". This information supports A, while other answers distort the content of the passage. Klaus didn't write "that often" (line 63), but his mother may still have meaningful knowledge of his activities from other channels (eliminating B). Klaus's mother has "never been easy" (line 57), but only one neighbor, the young woman, is described in detail and seems not to have any problems with Klaus's mother. And Klaus's mother has just "stepped out" (line 54) of her house, but is never described as wanting to leave her "community" itself.

QUESTION 7.

Choice C is correct. See above for the explanation of the correct answer. A describes the Bavarian town in general (not Klaus's mother), B offers a description of some items of mail, and D indicates that Klaus has been "busy" but has now decided to attend to his mother. None of these offer a precise characterization of the mother, yet be careful of wrongly taking B as a justification for Question 6 A.

QUESTION 8.

Choice B is correct. In the relevant paragraph, Klaus is reflecting on his mother's gate and his intention to "replace the supporting hinges" (line 21): this task is what Klaus has "promised" to fulfill. B is an effective answer while A ("burden") is much too negative. While C and D refer to themes from ELSEWHERE in the passage, they do not directly reference the TASK that Klaus is contemplating.

QUESTION 9.

Choice D is correct. As depicted in lines 49-50, the young woman is aware that Klaus has arrived and offers him a cup of tea: she is conscious both of details and of his needs, or "attentive" in these situations. While A ("awestruck") wrongly implies that the young woman is surprised or confused, B ("pompous" or stuck-up) wrongly introduces a negative. C ("idiosyncratic" or unusual) cannot describe the woman, who is presented mainly as trying to make pleasant dialogue, but COULD be taken as a description of Klaus or his mother, since their tastes and habits are better defined.

QUESTION 10.

Choice B is correct. See above for the explanation of the correct answer. A mainly establishes that the young woman is "timid", C depicts the young woman concurring with Klaus, and D mainly relates the young woman's actions and the sentiments of Klaus's mother. The traits that can be gleaned from these answers (timidity, acceptance, sympathy) are not among the answer choices for the previous question.

QUESTION 11.

Choice B is correct. The first paragraph explains how Esperanto functions as "a constructed language" (line 1) that could allow "diverse populations to communicate" (line 9). This focus on explanation and possible advantages supports B. Ultimately, the author constructs a thesis AGAINST the applicability of Esperanto (eliminating positive answers A and C) and ONLY talks about Esperanto itself (eliminating A and D, which both assume that multiple constructed languages are analyzed in the passage).

QUESTION 12.

Choice D is correct. While the author spends the early paragraphs (lines 1-27) explaining the modern language Esperanto, he spends later portions of the passage (lines 45-74) explaining that Esperanto is limited in usefulness but is still linked to the idea of "mutual understanding" (lines 73-74). This combination of analysis and assessment justifies D, while other answers focus on the wrong TOPICS: Esperanto, not a "linguist" (A), an "ancient" language (B), or a "philosophy" (C), is the focus of the passage.

QUESTION 13.

Choice C is correct. The author often calls attention to the limitations of Esperanto: in lines 25-28, it is observed that Esperanto relies on "Romance languages" and bypasses "non-European language structures entirely". This information aligns with C as a qualification of the idea of "political neutrality" (which is CONTRADICTED by such language bias). A and B both wrongly assume that the author ACCEPTS and is building off the idea that Esperanto is politically neutral, while D distorts the reasoning behind Esperanto's lack of popularity. As argued in lines 45-57, people avoid Esperanto because it seems confusing and unnecessary, NOT because it is a threat to cultures.

QUESTION 14.

Choice B is correct. See above for the explanation of the correct answer. A indicates that Esperanto can ease specific international tensions, C indicates that Esperanto bears resemblances to Romance languages, and D WEAKENS claims that Esperanto can bring cultures together. Be careful of answer A, which only refers to a SPECIFIC set of relationships but can be confused as justification for the GENERAL idea of political neutrality.

QUESTION 15.

Choice D is correct. In lines 52-54, the author points out a criticism of Esperanto: English speakers have difficulty with the language, which derives from languages spoken in Continental Europe. This information supports D, while other answers distort arguments from the passage. Although the author points out that English is prevalent in lines 49-50, this does NOT mean that other languages are unnecessary (eliminating trap answer A). And while B and C apply negative tones to Esperanto, these answers indicate problems with the DEVELOPMENT or SOPHISTICATION of Esperanto, not objections to its USEFULNESS as cited by the author.

QUESTION 16.

Choice C is correct. See above for the explanation of the correct answer. A points out that Esperanto is both belittled and taken seriously, B simply explains an Esperanto translation, and D indicates that Esperanto will probably not become widely popular. Be careful of taking A as a justification for Question 15 B or C (which deal with Esperanto's STRUCTURE, an issue that is not raised here) and of taking D as a justification for Question 15 D (which raises the issue of English usage, which is not discussed in the line reference).

QUESTION 17.

Choice D is correct. The phrase "partake so fluidly of" refers to Esperanto, which (as established in the previous paragraph) is strongly indebted to "Romance languages" (line 39). It thus includes parts of these languages or "samples" them, making D the best answer. A would indicate that Esperanto is being portioned or split, while B refers primarily to actions that PEOPLE would perform, as does trap answer C: people can "engage" with Esperanto, but it cannot itself engage them.

QUESTION 18.

Choice A is correct. The word "common" refers to English, which is widely and efficiently used in certain settings. A, "prevalent", is an effective usage: both B and D indicate negatives while C emphasizes the wrong issue. The author is concerned with how widespread English is, not with whether it is granted "approval" in any formal way.

QUESTION 19.

Choice A is correct. The author begins this paragraph by noting how "unlikely" it is that Esperanto "will ever achieve linguistic ascendancy" (lines 59-60); however, it is then pointed out that Esperanto could "unite far-flung factions" (line 73), an ability that is similar to Zamenhof's intent (lines 3-7) in creating the language. This information supports A and eliminates B (since the paragraph ends in a positive fashion). C and D both wrongly assume that the paragraph begins in a neutral fashion and introduces contexts (the media and school settings, respectively) that are not of interest to the author here.

QUESTION 20.

Choice C is correct. In the passage, the author calls attention to Esperanto associations (lines 11 and 17) and continues to be motivated by "idealism" (line 65). This information supports C, since mature linguists would be likely to form such associations. A and D are contradicted by the author's argument that Esperanto has not been instituted at large in the realms of business or politics, while B is problematic because the author is concerned with how adults, NOT children, respond to Esperanto.

QUESTION 21.

Choice D is correct. In the passage, the author indicates that English is "already the common language of expediency" (lines 49-50) and that Esperanto is unlikely as a popular replacement. The graph substantiates this idea by showing that English (at 46.40%) is a more popular second language than Esperanto (at 0.90%). The graph only lists Esperanto speakers in the European Union: eliminate A and C because the graph does not show how the popularity of Esperanto has changed OVER TIME, and eliminate B because the graph says nothing about the AGE or MOTIVES of people who learn Esperanto.

QUESTION 22.

Choice B is correct. The passage discusses indications that "water flows on the Martian surface" (lines 34-35) and goes on to consider the implications of such a "monumental discovery" (line 49), including new missions, the possibility of life on Mars, and the danger of contamination. This information supports B, while A is inaccurate (since humans have only explored Mars using probes) and C is too extreme (since the author considers possible liabilities of exploring Mars but does not argue that Mars should NOT be explored). D misstates the final stages of the passage, which introduce the positives and negatives of a course of action but do not define sides in a "controversy".

QUESTION 23.

Choice B is correct. In lines 6-7, the author explains that life could "theoretically evolve in dry conditions" such as those that exist on Mars: this information supports B and eliminates A, which wrongly states that life definitively CANNOT exist on Mars. C and D overstate the other side of the issue: the author describes life on Mars as a "possibility" (line 52) while these answers wrongly assume that there definitely is life on Mars.

QUESTION 24.

Choice A is correct. See above for the explanation of the correct answer. B explains that massive dust storms take place on Mars, C explains that Mars has polar ice caps, and D notes the presence of liquid water on Mars. None of these answers directly states whether Mars harbors life or not, though make sure not to wrongly align B with Question 23 A or C with Question 23 C.

QUESTION 25.

Choice A is correct. The word "definitive" refers to "evidence" of liquid water: this evidence is certain or occurs at the end of a rigorous and "conclusive" study, making A the best answer. The author is concerned with how VALID the evidence is on its own merits, not with the level of DETAIL (eliminating B and D) or the level of ACCEPTANCE (eliminating C).

QUESTION 26.

Choice C is correct. In lines 32-35, the author explains that, despite years of difficulties, researchers found "new evidence" of liquid water on Mars in 2011. This information supports C and can be used to eliminate A (which cites the wrong year and the wrong factor as part of the research breakthrough) and B (which wrongly indicates that scientists were uninterested in the issues of liquid water and life on Mars). D misconstrues part of the passage: "hydrated salts" were DISCOVERED on Mars, not USED as research tools.

QUESTION 27.

Choice C is correct. See above for the explanation of the correct answer. A indicates that life has not yet been discovered on Mars, B indicates that ice (but not life or liquid water) has been found on Mars, and D refers to a research breakthrough that took place in 2015 (not 2011, as demanded by the correct answer to the previous question). Make sure not to wrongly take A as evidence for Question 26 A.

QUESTION 28.

Choice D is correct. In lines 40-48, the author explains that "evidence of hydrated salts" (line 43), when combined with earlier findings involving recurring slope lineae, substantiated the idea that water flows on Mars. This information supports D, while the passage never definitively states that Mars harbors life (eliminating B) or draws an explicit link between the RSL and the ice caps on Mars (eliminating C). A is a trap answer: the "perchlorates" (line 44) accompanied the RSL, but did not necessarily CAUSE the RSL.

QUESTION 29.

Choice D is correct. Near the end of the passage, the author notes that Martian micro-organisms would present a "huge contamination risk" (lines 54-55) on Earth, and that micro-organisms from Earth could reach Mars and "contaminate the planet irreversibly" (line 63). This information directly supports D, while A (writers and artists), B (settlements and cities), and C (planets beyond Mars) touch on topics in space exploration that are not major considerations of the passage.

QUESTION 30.

Choice C is correct. The word "meticulous" refers to the "science" methods that would be necessary to prevent contamination on Mars and Earth: such methods would involve caution, making C the best answer. A refers to MEASUREMENT, not to AVOIDING a danger, while B ("creative") and D ("ethical") refer to issues that have more to do with JUDGMENT and little to do with a straightforward PRACTICAL problem such as contamination.

QUESTION 31.

Choice B is correct. In the graph, the bar for "Bradbury to Rocknest" is highest, thus indicating the greatest depth of water. Rapidly eliminate A, C, and D, but make sure not to wrongly assume that the LOWEST bar (A) signifies the greatest depth.

QUESTION 32.

Choice D is correct. While the passage discusses the water that "flows on the Martian surface" (lines 34-35), the graph considers the depth of water relative to or BELOW the surface of Mars (since the water levels are consistently below the topography levels). D correctly reflects this information, while A is directly contradicted by the graph and B is contradicted by the passage (which only states that ICE can be found below the surface of Mars). C is a faulty answer: while the passage FOCUSES on water aboveground, the author of the passage never argues that water CANNOT be found below the surface of Mars.

QUESTION 33.

Choice C is correct. After attributing recent revolutionary activity in Europe to justifiable "social want" (line 24), Marx transitions to an "inquiry into" (line 55) the forces behind the rise and fall of such activity. This information supports C, while A wrongly assumes that Marx takes a negative stance towards revolutionary activity, B wrongly focuses on a SINGLE revolutionary (not on broad revolutionary conditions), and D misstates as positive the tone of later portions of the passage (which delve into the negative misperceptions that surround revolution).

QUESTION 34.

Choice A is correct. The word "irresistible" is used to describe the result of "wants and necessities" (lines 41-42), which would result in an unavoidable or "inevitable" manifestation. A is the best answer: B and C wrongly focus on OPINIONS or EMOTIONS, rather than on the idea of being strongly needed. Trap answer D is incorrect in context: the movements and "manifestations" that Marx saw as inevitable were in fact defeated for a time, so that "powerful" is not the best possible fit.

QUESTION 35.

Choice A is correct. In lines 21-23, Marx argues that revolutions are no longer seen as the activity of a few disgruntled agitators: A effectively reflects Marx's rejection of such an earlier, outdated opinion. Although Marx does argue that revolutions can face setbacks, this line reference indicates that Marx's attitude towards revolution is positive overall. Eliminate B, C, and even D (since Marx is mostly interested in the nature of revolution, now in how individuals "experience" revolution) as too negative.

QUESTION 36.

Choice B is correct. See above for the explanation of the correct answer. A records the outcome of a single revolutionary movement (not of revolution in general), C rejects a specific inquiry as unimportant (and again does not address revolution in general), and D notes that specific nationalities may have little concern with specific national quarrels. Only in B does Marx offer a broad characterization of "revolution" as demanded by the previous question.

QUESTION 37.

Choice B is correct. The phrase "bursts its fetters" refers directly to a revolutionary movement or "convulsion" (line 24) that eventually overpowers and defeats "forcible repression" (line 28). This information directly supports B, while A ("events of 1848") and C (social class) refer to issues that may interest Marx but that are NOT directly relevant to the line reference. D is relevant to events described earlier (lines 1-12), but NOT to Marx's optimistic prediction that repression can eventually be defeated.

QUESTION 38.

Choice C is correct. In the second paragraph, Marx depicts revolution as a broad-based struggle driven by "social want" (line 24), but often believed to be doomed by a single individual who "betrayed" (line 47) the people. This information supports C, while Marx would disagree with A (since it only SEEMS that a small effort or single betrayal compromises a revolution) and B (since Marx acknowledges that some repressive efforts have in fact been successful). D wrongly focuses on the "mindset" of revolutionaries: in fact, Marx is mostly interested in the practical OUTCOMES of revolutions, not the principles that motivate them.

QUESTION 39.

Choice C is correct. The word "light" refers to the result of how an "American or Englishman" (line 64) would observe distant event. Because the "details" (line 66) could not be effectively taken in, the American or Englishman would have poor "context" for understanding political events abroad. C is thus the best answer: A and D both wrongly assume that the events would be serve a PRACTICAL purpose (rather than simply being OBSERVED), while B is ineffective in a different way. The American or Englishman could still form an "opinion" of distant events, though such opinions would be faulty.

QUESTION 40.

Choice A is correct. Marx notes that the figures named in the line reference were subjected to "petty" (line 58) accusations and "contradictory assertions" (line 59) concerning revolutionary matters. These men were thus unfairly criticized, making A an effective answer and eliminating B and D (which ultimately describe the figures negatively). C uses flawed logic: although Marx notes that the figures may not deserve strong blame, he never notes that they committed great or heroic actions in promoting political ideals.

QUESTION 41.

Choice B is correct. In lines 55-58, Marx argues that inquiring into the nature of revolutionary activity and its suppression is "of paramount [or supreme] importance" (line 57). This information supports B. While Marx often speaks positively of revolution and its eventual chances of success, he does not necessarily endorse political reform (A), education in socialism (C), or legislation and elections (D). In fact, because he believes that "single individuals" (line 40) are often beside the point and expresses faith in political upheaval, these answer may be too moderate to fit his argument.

QUESTION 42.

Choice D is correct. See above for the explanation of the correct answer. A notes and dismisses a political and revolutionary defeat, B notes that revolutionary efforts will eventually overcome suppression, and C notes that political parties cannot premise their success on distrust of individuals. None of these answers aligns with an answer to the previous question, though make sure not to mistake the positive B as a justification for either Question 41 B or another, positive answer to Question 41.

QUESTION 43.

Choice C is correct. In discussing the Mozart Effect, Passage 1 develops the position that there have not been "particularly conclusive results" (line 4) about the validity of the Effect; Passage 2 makes the argument that the Mozart Effect "is a reality" (line 68) but has not been sufficiently assessed. This information justifies C, while A and D wrongly attribute a harsh tone to the skeptical (but not sharply condemning or broadly critical) Passage 1. B misconstrues Passage 2, which argues that the Mozart Effect has been "formulated simplistically" (line 69) and thus does NOT advocate all the reasoning behind the effect.

QUESTION 44.

Choice C is correct. While Passage 1 indicates that research on the Mozart Effect has not resolved "the issue of whether or not the effect exists" (line 36), the author of Passage 2 wants to "re-evaluate" (line 40) the Mozart Effect and consider responses to non-classical music, which have typically not played a part in Mozart Effect research. This information supports C, while the inconclusive Passage 1 contradicts A and Passage 2, which mostly accepts the Mozart Effect, contradicts B. Only Passage 2 considers "musical genres besides classical", making D a faulty answer.

QUESTION 45.

Choice D is correct. In lines 15-18, the author explains that the flaws in the 1993 study included small sample size, consideration of only a single age group, and a focus only on short-term changes. This information supports D and is linked to the author's generally skeptical stance on the Mozart Effect. A, B, and C all identify the wrong flaws: data manipulation, outdated technology, and inability to reproduce results are not mentioned. Rather, the TYPE of people and CONSIDERATIONS involved in testing the Mozart Effect were both much too narrow.

QUESTION 46.

Choice B is correct. See above for the explanation of the correct answer. A notes a possible positive result linked to the Mozart Effect, C indicates that the Mozart Effect was attractive despite a seeming drawback, and D notes measures that indicate the popularity of the Mozart Effect as a premise. While all of the answers to Question 45 are to some extent negative, these answer choices are all positive and should be eliminated.

QUESTION 47.

Choice D is correct. The word "modest" describes the results of a specialized study: these results were not large in scope or were "limited" in scope, since they are contrasted with a broader notion that "captured the public's imagination" (line 21). D is the best answer, while A refers to complexity and B refers to temperament (two issues unrelated to the author's discussion of EXTENT and limitation). C is a trap answer: the results were limited in extent, but were not truly "insignificant" since they did attract public attention and have a clear impact.

QUESTION 48.

Choice B is correct. The different music-based "Effects" mentioned in the line reference precede a discussion of how different genres of music can in fact help people "think more effectively" (line 49): B is thus a highly effective answer, since the line reference refers to non-classical musical genres. A refers primarily to Passage 1 ("spatial reasoning test"), C contradicts Passage 2 (which ultimately argues that listening to music can aid cognition), and D combines an accurate tone ("lighthearted") with an overly strong negative ("pessimistic") that is nowhere present in the mostly analytic Passage 2.

QUESTION 49.

Choice A is correct. The word "formulated" refers to the Mozart Effect "phenomenon" that has been analyzed and summed up, or "described", by two researchers. A is thus the best answer, while B, C, and D wrongly assume that the Mozart Effect was a fabricated RESULT of specific activities by Shaw and Rauscher, not an OBSERVATION of something that existed independent of them.

QUESTION 50.

Choice C is correct. In lines 2-4, the author of Passage 1 observes that experimentation surrounding the Mozart Effect has "not yet arrived at particularly conclusive results": however, the author of Passage 2 declares that "The Mozart Effect is a reality" (line 68). This information supports C and can be used to eliminate both A and B, which wrongly assume that the author of Passage 1 ultimately accepts the Mozart Effect as an effective explanation. However, D is much too negative, since the author of Passage 1 argues that the Mozart Effect is not fully verified, NOT that it is definitively a "hoax" or a deception.

QUESTION 51.

Choice A is correct. See above for the explanation of the correct answer. B indicates that the Mozart Effect was an effective marketing premise, C indicates that numerous experiments have been devoted to the Mozart Effect, and D records the results of an analysis. While B and C are purely factual (and thus do not offer the perspective of the author of Passage 1), D offers a DIFFERENT perspective that should not readily be attributed to the author of Passage 1.

QUESTION 52.

Choice B is correct. The words "less lofty" refer to a source other than Mozart, such as popular music. Such music, as described by the author of Passage 2, would be widely regarded as less impressive or "more humble" than Mozart's music. B is a correct answer, while A refers to physical form, C refers to the ability to recover, and D indicates a negative EXCESS rather than a simple COMPARISON as demanded by the passage.

Section 2: Writing
Passage 1, Restaurant Woes

QUESTION 1.

Choice C is correct. The underlined portion should be a singular possessive that refers to the "New York restaurant" mentioned earlier. C is exactly the possessive required: A is a nonexistent form, B is the contraction of "it is", and D is plural.

QUESTION 2.

Choice A is correct. The underlined verb should refer to the restaurant Alder and its position on a piece of "real estate": Alder "occupied" this area. While A is an effective answer, B and D both wrongly assume that Alder had a negative effect or was difficult to oppose. C would best refer to a person who is "preoccupied", not to the "occupation" of an area.

QUESTION 3.

Choice D is correct. Without the underlined portion, there is no other context in the passage that directly explains who Pete Wells is: D is the best answer. While Wells is never again mentioned (eliminating B) and no other newspapers are mentioned in the passage (eliminating C), the author still needs to clarify Wells's role (eliminating A, despite its deceptively good logic).

QUESTION 4.

Choice D is correct. This question requires a concise and logical description of the "restaurant industry". A and B are both redundant because they use the synonyms "unstable" and "volatile", while C wrongly assumes that the restaurant industry is "notorious" or highly negative OVERALL, rather than that its lack of stability is a well-known negative. D is thus the best answer in the context of the passage.

146

QUESTION 5.

Choice D is correct. The relevant sentence describes two different problems with Alder, which are linked by the underlined portion. D, "while", rightly indicates that these problems were simultaneous and complementary. A wrongly assumes that the dining room CAUSED the problems with the serving portions, B creates a contrast, and C indicates that one problem ENDED when the other began when in fact both problems with Alder were present at once.

QUESTION 6.

Choice D is correct. In this paragraph, the author explains a few of the further troubles that face restaurants, so that a general statement about "why restaurants fail" effectively introduces this discussion. Nowhere in the paragraph are celebrity chefs (A), food critics (B), or individual restaurant owners (C) mentioned, so that all of the other answers must be eliminated even though they are negative in tone.

QUESTION 7.

Choice D is correct. The underlined noun refers to "customers": because customers can be counted individually, the word "number" (not "amount", which refers to NON-COUNTABLE quantities) must be used. Eliminate A and B, but also eliminate the singular C, since plural "urban areas" would involve plural and perhaps different "numbers" of customers.

QUESTION 8.

Choice C is correct. The underlined portion must be in parallel with the phrase "interrupt business", since these are two hypothetical situations that are being presented together. Only C, "halt cash flow", creates effective parallelism: A is in past tense, B is not grammatically correct ("would . . . halts"), and D is wordier and less clearly in parallel than C.

QUESTION 9.

Choice C is correct. This sentence is structured to compare the "negative publicity" that met Chipotle to the publicity that would confront smaller restaurants: C properly uses the phrase "that which met" to refer to the publicity that met Chipotle. A wrongly compares publicity to Chipotle itself, B wrongly compares publicity to restaurants, and D wrongly uses the plural pronoun "those" to refer to the singular "publicity".

QUESTION 10.

Choice A is correct. The proper English idiom for this sentence is "slated for", which means "intended for". B, C, and D all supply the wrong preposition. Be careful of some of these choices in context, however, since a building is being described but is not in fact being covered "with" slate.

QUESTION 11.

Choice C is correct. Sentence 4 calls attention to the topic of "real estate": while sentence 2 raises the issue of Wylie Dufresne's "weak point," sentence 3 explains that "zoning strictures" or real estate problems undermined one of his restaurants. Thus, sentence 4 effectively transitions from sentence 2 to sentence 3. While A and D wrongly re-introduce the issue of real estate AFTER the issue is raised in sentence 3, B places the issue of real estate too early and renders the pronoun "It" ambiguous.

Passage 2, How Shakespeare Works

QUESTION 12.

Choice A is correct. Because the sentence involves a hypothetical situation, use the subjunctive: in cases such as this, "were" is the proper verb form for a hypothetical cause and "would" is the proper verb form for a hypothetical effect. A is thus the best answer. While B and C are not subjunctive forms, D presents a "would" form for a CAUSE rather than an EFFECT.

QUESTION 13.

Choice B is correct. The underlined portion should link two independent clauses, and should contrast two pursuits ("short-run plays", "show business") that are connected to Shakespeare. A involves a comma splice, C wrongly states a similarity, and D places a fragment after a semicolon. (When linking two independent clauses, "but" should be preceded by a comma.) B involves both effective grammar and the correct sentence relationship.

QUESTION 14.

Choice A is correct. The underlined portion occurs in a series and should be in parallel with "his appearances" and "his stints": "his remarks" is the best choice. B is an awkward phrasing that does not involve a plural noun, and C and D both break parallelism by introducing verbs.

QUESTION 15.

Choice D is correct. This portion of the passage calls for the idiomatic expression "invited to", since Shakespeare would be invited "to a place" or "to a location". All the other answers break this common idiom and assume different relationships: A indicates that he is already present ("at"), B indicates that his only purpose is to see the White House ("for"), and C mainly indicates that he is leaving ("from").

QUESTION 16.

Choice B is correct. The underlined portion, Shakespeare is described, not people in general: eliminate A and C. Furthermore, in subjunctive-form sentences such as this, a hypothetical cause must be phrased using "were" and a hypothetical effect must be phrased using "would". Because the underlined portion describes the effect or condition Shakespeare would face, eliminate the simple present D and choose B for proper subjunctive phrasing.

QUESTION 17.

Choice C is correct. In this paragraph, the writer addresses the documentation efforts of Hemminge and Condell, who faced challenges because the "plays were ephemeral" or short-lived. This content makes the negative answer C effective. A focuses on scholars (not mentioned here at all), and B attributes the wrong difficulty (writing background and reputation) to the project undertaken by Hemminge and Condell. D refers to the issue of money, which is important only in previous paragraphs.

QUESTION 18.

Choice A is correct. Before he "oversaw" the printing process, Ben Jonson "had written" the plays that were being printed: to register this difference in timing, choose A and eliminate B, which uses an improper verb form. C and D ("has" forms) both describe action that continues from the past into the present: because Jonson lived centuries ago, these choices are automatically illogical.

QUESTION 19.

Choice B is correct. The underlined portion should indicate similarity or simultaneity, since the publication of "Shakespeare's works" was designed as "an act of homage" that would have a positive effect. Eliminate A, which wrongly indicates a contrast, and choose B. Both C and D result in comma splices.

QUESTION 20.

Choice C is correct. The underlined word should refer to "scripts" that were searched out and utilized when other documents "were not available": "unearthed" is a word that can mean "discovered" or "found" in standard written English. A and D both refer literally to the act of removing a body from the ground, while B is needlessly wordy.

QUESTION 21.

Choice C is correct. In this sentence, the subject "Shakespeare Industry" takes the verb "was set": a subject and verb cannot be divided by a single dash, but may be interrupted by information that is placed between two dashes. C creates this sentence structure, while A, B, and D all wrongly involve only a single interrupting dash.

QUESTION 22.

Choice D is correct. Watch for redundancy in this question: A and B both contain content that is interchangeable with the earlier phrase "worldwide", while C pairs the interchangeable phrases "a year" and "annual". D is the most concise option and does not present any redundant content.

Passage 3, Somebody's Got a Date . . . with Carbon

QUESTION 23.

Choice B is correct. The underlined portion requires a noun which will serve as the subject of "can give": this noun must be modified by an adjective. A and C both employ adverbs, NOT adjectives: for the remaining answers, "behavior" as opposed to "behaving" is the noun expected in common English usage. Thus, eliminate D and choose B.

QUESTION 24.

Choice C is correct. The underlined pronoun should refer to "carbon dating", which is what can give "a reasonably accurate" estimate of the true age of a sample. While A and D are plural and B would only refer to people, C properly refers to carbon dating as "it".

QUESTION 25.

Choice A is correct. Sentence 4 transitions from a discussion of how carbon dating works to a discussion of the "accurate dating" of materials, a topic that is discussed primarily in sentence 5. Thus, sentence 4 should be left in its current position: B, C, and D would all interrupt the introductory explanation of how carbon dating works.

QUESTION 26.

Choice B is correct. While the previous paragraph has pointed out an asset of carbon dating (its accuracy), this sentence points to a possible negative (its questionable naming). The underlined portion should thus introduce a contrast in tone, not a causal relationship (A), a dismissal of the earlier information (C), or an indication of similarity (D).

QUESTION 27.

Choice D is correct. Because the sentence has already established that carbon-14 is one of "18 or so elements", it is not necessary to repeat the fact that carbon-14 is an element. A, B, and C are thus redundant, while D is the most concise and effective answer.

QUESTION 28.

Choice B is correct. The paragraph as a whole explains the decay of carbon samples in order to explain how "applicable" carbon is for estimating sample ages: the author is thus concerned with the effectiveness of the measurements, so that B is the best answer. Specific researchers (A) and specific objects (C) are never mentioned directly, while the author has established why carbon dating is important in the PREVIOUS paragraphs and mostly explains its specifics in this one.

QUESTION 29.

Choice D is correct. Because atoms (at least in theory) are individual things that can be counted, eliminate A and B, since "much" is used for NON-COUNTABLE quantities. While C breaks noun to noun agreement (since the "atoms" should decay into "forms"), D creates such agreement and is thus the best answer.

QUESTION 30.

Choice B is correct. The information in the graph lists the "relatively short timeline" of the half-life for Carbon-14, 5730 years. Since this half-life is used for dating measurements, it would be used primarily to estimate the ages of samples that are thousands of years old: B is an effective answer, while A, C, and D all wrongly assume that Carbon-14 would be effective on much longer timelines.

QUESTION 31.

Choice B is correct. While the half-life of Uranium-238 is 4.5 billion years, the half-life of Samarium-147 is 106 billion years, a much larger number. B effectively states information from the graph, while A and C state faulty relationships and D wrongly assumes that the half-life for Samarium-147 has not been measured at all.

QUESTION 32.

Choice C is correct. In the underlined portion, the singular subject "dating" is wrongly paired with the plural verb "are". Eliminate A, B ("using . . . are"), and D ("samples . . . is") on account of subject-verb disagreement, and choose C ("sampling . . . is") as the only grammatically correct answer.

QUESTION 33.

Choice A is correct. The passage as a whole has addressed the fact that carbon dating is an imperfect yet generally effective method that has undergone improvement and revision: this qualified positive tone toward "Data determination" aligns best with A. While B and C both distract from the topic of age measurement to address "different atoms" and "more accurate ways", trap answer D is mostly about the EFFECTS of carbon dating on research at large, not about HOW carbon dating functions and how it has been improved.

Passage 4, Whose Business Is Social Media?

QUESTION 34.

Choice A is correct. In context, the underlined portion should refer to a "way" that was observed "a few decades" ago but has been disregarded as a result of the growth of social media. A is the best answer: B and D both assume continuation into the present, while C introduces a remote past form that is unnecessary in a sentence that describes a single practice that "was" once customary.

QUESTION 35.

Choice D is correct. The "employers" described in the sentence would naturally want to research possible or "prospective" employees before hiring them, making D the best choice in context. The other answers involve diction errors and would best fit other contexts: A distinguishes between two things, B refers to a viewpoint, and C is a term of praise.

QUESTION 36.

Choice C is correct. The subject of the underlined verb is the plural "Various [different] social media", so that C is the only choice that provides an acceptable plural form. A and D are both singular while B creates a sentence fragment.

QUESTION 37.

Choice A is correct. According to the graph, over 80% of employers consult Facebook and over 70 % consult LinkedIn: thus, at least some employers must consult both of these sites. This information supports A, while the much more infrequent use of the two other social medial platforms listed in the chart disqualifies B. Neither location nor background checks are considered in the graph, so that C and D must be eliminated.

QUESTION 38.

Choice C is correct. According to the graph, the only social media platform that employers use to a greater extent than LinkedIn is Facebook; this information justifies C and eliminates A, B, and trap answer D, which wrongly assumes that Facebook and Twitter are COMPARABLE in terms of employer preference, while the figure for Twitter is in fact significantly LOWER than the figure for Facebook.

QUESTION 39.

Choice C is correct. The phrase "By scanning social media accounts" must refer directly to the people doing the scanning. Both A ("professionalism") and D ("it") create misplaced modifiers. B introduces a misplaced modifier at the end of the sentence, since the "culture" belongs to the "company" and is not the "culture of the applicant". Eliminate this answer and choose C as the best-coordinated and most logical choice.

QUESTION 40.

Choice C is correct. As a whole, this paragraph describes problems in early uses of social media by employers: C effectively captures this negative topic. A refers to new measures (not early mistakes), B refers to a variety of platforms (not to specific uses by employers), and D makes a distinction between employers that is not explored at length and that does not capture the negatives that this paragraph addresses.

QUESTION 41.

Choice B is correct. The underlined word should refer to "reasons", which are distinct and countable: "much" refers to non-countable quantities (eliminating A and C), while the preposition "of" is not necessary (eliminating D). B properly phrases the "many reasons" why a particular social media strategy would be foolish.

QUESTION 42.

Choice C is correct. In order to properly address this question, pay attention to closely-related phrases that are redundant: "Additionally" and "also" (A), "Additionally" and "as well" (B), and "also" and "too" (D). Eliminate all of these answers and choose C, which only involves the qualifier "also".

QUESTION 43.

Choice B is correct. The question demands a specific "example", and the "Facebook friend request" mentioned in B would be one such example. Although the other answers are roughly on-topic, they do not add examples or detail: A simply qualifies the preceding statement, C lists a general preference, and D refers to "specific employee search methods" without explaining what exactly these methods are.

QUESTION 44.

Choice A is correct. The underlined word should be a possessive that modifies "personal lives", which belong to multiple "people": "people's" in A is the best choice. B is a plural noun, C is a nonexistent form, and D is a singular possessive.

Section 3: Math Test - No Calculator

QUESTION 1.

Choice A is correct. Dividing both sides of $4x = 12$ by 2 yields $2x = 6$. Subtracting 1 from both sides yields $2x - 1 = 5$.

Choice B is incorrect and may result from adding 1 to both sides after dividing by 2 instead of subtracting 1 from both sides. Choice C is incorrect and may result from multiplying both sides by 2 then subtracting 1 from each side. Choice D is incorrect and may result from multiplying both sides by 2 and adding 1 to each side.

QUESTION 2.

Choice D is correct. The remaining value on the gift card is calculated using the equation $f(v) = 75 - 12.50v$, where 75 is a fixed dollar value and $-12.50v$ is the expression that represents the amount of money removed for v visits to the gym. Substituting 0 for v in the original equation gives $f(0) = 75 - 12.50(0)$, or $f(0) = 75$. With 0 visits to the gym, the remaining balance on the gift card is $75. Thus, the initial value of the gift card is $75.

Choice A is incorrect because the coefficient 75 is neither negative nor attached to the variable v, which represents the number of visits. Choice B is incorrect because the equation is built around the number of visits, v, not the number of days at the gym. Choice C is incorrect because if you substitute 8 for v in the original equation, it yields $f(8) = 75 - 12.50(8)$, or $f(8) = -25$. This results in a negative gift card balance, which is impossible.

QUESTION 3.

Choice B is correct. Since line k is perpendicular to the line $y = -4x + 2$, line k has an opposite reciprocal slope of $\frac{1}{4}$. Additionally, since the y-intercept is given, $(0, -2)$, the equation for line k can be written as $y = \frac{1}{4}x - 2$. Substituting the point $(20, m)$ into the equation for line k gives $m = \frac{1}{4}(20) - 2$, or $m = 3$.

Choices A, C, and D are incorrect and may result from errors in conceptual understanding or errors in calculation.

QUESTION 4.

Choice C is correct. Given an arc length of 22π, one can create the equation $22\pi = \frac{\theta}{360}(2\pi r)$. Solving this equation for θ yields $\frac{360(22\pi)}{(2\pi r)} = \theta$, or more simply $\frac{3960}{r} = \theta$. Since θ is at least $45°$, then $\frac{3960}{r} \leq 45$. Solving for r yields $r \geq 88$. The shortest possible measure of r is 88.

Choices A and B are incorrect because the values of $\frac{11}{2}$ and 11 are both less than 88 which is the lowest possible value for the radius. Choice D is incorrect. 176 could be the measure of the radius, but it is not the shortest possible measure of the radius.

QUESTION 5.

Choice A is correct. Multiplying each side of $-3x + y = -10$ by 2 gives the equation $-6x + 2y = -20$. Adding $-6x + 2y = -20$ to $6x - 2y = 10$ gives $0 = -10$. Since both variables are eliminated and the final statement makes no sense, the two lines are parallel, which yields 0 solutions.

Choices B, C, and D are incorrect and may result from computational errors when solving the system of linear equations.

QUESTION 6.

Choice D is correct. Factoring a 3 out of the binomial $(3a + 3b)$ yields the expression $3(a + b)(a - b)$. From this form, one can see the factors of the difference of perfect squares which, when multiplied, give the expression $3(a^2 - b^2)$, or $3a^2 - 3b^2$.

Choices A and B are incorrect and may result from errors in expanding the expression $(3a + 3b)(a - b)$. Choice C is incorrect and may result from errors in conceptual understanding of the difference of perfect squares.

QUESTION 7.

Choice D is correct. Since $(x - 3)^2 = h$ and $h = 25$, one can substitute h with 25 which yields $(x - 3)^2 = 25$. Taking the square root of both sides of the equation $(x - 3)^2 = 25$ yields $x - 3 = \pm 5$. Since $x > 0$, one would solve the equation $x - 3 = 5$ which gives $x = 8$.

Choice A is incorrect because -2 is less than 0 and $x > 0$. Choices B and C are incorrect because substituting 2 or 5 into the expression $(x - 3)^2$ is not equivalent to 25.

QUESTION 8.

Choice C is correct. By the laws of exponents, the equation $f(x) = \dfrac{x^a x^b}{x^3}$ can be rewritten as $f(x) = \dfrac{x^{a+b}}{x^3}$, which can be further simplified to $f(x) = x^{(a+b)-3}$. Substituting 2 for x and 12 for $a + b$ gives $f(2) = 2^{(12)-3}$, or $f(2) = 2^9$. Therefore, $f(2) = 512$.

Choices A, B, and D are incorrect and may result from errors in applying the laws of exponents. For example, Choice A is incorrect because if one applies the exponent division rule incorrectly and divides the power of 12 by 3 instead of subtracting 3, the equation would give $2^4 = 16$.

QUESTION 9.

Choice C is correct. Since the absolute value makes every value inside greater than or equal to 0, the equation $f(x) = |x-1|$ would only have solutions greater than or equal to zero. Inverting the equation and making it $f(x) = -|x-1|$ would only give solutions that are less than or equal to zero. These solutions would all occur at or below the x-axis, or in Quadrants III and IV. By adding 2 and creating the equation $f(x) = 2 - |x-1|$, the graph of the function $f(x) = -|x-1|$ is shifted vertically creating solutions in both Quadrants I and II as well. Therefore, $f(x) = 2 - |x-1|$ has solutions in all four quadrants of the xy-plane.

Choice A is incorrect because its graph in the xy-plane only has solutions in Quadrants I and II. Choice B is incorrect because its graph in the xy-plane only has solutions in Quadrants I and III. Choice D is incorrect because it is an inverted absolute value function with a negative y-intercept and its graph in the xy-plane only has solutions in Quadrants III and IV.

QUESTION 10.

Choice B is correct. Multiplying both sides of $P = \dfrac{2(s-c)}{5}$ by 5 yields $5P = 2(s-c)$.

Distributing the 2 gives $5P = 2s - 2c$ which can be further simplified $5P - 2s = -2c$.

Dividing both sides by -2 yields $-\dfrac{5P}{2} + s = c$. Finally, rearranging the equation gives the solution $c = s - \dfrac{5P}{2}$.

Choices A, C, and D are incorrect and may result from errors in calculation or errors in mental math when attempting to manipulate the form of the given equation.

QUESTION 11.

Choice B is correct. Since line k goes through $(-4, 0)$ and $(3, 2)$, one can use the slope formula $m = \dfrac{y_2 - y_1}{x_2 - x_1}$ to calculate the slope. Therefore, $m = \dfrac{(2)-(0)}{(3)-(-4)} = \dfrac{2}{7}$. Then, substituting the point $(-4, 0)$ into $y = \dfrac{2}{7}x + b$ yields $(0) = \dfrac{2}{7}(-4) + b$, which gives $b = \dfrac{8}{7}$. The equation for line k is $y = \dfrac{2}{7}x + \dfrac{8}{7}$. Similarly, since line m contains $(4, 0)$ and $(-3, 2)$, one can use the slope formula to get $m = \dfrac{(2)-(0)}{(-3)-(4)} = -\dfrac{2}{7}$. Then, substituting the point $(4, 0)$ into $y = -\dfrac{2}{7}x + b$ yields $b = \dfrac{8}{7}$. The equation for line m is $y = -\dfrac{2}{7}x + \dfrac{8}{7}$.

Finally, substituting into $m_1 b_2 + m_2 b_1$ yields $(\dfrac{2}{7})(\dfrac{8}{7}) + (-\dfrac{2}{7})(\dfrac{8}{7})$, or 0.

Choices A, C, and D are incorrect and may be the result of errors in calculating the appropriate y-intercepts for the equations of line k and line m.

QUESTION 12.

Choice D is correct. In order to simplify $i(3+2i)(12-8i)$, multiply the binomials first, which yields $i(3(12)+3(-8i)+2i(12)+2i(-8i))$, or $i(36-16i^2)$. Substituting -1 for i^2 yields $i(36-16(-1))$, which simplifies to $52i$.

Choices A, B, and C are incorrect and may be the result of errors in expanding the portion of the complex expression $(3+2i)(12-8i)$.

QUESTION 13.

Choice B is correct. Every year, the mass of a fallen tree branch decays by 25 percent from the previous year's mass. So, each year, 75 percent of the previous year's amount remains. Since the initial mass of the fallen tree branch is 55 kilograms, the remaining amount after one year is equivalent to $55(.75)$. After two years, the remaining amount would be equivalent to $55(.75)(.75)$, or $55(.75)^2$. Therefore, after t years have passed, the remaining mass of the fallen tree branch is $55(.75)^t$. So, $f(t) = 55(.75)^t$.

Choice A is incorrect and may result from multiplying the initial mass by the percent of decay rather than the decay factor of $1-.25=.75$. Choices C and D are incorrect because they are both linear models and not exponential as defined by the context of the problem.

QUESTION 14.

Choice C is correct. Dividing $x^3 - 2x^2 + 4x + 6$ by $x-4$ yields:

$$
\begin{array}{r}
x^2 + 2x + 12 \\
x-4 \overline{\smash{\big)}\ x^3 - 2x^2 + 4x + 6} \\
\underline{-(x^3 - 4x^2)} \\
2x^2 + 4x \\
\underline{-(2x^2 - 8x)} \\
12x + 6 \\
\underline{-(12x - 48)} \\
54
\end{array}
$$

Therefore, the expression $\dfrac{x^3 - 2x^2 + 4x + 6}{x-4}$ can be rewritten as $x^2 + 2x + 12 + \dfrac{54}{x-4}$. So, in the form $ax^2 + bx + c + \dfrac{k}{x-4}$, k is equivalent to 54.

Choices A, B, and D are incorrect and may result from finding the incorrect remainder when using long division.

QUESTION 15.

Choice A is correct. In order to find the product of all of the solutions of the equation

$2x^2 + 10x + 1 = 0$, one must substitute into the quadratic formula, $\dfrac{-b \pm \sqrt{b^2 - 4ac}}{2a}$.

Substituting $a = 2$, $b = 10$, and $c = 1$ yields $\dfrac{-(10) \pm \sqrt{(10)^2 - 4(2)(1)}}{2(2)}$, or

$\dfrac{-10 \pm \sqrt{92}}{4}$. This simplifies to $\dfrac{-5 \pm \sqrt{23}}{2}$. So, multiplying the two roots yields

$\dfrac{-5 + \sqrt{23}}{2} \bullet \dfrac{-5 - \sqrt{23}}{2} = \dfrac{25 - 23}{4} = \dfrac{1}{2}$.

Choices B, C, and D are incorrect and may result from errors in applying the quadratic formula or errors when multiplying the roots of the equation.

QUESTION 16.

The correct answer is 10. Given that $\triangle ACF$ and $\triangle ABE$ are both right triangles and share a common angle at A, the two triangles are similar and thus have sides of proportional length. In $\triangle ACF$, $\overline{AC}$ measures 6 and $\overline{CF}$ measures 15. In $\triangle ABE$, $\overline{AB}$

measures 4 and the measure of $\overline{BE}$ is the unknown. Using the proportion $\dfrac{\overline{AC}}{\overline{CF}} = \dfrac{\overline{AB}}{\overline{BE}}$,

one can solve for $\overline{BE}$. Substituting gives $\dfrac{6}{15} = \dfrac{4}{\overline{BE}}$. Cross-multiplying yields

$6\overline{BE} = 60$, or $\overline{BE} = 10$.

QUESTION 17.

The correct answer is 3. Let p be the number of mini pumpkin pies consumed and let f be the number of blocks of fudge consumed. Since 16 people ate dessert, each pie feeds 4 people, each block of fudge feeds 2 people, and at least one pie and one block of fudge were consumed, one can conclude that p and f are positive integers and the equation

$4p + 2f = 16$ is true. Solving for p yields $p = 4 - \dfrac{1}{2}f$. Since the question is asking for

the greatest number of pies, p, that could have been consumed and p is a positive integer, one must substitute the lowest positive integer value for f that gives a positive value of p.

This is 2. Substituting 2 for f yields $p = 4 - \dfrac{1}{2}(2)$, or $p = 3$.

QUESTION 18.

The correct answer is 35. Since $(ax - c)(bx + c) = 5x^2 - 49$ is true for all values of x, the two sides of the equation must be equal to each other. Expanding the left hand side gives $(ab)x^2 + (ac)x - (bc)x - c^2 = 5x^2 - 49$, which can be rewritten as $(ab)x^2 + (ac - bc)x - c^2 = 5x^2 - 49$. Given that both sides of the equation are equal, one can see that $ab = 5$, $ac - bc = 0$, which only means that a and b are equal, and $c^2 = 49$. Solving $c^2 = 49$ for a positive value of c yields $c = 7$ and substituting 5 for ab and 7 for c yields the product $abc = (5)(7) = 35$.

QUESTION 19.

The correct answer is 125. If a circle is centered on the origin, its equation follows the form $x^2 + y^2 = r^2$. Since the question states that the circle's equation follows the form $x^2 + y^2 = D$, then $D = r^2$. Given that $\overline{AB}$ measures $10\sqrt{5}$ and $\overline{AB}$ is a diameter, the radius is equivalent to $5\sqrt{5}$. Substituting $5\sqrt{5}$ for r yields $D = (5\sqrt{5})^2$, which is equivalent to 125.

QUESTION 20.

The correct answer is 25 or 4. Since the system of equations has only one solution, one can eliminate y, find K, and finally square to get K^2. Multiplying the second equation by -2 yields $-2(\frac{K}{2}x + 4y) = -2(5)$, or $-Kx - 8y = -10$. Adding $K^2x + 8y = 30$

to $-Kx - 8y = -10$ yields $K^2x - Kx = 20$. Factoring out a K and an x gives

$K(K-1)x = 20$. One can see that K and $K - 1$ are two numbers that are one apart, and since K and x are positive integers, K, $K - 1$, and x must be three factors of 20 that have a product of 20, two of which are one apart. Since K and $K - 1$ are the two numbers that are one apart, if x is 1, K and $K - 1$ are 5 and 4. If x is 10, K and $K - 1$ are 2 and 1. Therefore, it follows that if K is 5 or 2, $K^2 = 25$ or $K^2 = 4$.

Section 4: Math Test - Calculator

QUESTION 1.

Choice C is correct. If a Goodwill store donates 5 of every 120 donated articles of clothing it receives to a local shelter and the store donated 24 articles of clothing to the local shelter, one can solve the proportion $\frac{5}{120} = \frac{24}{x}$, where x represents the total number of articles of clothing donated to the goodwill store. Cross-multiplying yields $5x = 2880$ and then dividing both sides of the equation by 5 gives $x = 576$.

Choices A, B, and D are incorrect and may result from errors in setting up the appropriate proportion or errors in calculation. For example, Choice A is incorrect because it is the solution to the proportion $\frac{5}{120} = \frac{x}{24}$, an error in which the 24 articles of clothing are assumed to be the donations made to the Goodwill store, not the denotations made by the Goodwill store to the local shelter as was stated in the question.

QUESTION 2.

Choice C is correct. If $6x + 2 = 8$ and the question asks for the value of $6x - 2$, one can simply subtract 4 from both sides of $6x + 2 = 8$, which yields $(6x + 2) - 4 = (8) - 4$. Simplifying gives the answer $6x - 2 = 4$.

Choice B is incorrect because 1 is the answer if one were to solve for x. Choices A and D are incorrect and may result from errors in calculating the value of $6x - 2$.

QUESTION 3.

Choice C is correct. The number of days worth of emergency food rations is inversely proportional to the number of passengers aboard the lifeboat. By the definition of an inversely proportional relationship, $R = \dfrac{k}{P}$, where R is the number of days of emergency food rations and P is the number of passengers aboard the lifeboat. However, this can be rewritten as $RP = k$, which shows that the number of days of emergency food rations multiplied by the number of passengers must always equal the same constant. Therefore, the number of current days worth of rations, 4, times the number of current passengers, 18, must be equal to the unknown number of days worth of emergency rations, x, times the new number of passengers, $18 + 6 = 24$. This yields $4(18) = x(24)$, or simply $x = 3$.

Choice A is incorrect and may result from using a directly proportional relationship, $R = kP$, instead of the inversely proportional relationship defined by $R = \dfrac{k}{P}$. Choice B is incorrect and may result from a calculation error when solving for the unknown number of days worth of emergency rations. Choice D is incorrect and may result from calculating the inverse relationship with 6 passengers instead of 24 passengers on the lifeboat.

QUESTION 4.

Choice B is correct. If the current amount of emergency food rations allows the 18 passengers on the lifeboat to survive for 4 days and this is only 25% of the original amount of food rations, then 75% of the initial amount of rations have already been used or lost at sea. Since 75% is three times 25%, the 18 passengers could have survived for $3(4) = 12$ additional days.

Choices A, C, and D are incorrect and may result from errors in calculation or comprehension of the question. For example, Choice A is incorrect because 16 days would have been the total number of days the 18 passengers could have survived with all of the initial emergency food rations, not the *additional* number of days that the passengers could have survived.

QUESTION 5.

Choice A is correct. Since the tailor receives $8 for each shirt that he repairs, the tailor will earn $8s$ dollars if he repairs s shirts. In addition, since the tailor receives $22.50 for each suit that he repairs, the tailor will earn $22.50u$ dollars if he repairs u suits. So, the amount of money that they tailor makes, M, for repairing s shirts and u suits is represented by the equation $M = 8s + 22.5u$.

Choice B is incorrect because the fee for repairing a pair of pants, $10, was substituted for the fee for repairing a shirt. Choice C is incorrect because the fee for repairing a pair of pants, $10, was substituted for the fee for repairing a suit. Choice D is incorrect because it includes the money the tailor would have earned for also repairing p pairs of pants, which was not stated in the question.

QUESTION 6.

Choice B is correct. The number of hours worked, h, can be found by substituting the $860 earned by the webmaster for $P(h,v)$ and substituting 200,000 for v, the number of visits to the website. Making these substitutions into the equation $P(h,v) = 28h + .0001v$ yields $860 = 28h + .0001(200,000)$, or $860 = 28h + 20$. Subtracting 20 from each side and dividing by 28 yields $h = 30$ hours

Choice A is incorrect and may result from calculating $.0001(200,000)$ as 200 instead of 20. Choice C is incorrect and may result from adding 20 to each side instead of subtracting 20 from each side. Choice D is incorrect and may result from calculating $.0001(200,000)$ as 200 instead of 20 and adding it to both sides instead of subtracting.

QUESTION 7.

Choice B is correct. Since a student receives 5 points for every minute of physical activity and 1 point for every jumping jack that is performed, using m for minutes of continuous exercise, j for the number of jumping jacks, and P for total points, one can solve the equation $P = 5m + 1j$ to find the number of minutes of continuous physical activity the student performed. Substituting 95 points for P and 80 for j yields the expresssion $(95) = 5m + 1(80)$. Subtracting 80 from both sides of the equation yields $15 = 5m$, which simplifies to $m = 3$ minutes.

Choices A, C, and D are incorrect and may result from calculation errors when solving or errors in solving for the appropriate value. For example, Choice D is incorrect because 15 is the total number of points earned for the minutes of continuous physical activity, not the number of minutes for which the student had continuous activity.

QUESTION 8.

Choice C is correct. Given that $f(x) = x - g(x)$ and $g(x) = x - 1$, substituting $x - 1$ for $g(x)$ in the first equation yields $f(x) = x - (x - 1)$, or $f(x) = 1$. $f(x) = 1$ is a constant function which means that regardless of the input, the output will always be 1. Therefore, $f(g(x)) = 1$.

Choices A, B, and D are incorrect and may result from errors in substitution or calculation errors involved in distributing the negative sign when $x - 1$ is substituted for $g(x)$.

QUESTION 9.

Choice D is correct. Linear equations can be written in three forms: slope-intercept form ($y = mx + b$), point-slope form ($y - y_1 = m(x - x_1)$), and standard form ($Ax + By = C$). The question asks for the equation of a line that has both the x and y coordinates of a point that lies on the line as constants in the equation. This would be an equation in point slope form. Looking at the equation in point-slope form given in answer choice D, $y - 1 = 2(x - 1)$, one can distribute the 2 which yields $y - 1 = 2x - 2$, and after adding 1 to both sides, the equation yields our original linear equation $y = 2x - 1$. $y - 1 = 2(x - 1)$ is an equivalent form of $y = 2x - 1$ that has the constants of the point $(1,1)$, within the equation.

Choices A and B are incorrect because they are not linear equations in point-slope form. Choice C is incorrect because it is not equivalent to the given equation $y = 2x - 1$.

QUESTION 10.

Choice C is correct. The inequality $a + b \leq 200$, where a represents the number of boxes of toilet paper and b represents the number of boxes of paper towels, dicatates that the elevator is filled to capacity when it is carrying a total of 200 boxes. In order for the elevator to be filled to capacity and have an equal number of boxes of toilet paper and paper towels, there would have to be 100 boxes of each. If the elevator were carrying 100 boxes of toilet paper and 100 boxes of paper towels, the overall weight could be checked using the other equation, $15a + 10b \leq 2500$. Substituting 100 for a and 100 for b yields $15(100) + 10(100) \leq 2500$, or $1500 + 1000 \leq 2500$. Since this is also a true statement, answer choice C is correct.

Choice A is incorrect because the elevator can only transport a maximum of 200 boxes of any type. Choice B is incorrect because 200 boxes of toilet paper would weigh $15(200) = 3000$ pounds. This is heavier than the maximum 2,500 pounds. Choice D is incorrect because the elevator can transport just boxes of toilet paper as long as the weight of those boxes does not exceed 2,500 pounds

QUESTION 11.

Choice A is correct. The total number of miles driven in a week for any person can be calculated by multiplying the total number of hours of driving by the average speed in miles per hour ($D = rt$). If Meryl drives 6 hours a day and 5 days a week, her total weekly hours of driving are $6(5) = 30$ hours. Multiplying Meryl's weekly hours of driving by her average speed of 50 miles per hour yields $30(50) = 1500$ miles. If Dana drives 8 hours a day and 4 days a week, her total weekly hours of driving are $8(4) = 32$ hours. Multiplying Dana's weekly hours of driving by her average speed of 40 miles per hour yields $32(40) = 1280$ miles. Subtracting Dana's total miles from Meryl's total miles yields $1500 - 1280 = 220$ miles. Meryl drives 220 more miles per week than Dana.

Choices B, C, and D are incorrect and may be the results of a comprehension error in solving for the incorrect difference in mileage. For example, Choice B is incorrect because 300 miles is the number of additional miles that Randy drives over Meryl.

QUESTION 12.

Choice C is correct. The research study is attempting to get an idea through sampling as to the true percentage of people in this large metropolitan area that prefer to shop online rather than in person. Although the survey selected people randomly, the location of the selection creates bias. The only people surveyed were exiting a mall. These are people who were shopping "in-person" already. This means that the results of the surveyed would be skewed towards shopping in person. since the only people selected were already shopping in person. Hence, the location of the survey creates bias.

Choices A is incorrect because an inference can only be made if the sampling was conducted appropriately. Choice B is incorrect because it is the opposite of the result that was attained, regardless of sampling error. Choice D is incorrect because a sample size of 200 is sufficiently large.

QUESTION 13.

Choice D is correct. First, one must convert to the units that the question requires. Since the question is asking for the speed of the rocket in kilometers per hour, one must convert miles to kilometers. Multiplying 240,000 miles by 1.609 kilometers will yield $240,000(1.609) = 386,160$ kilometers. Dividing 386,160 kilometers by 24 hours will give the speed of the rocket in kilometers per hour which is $\frac{386,160}{24} = 16,090$ kilometers per hour.

Choices A, B, and C are incorrect and may result from calculation errors when converting from miles to kilometers.

QUESTION 14.

Choice D is correct. If an adult male Maine Coon is 125% larger than its female counterpart, it is $(1+1.25) = 2.25$ times the size of its female counterpart. Therefore, if a female Maine Coon weighs 12 pounds, its male counterpart weighs $12(2.25) = 27$ pounds.

Choice A is incorrect and may result from a error in solving for the size of a female Maine Coon when the male weighs 12 pounds. Choice B is incorrect and may result from calculating the size of a female Maine Coon when assuming the male Maine Coon is 12 pounds and only 25% larger. Choice C is incorrect and may result from calculating the size of a male Maine Coon at only 25% larger than the female, not 125% larger.

QUESTION 15.

Choice C is correct. Factoring the right hand side of the function $p(x) = -x^2 + 12x - 20$ yields $p(x) = -(x-2)(x-10)$. Looking at the new function, one can see that the zeros occur at 2 and 10. Checking a value in between 2 and 10, such as 3, yields $p(3) = -((3)-2)((3)-10)$, or $p(3) = 7$. Since this is positive, all values that fall between 2 and 10 make the equation positive. Therefore, the company broke even or returned a positive profit during the duration from 1982 to 1990. Subtracting 1982 from 1990 yields 8 years.

Choices A, B, and D are incorrect and may result from errors in factoring and/or solving for the incorrect quantity.

QUESTION 16.

Choice B is correct. Given that the model $G(x) = 13.8 - 0.06x$ can be used to estimate the number of gallons remaining, $G(x)$, given x, the number of miles driven, one must simply substitute 150 miles for x to estimate the number of remaining gallons of gas. Substituting 150 for x yields $G(x) = 13.8 - 0.06(150)$, or $G(x) = 13.8 - 9$. Therefore, the estimated number of remaining gallons given 150 miles driven is $G(x) = 4.8$ gallons, or approximately 5 gallons.

Choices A, C, and D are incorrect and may result from calculation errors while utilizing the equation for the line of best fit or through estimating the remaining gallons of gas visually as opposed to using the best fit model.

QUESTION 17.

Choice B is correct. In order to calculate the average number of family vacations taken during a school year for all 52 students surveyed, one must add up the total number of vacations taken and divide by 52. Looking at the bar chart and accounting for both bars in each category, one can see that $8+3=11$ students took 0 vacations, $6+6=12$ students took 1 vacation, $6+8=14$ students took 2 vacations, $4+6=10$ students took 3 vacations, and $2+3=5$ took 4 vacations. Multiplying the number of students in each category by the number of vacations taken, then summing the results yields $11(0)+12(1)+14(2)+10(3)+5(4)=90$ total vacations. Dividing the 90 total vacations by the 52 total students yields an average of $\frac{90}{52}=1.73$ vacations per student.

Choice A is incorrect because it is the average number of family vacations per year for the students from Century High School only. Choice C is incorrect because it is the average number of family vacations for the students from Krane High School only. Choice D is incorrect and may result from errors in calculation.

QUESTION 18.

Choice A is correct. In Krane High School, 6 of the 26 surveyed students reported that they take 1 family vacation per year. Given that there are 2,600 students in Krane High School, one can estimate that $\frac{6}{26}$, or $\frac{3}{13}$ of the students at Krane High School will take one family vacation in a school year. Therefore, one can estimate that $\frac{3}{13}(2,600)=600$ students from Krane High School will take one vacation in a school year. In Century High School, similarly, 6 of the 26 students reported that they take 1 vacation per year. Given that there are 1,820 students in Century High School, one can estimate that $\frac{6}{26}$, or $\frac{3}{13}$ of the students at Century High School will take one family vacation in a school year. Therefore, one can estimate that $\frac{3}{13}(1,820)=420$ students from Century High School will take one vacation in a school year. So, the number of students who take one family vacation in Krane High School exceeds the number of students who take one family vacation in Century High School by $600-420=180$ students.

Choice B is incorrect because it is the number of total students that are estimated to take one family vacation at Krane High School, not the number of additional students over Century High School. Choice C is incorrect because the two schools have the same percent of students in the survey that take one family vacation, but not the same number of total students estimated to take one family vacation. Choice D is incorrect because Krane High School clearly has more students estimated to take one family vacation in a school year than Century High School.

QUESTION 19.

Choice B is correct. If a solution with a pH level of 1-4 is selected at random, the population has changed to only solutions with pH levels between 1 and 4. This means our total population is 10, two with blue tint and eight with red tint. The probability of randomly selecting one with a blue tint is $\dfrac{blue}{pH \rightarrow 1-4} = \dfrac{2}{10} = \dfrac{1}{5}$.

Choice A is incorrect because $\dfrac{1}{4}$ are the odds of selecting blue as opposed to red given a pH level of 1-4. Choice C is incorrect because $\dfrac{2}{15}$ is the probability of selecting a pH of 1-4 given that a blue tint was chosen. Choice D is incorrect because $\dfrac{1}{14}$ is the probability that a solution with a pH level of 1-4 and a blue tint is selected from all of the solutions.

QUESTION 20.

Choice A is correct. Calculating height, h, from a given radius, r, and a given print area, A_p, can be achieved by solving the equation $A_p = (2\pi r + 2)(h + 2)$ for h. First, divide both sides of the equation by the expression $2\pi r + 2$, which yields $\dfrac{A_p}{2\pi r + 2} = h + 2$. Subtracting 2 from both sides yields $h = \dfrac{A_p}{2\pi r + 2} - 2$.

Choices B, C, and D are incorrect and may result from calculation errors or errors in correctly applying the order of operations.

QUESTION 21.

Choice A is correct. Calculating the print area for Cylinder A by substituting 4 for h and 1 for r yields $A_p = (2\pi(1) - 2)((4) + 2)$, which can be simplified to $A_p = (2\pi - 2)(6)$, or $A_p = 12\pi - 12$. Calculating the print area for Cylinder B by substituting 8 for h and 1 for r yields $A_p = (2\pi(1) - 2)((8) + 2)$, which can be simplified to $A_p = (2\pi - 2)10$, or $A_p = 20\pi - 20$. In order to calculate what percent smaller the print area required for Cylinder A is compared to Cylinder B, one can multiply the print area for the larger cylinder, Cylinder B, by an unknown decay factor, x, to get to the print area for Cylinder A, and then subtract from one. Therefore, $(20\pi - 20)x = (12\pi - 12)$ which simplifies to $x = \dfrac{12\pi - 12}{20\pi - 20} = \dfrac{12(\pi - 1)}{20(\pi - 1)} = \dfrac{12}{20} = \dfrac{3}{5}$. This means that the print area required for Cylinder A is $\dfrac{3}{5}$, or 60% of the print area required for Cylinder B. Therefore the print area required for Cylinder A is $1 - \dfrac{3}{5} = \dfrac{2}{5}$, or 40% smaller than the print area required for Cylinder B.

Choices A, B, and C are incorrect and may result from calculation errors or errors in comprehension of the question. For example, choice B is incorrect because 60% is the percent of Cylinder B's print area required by Cylinder A, not the percent *smaller*.

QUESTION 22.

Choice B is correct. An average can be strongly affected by an outlier. For example, the average of the consecutive numbers 1, 2, 3, 4, and 5 is 3. However, if the top number, 5, is changed to a 10, the average jumps to 4. Now, look at the median. The median of the consecutive numbers 1, 2, 3, 4, and 5 is 3. However, when the top number, 5, is changed to a 10, the median is still 3. Therefore, averages are more strongly effected by outliers. If the company in question advertised its average salary, this average salary could be skewed based upon a few employees that have very high salaries. A new hire may begin work for the company seeing that there is a very high average salary, but the average salary may only be that high because of a few employees, maybe the owners of the company, who have very high salaries. The company may change to reporting the median salary because the median would be affected much less by the outlers pulling the average salary upward, which would give new hires a more realistic idea about the salaries they may receive.

Choice A is incorrect because if a few employees were paid much less than the rest, the average salary would be skewed downward; a case in which new employees would most likely be happier with the salaries they receive. Choices C and D are incorrect because the spread of the data has little bearing on the difference between the average and the median unless there are outliers. If anything, highly scattered data with no outliers would be better represented by an average due to potentially large gaps between different employee salaries that could make the median jump sufficiently in either direction.

QUESTION 23.

Choice A is correct. One way to see if an absolute value meets the criteria is to check the extremes of each end of the weigh range and see if the statement is true. Substituting 17.5 into the equation $|x - 18.5| < 1$ yields $|(17.5) - 18.5| < 1$, or $1 < 1$. This statement is not true, which means that a value greater than 17.5 must be input to make the statement true. Substituting the other extreme value, 195, into the equation yields $|(19.5) - 18.5| < 1$, or $1 < 1$. This statement is not true. However, this time it means that a value lower than 19.5 must be entered. Combining the two statements yields $17.5 < x < 19.5$ which is what the manufacturer requires.

Alternatively, one can use the formula $|Variable - Middle| < or \leq \frac{Range}{2}$. One would elect to use < because the manufacturer requires that the weights are strictly *between* 17.5 and 19.5. Then substituting x for the randomly selected box's weight, substituting 18.5 for the middle, and substituting $19.5 - 17.5 = 2$ for the range yields $|x - 18.5| < 1$.

Choices B, C, and D are incorrect because for each equation there are input values that satisfy the equation, but do not meet the criteria defined by the manufacturer. For example, choice C is incorrect because if one inputs a weight of 17 ounces, the equation yields $|(17) - 1| < 18.5$, or $16 < 18.5$. The statement is true, however, that a cereal box that weighs 17 ounces is not accepted by the manufacturer.

QUESTION 24.

Choice B is correct. Factoring the right side of the equation $f(x) = x^2 - 4x - 12$ yields $f(x) = (x-6)(x+2)$. Substituting 0 for $f(x)$ yields $0 = (x-6)(x+2)$ which gives the x-intercepts of $(6,0)$ and $(-2,0)$. Since d is greater than e, d is equivalent to 6 and e is equivalent to -2. Substituting 6 and -2 for d and e in the expression $2e+d$ yields $2(-2)+(6)=2$. The x-coordinate of the vertex of any quadratic equation is the average of its roots. The average of 6 and -2 is 2. Therefore, $2e+d$ is equivalent to the average of 6 and -2 making $f(x) = x^2 - 4x - 12$ a possible definition of f.

Choices A, C, and D are incorrect and may result from calculation errors, errors in factoring, and/or errors in substituting.

QUESTION 25.

Choice C is correct. Going to -6 on the x-axis and tracing downward yields $f(-6) = -4$. Going to 4 on the x-axis and tracing downward yields $f(4) = -8$. Adding 2 to both sides yields $f(4)+2 = -6$. Therefore, since $f(4)+2 = -6$ and $f(-6) = -4$, $f(4)+2 \neq f(-6)$.

Choices A, B, and D are incorrect because all three expressions yield the same value as $f(-6)$, -4.

QUESTION 26.

Choice C is correct. The equation $x^2 + y^2 - 8y = 9$ must be written in the the the form of a circle that is not centered on the origin: $(x-a)^2 + (y-b)^2 = r^2$, where (a,b) is the coordinate center of the circle. This can be accomplished by completing the square for the y expressions in the equation:

$$x^2 + y^2 - 8y + \underline{\quad} = 9 + \underline{\quad}$$
$$x^2 + y^2 - 8y + \underline{16} = 9 + \underline{16}$$
$$x^2 + (y^2 - 8y + 16) = 25$$
$$x^2 + (y-4)^2 = 25$$

$$(x-0)^2 + (y-4)^2 = 25$$

Given that $(x-0)^2 + (y-4)^2 = 25$ follows the form $(x-a)^2 + (y-b)^2 = r^2$, $r^2 = 25$. This yields a radius of $r = 5$. Therefore, using the area formula for a circle, $A = \pi r^2$, yields an area of of the circle is $A = \pi(5)^2 = 25\pi$.

Choice A is incorrect and may result from neglecting to complete the square before calculating the circle's area. Choice B is incorrect and may result from incorrectly calculating the radius after completeing the square. Choice D is incorrect and may result from neglecting to complete the square and also misinterpreting the equation of a circle as $x^2 + y^2 = r$, rather than r^2.

QUESTION 27.

Choice C is correct. In the equation $y = -2x^2 + 18$, the y-intercept occurs at the point $C(0,18)$. In order to calculate the x-intercepts, substitute 0 for y and solve for x in the equation $y = -2x^2 + 18$. Doing so yields $0 = -2x^2 + 18$, which simplifies to $-18 = -2x^2$, or $9 = x^2$. Taking the square root of both sides yields $x = \pm 3$, which reveals the two x-intercepts $A(-3,0)$ and $B(3,0)$. D is the point that is one fourth of the distance from A to B. One fourth of the distance from A to B can be calculated by simplifying the expression $\dfrac{|3-(-3)|}{4}$, which yields 1.5. The point that is 1.5 units to the right of $(-3,0)$ is $D(-1.5,0)$. The slope of the line that goes through the points C and D can be calculated by substituting the points $(0,18)$ and $(-1.5,0)$ into the slope equation $m = \dfrac{y_2 - y_1}{x_2 - x_1}$ which yields $m = \dfrac{(0)-(18)}{(-1.5)-(0)} = \dfrac{-18}{-1.5} = 12$.

Choices A, B, and D are incorrect and may result from calculation errors resulting in an incorrect value for the coordinates of point D.

QUESTION 28.

Choice D is correct. The area of an equilateral triangle can be calculated using the formula $A = \dfrac{s^2\sqrt{3}}{4}$. Substituting $16\sqrt{3}$ for the area yields $16\sqrt{3} = \dfrac{s^2\sqrt{3}}{4}$. Multiplying by 4 on either side gives $64\sqrt{3} = s^2\sqrt{3}$ and dividing by $\sqrt{3}$ yields $64 = s^2$, or $s = 8$. If the side length of $\triangle ABC$ is 8, it follows that the area of square $BCED$ is $8 \times 8 = 64$. The area of the pentagon $ACEDB$ is the sum of the area of $\triangle ABC$, $16\sqrt{3}$, and square $BCED$, 64, which is $64 + 16\sqrt{3}$.

Choices A, B, and C are incorrect and may result from errors in calculating the side length of $\triangle ABC$ and ultimately the area of square $BCED$.

QUESTION 29.

Choice A is correct. Expanding the left side of the equation $(x^2 + bx) + c(x + d) = x^2 + 5x + 12$ yields $x^2 + bx + cx + cd = x^2 + 5x + 12$. Factoring out an x from $bx + cx$ on the left hand side yields $x^2 + (b+c)x + cd = x^2 + 5x + 12$. Looking at both sides of the equation, one can see that $b + c = 5$ and $cd = 12$. If d were equal to 2, than c would have to equal 6 so that $cd = 12$. However, if c were equal to 6 then b would have to equal -1 in order for $b + c = 5$. Since b, c, and d must be positive integers, -1 cannot be a value of b. Therefore, d cannot be equal to 2.

Choices B, C, and D are incorrect because all three values for d yield values of b and c that are positive integers.

QUESTION 30.

Choice A is correct. Substituting a value of 0.5 for t into the moped's value equation $V_1(t) = 10,000 - 1,000t$ yields $V_1(0.5) = 10,000 - 1,000(0.5)$, or $V_1(0.5) = 9,500$. Substituting a value of t into the dirt bike's value equation $V_2(t) = 10,000(0.9)^t$ yields $V_2(0.5) = 10,000(0.9)^{(0.5)}$, or $V_2(0.5) = 9,486.83$. Therefore, between 0 and 1 years the value of the moped is higher than the value of the dirt bike.

Choices B and C are incorrect and may result from calculation errors while substituting values for t. Choice D is incorrect and may result from substituting only integer values for t.

QUESTION 31.

The correct answer is 11. There are 12 inches in every foot. Using the equation $N = Dx + R$, where N is the larger number, D is the divisor, and R is the remainder when N is divided by D, one can see that $77 = 12(6) + 5$ is a true statement. Since there are 6 feet with a remainder of 5 inches in a total of 77 inches, 77 inches can be written as, "6 feet, 5 inches." This would make $F + I = (6) + (5) = 11$.

QUESTION 32.

The correct answer is 68. Using S for the number of photos that Sadie had on her cell phone and E for the number of photos Enrique had on his cell phone, if Enrique had 20 more than half the number of photos on his cell phone that Sadie had on her cell phone, this can be written as $E = \frac{1}{2}S + 20$. If Sadie and Enrique sold a took at total of 124 photos, then $S + E = 122$. Substituting E with $\frac{1}{2}S + 20$ yields $S + (\frac{1}{2}S + 20) = 122$. Combining like terms yields $\frac{3}{2}S + 20 = 122$ and subtracting 20 from both sides yields $\frac{3}{2}S = 102$. Finally, multiplying both sides by $\frac{2}{3}$ yields $\frac{2}{3}(\frac{3}{2}S) = \frac{2}{3}(102)$, or $S = 68$.

QUESTION 33.

The correct answer is 8.8 or $\frac{44}{5}$. Since the area of the circle is 121π, setting 121π equal to πr^2 yields $\pi r^2 = 121\pi$. Dividing both sides by π and taking the square root of each side reveals the length of the radius, $r = 11$.

A regular pentagon that is inscribed in a circle divides the circle into 5 arcs of equal length. $\overset{\frown}{ABC}$ is visibly $\frac{2}{5}$ of the circumference of the circle. Using the equation $\frac{2}{5}(2\pi r)$ to find the length of $\overset{\frown}{ABC}$ and substituting 11 for r yields $\frac{2}{5}(2\pi(11))$, or $\frac{44}{5}\pi$. Therefore, D is equivalent to $\frac{44}{5}$.

QUESTION 34.

The correct answer is 4. If the freshman class grows steadily over the course of 17 years, it follows a linear model in the form of $y = mx + b$, where x is the number of years that have passed since the professor began teaching and y is the enrollment in the class. If the enrollment was 54 students at a time of 0 years, that corresponds to the coordinate point $(0, 54)$, which is the y-intercept of the model. At a time of 17 years, the enrollment grew to 122, which corresponds to the coordinate point $(17, 122)$. The average increase in enrollment per year would be equivalent to m, the slope of the line. Substituting into the slope formula $m = \dfrac{y_2 - y_1}{x_2 - x_1}$ yields $m = \dfrac{(122) - (54)}{(17) - (0)} = \dfrac{68}{17} = 4$. Therefore, the course enrollment had an average increase of 4 students per year.

QUESTION 35.

The correct answer is 13. The linear equation $5y - 12x = 5$ can be rewritten to the form $y = \dfrac{12}{5}x + 1$. If line k is parallel to $y = \dfrac{12}{5}x + 1$, it has the same slope, which is $\dfrac{12}{5}$. Since line k intercepts the x-axis at 5, the x-intercept is $(5, 0)$. Using the equation $y = \dfrac{12}{5}x + b$ to represent line k and substituting the coordinate point $(5, 0)$ yields $(0) = \dfrac{12}{5}(5) + b$, or $0 = 12 + b$. Solving for b yields $b = -12$, which makes the y-intercept $(0, -12)$. Substituting the x-intercept and the y-intercept into the distance formula $D = \sqrt{(x_2 - x_1)^2 + (y_2 - y_1)^2}$ yields

$$D = \sqrt{((0) - (5))^2 + ((-12) - (0))^2} = \sqrt{25 + 144} = \sqrt{169} = 13.$$

Alternatively, one can recognize that the points $(5, 0)$ and $(0, -12)$ form a 5-12-13 special right triangle with the origin, thus making the distance from $(5, 0)$ to $(0, -12)$ equivalent to 13.

QUESTION 36.

The correct answer is 48.8. The equation $B = 3,520(0.8)^m$ dictates that the account balance of 3,520 euros will reduce to 0.8 times or 80% of its current value each month that passes. After 3 months, the 3,520 euros would reduce to $(0.8)^3$, 0.512 times or 51.2% of its original value. This is a reduction of $100\% - 51.2\%$, or 48.8%. The answer is 48.8.

QUESTION 37.

The correct answer is 6552. The manufacturer's current profit, $P_{Current}$, is equivalent to 120% of last year's profit, or $1.2(P_{Last})$. Substituting $1.2(P_{Last})$ for $P_{Current}$ and 5,200 for A_{Last} in the equation $A_{Current} = 1.05(\dfrac{P_{Current}}{P_{Last}})(A_{Last})$ yields $A_{Current} = 1.05(\dfrac{1.2(P_{Last})}{P_{Last}})(5,200)$.

Simplifying yields $A_{Current} = 1.05(1.2)(5,200) = 6,552$. Therefore, the company can expect to spend $6,552 on advertising in the current year. Disregard the comma when griding your answer. The answer is 6552.

QUESTION 38.

The correct answer is 7500. Substituting 5,187 for $A_{Current}$, 142,500 for $P_{Current}$, and 5,200 for A_{Last} in the equation $A_{Current} = 1.05(\frac{P_{Current}}{P_{Last}})(A_{Last})$ yields $(5,187) = 1.05(\frac{142,500}{P_{Last}})(5,200)$. Dividing both sides by 1.05 and 5,200 yields $0.95 = \frac{142,500}{P_{Last}}$. Multiplying both sides by P_{Last} and dividing both sides by 0.95 yields $P_{Last} = \frac{142,500}{0.95} = 150,000$. Therefore, last year's net profit of $150,000 was $150,000 - $142,500$, or $7,500 larger than this year's net profit. Disregard the comma when gridding your answer. The answer is 7500.

TEST 3

Reading Test
65 MINUTES, 52 QUESTIONS

Turn to Section 1 of your answer sheet to answer the questions in this section.

DIRECTIONS

Each passage or pair of passages below is followed by a number of questions. After reading each passage or pair, choose the best answer to each question based on what is stated or implied in the passage or passages and in any accompanying graphics (such as a table or graph).

Questions 1-10 are based on the following passage.

This passage is adapted from Kate Chopin, "A Respectable Woman." Originally published in 1894

Mrs. Baroda was a little provoked to learn that her husband expected his friend, Gouvernail, up to spend a week or two on the plantation.

Line
5 They had entertained a good deal during the winter; much of the time had also been passed in New Orleans in various forms of mild dissipation. She was looking forward to a period of unbroken rest, now, and undisturbed *tete-a-tete* with her husband, when he informed her that Gouvernail was coming up to stay a week or two.

10 This was a man she had heard much of but never seen. He had been her husband's college friend; was now a journalist, and in no sense a society man or "a man about town," which were, perhaps, some of the reasons she had never met him. But she had unconsciously formed an image of him in her mind.

15 She pictured him tall, slim, cynical; with eye-glasses, and his hands in his pockets; and she did not like him. Gouvernail was slim enough, but he wasn't very tall or very cynical; neither did he wear eyeglasses nor carry his hands in his pockets. And she rather liked him when he first presented himself.

20 But why she liked him she could not explain satisfactorily to herself when she partly attempted to do so. She could discover in him none of those brilliant and promising traits which Gaston, her husband, had often assured her that he possessed. On the contrary, he sat rather mute and receptive
25 before her chatty eagerness to make him feel at home and in face of Gaston's frank and wordy hospitality. His manner was as courteous toward her as the most exacting woman could require; but he made no direct appeal to her approval or even esteem.
30 Once settled at the plantation he seemed to like to sit upon the wide portico in the shade of one of the big Corinthian pillars, smoking his cigar lazily and listening attentively to Gaston's experience as a sugar planter.

"This is what I call living," he would utter with deep
35 satisfaction, as the air that swept across the sugar field caressed him with its warm and scented velvety touch. It pleased him also to get on familiar terms with the big dogs that came about him, rubbing themselves sociably against his legs. He did not care to fish, and displayed no eagerness to go out and kill
40 grosbecs when Gaston proposed doing so.

Gouvernail's personality puzzled Mrs. Baroda, but she liked him. Indeed, he was a lovable, inoffensive fellow. After a few days, when she could understand him no better than at first, she gave over being puzzled and remained piqued. In this
45 mood she left her husband and her guest, for the most part, alone together. Then finding that Gouvernail took no manner of exception to her action, she imposed her society upon him, accompanying him in his idle strolls to the mill and walks along the batture. She persistently sought to penetrate the
50 reserve in which he had unconsciously enveloped himself.

"When is he going—your friend?" she one day asked her husband. "For my part, he tires me frightfully."

"Not for a week yet, dear. I can't understand; he gives you no trouble."
55 "No. I should like him better if he did; if he were more like others, and I had to plan somewhat for his comfort and enjoyment."

Gaston took his wife's pretty face between his hands and looked tenderly and laughingly into her troubled eyes.
60 They were making a bit of toilet sociably together in Mrs. Baroda's dressing-room.

"You are full of surprises, *ma belle*," he said to her. "Even I can never count upon how you are going to act under given conditions." He kissed her and turned to fasten his cravat
65 before the mirror.

174

CONTINUE

©Integrated Educational Services, 2015 www.ies2400.com | Unauthorized copying or reuse of any part of this page is illegal.

1

Which choice best summarizes the passage?

A) One character reminisces about a friend from college and recalls the times they spent together.

B) One character has an argument with another character who has unexpectedly visited her home.

C) One character who is unhappy with her marriage falls in love with the friend of another character.

D) One character is fascinated by a mysterious and interesting character who is a guest in her home.

2

As used in line 1, "provoked" most nearly means

A) annoyed.

B) infuriated.

C) excited.

D) scandalized.

3

In the third paragraph (lines 10-19) the passage establishes a contrast between

A) Gouvernail's reputation as a sophisticated, urbane gentleman and his behavior in actuality.

B) the way Mr. Baroda acted towards his wife and the way Gouvernail treated her.

C) Mrs. Baroda's expectations of Gouvernail and what he was like in reality.

D) Mrs. Baroda's loquacious style of hospitality and Gouvernail's seemingly unresponsive reactions.

4

The author indicates that Gouvernail

A) was a wealthy and powerful man who was a business partner of Gaston but had never met Mrs. Baroda personally.

B) was much more sophisticated, intellectual, and distinguished than either Mrs. Baroda or Gaston had imagined.

C) was a close friend of Gaston but was not well liked by Mrs. Baroda because of his lackadaisical personality.

D) pleasantly surprised Mrs. Baroda upon his arrival because he did not look or act like she had assumed he would.

5

As used in line 27, "exacting" most nearly means

A) intimidating.

B) demanding.

C) punishing.

D) laborious.

6

Throughout the passage, Mrs. Baroda notices that Gouvernail

A) was polite and cordial towards her but did not make any effort to impress her or get her attention.

B) harbored a secret about himself that he desperately tried to hide from the Barodas.

C) was lazy and did not write his own work despite having won awards as a journalist.

D) was crude and ignorant, possessing none of the traits that she admired in Gaston.

7

Which choice provides the best evidence for the answer to the previous question?

A) Lines 13-16 ("But . . . him")

B) Lines 21-24 ("She . . . possessed")

C) Lines 26-29 ("His . . . esteem")

D) Lines 30-33 ("Once . . . planter")

8

Mrs. Baroda's attitude towards Gouvernail is best described as one of

A) awe.

B) intrigue.

C) distrust.

D) disdain.

9

The author suggests that many of Mrs. Baroda's actions were intended primarily to

A) reform Gouvernail's actions and change his personality to become more like her husband's.

B) understand Gouvernail and break through the front that had made him inscrutable and perplexing to her.

C) prolong Gouvernail's stay as long as possible and prevent him from leaving.

D) persuade Governail to offer her a job as a journalist and liberate her from her husband.

CONTINUE

10

Which choice provides the best evidence for the answer to the previous question?

A) Lines 24-26 ("On the contrary . . . hospitality")

B) Lines 36-38 ("It . . . him")

C) Lines 49-50 ("She . . . himself")

D) Lines 51-52 ("When . . . frightfully")

Questions 11-20 are based on the following passages.

In these two excerpts from recent articles, two journalists consider new ideas about the modern workplace.

Passage 1

While people and their personalities range across a complex spectrum, the classic distinction between extroverts and introverts can offer a useful model for understanding
Line behaviors. Introverts tend to prefer to socialize in small groups
5 and to work independently, and need time alone in order to "re-charge."

It is often assumed that contemporary culture, especially within competitive academic or business environments, rewards extroverts. However, individuals with introverted personalities
10 have a number of innate strengths that can enable them to thrive just as much as their extroverted counterparts. Despite their reputation for being shy and reserved, introverts can be highly successful at relationship building. A boisterous extrovert may appear to make six new best friends at every party he or she
15 attends, but these interactions are usually temporary in nature, whereas an introvert is more likely to forge a deep and lasting connection with just one or two individuals.

Introverts also tend to be particularly good at listening, which can translate both to strong personal relationships and
20 to success in the workplace. A research team at the Wharton School of Business found that introverted executives tended to be recognized for more effective team leadership abilities, since they were better able to foster inclusion and idea sharing. Jennifer Kahnweiler, who has coined the term "quiet leaders"
25 to describe successful introverts, notes that the leadership displayed by introverts may translate more effectively in non-Western business contexts: modesty and humility are often highly prized virtues in such settings.

Moreover, brain scans have shown that, when exposed to
30 stimulation, individuals with introverted personalities show more activity in brain regions associated with information processing and problem solving. "An introvert who's quiet in a meeting may be taking everything in, making mental connections, doing deeper processing," psychologist Laurie
35 Helgoe notes. That ability to quietly reflect is a great asset, and just one strength among the many that introverts possess.

Passage 2

It is easy to mistake the headquarters of Google—a sprawling installation known as the Googleplex—for a university campus. There are volleyball courts, cafeterias
40 decorated with quirky paintings, rooms with giant whiteboards, and many of the other amenities of a typical college, though Google is surely interested in more than stirring up nostalgia in its employees. What the $550 billion company has figured out is that the same skills of contemplation that college life can

CONTINUE

45 foster are also invaluable business assets. Employees wander about, get lost in their work, and occasionally break into tight, intense conversations. Somewhere in this pleasant, meandering mix of thoughts, great ideas emerge.

The Google model is only the most visible manifestation
50 of a shift in thinking about success and innovation that has swept over American corporate culture. The ideal of the fast-talking, deal-cutting, suit-wearing, always-busy executive has been swept away and replaced with a completely new image: the executive of today has time to contemplate, to sympathize,
55 and to get enough sleep. As explained by Greg McKeown, author of *Essentialism: The Disciplined Pursuit of Less*, we are currently shaking off a myth "celebrated in modern culture: it's someone who is capable, driven, and wants to win and be popular." Different virtues are needed: selectivity, serenity, and
60 imagination.

While the allure of these virtues may be obvious, the reasoning might not be. But as McKeown has also argued, more active, less thoughtful workers are in fact *less likely* to achieve their goals: people with this cast of mind are simply
65 not as good at setting priorities, or at weighing short-term plans against long-term outcomes. The unwillingness to reflect and listen is what, for McKeown, "holds otherwise hard working, capable people back from our highest contribution."

11

Which choice best describes the relationship between the two passages?

A) Passage 1 is concerned with describing the differences between introverts and extroverts, while Passage 2 focuses on the skills both have in common.

B) Passage 1 argues for greater acceptance of introverts in the workplace, while Passage 2 states that introverted qualities are already valued over extroverted qualities.

C) Passage 1 focuses on the way introverts act in their personal lives, while Passage 2 focuses on the advantages and roles of introverts in the workplace.

D) Passage 1 describes the ways in which introverts have been beneficial to businesses, while Passage 2 recounts a shift in ideals in the business world.

12

Passage 1 indicates that introverted qualities

A) have generally been less valued by Western businesses.

B) are only more valued than extroverted qualities in specific fields.

C) have been gaining acceptance by employers because of studies revealing their benefits.

D) are currently in high demand by employers who seek long-term workers.

13

Which choice provides the best evidence for the answer to the previous question?

A) Lines 1-4 ("While . . . behaviors")

B) Lines 7-10 ("It is . . . strengths")

C) Lines 25-28 ("the leadership . . . settings")

D) Lines 32-35 ("An introvert . . . notes")

14

The second paragraph of Passage 1 (lines 7-17) is primarily concerned with establishing a contrast between

A) more well known traits of introverts and lesser known traits of extroverts.

B) the assumed superiority of extroverts and the more subtle advantages of introverts.

C) how introverts seem to strangers and how introverts actually behave.

D) how introverts are depicted in the media and pop culture and how introverts act in the real world.

15

As used in line 46, "get lost in" most nearly means

A) become disoriented by.

B) become obsessed with.

C) become distracted by.

D) become immersed in.

CONTINUE

16

As used in line 49, "visible" most nearly means

A) transparent.

B) attractive.

C) apparent.

D) eye-catching.

17

According to Passage 2, the traditional "ideal" (line 51) in the business world

A) was more successful economically in the past.

B) is less productive and successful than it seems.

C) has many traits in common with successful introverts.

D) is still preferred over introverts by most companies.

18

Which choice provides the best evidence for the answer to the previous question?

A) Lines 47-48 ("Somewhere . . . emerge")

B) Lines 54-55 ("the executive . . . sleep")

C) Lines 58-59 ("it's someone . . . popular")

D) Lines 63-64 ("more . . . goals")

19

The author of Passage 1 would most likely react to the "Googleplex" (line 38) with

A) approval, because promoting introverted qualities such as thoughtfulness can contribute to success in the workplace.

B) ambivalence, because the system is still inherently biased towards extroverts who are able to share their ideas freely in large groups.

C) skepticism, because unrestricted time to reflect and think might cause employees to become distracted and unproductive.

D) dissatisfaction, because the Googleplex is unique among companies and many corporations still value extroverted workers over introverted ones.

20

Both passages would most likely agree that success in the workplace

A) can be achieved with deep contemplation.

B) requires a degree of ambition.

C) depends on establishing clear priorities.

D) fosters a humble attitude.

CONTINUE

Questions 21-31 are based on the following passage and supplementary material.

Adapted from Nathaniel Hunt, "Consider (Destroying) the Mosquito: The Possible Benefits of Vector Species Extinction."

Humans have been accidentally driving species to extinction for hundreds, if not thousands, of years. Yet the implications of causing extinctions on purpose remain unclear;
Line nowhere is this more true than in the case of disease-carrying
5 mosquitoes. These flying bloodsuckers are the main "vector species" responsible for propagating numerous deadly diseases, including malaria, dengue, and chikungunya. Eradicating disease-carrying mosquito species would mean millions of saved human lives, as well as billions of dollars economized.
10 But can humans reliably predict what will happen if we drive a common insect to extinction? Is the potential damage to fragile ecosystems enough to deter us from such "specicide?"

The diseases that mosquitoes carry kill more than 1 million people per year—and the majority of these victims are children.
15 Malaria alone makes another 246 million people sick per year. The effects are mostly concentrated in emerging countries in tropical zones, including nations in South America and Africa. One study estimates that mosquitoes can directly affect a country's GDP (gross domestic product), lowering production.
20 So eliminating disease-carrying mosquito species would benefit humanity. The knottier issue is whether the potential damage to the Earth and its ecosystems would outweigh the gains. For many, the answer is an absolute yes. It is important to make the distinction that not all species of mosquitoes carry
25 deadly diseases. Of the 3,500 species, only 30 to 40 are actually dangerous to humans, and those are the only ones that humans are considering driving to extinction.

Current research has indicated that ridding the world of a few species of mosquitoes would not impact the planet very
30 much. Ecosystems are often pictured as intricate webs of life, in which each species plays an integral part. This romanticized notion does not correspond to reality very well, since many species will inevitably go extinct—with or without human involvement. Most scientists agree that ecosystems wouldn't
35 miss mosquitoes very much: whatever niche mosquitoes occupy in a specific ecosystem, they are not irreplaceable. As stated in a recent *Nature* Magazine article, "in many cases, scientists acknowledge that the ecological scar left by a missing mosquito would heal quickly as the niche was filled by other organisms."
40 Take bats, for instance. Before formal research was conducted, some in the scientific community were concerned that wiping out mosquitoes would deprive bats of a vital source of food. Yet studies have found that less than 2% of bats' stomach contents are typically composed of mosquitoes.
45 Similarly, scientists predict that mosquito-devouring fish

species could simply feed on other species of insects. Most bird species, too, could easily switch to other prey.

There are troubling possibilities involved in eradicating an entire species, however. Some scientists
50 doubt that highly specialized mosquito predators, like the mosquitofish, could find a source of food if mosquitoes were to be eradicated. More threatened still are the plant species that mosquitoes pollinate. These are not plant species that humans use or depend on, but if they did go
55 extinct, their disappearance could cause a chain reaction that could deeply impact the ecology of the Earth at large.

Humans can play the "what if" game forever, but the fact remains that mosquitoes must be fought somehow— and the current methods that humans are using are far
60 more destructive than the elegant genetics-based solutions that could eradicate disease-carrying mosquitoes once and for all. Contemporary mosquito-fighting techniques are not nearly as harmful as the DDT-fueled techniques of the past, but they do often involve destruction of wetlands or
65 the use of dangerous chemicals.

Yet even though manipulating ecosystems to wipe out disease-carrying mosquitoes seems like a way to wipe out malaria overnight—a benefit that could outweigh many environmental costs—not all scientists are optimistic. Phil
70 Lounibos, an ecologist at the Florida Medical Entomology Laboratory in Vero Beach, has found evidence that "efforts to eradicate one vector species would be futile, as its niche would quickly be filled by another." What if humans actually did eradicate mosquitoes, only to usher
75 in a new and even worse disease-carrying species? It's impossible to know the end results, but even this kind of "what if" should not stop us from improving the lives of millions.

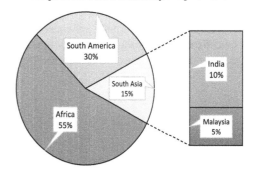

Percentage Breakdown of Annual Human Death Due to Mosquito-Related Diseases by Tropical Zone

☐ Africa ☐ South America ☐ India ☐ Malaysia

CONTINUE

21

Which of the following best describes the passage?

A) An analysis of how specicide is defined and a listing of various events in recent times that would be considered specicide.

B) A synopsis of the life cycle of one mosquito species and a detailed explanation of the diseases carried by this species.

C) A summary of the various arguments for and against the extermination of mosquitoes and the rejection of such debate as ultimately insignificant.

D) A careful weighing of the possible benefits as well as damage that could arise from the human-caused extinction of mosquitoes.

22

As used in line 9, "saved" most nearly means

A) spared.

B) improved.

C) rescued.

D) prolonged.

23

In the second paragraph, the discussion of malaria and the damage it causes primarily serves what purpose?

A) It offers an example of a disease that is only transmitted by mosquitoes and would be completely eradicated if mosquitoes were to become extinct.

B) It provides both ethical and economic justifications for the extinction of certain mosquito species.

C) It supports the author's thesis that the mass destruction of mosquitoes would not be beneficial.

D) It creates a transition from a previously lighthearted consideration of mosquitoes to a more serious one concerning the damage mosquitoes cause.

24

The author uses the phrase "romanticized notion" (lines 31-32) in order to

A) characterize the scientists who believe that the extinction of mosquitoes would be beneficial as wishful thinkers and idealists.

B) suggest that the belief that mosquitoes are an integral part of an ecosystem is incorrect and that researchers spreading this idea are mistaken.

C) imply that a world without disease or harm caused by mosquitoes is a concept that cannot be accomplished in the next century.

D) indicate that the idea that everything in an ecosystem is interconnected and intertwined does not always play out in reality.

25

With which statement would Phil Lounibos (lines 68-69) most likely agree?

A) Lines 28-30 ("Current . . . much")

B) Lines 34-36 ("Most . . . irreplaceable")

C) Lines 62-64 ("Contemporary . . . past")

D) Lines 66-68 ("manipulating . . . overnight")

26

The passage indicates which of the following about mosquito extinction?

A) It could lead to another species taking the position in the ecosystem that the mosquito had originally held, for better or for worse.

B) It would cause the mass extinction of other insect and amphibian species and consequently cause a chain reaction affecting all levels of the ecosystem.

C) It could preserve fragile ecosystems like the wetlands that suffer from an excessive mosquito population.

D) It would have no effect on plant species that depend on mosquitoes for pollination.

CONTINUE

27

Which choice provides the best evidence for the answer to the previous question?

A) Lines 41-43 ("some . . . food")

B) Lines 49-52 ("Some . . . eradicated")

C) Lines 59-62 ("current . . . all")

D) Lines 72-73 ("efforts . . . another")

28

As used in line 60, "elegant" most nearly means

A) graceful.

B) harmless.

C) practical.

D) delicate.

29

In the last paragraph, the author's attitude towards mosquito extinction is ultimately one of

A) wholehearted agreement.

B) tempered approval.

C) rightful apprehension.

D) outright disapproval.

30

According to the data in the figure and the passage, the author would most likely attribute the highest GDP loss to

A) Africa

B) South America

C) India

D) Malaysia

31

The author of the passage would most likely consider the information in the figure to be

A) useful evidence that supports the central argument of the passage.

B) incomplete for its lack of information on specific diseases.

C) compelling but does not indicate enough information about environmental impact.

D) representative of a perspective with which the author disagrees.

Questions 32-41 are based on the following passage.

Adapted from Harriet Beecher Stowe, "The Lady Who Does Her Own Work," issued as a chapter of Stowe's *Household Papers and Other Stories* (1896).

"The *lady* who *does her own work*."

America is the only country where such a title is possible—the only country where there is a class of women who may be

Line described as *ladies* who do their own work. By a lady we mean
5 a woman of education, cultivation, and refinement, of liberal tastes and ideas, who, without any very material additions or changes, would be recognized as a lady in any circle of the Old World or the New.

What I have said is, that the existence of such a class is a
10 fact peculiar to American society, a clear, plain result of the new principles involved in the doctrine of universal equality.

When the colonists first came to this country, of however mixed ingredients their ranks might have been composed, and however imbued with the spirit of feudal and aristocratic
15 ideas, the discipline of the wilderness soon brought them to a democratic level; the gentleman felled the wood for his log-cabin side by side with the ploughman, and thews and sinews rose in the market. "A man was deemed honorable in proportion as he lifted his hand upon the high trees of the forest." So in
20 the interior domestic circle. Mistress and maid, living in a log-cabin together, became companions, and sometimes the maid, as the more accomplished and stronger, took precedence of the mistress. It became natural and unavoidable that children should begin to work as early as they were capable of it. The
25 result was a generation of intelligent people brought up to labor from necessity, but turning on the problem of labor the acuteness of a disciplined brain. The mistress, outdone in sinews and muscles by her maid, kept her superiority by skill and contrivance. If she could not lift a pail of water she could
30 invent methods which made lifting the pail unnecessary; if she could not take a hundred steps without weariness, she could make twenty answer the purpose of a hundred.

Slavery, it is true, was to some extent introduced into New England, but it never suited the genius of the people, never
35 struck deep root, or spread so as to choke the good seed of self-helpfulness. Many were opposed to it from conscientious principle—many from far-sighted thrift, and from a love of thoroughness and well-doing which despised the rude, unskilled work of barbarians. People, having once felt the thorough
40 neatness and beauty of execution which came of free, educated, and thoughtful labor, could not tolerate the clumsiness of slavery. Thus it came to pass that for many years the rural population of New England, as a general rule, did their own work, both out doors and in. If there were a black man or black
45 woman or bound girl, they were emphatically only the *helps*, following humbly the steps of master and mistress, and used

CONTINUE

by them as instruments of lightening certain portions of their toil. The master and mistress with their children were the head workers.

50   Great merriment has been excited in the Old Country because years ago the first English travelers found that the class of persons by them denominated servants were in America denominated help or helpers. But the term was the very best exponent of the state of society. There were few servants in the

55 European sense of the word; there was a society of educated workers, where all were practically equal, and where, if there was a deficiency in one family and an excess in another, a *helper*, not a servant, was hired. Mrs. Brown, who has six sons and no daughters, enters into agreement with Mrs. Jones,

60 who has six daughters and no sons. She borrows a daughter, and pays her good wages to help in her domestic toil, and sends a son to help the labors of Mr. Jones. These two young people go into the families in which they are to be employed in all respects as equals and companions, and so the work of

65 the community is equalized. Hence arose, and for many years continued, a state of society more nearly solving than any other ever did the problem of combining the highest culture of the mind with the highest culture of the muscles and the physical faculties.

32

It is implied by the passage that in countries other than America

A) early feminist ideology and philosophy were virtually unheard of.

B) a maid could sometimes possess equal or even greater power than her mistress.

C) women were given leadership positions comparable to men in certain fields.

D) there was no such thing as an upper class of women responsible for their own work.

33

Which choice provides the best evidence for the answer to the previous question?

A) Lines 4-6 ("By . . . ideas")

B) Lines 9-11 ("the existence . . . equality")

C) Lines 21-23 ("sometimes . . . mistress")

D) Lines 27-29 ("The mistress . . . contrivance")

34

As used in line 10, "peculiar to" most nearly means

A) outlandish in.

B) unique to.

C) unconventional for.

D) unusual within.

35

Stowe indicates that early American colonists

A) primarily lived in rural areas surrounding small towns, which affected their views on equality.

B) often sacrificed education for the practicality of physical labor and harvesting crops.

C) were some of the first to oppose and protest slavery and publish abolitionist texts.

D) may have possessed prejudices but became more democratic after their arrival in America.

36

Which choice provides the best evidence for the answer to the previous question?

A) Lines 14-16 ("however . . . level")

B) Lines 24-26 ("The result . . . necessity")

C) Lines 36-38 ("Many . . . well-doing")

D) Lines 42-44 ("for many . . . and in")

37

According to the passage, women who were not as strong physically

A) hired slaves or indentured servants to perform their labor more easily.

B) finished their educations by going to college or pursued careers by learning a trade.

C) married into wealthier families or relied on stronger family members.

D) used their intellectual skills to find methods to complete their tasks more efficiently.

38

As used in line 38, "rude" most nearly means

A) violent.

B) impolite.

C) crude.

D) ignorant.

CONTINUE

39

Stowe uses the words "beauty," "educated," and "thoughtful" (lines 40-41) primarily in order to

A) juxtapose the thoroughness of labor accomplished by New Englanders with work done by slaves.

B) sarcastically comment on the methods taken to discipline workers under slavery.

C) characterize the New Englanders as a whole as intelligent and conscientious.

D) describe a proposed solution to the practice of slavery in New England.

40

According to Stowe, slavery was introduced to New England but

A) was only prevalent in rural and suburban areas and was considered unnecessary in cities.

B) was popular in New England for a few years but became more expensive as time went on.

C) went against many New Englanders' morals and was not an acceptable substitute for labor done by citizens.

D) was abolished shortly after its arrival because citizens were appalled by the cruelty of the practice.

41

Stowe draws a distinction between a "helper" and a "servant" by stating that

A) helpers were hired in European countries, whereas servants were a predominantly American phenomenon.

B) servants were slaves who were kept in captivity by their masters, while helpers were lower-class citizens bound by debt.

C) servants were considered inferior to their masters, while helpers were considered equal and were hired to assist their masters in their work.

D) helpers were generally black or mixed-race and stood lower on the social hierarchy, while servants were often white and privileged citizens.

Questions 42-52 are based on the following passage and supplementary material.

Adapted from Patrick Kennedy, "2014: An Underwater Odyssey."

The deep sea is widely regarded as one of human exploration's final frontiers, and with good reason: as of this writing, 95% of the Earth's ocean-covered territory remains
Line completely unexplored. What creatures have been found in the
5 farthest and deepest reaches of the world's oceans often seem to be figments of dreams or nightmares—goblin-visaged fish, twining anemones, monstrous and wide-eyed squids. But as researchers realize, studying these extraordinary organisms can help us to better understand the exact biological traits
10 and the overall classification systems we thought we knew. Insight, sometimes, is to be found at the extremes of the world's geography.

Scientists interested in such extreme organisms have had banner years between 2014 and 2015, years that featured both
15 giant squid sightings (which are preciously rare occurrences) and the discovery of several new and unusual underwater species. Among the absolute most unusual of these is a new species of the Ceratioid Anglerfish, which researchers from Florida's Nova Southeastern University discovered during a
20 deep-sea excursion in the Gulf of Mexico. The researchers caught three of these fish, all female, in a region of the ocean known as the "Midnight Zone": no natural sunlight can penetrate to this region, which begins at just over 3000 feet under the ocean, making the water pitch black and plant growth
25 nonexistent. Carnivorous anglerfish thrive in these reaches of the ocean, using the "angling" appendages that sprout from their backs to lure their prey.

However, in a paper published in the zoological journal *Copeia*, Theodore W. Pietsch and Tracey T. Sutton argued
30 that the newly-found anglerfish is "not especially similar to any of the five previously described members of the genus" *Lasiognathus*, which encompasses the earlier-known anglerfish. It is perhaps too early to say what effect the revelation of the new Ceratioid Anglerfish will have on existing classifications—
35 if any. But even though the new species is an anomaly among anglerfish, it exhibits traits that are familiar from land-based organisms. One such trait is a pronounced disparity on size and development based on sex, or a "sexual dimorphism," that favors females. While animals as different as birds of
40 prey and praying mantises exhibit such a gender-determined biological structure, the form of sexual dimorphism that can be found among the new anglerfish and some related species is particularly extreme: in this case, females are a yellowish brown color and have long, angled lures, while males have
45 so far only been found as parasites attached to the females' bodies. (At first, adult males are easy to mistake for warts or

CONTINUE

other growths.) Eventually, adhering males will degenerate completely and function almost like sexual organs, not as autonomous organisms.

50   It is thought that this sexual dimorphism is present in the aphotic "Midnight Zone" because of a lower density of species population due to frigid temperatures and extreme environmental pressure. Finding a mate could prove difficult, so years of evolution may have favored this reproductive
55 sexual parasitism as a means of survival for the Ceratioid Anglerfish. After all, there's no need to find a mate if he's simply attached to you.

    If the anglerfish discovery could help us understand new variations on well-known biological mechanisms, another
60 recent finding could upend some of what we think we know about biology itself. Researchers from the University of Copenhagen spent 2014 studying new samples of an organism that partially resembles a jellyfish, partially a mushroom. According to Paul Rincon, Science Editor at BBC News,
65 these organisms "have proven difficult to categorise and some researchers have even suggested they were failed experiments in multi-cellular life." Jorgen Olesen, one of the University of Copenhagen researchers involved in studying these puzzling organisms, has stated that these life forms probably belong "in
70 the animal kingdom somewhere; the question is where." But in all this indeterminacy, there is one certainty: that the darkest regions of the sea continue to be sites of scientific intrigue. The organisms that currently preoccupy the University of Copenhagen team were first detected off the coast of Australia
75 in 1986, at depths of 1300 to 3300 feet.

42

The main purpose of the passage is to

A) describe the different kinds of organisms found in the deep sea and reveal the qualities they share that enable them to survive.

B) detail the purpose and procedure of a study in the deep sea and explain the implications and significance of the results of that study.

C) summarize the history of the study of biological anomalies and depict two examples of such abnormalities.

D) recount the recent developments and discoveries in the deep sea and analyze the importance of two of these discoveries.

43

Which of the following best describes the developmental pattern of the second paragraph (lines 13-27)?

A) A summary of the research done in the deep sea to a description of a highly researched region where squid and fish have been found.

B) A reiteration of the author's main argument about deep sea creatures to a list of supporting points that will be explained later in the passage.

C) An outline of the recent progress made by scientists in the deep sea to a more detailed characterization of a particular discovery.

D) A scientific depiction of an abrasive and barren habitat to a more subjective musing about the organisms that survive in this setting.

Marine-life Sexual Reproductive Practices by Ocean Zone

Ocean Zone	Depth (Average)	Environmental Pressure	Temperature Range	Average Species Population Density	Percentage of Species exhibiting Sexual Dimorphism	Percentage of Species exhibiting Sexual Parasitism
Euphotic	Above 660 ft.	Low	27 to 90 F	High	80%	4.9%
Disphotic	Begins at 660 ft.	High	33 to 41 F	Medium	65%	9.6%
Aphotic	Begins at 3300 ft.	Very High	Below 33 F	Low	75%	15%

CONTINUE

44

The author indicates that the recently-found Ceratioid Anglerfish

A) are speculated by scientists to actually be the descendants of land animals.

B) had previously never been encountered as far west as the Gulf of Mexico.

C) look and behave differently than species of anglerfish living above the deep sea.

D) inhabit an environment that is otherwise hostile to many forms of life.

45

Which choice provides the best evidence for the answer to the previous question?

A) Lines 17-20 ("Among . . . Mexico")

B) Lines 22-25 ("no natural . . . nonexistent")

C) Lines 29-32 ("Theodore . . . anglerfish")

D) Lines 35-38 ("even . . . dimorphism")

46

As used in line 41, "form" most nearly means

A) condition.

B) expression.

C) shape.

D) structure.

47

As used in lines 66-67, "experiments in" most nearly means

A) attempts at.

B) experiences in.

C) examinations of.

D) trials on.

48

The parenthetical statement in lines 46-47 ("At . . . growths") primarily serves to

A) provide a humorous interlude about the appearance of anglerfish in a predominantly serious passage.

B) suggest a potential explanation for the disparity between male and female anglerfish discoveries.

C) highlight the intensity of the effects of sexual dimorphism among the new anglerfish.

D) give helpful advice to aspiring deep sea scientists on finding and identifying male anglerfish.

49

According to the passage, some scientists believe that recently discovered deep-sea organisms

A) have evolved over millennia.

B) are able to reproduce by themselves asexually.

C) live even deeper in the ocean than researchers thought.

D) can blur the distinction between animal kingdoms.

50

Which choice provides the best evidence for the answer to the previous question?

A) Lines 59-62 ("another . . . itself")

B) Lines 64-65 ("According . . . categorise")

C) Lines 70-72 ("But . . . intrigue")

D) Lines 73-75 ("The organisms . . . feet")

CONTINUE

51

Based on the table and the passage, which choice gives the correct percentage of sexual parasitism for the "Midnight Zone"?

A) 4.9%

B) 9.6%

C) 15%

D) 75%

52

Do the data in the table provide support for the author's claim about sexual parasitism?

A) Yes, because the environmental conditions of the aphotic zone are conducive to sexual parasitism.

B) Yes, because the average species population density is significantly high in the euphotic zone.

C) No, because the environmental pressure is indicated as too high to allow for sexual parasitism in the aphotic zone.

D) No, because the percentage of sexual dimorphism in the aphotic zone is not directly proportional to average population density.

STOP
If you finish before time is called, you may check your work on this section only.
Do not turn to any other section.

Writing Test
35 MINUTES, 44 QUESTIONS

Turn to Section 2 of your answer sheet to answer the questions in this section.

DIRECTIONS

Each passage below is accompanied by a number of questions. For some questions, you will consider how the passage might be revised to improve the expression of ideas. For other questions, you will consider how the passage might be edited to correct errors in sentence structure, usage, or punctuation. A passage or a question may be accompanied by one or more graphics (such as a table or graph) that you will consider as you make revising and editing decisions.

Some questions will direct you to an underlined portion of a passage. Other questions will direct you to a location in a passage or ask you to think about the passage as a whole.

After reading each passage, choose the answer to each question that most effectively improves the quality of writing in the passage or that makes the passage conform to the conventions of standard written English. Many questions include a "NO CHANGE" option. Choose that option if you think the best choice is to leave the relevant portion of the passage as it is.

Questions 1-11 are based on the following passage and supplementary material.

All in the Elephant Family

In 1998, a group of researchers set out to study the elephant populations of the Samburu and Buffalo Springs National Reserves, both located in Kenya. This project was motivated in part by the same concern that informs other large animal fieldwork that has been performed in Africa—the fear that majestic mammals such as lions, gorillas, and elephants are increasingly **1** scared by human poaching and development. Indeed, over the course of sixteen years of fieldwork, the elephant research team found yet more reasons to protect the elephants. Elephants are social animals: **2** they form tight-knit communities led by elder females. By monitoring

1
A) NO CHANGE
B) vilified
C) subverted
D) endangered

2
Which choice best supports the writer's description of elephant society?
A) NO CHANGE
B) comparing them to lions or gorillas is a futile line of inquiry.
C) there is much about them that we still do not comprehend.
D) however, it is difficult reconcile this image with the solitary, fearsome elephants of popular culture.

CONTINUE

these communities well into the future—and by making sure

that they remain intact—zoologists and ecologists could make

further contributions to new and exciting fields, **3** being animal

psychology and animal sociology.

Elephants tend to form small groups based on familial ties,

but these groups interact in valuable ways. According to Shifra

Goldenberg of Colorado State University, broader elephant

social structures are analogous to human social networks: a small

group of elephants with a few dominant females is like a

4 family that "is one of several that make up our university

department," while the department itself is only one among

many. **5** Goldenberg envisions elephant society as made up of

"nested groupings" with "clearly defined tiers."

3
A) NO CHANGE
B) including
C) they are
D) those are

4
A) NO CHANGE
B) research group
C) researcher
D) society

5
The writer is considering deleting the underlined portion. Should the writer make this deletion?
A) Yes, because universities do not entail groupings and tiers such as those described.
B) Yes, because the paragraph focuses primarily on establishing Goldenberg's reputation as a scholar.
C) No, because it is otherwise unclear why Goldenberg compares elephant society to a social network.
D) No, because it adds detail that explains Goldenberg's ideas about elephant society.

CONTINUE

However, this somewhat regimented social structure can be shifted and transformed depending on elephants' needs and on the time of year. Elephants tend to splinter off into small foraging groups (10 or 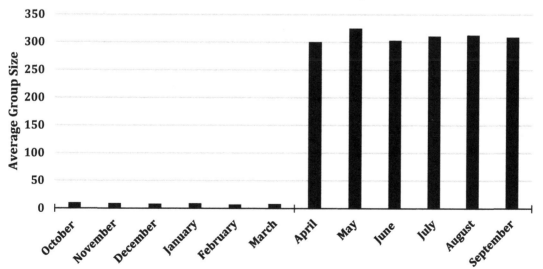 **6** less) during the dry season, but will normally congregate in large numbers **7** (300 or more) during the more comfortable and stable wet season. Goldenberg notes that "these large groupings when life is good facilitate information exchange and mating"—just as large groupings do among humans.

6

A) NO CHANGE
B) fewer
C) least
D) fewest

7

Which choice provides the most accurate and relevant interpretation of the graph?

A) NO CHANGE
B) (300 or more) in times when survival becomes especially difficult
C) (though never exceeding 100) during the more comfortable and stable wet season
D) (though never exceeding 100) in times when survival becomes especially difficult

Average Elephant Group Size Throughout Year

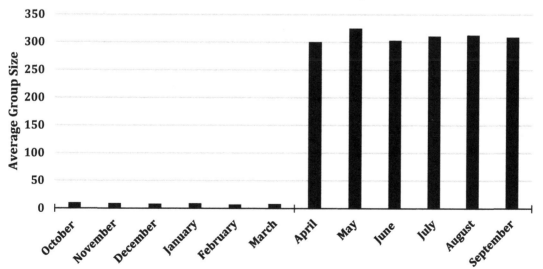

October to March (Dry Season) | April to September (Wet Season)

[1] The use of **8** relatively sophisticated social structures also allows elephant communities remain strong even in the face of resource scarcity, natural disasters, and poaching.

[2] Here, the leadership provided by female elephants is key: bull elephants form tiny all-male groups and sometimes wander **9** alone, they interact with the larger, matriarch-dominated groups mostly during mating. [3] It is not uncommon to find two closely cooperative family groups that have roamed the same territory through the generations, led by two allied matriarchs and then their younger counterparts—daughters and even granddaughters. [4] Yet perhaps the most remarkable of elephants' social traits **10** are a sense of compassion.

[5] Even elephants that are committed to set ways of life will make exceptions, welcoming abandoned or orphaned younger elephants into the family group. **11**

8
A) NO CHANGE
B) relative sophisticated
C) sophisticatedly relatively
D) sophisticated and relative

9
A) NO CHANGE
B) alone, which interacts
C) alone; interacting
D) alone, interacting

10
A) NO CHANGE
B) is
C) were
D) was

11
The writer wishes to add the following statement to the paragraph

In fact, elephant matriarchs can "train" their daughters to preserve longstanding social ties.

The best place to insert this statement would be
A) after sentence 1.
B) after sentence 2.
C) after sentence 3.
D) after sentence 4.

CONTINUE

Questions 12-22 are based on the following passage.

Flexing Your Time

Tammy Hunter, a financial services professional and mother of three **12** children, who found it very difficult to balance the demands of her career with the commitments of parenthood. Even when she was at home, she was "at work," bound moment-to-moment to her cell phone. Whenever she received a work-related call at home, she would immediately take the call, **13** even while having a meal with her children.

Hunter then decided to switch over to flex scheduling (also known as flextime), an increasingly popular arrangement **14** in which employees fit their 40 hours per week into a format other than 9:00-5:00, Monday to Friday. Some employees choose to work four 10-hour days in order to reduce the number of hours that they spend commuting each week, **15** while another chooses to work from 10:00-6:00 or 8:00-4:00 to better fit their children's schedules. In Hunter's case, she leaves work at 3:00 pm on Fridays during the summer, since her children are home from school, and **16** making other adjustments as needed to allow her to take part in her children's activities.

12
A) NO CHANGE
B) children, she found
C) children, finding
D) children, found

13
Which choice most effectively indicates that Hunter's work obligations interrupted her personal life?
A) NO CHANGE
B) even though some of the calls were ultimately unimportant.
C) a practice she developed over time.
D) as many other finance professionals would in her situation.

14
The author is considering deleting the underlined portion (ending the sentence with a period). Should the author make this deletion?
A) Yes, because it presents information that occurs elsewhere in the passage.
B) Yes, because it distracts from the discussion of the problems that Hunter faced.
C) No, because it defines a term that is of great importance to the passage.
D) No, because it anticipates an objection that will be raised later in the passage.

15
A) NO CHANGE
B) while others choose
C) and another chooses
D) and others choose

16
A) NO CHANGE
B) makes
C) made
D) had made

Hunter's employer is KPMG, a tax and financial services firm in Atlanta. Approximately half of KPMG's workforce uses flextime. Other major companies that offer flex scheduling include Kraft Foods and Texas Instruments. Many government agencies offer flextime as well. **17** They realize that flex scheduling not only facilitates their employees' work-life balance but also helps to increase employee retention and productivity, and to decrease unplanned absences from work. That is not a trifling **18** matter; a recent Georgetown University study found that unplanned employee absences cost some companies almost $1 million annually.

19 Indeed, Hunter's case is not unique. For example, David Lewis, a chief executive at a human resources consulting firm, pointed out that many companies only offer flex scheduling for certain positions, namely those for which working at home works well. A 2014 study found that 81% of U.S. companies allowed certain employees to periodically change their work hours, while only 27% allowed most or all employees to do so. **20** Having some positions with flextime options and some without sometimes creates tension: employees who do not have the option of flex scheduling may experience jealousy or feel as though they are not trusted to work productively at home.

17

Which of the following is the best replacement for the underlined portion?
A) The government realizes
B) Employees realize
C) These employers realize
D) The workforce realizes

18

A) NO CHANGE
B) matter, a recent
C) matter, if a recent
D) matter, although a recent

19

Which choice most effectively sets up the paragraph?
A) NO CHANGE
B) Flex scheduling does have its downsides, though.
C) Will flex scheduling ever be mandated by law?
D) The findings of the Georgetown University study, however, have been disputed.

20

A) NO CHANGE
B) When you have
C) When they have
D) DELETE the underlined portion and begin the sentence with the word "Some".

CONTINUE

Lewis also noted that employees who [21] are prominent opportunists about flextime may be less likely to be promoted if their choice to work at home is perceived as reflecting a decreased commitment to their careers. However, as flextime becomes more prevalent, perhaps its [22] negatively associations will diminish. For now, many employees—particularly those who would otherwise be likely to leave their careers behind—are willing to take the risk.

21

A) NO CHANGE
B) take advantage of
C) make a lot of
D) get a huge deal of

22

A) NO CHANGE
B) associated negatively
C) associating negatively
D) negative associations

Questions 23-33 are based on the following passage.

Nyoka, Queen of the Jungle

— 1 —

As a child growing up just after the Second World War, I loved going to "the pictures." Wild west films were some of my favorites, especially if the Apache were on the warpath, which they **23** usually were during these movies. I rooted for them every time, but neither their superiority in numbers, nor **24** the fact that they were defending their own land, helped them to win a single victory.

— 2 —

Finally, after a few song and dance segments, the climax of the morning's entertainment arrived: the latest installment of the adventure series! Often, it was Flash Gordon on the screen. Each week, with courage, resourcefulness, and daring, **25** we battled Ming the Merciless. Occasionally, it was Zorro who upheld justice **26** for the poorer inhabitants of California. Each week, justice and fairness and freedom were threatened, seemingly doomed, yet each hero escaped and liberty was allowed to survive. Flash, Zorro, the Lone Ranger: I believed in them all.

23
A) NO CHANGE
B) usually did during the Westerns.
C) usually were.
D) usually did.

24
A) NO CHANGE
B) when they were
C) them
D) DELETE the underlined portion.

25
A) NO CHANGE
B) they
C) he
D) one

26
The writer is considering deleting the underlined portion (ending the sentence with a period). Should the writer make this deletion?
A) Yes, because it undermines the author's claim that Zorro and Flash Gordon are indistinguishable.
B) Yes, because most readers would already be familiar with this information.
C) No, because the author discusses Zorro at greater length later on.
D) No, because it offers a specific example of how Zorro upheld the values the author praises.

CONTINUE

— 3 —

On Saturday mornings, the local cinema offered a program for children, a kind of exclusive club: no adults allowed, apart from the cinema staff. The program always [27] began with a short informative film about something encouraging for a country not long out of a war. We scorned this segment, unless it was about steam trains or breaking land speed records. Relief was [28] at hand: a comic short film, hopefully Laurel and Hardy with another "fine mess" they had gotten themselves into. We laughed till the tears came! The lights came up for a small break, for advertisements and the ice cream lady, who was making her way up the aisle. She was besieged.

— 4 —

Yet for me, only one hero meant anything: Nyoka, Jungle Girl. She was a sort of female Tarzan, [29] although she was a female character. She lived in the jungle, through which she ran barefoot, repelling lions and grappling with giant crocodiles. She rescued poor natives from the tyranny of by crooked hunters. She was resourceful, [30] tough, and intelligent: no problem, discouraged her for long. Every week she was left facing a dilemma that was seemingly impossible to escape; by the following week, she had come up with a solution. After an hour with her, I felt as though I could do anything.

27

A) NO CHANGE
B) has begun
C) have begun
D) will begin

28

A) NO CHANGE
B) local
C) proximate
D) going to happen soon

29

The writer wants to call attention to a meaningful difference between Nyoka and Tarzan. Which choice best accomplishes this goal?

A) NO CHANGE
B) although Tarzan had his own adventure series.
C) although more relatable to me.
D) although I am not sure which character was more popular at the time.

30

A) NO CHANGE
B) tough, and intelligent: no problem
C) tough, and intelligent, no problem
D) tough—and intelligent, no problem

— 5 —

Nowadays, I laugh at the schematic storylines and general naïveté of **31** them. Yet Nyoka reminded us children of the necessity of resilience in life. Our parents did not need to be reminded of that: they had just lived through World War II, but we needed Nyoka as a symbol of hope. And, if ever I find myself in the jungle, before me a lake covered in burning oil, **32** and then native hordes with poisoned spears, I shall know exactly what to do.

Question 33 asks about the previous passage as a whole.

31

Which of the following is the best replacement for the underlined portion?

A) the other children at the cinema.
B) the values I once admired.
C) the staff of the movie theater.
D) those Saturday morning films.

32

A) NO CHANGE
B) but also
C) behind me
D) despite me

Think about the previous passage as a whole as you answer question 33.

33

To make the passage most logical, paragraph 2 should be placed

A) where it is now.
B) before paragraph 1.
C) before paragraph 4.
D) before paragraph 5.

CONTINUE

Questions 34-44 are based on the following passage.

Vacation, Without the Travel

A few years ago, while taking a guided tour of Russia, I encountered a strange sight. I [34] have just checked into a hotel on the outskirts of St. Petersburg and was making my way to my room when I noticed a full-sized go-cart track, right in the middle of the hotel's atrium. [35] All of this struck me as very unusual. Intrigued, I decided to explore the hotel further: on the second floor, I discovered a large room that contained almost two dozen billiards tables and almost four dozen pinball machines. Yet as I learned from my tour guide later that day, the Russians had [36] massive things in mind for stocking their hotel with these forms of entertainment—which were actually holdovers from the 1960s and 1970s, when Russian society was quite different. Because the Russians of that era lived under a strict communist regime and were not allowed to travel freely, they created a type of "vacation" that did not involve international travel. [37] They would simply take time off from work, drive to a hotel, and enjoy a few days of light games and challenges.

34

A) NO CHANGE
B) had just checked
C) could just check
D) am just checking

35

The writer is considering deleting the underlined portion. Should the writer make this deletion?

A) Yes, because the sentence simply re-formulates a thought expressed earlier in the passage.
B) Yes, because it is not clear why the writer finds the sights that are described unusual.
C) No, because this sentence articulates the main idea of the passage.
D) No, because this sentence anticipates the later discussion of attractions that the writer of the passage finds unusual.

36

A) NO CHANGE
B) valid reasons
C) lots of ideas
D) verified musings

37

Which of the following is the best replacement for the underlined portion?

A) The Russians of those decades
B) High-ranking communist officials
C) My fellow tourists
D) Hotel employees

Russians today don't seem to have much use [38] with the forms of entertainment I discovered in that hotel: the go-cart track was completely defunct, and only a handful of teenagers seemed to take an interest in the billiards tables. However, contemporary business has made excellent use of one of the principles behind the Russians' close-to-home "vacations." Time-consuming travel is one of the nuisances that face many vacationers, [39] and in a somewhat desperate maneuver, American leisure and entertainment companies have created sites and attractions that are not too far in spirit from that Russian hotel.

A) NO CHANGE
B) in the forms
C) from the forms
D) for the forms

A) NO CHANGE
B) and in order to stimulate tourism to Russia,
C) and with this modern reality in mind,
D) DELETE the underlined portion.

CONTINUE

One business that has successfully put a close-to-home strategy into practice is Great Wolf Lodge, which has locations in Pennsylvania and Virginia. These two states have [40] growing and prospering suburban communities—large numbers of people, in other words, [41] which may not be able to abandon their day-to-day obligations to travel across the world but who probably need a fun weekend every few months. Each Great Wolf Lodge is designed to meet these desires. Visitors to a Great Wolf Lodge will find hotel rooms, restaurants, an indoor water park, [42] and seasonal attractions—such as life-size gingerbread houses for the winter holidays—all under one roof.

Best of all, the hassle involved in finding and then navigating a Great Wolf Lodge is minimal: you simply find a parking space, drop your bags in your hotel room, and [43] you settle in for a couple days of uninterrupted recreation. There are no plane tickets to buy, no flight delays to fear. [44] Will the Great Wolf Lodge ever go the way of those now-neglected Russian hotels?

[40]
A) NO CHANGE
B) prospered growingly
C) growingly prosperingly
D) growingly and prospered

[41]
A) NO CHANGE
B) who
C) where they
D) because they

[42]
A) NO CHANGE
B) and seasonal attractions, such as—life-size gingerbread houses for the winter holidays—all
C) and seasonal—attractions such as life-size gingerbread houses for the winter holidays—all
D) and—seasonal attractions—such as life-size gingerbread houses for the winter holidays, all

[43]
A) NO CHANGE
B) settle
C) settled
D) settling

[44]
Which choice most effectively concludes the writer's discussion of the relative ease of visiting a Great Wolf Lodge?
A) NO CHANGE
B) Will airlines ever address the many inconveniences associated with travel by plane?
C) After all, when was the last time you went to a water park of any sort?
D) Whoever said that a great vacation can't be only a short car-ride away?

STOP
If you finish before time is called, you may check your work on this section only.
Do not turn to any other section.

Math Test - No Calculator

25 MINUTES, 20 QUESTIONS

DIRECTIONS

For each question from 1-15, choose the best answer choice provided in the multiple choice bank and fill in the appropriate circle in the provided answer key. Alternatively, for questions **16-20**, answer the problem and enter your answer in the grid-in section of the answer key. Refer to the directions given before question 16 as to how to enter your answers for the grid-in questions. You may complete scratch work in any empty space in your test booklet.

NOTES

A. Calculator usage **is not allowed** in this section.
B. Variables, constants, and coefficients used represent real numbers unless indicated otherwise.
C. All figures are created to appropriate scale unless the question states otherwise.
D. All figures are two-dimensional unless the question states otherwise.
E. The domain of any given function is all real numbers x for which the function, $f(x)$, is a real number unless the question states otherwise.

REFERENCE

$A = \pi r^2$
$C = 2\pi r$

$A = lw$

$A = \frac{1}{2}bh$

$c^2 = a^2 + b^2$

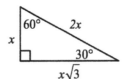
Special Right Triangle

Special Right Triangle

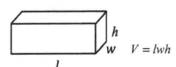
$V = lwh$

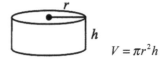
$V = \pi r^2 h$

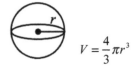
$V = \frac{4}{3}\pi r^3$

$V = \frac{1}{3}\pi r^2 h$

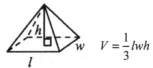
$V = \frac{1}{3}lwh$

There are $360°$ in a circle.
There are 2π radians in a circle.
There are $180°$ in a triangle.

CONTINUE ➡

1

If $3 + h(x - 4) = 33$ and $h = 5$, what is the value of x?

A) $\dfrac{16}{5}$

B) $\dfrac{34}{5}$

C) 10

D) 50

2

Manny can ride his bicycle 5 miles in h hours. If Manny rides his bicycle h hours each day for d days, which of the following expressions represents the total number of miles that Manny rode on his bicycle?

A) $5d$

B) $5hd$

C) $\dfrac{5h}{d}$

D) $\dfrac{5d}{h}$

3

$$\dfrac{5x^2 - 20xy}{3xy - 12y^2}$$

If $x \ne 4y$ and $y \ne 0$, the expression above is equivalent to which of the following?

A) 1

B) $x - 4$

C) $\dfrac{5x}{3y}$

D) $\dfrac{5x(x - 20y)}{3y(x - 12y)}$

4

$$(-1 + i)(-3 + 2i)$$

Which of the following is equivalent to the value of the expression above? (Note: $i = \sqrt{-1}$)

A) $1 - i$

B) $1 - 5i$

C) $-5 - 5i$

D) $5 - 5i$

CONTINUE

5

Hernando owns and operates an ice cream parlor in the city of Highgate. When the ice cream parlor opened, Hernando opened a savings account at a local bank. Not counting any deposits, the balance in Hernando's savings account closely follows the model $B = 5,500(1.01)^t$, where B is the account balance t years after the account was opened. The constant 1.01 indicates which of the following in the context of Hernando's savings account balance?

A) The account balance will decrease by 1% each year.

B) The account balance will increase by .01% each year.

C) The account balance will increase by .1% each year.

D) The account balance will increase by 1% each year.

6

$$3p - 9c = 120$$

A video gamer's point total, p, and number of competitions entered, c, closely follows the linear relationship above. If the gamer were to use the equation to estimate the point total based on the number of competitions he had entered, the gamer could expect an increase of how many points per competition?

A) 3

B) 9

C) 12

D) 120

7

If a is not equivalent to 0 and $b = \dfrac{a}{5}$, what is the value of $\dfrac{25b}{a}$?

A) $\dfrac{1}{5}$

B) 5

C) 25

D) 125

8

Given $f(x) = \dfrac{b}{2}x^2$ and $f(8) = 96$, what is the value of $f(2)$?

A) 2

B) 3

C) 4

D) 6

CONTINUE

9

$$y = -\frac{1}{2}x + 7$$

Line k is perpendicular to the line defined by the equation above and passes through the point $(4,0)$. Which of the following points also lies on line k?

A) $(0,8)$

B) $(2,-4)$

C) $(2,-2)$

D) $(2,8)$

10

$$S = \frac{(\frac{320}{h})(h-8)}{64B} - MPh$$

The final selling price per bottle, S, for B bottles of breath mints can be calculated based on the number of hours, h, that the manufacturing machines have been running, M, the number of men operating the machines, and P, the current hourly wage for the machine workers. Which of the following gives B in terms of S, h, M, and P?

A) $B = \dfrac{(\frac{320}{h})(h-8) - MPh}{64S}$

B) $B = \dfrac{(\frac{320}{h})(h-8)}{64S + MPh}$

C) $B = \dfrac{(\frac{320}{h})(h-8)}{64(S + MPh)}$

D) $B = \dfrac{64S - 64MPh}{(\frac{320}{h})(h-8)}$

11

$$12x - 2y = 21$$
$$-4x + Ay = -7$$

If the system of equations above is true for all values of x and y, what is the value of A?

A) $-\dfrac{1}{3}$

B) -1

C) 1

D) $\dfrac{2}{3}$

12

One phone service provider charges \$1 for the first two minutes of a long-distance phone call and \$0.03 per minute thereafter. Another phone service provider charges \$0.05 per minute for long-distance calls of any length. What is the price, in dollars, of a long-distance phone call that costs the same from both providers?

A) 2.35

B) 2.65

C) 47

D) 53

203

CONTINUE

13

$$\frac{16^x \bullet 4^y}{2}$$

If $4x + 2y - 1 = 5$, what is the value of the expression above?

A) 1

B) 32

C) 64

D) 1024

14

$$m(x^2 - b^2) = (2x - 1)(2x + 1)$$

If the equation above is true for all values of x, m is a constant, and $b < 0$, what is the value of b?

A) $-\dfrac{1}{2}$

B) $-\dfrac{1}{16}$

C) $\dfrac{1}{16}$

D) $\dfrac{1}{2}$

15

Given that $x < 0$, which of the following is equivalent to the expression $\dfrac{\dfrac{1}{x-1} + \dfrac{1}{x-2}}{4x - 6}$?

A) $\dfrac{1}{2x^2 - 6x + 4}$

B) $\dfrac{2}{x^2 - 3x + 2}$

C) $\dfrac{8x^2 - 24x + 18}{x^2 - 3x + 2}$

D) $\dfrac{1}{2}$

CONTINUE

DIRECTIONS

For each question from 16-20, solve and enter your answer in the grid-in section of your answer sheet as described below.

A. Write out your answers in the boxes at the top of each column in order to help you fill in the circles accurately. Remember, you will only receive credit for the circles that are filled in correctly, not for the written answer at the top of the columns.

B. Mark only a single circle in each column.

C. There are no negative answers.

D. If the problem has more than one correct answer, grid only one of the correct answers.

E. When your answer is a **mixed number**, such as $1\frac{1}{2}$, it should be entered as 1.5 or $3/2$. You cannot enter a mixed number because there is no room to fill in a circle that represents a space.

F. If you enter a **decimal answer** with more digits then the grid can handle, the answer may be rounded or truncated, but it absolutely must fill the entire grid.

Answer: 102 - both positions are correct

REMEMBER: You can begin writing your answers in any column as long as there is enough space. Leave unused columns blank.

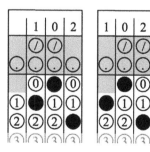

Answer: $\frac{8}{21}$

Answer: 6.4

Written answer →
Decimal → point
← Fraction line

The ways to correctly grid $\frac{7}{9}$ are:

CONTINUE ➡

16

How many integer values of x satisfy the inequality $2x^2 - 9x + 4 < 0$?

18

In a right triangle, the smaller acute angle measures $x°$ and the larger acute angle measures $y°$. If $\sin x° = \dfrac{5}{13}$, what is $\tan y°$?

17

$$y = x^2 - 2x + 1$$
$$y = -2x + \frac{13}{4}$$

If the point (x_1, y_1) is a solution to the system of equations above in which $x_1 > 0$, what is the value of y_1?

19

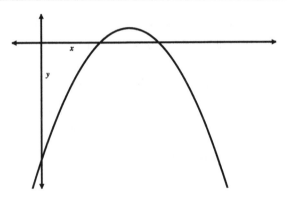

The equation of the function graphed above in the y-plane can be written in the form $y = -a(x - h)^2 + 1$ where a and h are positive constants. If the function crosses the x-axis at 2 and 4, what is the value of a?

CONTINUE

3 3

20

A triangle has two sides that measure 6 inches and 26 inches. A similar triangle has sides that measure exactly half of the length of the original triangle What is the greatest possible area of the smaller triangle?

STOP

If you finish before time is called, you may check your work on this section only.

Do not turn to any other section.

207

©Integrated Educational Services, 2016 **www.ies2400.com** | Unauthorized copying or reuse of any part of this page is illegal.

Math Test - Calculator

55 MINUTES, 38 QUESTIONS

DIRECTIONS

For each question from 1-30, choose the best answer choice provided in the multiple choice bank and fill in the appropriate circle in the provided answer key. Alternatively, for questions **31-38**, answer the problem and enter your answer in the grid-in section of the answer key. Refer to the directions given before question 31 as to how to enter your answers for the grid-in questions. You may complete scratch work in any empty space in your test booklet.

NOTES

A. Calculator usage **is allowed**.
B. Variables, constants, and coefficients used represent real numbers unless indicated otherwise.
C. All figures are created to appropriate scale unless the question states otherwise.
D. All figures are two-dimensional unless the question states otherwise.
E. The domain of any given function is all real numbers x for which the function, $f(x)$, is a real number unless the question states otherwise.

REFERENCE

$A = \pi r^2$
$C = 2\pi r$

$A = lw$

$A = \frac{1}{2}bh$

$c^2 = a^2 + b^2$

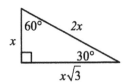
Special Right Triangle

Special Right Triangle

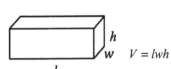
$V = lwh$

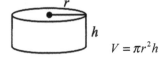
$V = \pi r^2 h$

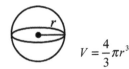
$V = \frac{4}{3}\pi r^3$

$V = \frac{1}{3}\pi r^2 h$

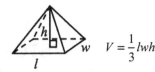
$V = \frac{1}{3}lwh$

There are $360°$ in a circle.
There are 2π radians in a circle.
There are $180°$ in a triangle.

CONTINUE ➡

1

$\frac{y}{x} = k$ where k is a positive constant. If $y = 12$ when $x = 60$, what is the value of y when $x = 35$?

A) 5

B) 7

C) 25

D) 175

2

Three less than one half of a number is twelve more than the number. What is the number?

A) -30

B) -15

C) $-\frac{15}{2}$

D) 30

3

There are 128 ounces in a gallon of orange juice. A one pint glass can hold exactly 16 ounces of liquid. Three half-gallon containers of orange juice can fill exactly how many pint glasses with orange juice?

A) 6

B) 8

C) 12

D) 24

4

For how many integer values of x is $x^2 + 16 \leq 7$?

A) 0

B) 1

C) 2

D) Infinitely many

CONTINUE

5

Triatholon Distance vs. Time

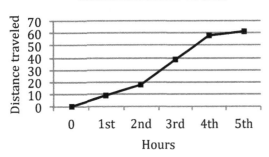

Tom recently entered a triatholon where he had to swim, run, and cycle a course that totaled 61 miles. If Tom cycles faster than he runs and runs faster than he swims, during which of the following intervals could Tom have been running?

A) 0-2 hours

B) 0-4 hours

C) 2-4 hours

D) 4-5 hours

6

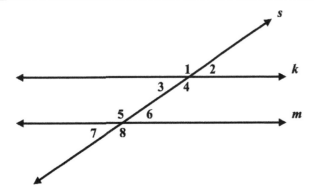

If line k is parallel to line m and $\angle 1$ has twice the measure of $\angle 3$, what is the measure of $\angle 5 + \angle 8$ in degrees?

A) 60

B) 120

C) 240

D) 270

7

A scatterplot created in the xy-plane is populated by a group of 24 points that closely approximates a line with little to no outliers. A best fit line has been calculated for the data and has the equation $y = -0.5x + 6.5$. Which of the following best describes the association between the variables x and y?

A) Strong positive linear association

B) Weak positive linear association

C) Strong negative linear association

D) Weak negative linear association

8

SAT Prep Cumulative Revenue from 2004 to 2009

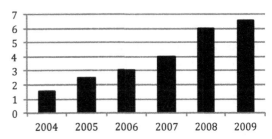

The cumulative revenue for an SAT preparation company for the years 2004 through 2009 is shown in the bar graph above. If $500,000 was made by the company over the course of the year 2005, which of the following would be an appropriate label for the vertical axis of the graph?

A) Cumulative revenue as per the first of the year in millions of dollars.

B) Cumulative revenue as per the first of the year in thousands of dollars.

C) Cumulative revenue as per the last day of the year in millions of dollars.

D) Cumulative revenue as per the last day of the year in thousands of dollars.

CONTINUE

9

If b is a prime number and the product bc is equivalent to 30 for some positive integer value of c, which of the following could NOT be the value of b?

A) 2

B) 3

C) 5

D) 7

10

The average of 11 consecutive numbers is 9. If the largest number is increased by 55, by how much does the average increase?

A) 3

B) 5

C) 9

D) 14

Questions 11 and 12 refer to the following information.

Holistic Treatments Effect on
Diastolic Blood Pressure

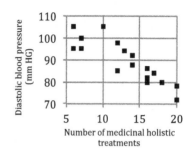

A random sample of 17 adults diagnosed with high blood pressure who have been undergoing medicinal holistic treatments to reduce their diastolic blood pressure were asked the number of treatments they have received and their current diastolic blood pressure. The results are gathered in the scatterplot above.

11

Which of the following linear models could best be used as a line of best fit to predict diastolic blood pressure, D, in mm HG as defined by t, the number of medicinal holistic treatments received?

A) $D = -2.3t + 110$

B) $D = -2.3t + 122$

C) $D = -3.5t + 110$

D) $D = -3.5t + 122$

12

For the one patient who reported 10 treatments, what is the approximate difference between the patient's observed diastolic blood pressure and the diastolic blood pressure that would have been predicted using the best fit model?

A) 0

B) 6

C) 18

D) 30

CONTINUE

13

Runner	Time
Daniel	4:30
Bill	5:05
Geraldine	5:25
Gregory	4:45
Angela	5:05
Samantha	4:50

The table above includes the times, in minutes and seconds, that it took 6 runners to complete a one-mile run. Geraldine's time was accidentally recorded as a minute longer than she actually ran. If Geraldine's time were adjusted appropriately, which of the following would change?

A) Range

B) Median

C) Mean

D) They will all change.

14

If $f(x) = 3x^2 - 6x + 2$, what is the least possible value of $f(x)$?

A) -1

B) 1

C) Infinite

D) The minimum value cannot be determined.

Questions 15 and 16 refer to the following information.

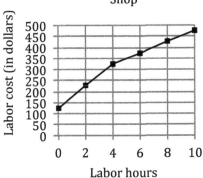

Labor Costs at an Autobody Shop

The graph above displays the total cost of labor for an autobody repair job that lasts between 0 and 10 hours.

15

What does the point at $(0,125)$ represent in the graph?

A) The total number of laborers required.

B) The initial cost of parts required for the job.

C) The initial fixed cost of a repair.

D) The total cost of repair and labor if no additional labor hours are required.

16

What is the difference in the price of additional labor per hour, in dollars, during the period from 0 to 4 hours as compared to the period from 4 to 10 hours?

A) 25

B) 35

C) 50

D) 100

CONTINUE

Questions 17 and 18 refer to the following information.

	Business	Science	TOTAL:
Undergraduate	18	9	27
Graduate	27	9	36
TOTAL:	45	18	63

63 students studying business or science at a local university were asked which degree they were working toward and if they were undergraduates or graduate students. The results were collected in the table above.

17

Which of the following categories accounts for approximately 43% of the students in the sample?

A) Graduate students studying Business
B) Graduate students
C) Undergraduate students studying Business
D) Undergraduate students studying Science

18

If a student studying business were to be selected at random, what is the probability that the student is an Undergraduate?

A) $\frac{2}{5}$

B) $\frac{3}{7}$

C) $\frac{2}{3}$

D) $\frac{5}{7}$

19

The drama club at a high school is charging $5 for tickets sold in advance to the performance of the spring play and $7 for tickets sold on the day of the performance. If the club sold a total of 200 tickets and raised a total of $1,150, how many tickets were sold on the day of the performance?

A) 50
B) 75
C) 125
D) 150

20

$$y = 2x + a$$
$$y = ax + 2$$

If the coordinate point $(1,s)$ is the only solution to the system of linear equations above, which of the following statements is true about a and s?

A) $a + s = 2$
B) $a = s + 2$
C) $a + 2 = s$
D) $a = \frac{s}{2}$

CONTINUE

21

$$x^2 + y^2 - 2y = 3$$

Which of the following coordinate points is the center of the circle represented by the equation above?

A) $(0,-1)$

B) $(0,2)$

C) $(1,0)$

D) $(0,1)$

22

Helina bought a purse that was discounted by 35% and her receipt read that she paid d dollars. If Helina paid 6% sales tax, which of the following is equivalent to the original selling price of the purse?

A) $0.35(1.06)d$

B) $0.65(1.06)d$

C) $\dfrac{1.06d}{0.65}$

D) $\dfrac{d}{0.65(1.06)}$

23

A statistics professor at Knoll University noticed that the enrollment for Introductory Statistics was 30% lower than the enrollment for Intro to Statistics for Business. If there were 210 students enrolled in Introductory Statistics, how many students enrolled in Intro to Statistics for Business?

A) 63

B) 147

C) 300

D) 840

24

A tennis ball is thrown upward from the ground and its height, h, with respect to time, t, is given by the equation $h = 22t - t^2$. Some kids are sitting on the roof of a building that stands 21 feet tall. If the kids are sitting in such a position that they cannot see the ball until it reaches the height of the roof, for how many seconds of the tennis ball's flight can the kids see the ball?

A) 18

B) 20

C) 21

D) 22

CONTINUE

Questions 25 and 26 refer to the following information.

Net Profit for Multiple Income Streams of a Music Store

	2010	2011	2012	2013	2014
Classes	35	41	45	49	55
Book Sales	12	14	13	12	14
Equipment Sales	4	8	15	31	64
TOTAL:	51	63	73	92	133

The table above displays the net profit in thousands of dollars for the three sales divisions of a music store from the year 2010 through the year 2014.

25

The net profits of which of the following divisions of the music store would best be approximated by a linear equation of the form $y = b$ where b is a positive constant?

A) Classes

B) Book Sales

C) Equipment Sales

D) None of the divisions

26

Which of the following best approximates the average change in dollars per year of net profits from the sale of classes?

A) 4

B) 5

C) 4,000

D) 5,000

27

$$x + y < -1$$
$$x - 2y \geq 2$$

Which of the following is true of all solutions (x, y) in the solution set of the system of linear inequalities above?

A) $x < y$

B) $y \leq x$

C) $x \leq -1$

D) $y < -1$

28

When the polynomial $f(x)$ is divided by $x - 4$, the remainder is equivalent to $\dfrac{5}{x-4}$. Which of the following statements must be true?

A) $f(4) = 5$

B) $f(-4) = 5$

C) $f(5) = 4$

D) $f(4) = 0$

CONTINUE

29

	Number of Gold Awards
Student 1	5
Student 2	8
Student 3	2
Student 4	4
Student 5	1
Student 6	10

6 students were each asked to play 50 simple mind games generated by an educational website and to record the number of Gold Awards they received in those 50 games. The website states that any student who earns over 500 Gold Awards will be entered in a lottery to win a free iPad. A new student would like to know how many Gold Awards he could expect to win if he played all of the games generated by the website. Using the data in the table above, if the website boasts that it has 45,000 games available, how many Gold Awards can the student reasonably expect to receive if he plays all of the games generated by the website?

A) 450

B) 500

C) 4,500

D) 7,500

30

$$y = -x^2 + 6x - 5$$

The quadratic equation above reaches its maximum at the point (a, b). A second quadratic equation intercepts the x-axis at the same points as the equation above, except it has an absolute minimum at the point $(a, -b)$. Which of the following is an equivalent form of the second quadratic equation in which a and $-b$ appear as constants in the equation?

A) $y = (x-1)(x-5)$

B) $y = (x+1)(x+5)$

C) $y = (x-3)^2 - 4$

D) $y = -1(x-3)^2 + 4$

CONTINUE

DIRECTIONS

For each question from 31-38, solve and enter your answer in the grid-in section of your answer sheet as described below.

A. Write out your answers in the boxes at the top of each column in order to help you fill in the circles accurately. Remember, you will only receive credit for the circles that are filled in correctly, not for the written answer at the top of the columns.

B. Mark only a single circle in each column.

C. There are no negative answers.

D. If the problem has more than one correct answer, grid only one of the correct answers.

E. When your answer is a **mixed number**, such as $1\frac{1}{2}$, it should be entered as 1.5 or 3/2. You cannot enter a mixed number because there is no room to fill in a circle that represents a space.

F. If you enter a **decimal answer** with more digits then the grid can handle, the answer may be rounded or truncated, but it absolutely must fill the entire grid.

Answer: $\frac{8}{21}$ Answer: 6.4

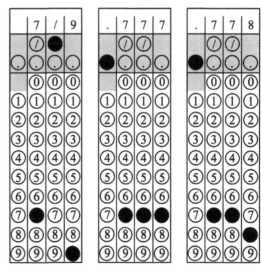

The ways to correctly grid $\frac{7}{9}$ are:

Answer: 102 - both positions are correct

REMEMBER: You can begin writing your answers in any column as long as there is enough space. Leave unused columns blank.

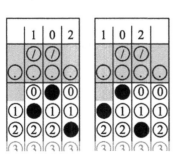

CONTINUE →

31

Justine makes homemade candles as a small side business to make extra money. Justine ships her candles in pre-paid shipping boxes that allow her to ship a maximum weight of 28 pounds in each box before she is charged additional postage. Justine knows that the packaging material for each box of candles weighs 3 pounds and she knows that each candle weighs 1.5 pounds. If x is the maximum number of candles that Justine can pack in the shipping box without going over weight, what is the value of x?

32

Felipe rents self-storage spaces that measure 320 cubic feet each. Each warehouse that Felipe owns has a total of 17,600 cubic feet of available rental space. If Felipe owns two warehouses, how many total self-storage spaces can he rent?

33

Daniella trains for long distance road races. In her most recent training cycle, her lowest average pace for a single run was 5 miles per hour, whereas her fastest pace was completed on a day where she ran 14 miles in 2 hours. If Daniella were to run for 2 and a half hours, what is one possible distance, in miles, she could have run?

34

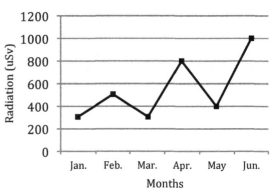

Radiation Readings for the Months of January Through June

According to the radiation readings in the line graph above, the radiation reading in June was what percent larger than the radiation reading in April?

CONTINUE

35

A square with an area of 16 square centimeters is inscribed in a circle. If the area of the square is $\dfrac{a}{\pi}$% of the area of the circle, what is the value of a?

36

$$g(x) = \dfrac{x-2}{x^3 - \dfrac{5}{2}x^2 + x}$$

For how many values of x is the function above undefined?

CONTINUE

Questions 37-38 refer to the following information.

$$\$2{,}100(1+\frac{r}{100})^{\frac{m}{12}}$$

The account balance of a savings account at a bank can be calculated using the expression above, where r is the annual interest rate of the account and m is the number of months that have passed since the initial deposit of \$2,100 was placed in the account.

37

If the account balance after 24 months was \$2,227.89, what is the value of r?

38

If the account balance was \$2,227.89 after 24 months had passed, by exactly what rational number of percentage points must the annual interest rate, r, be increased in order for the account to grow to the same value in half the amount of time?

STOP

If you finish before time is called, you may check your work on this section only.

Do not turn to any other section.

Answer Key: TEST 3

SAT

SECTION 1—READING

1.	D	11.	D	21.	D	32.	D	42.	D
2.	A	12.	A	22.	A	33.	B	43.	C
3.	C	13.	C	23.	B	34.	B	44.	D
4.	D	14.	B	24.	D	35.	D	45.	B
5.	B	15.	D	25.	B	36.	A	46.	B
6.	A	16.	C	26.	A	37.	D	47.	A
7.	C	17.	B	27.	D	38.	C	48.	C
8.	B	18.	D	28.	C	39.	A	49.	D
9.	B	19.	A	29.	B	40.	C	50.	B
10.	C	20.	A	30.	A	41.	C	51.	C
				31.	A			52.	A

SECTION 2—WRITING

1.	D	12.	D	23.	C	34.	B
2.	A	13.	A	24.	A	35.	A
3.	B	14.	C	25.	C	36.	B
4.	B	15.	B	26.	D	37.	A
5.	D	16.	B	27.	A	38.	D
6.	B	17.	C	28.	A	39.	C
7.	A	18.	A	29.	C	40.	A
8.	A	19.	B	30.	B	41.	B
9.	D	20.	A	31.	D	42.	A
10.	B	21.	B	32.	C	43.	B
11.	B	22.	D	33.	C	44.	D

SECTION 3—MATH

1.	C	12.	A
2.	A	13.	B
3.	C	14.	A
4.	B	15.	A
5.	D		
6.	A	**Fill-Ins:**	
7.	B	16.	3
8.	D	17.	1/4 or .25
9.	B	18.	12/5 or 2.4
10.	C	19.	1
11.	D	20.	39/2 or 19.5

SECTION 4—MATH

1.	B	13.	D	24.	B	**Fill-Ins:**	
2.	A	14.	A	25.	B	31.	16
3.	C	15.	C	26.	D	32.	110
4.	A	16.	A	27.	D	33.	$12.5 < x < 17.5$
5.	A	17.	A	28.	A	34.	25
6.	C	18.	A	29.	C	35.	200
7.	C	19.	B	30.	C	36.	3
8.	A	20.	C			37.	3
9.	D	21.	D			38.	3.09
10.	B	22.	D				
11.	B	23.	C				
12.	B						

Answer Explanations

SAT Practice Test #3

Section 1: Reading

QUESTION 1.

Choice D is correct. The passage deals with the perspective of "Mrs. Baroda" (line 1) as she observes Gouvernail, a family friend whose "personality puzzled Mrs. Baroda" (line 41). This information supports D. A is inaccurate because it assumes that the passage is from the perspective of Mrs. Baroda's husband, B is inaccurate because Gouvernail and Mrs. Baroda do not argue (or talk at any length), and C is inaccurate because it mistakes Mrs. Baroda's fascination with Gouvernail for dissatisfaction with her marriage (which is not anywhere described in explicitly negative terms).

QUESTION 2.

Choice A is correct. The word "provoked" describes Mrs. Baroda, who "was looking forward to a period of unbroken rest" (lines 6-7) but would instead need to entertain a guest. She would thus be a little "annoyed" to have these pleasant plans interrupted. B and D are both negative but much too extreme, while C is a positive that does not fit the context of a somewhat unwelcome change.

QUESTION 3

Choice C is correct. The paragraph explains that Mrs. Baroda had "never seen" (line 10) Gouvernail but "formed an image of him in her mind" (line 14). However, Gouvernail's actual appearance contradicts this image, and Mrs. Baroda, who expected to dislike him, "rather liked him" (line 19) in reality. This information supports C, while A refers to an issue that is SETTLED (since line 12 explains that Gouvernail was not a "society man" or "a man about town") not to a CONTRADICTION. B (Mr. Baroda's behavior) and D (Mrs. Baroda's presumed talkativeness) refer to issues that distract from the paragraph's emphasis on Mrs. Baroda's perceptions.

QUESTION 4.

Choice D is correct. As explained in the lines 10-19, Mrs. Baroda formed a mental image of Gouvernail and expected that she would not like him, but in fact found his looks unexpected and "rather liked him" (line 19). This information supports D and contradicts C, which assumes that Mrs. Baroda disliked Gouvernail. Although a likable man, Gouvernail is a "journalist" but not a "society man" (lines 11-12): in other words, he is not a powerful or prominent figure. A and B wrongly assume that he is, so eliminate these answers.

QUESTION 5.

Choice B is correct. The word "exacting" is used to explain Gouvernail's behavior, which would meet the approval of "exacting" women or women who demand excellent manners. B is thus the best answer. While A and C are inappropriate negatives, D would be most appropriate in the context of a difficult task or challenge, NOT in reference to firm standards of behavior.

223

QUESTION 6.

Choice A is correct. In lines 26-29, the author notes that Gouvernail was extremely "courteous" but made no strong attempt to win Mrs. Baroda's "approval or even esteem". This information supports A and can be used to disqualify the strong negatives C and D. (Gouvernail is easygoing, but there is no reason to assume that he is a lazy or unprincipled journalist.) B misrepresents Mrs. Baroda's true responses: Gouvernail "puzzled" (line 41) her, but mostly because she finds his personality intriguing, NOT because he is trying to hide something. In fact, his easygoing personality suggests that he is not anxious to hide anything.

QUESTION 7.

Choice C is correct. See above for the explanation of the correct answer. A describes Mrs. Baroda's preconceptions (NOT the actual Gouvernail), B indicates that Gouvernail is not as remarkable as Mr. Baroda had claimed, and D indicates that Gouvernail has settled into life on the Baroda estate. Make sure not to wrongly take these line references as justifications for negative answers to the previous question, such as Question 6 C and D.

QUESTION 8.

Choice B is correct. The author explains that Mrs. Baroda found Gouvernail "lovable" (line 42) but was still puzzled by his personality and "sought to penetrate the reserve in which he had unconsciously enveloped himself" (lines 49-50). This information supports B and can be used to eliminate the strong negatives C and D. A distorts the content of the passage: Mrs. Baroda is puzzled but cannot be in "awe" of Gouvernail because she does not think he has "brilliant and promising traits" (line 22).

QUESTION 9.

Choice B is correct. In lines 49-50, the author explains that Mrs. Baroda tried to penetrate Gouvernail's "reserve" and thus comprehend him better. This information supports B, while Mrs. Baroda does not at any point express an interest in changing Gouvernail (eliminating A) or her own circumstances (eliminating D); she simply wishes to understand Gouvernail better. C is contradicted by the passage: while Mrs. Baroda is fascinated by Gouvernail, she finds his presence to be a mild burden, as indicated in lines 51-52.

QUESTION 10.

Choice C is correct. See above for the explanation of the correct answer. A indicates Gouvernail's passivity, B indicates how pleasant Gouvernail finds life with the Barodas, and D records a few of Mrs. Baroda's slightly negative sentiments about Governail. Do not wrongly assume that the negatives in these answers justify Question 9 A or D, which both deal with possible ACTIONS, not the PERCEPTIONS that are most important to this passage.

QUESTION 11.

Choice D is correct. While Passage 1 revolves around the thesis that "people with introverted personalities have a number of innate strengths" (lines 9-10), Passage 2 notes a "shift in thinking" (line 50) in business that has led to the prioritization of "selectivity, serenity, and imagination" (lines 59-60). This information supports D and disqualifies A (since Passage 2 relies on a very clear distinction similar to the introvert-extrovert contrast in Passage 1) and C (since Passage 1 focuses on the PROFESSIONAL lives of introverts). B is a trap answer: Passage 1 notes that introverts are underestimated, but there is no reason to believe that they are not tolerated or accepted by their fellow workers.

QUESTION 12.

Choice A is correct. In lines 25-28, the author of Passage 1 notes that introvert traits are "often highly prized" mainly outside of Western business contexts. This information supports A, while B ("fields") raises an introvert-extrovert distinction that the author never addresses. C and D are both rightly positive towards introverts, but address factors that are not analyzed by the author: the IMPACT of "studies" and the PREVALENCE of "high demand" are not strictly related to the content of Passage 1.

QUESTION 13.

Choice C is correct. See above for the explanation of the correct answer. A indicates the usefulness of the introvert-extrovert distinction, B counters an assumption about the overall strengths of extroverts, and D records a psychologist's ideas about the strengths of introverts. Make sure not to wrongly take D as a justification for Question 12 C.

QUESTION 14.

Choice B is correct. The author begins the relevant paragraph by introducing the assumption that contemporary culture "rewards extroverts" (lines 8-9), but then goes on to explain how introverts "can be highly successful at relationship building" (lines 12-13) despite perceptions in favor of extroverts. This information supports B and eliminates C (which does not actually describe a contrast, because introverts both behave in reserved ways AND actually are reserved). A wrongly focuses on how well-known introvert and extrovert traits are (while the author is really concerned with unexpected CONSEQUENCES of well-known introvert and extrovert traits). D is out of scope, since no specific media and pop culture sources are mentioned.

QUESTION 15.

Choice D is correct. The phrase "get lost in" is used to explain how thoughtful employees act within a business environment, the "Googleplex" (line 38). D would effectively describe these involved or "immersed" employees, while A, B, and C are all negatives and should be readily eliminated.

QUESTION 16.

Choice C is correct. The word "visible" is used to describe the business "model" (line 49) followed by Google, a prominent company that designed a massive facility based on this model. Google has thus created a clear or "apparent" sign of a shift in business practices: C is an effective answer, while A is a negative and B and D would describe PHYSICAL items, not an ABSTRACT model or set of practices.

QUESTION 17.

Choice B is correct. The formerly popular "ideal" mentioned in line 51 involves constant activity and little relaxation or thoughtfulness; in lines 63-64, the author paraphrases McKeown's view that "more active, less thoughtful" workers face obstacles to achieving their goals. This information supports B and can be used to eliminate C (which understates the contrast between the "ideal" and the behavior of introverts) and D (which wrongly describes the "ideal" positively). A misrepresents the content of the passage: while the "ideal" is SEEN as problematic by commentators such as McKeown, there is no argument that the "ideal" yielded poor economic RESULTS.

QUESTION 18.

Choice D is correct. See above for the explanation of the correct answer. A explains what working at the Googleplex is like, B explains some of the traits of contemporary executives, and C simply reiterates the traits of the "ideal". None of these choices refers to the negative perspective on the "ideal" that the author emphasizes.

QUESTION 19.

Choice A is correct. The author of Passage 1 praises the ability of introverts to "work independently" (line 5) and "quietly reflect" (line 35). Because the Googleplex fosters independence and "contemplation" (line 45), which are depicted as thoroughly positive qualities in Passage 1, choose A ("approval"). C and D wrongly introduce doubting or negative attitudes, while B contradicts the thesis of Passage 2, since the qualities of introverts are in fact becoming more heavily prioritized in business thinking.

QUESTION 20.

Choice A is correct. While the author of Passage 1 explains that the "ability to quietly reflect" (line 35) can be a clear workplace asset, the author of Passage 2 notes the value of specific "skills of contemplation" (line 44). This information supports A, while BOTH passages criticize over-ambitious workers (eliminating B), only Passage 2 focuses on setting priorities (eliminating C), and only Passage 1 focuses on humility (and mostly mentions humility as a cause of success, not as a quality that success itself "fosters", thus eliminating D)

QUESTION 21.

Choice D is correct. In this passage, the author indicates that driving mosquitoes to extinction could "benefit humanity" (line 21), but would also present "troubling possibilities" (line 48). This balance of positive and negative considerations makes D the best answer. A is too broad (since it deals with speciecide, not mosquitoes in particular), B avoids the crucial issue of extinction, and C misstates the author's final conclusion, since the debate is somewhat inconclusive but still ecologically important or "significant".

QUESTION 22.

Choice A is correct. The word "saved" refers to the "lives" that would not be taken if fewer people were killed by mosquito-transmitted diseases: these people would be "spared" from death, so that A is the best answer. In context, it is not clear that the lives would be impacted in any other way (eliminating B), while C and D refer to processes for helping LIVING people, not directly to saving people from DEATH.

QUESTION 23.

Choice B is correct. In the relevant paragraph, the author notes that mosquitoes carry malaria and thus can contribute to loss of human life and loss of GDP. Eliminating mosquitoes in certain areas would eliminate these problems: this information supports B and can be used to eliminate C, which makes opposite assumptions. A must be eliminated because mosquitoes, although malaria carriers, are not specified as the ONLY carriers; D must be eliminated because the first paragraph, which also notes human and economic costs, is not "lighthearted" in tone.

QUESTION 24.

Choice D is correct. The words "romanticized notion" refer most directly to the idea that ecosystems are "intricate webs of life" (line 30): the author does not endorse this idea as fully accurate, so that D is the best answer. Other answers misdirect the author's intended reference or avoid the author's larger emphasis on broad ideas about ecosystems: A wrongly refers to scientists, B wrongly refers to mosquitoes only, and C wrongly refers to the extinction of mosquitoes.

QUESTION 25.

Choice B is correct. Lounibos believes that eradicating a vector species would be futile because "its niche would quickly be filled by another" (line 73). This idea corresponds to the idea articulated in the line reference for B, which states that mosquitoes are "not irreplaceable". A refers to the fact that mosquito extinction would have a small impact (both NOT directly to Lounibos's main concern, the ability to be replaced), C discusses mosquito-fighting techniques (NOT a broad ecological idea), and D refers to the potential to eliminate malaria.

QUESTION 26.

Choice A is correct. In lines 72-73, the author approvingly cites the idea that it would "be futile" to eliminate mosquitoes since another vector species could take over their role. This information supports A and can be used to eliminate B, which posits that there would be massive ecological consequences to eliminating mosquitoes. C refers to an irrelevant issue (since the author is mostly interested in preserving human life), as does D (since mosquitoes are described in the passage as carriers of diseases, not as carriers of pollen).

QUESTION 27.

Choice D is correct. See above for the explanation of the correct answer. A indicates that bats are believed to depend on mosquitoes for food, B indicates that a fish species is believed to depend on mosquitoes for food, and C compares methods that could be used to eradicate species. None of these answers align with answers to the previous question, which only mention insect and amphibian species (Question 26 B) and plant species (Question 26 D).

QUESTION 28.

Choice C is correct. The word "elegant" refers to "genetics-based solutions" that, relative to other solutions, are not "destructive": a solution that achieves a desired end without causing undue destruction would be useful, effective, or "practical". C is an effective answer: A and D both refer to how PLEASING or SOPHISTICATED such a solution would be, while B is contradicted by the content of the passage, since the solutions involve the extinction of species and are (at least in this respect) harmful.

QUESTION 29.

Choice B is correct. Although the author notes that "not all scientists are optimistic" (line 69) about engineering the extinction of mosquitoes, the author himself ultimately notes that mosquito extinction efforts could improve "the lives of millions" (lines 77-78). This information supports B, which is a qualified positive. A neglects the author's awareness that eliminating mosquitoes could be problematic, while C and D must be eliminated because they are negative overall.

QUESTION 30.

Choice A is correct. The author notes that mosquitoes can "directly affect a country's GDP" (lines 18-19) in a negative fashion: according to the graph, Africa has the largest percentage of annual human deaths from mosquitoes (55%). Because the relation between the harmful activities of mosquitoes and GDP loss is direct, A is the best answer: B, C, and D all represent continents or countries with significantly smaller percentages.

QUESTION 31.

Choice A is correct. According to the passage, diseases carried by mosquitoes are concentrated "in emerging countries in tropical zones, including nations in South America and Africa" (lines 16-17). The information in the graph directly supports this point in the author's argument about the effects of targeting and eradicating mosquitoes in order to prevent cases of such diseases. A is an effective answer while B wrongly assumes that the author (who already knows which diseases mosquitoes carry) would reject a chart that clarifies his ideas about disease locations. C misreads the graph, which (instead of not containing "enough" information about environmental impact) does not contain ANY information about environmental impact whatsoever. D is too clearly negative (and wrongly assumes that the author would disagree with a purely factual chart).

QUESTION 32.

Choice D is correct. In lines 9-11, Stowe explains that the existence of a "class" of educated and prosperous women who do their own work (as explained in lines 2-8) is "peculiar [or unique] to America". This information supports D. Stowe's main contrast in the passage is between women who work and women who do not: feminist ideology is not a major or direct consideration (eliminating A), maids are described as occupying an elevated role only in America ITSELF (eliminating B), and the contrast between men and women is not given substantial discussion (eliminating C).

QUESTION 33.

Choice B is correct. See above for the explanation of the correct answer. A offers Stowe's definition of a woman, C describes how American maids would sometimes take on new responsibilities, and D indicates that American ladies would maintain authority even over skilled maids. All of these answers describe America directly, rather than considering countries other than America.

QUESTION 34.

Choice B is correct. The phrase "peculiar to" is used to describe the "class" (line 9) of ladies who do their own work; earlier, Stowe notes that "America is the only country" where such a class can be found. The existence of such a class is thus "unique to" America; choose B and eliminate A, which is an unjustified negative. C and D indicate the exact OPPOSITE of Stowe's actual point, if women who do their own work are characteristic of America they cannot also be "unconventional" or "unusual" in this national context.

QUESTION 35.

Choice D is correct. In lines 14-16, Stowe explains that American "colonists" (line 12) abandoned "feudal and aristocratic" values for a "democratic" arrangement. This information supports D, while Stowe never mentions the geography of "small towns" (eliminating A) and describes the colonists as "intelligent people" in line 25 (eliminating B). Although Stowe does mention that the colonists in New England did not take well to slavery (lines 33-35), she focuses on slavery in this area ONLY and never in fact describes the abolitionist movement or the texts it produced (eliminating C).

QUESTION 36.

Choice A is correct. See above for the explanation of the correct answer. B offers praise for how the colonists approached the question of labor, C indicates that New England colonists opposed slavery, and D indicates that New England colonists did their own work. Make sure not to wrongly take C as a justification for Question 35 C.

QUESTION 37.

Choice D is correct. In the second paragraph, Stowe describes the situation of a "Mistress and maid" (line 20): if the maid were to prove physically stronger, the mistress would maintain "her superiority by skill and contrivance" (lines 28-29). This information supports D, while other answers distort the content of the passage. Stowe does describe slaves (fourth paragraph, A) and marriage (fifth paragraph C), but never in relation to the question of stronger and weaker women (primarily the second paragraph). Stowe is also concerned primarily with PRACTICAL knowledge, not with FORMAL education (eliminating B).

QUESTION 38.

Choice C is correct. The word "rude" is paired with the word "unskilled" (line 38) and indicates work that is not thorough or attractive: "crude" would properly reflect this context. A ("violent") is out of context and is too strongly negative, while B and D would both refer to the kind of PEOPLE who might perform the work, not to the work itself.

QUESTION 39.

Choice A is correct. The words in the relevant line references refer to the "execution" (line 40) of a specific, positive type of "labor" (line 41) favored by New England colonists: the taste for such work, and the distaste for the inferior work of slaves, explains why slavery "never suited" (line 34) New England. This information supports A and can be used to eliminate B (since disciplinary methods are never mentioned) and D (since the consequences of slavery, NOT the means of eliminating slavery, are Stowe's focus). C wrongly shifts the focus of the passage: the comparison between the work of New Englanders and the work of slaves is neglected entirely in this answer, even though this answer rightly characterizes New Englanders in a positive manner.

QUESTION 40.

Choice C is correct. In the fourth paragraph (lines 33-49), Stowe explains that New Englanders opposed slavery "from conscientious principle" (lines 36-37) because the "clumsiness" (line 41) of the work of slaves was incompatible with the high standards of work set by New Englanders. This information supports C and can be used to eliminate D (which rightly states opposition to slavery, but cites the wrong primary reason, "cruelty"). A and B both wrongly assume that slavery was "prevalent" or "popular" in New England, when it in fact "never suited" (line 34) the region in Stowe's account.

QUESTION 41.

Choice C is correct. In the fifth paragraph (lines 50-69), Stowe contrasts "helpers" (line 53) with "servants" (line 54): helpers were present in American society, which "was a society of educated workers, where all were practically equal" (lines 55-56), while servants had a different, unequal relationship with their masters. This information supports C and can be used to eliminate A (which wrongly assumes that servants were prominent in America) and D (which wrongly states unequal social status as a characteristic of helpers). B must be eliminated because Stowe indicates that helpers were part of cooperative and "equalized" (line 65) communities, NOT that they were motivated by debt or other negative forces.

QUESTION 42.

Choice D is correct. The passage discusses "extreme organisms" (line 13) in the deep sea and analyzes two such organisms that have recently been discovered, the "Ceratioid Anglerfish" (line 18) and an organism "that partially resembles a jellyfish, partially a mushroom" (line 63). This information supports D, while A is incorrect because the two organisms primarily considered are noticeably DIFFERENT and B is incorrect because the two organisms were not found as part of a SINGLE study. C rightly refers to biological anomalies, but wrongly refers to the "history" of such unusual organisms, since the author mainly considers events from the recent past.

QUESTION 43.

Choice C is correct. The paragraph begins by recording the findings of "Scientists" interested in "extreme organisms" (line 13) and transitions to a consideration of a specific fish species found in the "Midnight Zone" (line 22). This information supports C and can be used to eliminate elements of other answers. A wrongly characterizes the "Midnight Zone" as "highly researched" (when in fact only a few years worth of research are being considered), B wrongly indicates that the mostly informative opening of this paragraph involves an "argument", and D wrongly assumes that the author BEGINS with a description of the Midnight Zone.

QUESTION 44.

Choice D is correct. In lines 22-25, the author describes the area of the ocean where the Ceratioid Anglerfish have been found and where there is "no natural sunlight" and "plant growth" is nonexistent. This information supports D, since the area is hostile to a large group of organisms, plants. Although the new anglerfish is unlike other anglerfish species and exhibits land-animal traits such as female-favoring "sexual dimorphism" (line 38) the author never directly argues that these anglerfish are "descendants" of land animals (eliminating A) or that they inhabit a different location than other anglerfish (eliminating C). B is illogical because the Ceratioid Anglerfish is a NEW, never-before-encountered species.

QUESTION 45.

Choice B is correct. See above for the explanation of the correct answer. A states the location where the anglerfish was discovered, C states that the Ceratioid Anglerfish is unlike earlier-discovered anglerfish species, and D states that both Ceratioid Anglerfish and land-based organisms exhibit sexual dimorphism. Do not wrongly take A as evidence for Question 44 B, C as evidence for Question 44 C, and D as evidence for Question 44 A.

QUESTION 46.

Choice B is correct. The word "form" refers to "sexual dimorphism", a tendency that appears or is "expressed" in the Ceratioid Anglerfish and other animals. B is thus an effective answer. A would best refer to a rule or a necessity (not an expression or manifestation of a phenomenon), while C and D (though they seem relevant to the discussion of anglerfish anatomy) do not capture the idea of manifesting DIFFERENT TYPES as well as "expression" does.

QUESTION 47.

Choice A is correct. The word "experiments" refers to "organisms" (line 65) that puzzle researchers and that approximate "multi-cellular life" (line 67) in unusual ways. A, "attempts at", effectively describes organisms that approached a certain condition. B, C, and D refer to human ACTIVITIES or INITIATIVES: these choices are loosely relevant to a discussion of scientists but do not, as demanded by the structure of the sentence, describe the "organisms" that the author is analyzing.

QUESTION 48.

Choice C is correct. The parenthetical statement describes "adult males" (line 46) of the Ceratioid Anglerfish species; these males attach to the much larger females and can be mistaken for parts of the females' bodies (indicating a sexual dimorphism that favors females). This information supports C. The tone of the information in parentheses is objective and factual, not humorous (even though the information may seem strange, eliminating A). The author neither discusses a CAUSE nor offers ADVICE: thus, eliminate B and D as inaccurate in terms of how the information functions.

QUESTION 49.

Choice D is correct. In lines 65-66, the author relates the idea that a group of newly-discovered organisms has proven "difficult to categorise" (line 65). This information most directly supports D, which rightly cites a confused or blurred classification distinction. A and B may be true of recent organisms, but are never presented as major points of discussion among scientists; C wrongly turns a basic fact (that the new organisms live deep in the sea) into a faulty assumption (that they were believed to live higher up).

QUESTION 50.

Choice B is correct. See above for the explanation of the correct answer. A indicates that the discoveries are important (but does not specify exactly why), C notes that there is ongoing uncertainty and that deep sea areas fascinate scientists, and D records the depth at which a group of new organisms was discovered. None of these answers presents a BELIEF that aligns with the particulars of the previous question.

QUESTION 51.

Choice C is correct. According to the passage, the "Midnight Zone" begins at "just under 3000 feet under the ocean" (lines 23-24) and thus corresponds to the Aphotic Zone (3300 feet under). In this zone, 15% of species exhibit sexual parasitism. Choose C: do not wrongly determine sexual parasitism in the Euphotic Zone (corresponding to A) or in the Disphotic Zone (corresponding to B), and make sure not to determine sexual dimorphism in the Aphotic Zone (corresponding to D).

QUESTION 52.

Choice A is correct. The author indicates that sexual parasitism is a "means of survival" (line 55) in the harsh conditions of the "Midnight Zone": this could explain why, as temperatures lower and conditions become harsher lower in the ocean, an increasingly large percentage of species exhibit sexual parasitism. This information supports A: the author never considers population density even though the TABLE does, eliminating B and D. C is contradicted by the data, since this answer wrongly assumes that sexual parasitism is IMPOSSIBLE in the Aphotic Zone and the overlapping "Midnight Zone".

Section 2: Writing
Passage 1, All in the Elephant Family

QUESTION 1.

Choice D is correct. In this paragraph, this author describes dangers such as "poaching and development" and reasons to "protect" elephants. Thus, elephants would be threatened or "endangered" by such influences. Other answers, though negative, distort the passage's meaning: A primarily indicates that the elephants are frightened, B indicates that the elephants are seen as villains, and C refers to undermining or rebellion, not to basic dangers.

QUESTION 2.

Choice A is correct. The underlined portion must further describe how elephants interact with one another: A offers a specific explanation of the small, female-led elephant social structures, which are discussed further in the passage. The other answers refer to factors unrelated to the question's keywords: B introduces other animals, C voices incomprehension rather than offering an explanation, and D introduces popular culture.

QUESTION 3.

Choice B is correct. Make sure that the underlined portion follows proper style, grammar, and logic. While C and D both introduce comma splices, A presents an awkward phrasing and assumes that the "fields" are taking action or "being", when in fact the fields simply "include" different options. B, "including", is the best linkage.

QUESTION 4.

Choice B is correct. In context, the author is comparing "elephant social structures to human social networks": to extend this comparison, the underlined portion must refer to a smaller group within a "university department". B, "research group", is an effective choice. A and D refer to groups, but NOT groups within a "university department", while C only refers to a single individual.

QUESTION 5.

Choice D is correct. This statement concludes Goldenberg's discussion of elephant society by introducing new and specific terminology: she has already used and explained the social network analogy (eliminating C) and is here focusing primarily on elephant society itself. Because the paragraph does NOT in fact focus primarily on universities or Goldenberg's reputation, eliminate A and B, respectively.

QUESTION 6.

Choice B is correct. The underlined portion must describe a group of elephants: since elephants can be counted, A and C (which are normally used to describe NON-COUNTABLE quantities) must be eliminated. D, "fewest", would describe the smallest possible group: the sentence instead requires a group that numbers below ten, or "fewer" than ten, elephants. Thus, B is the best answer.

QUESTION 7.

Choice A is correct. The graph compares the dry season (when elephant groups number below 50) to the wet season (when elephant groups number 300 and above). A effectively sums up the size of elephant groupings during the "wet season", while C wrongly states that wet season groups are smaller than 100 elephants. Both B and D refer to times when survival is difficult, yet these times are not directly designated in the graph.

QUESTION 8.

Choice A is correct. The underlined portion should describe HOW "sophisticated" the social structures are: "relatively" is an effective modifying adverb for "sophisticated". B provides two adjectives, C provides two adverbs, and D changes the meaning of the sentence entirely.

QUESTION 9.

Choice D is correct. This question requires close attention to sentence structure: while A involves a comma splice, B involves a pronoun ("which") with an unclear reference and C introduces a sentence fragment after the semicolon. Only D offers a proper construction, since "interacting" effectively refers to the "bull elephants" mentioned earlier.

QUESTION 10.

Choice B is correct. This sentence involves an inverted subject-verb combination: the subject of the underlined portion is the "sense of compassion" that "is" remarkable. Eliminate plural answers A and C, and avoid D because elephants and their behavior are described in present tense throughout the paragraph.

QUESTION 11.

Choice B is correct. While sentence 2 introduces the topic of elephant matriarchs, sentence 3 provides an example of how matriarchs and their descendants preserve "longstanding social ties". The new statement should thus serve as a linkage between two sentences: A would wrongly place the new statement BEFORE the discussion of elephant matriarchs, while C and D would place the somewhat general statement AFTER the example that it should lead into.

Passage 2, Flexing Your Time

QUESTION 12.

Choice D is correct. The underlined portion should provide a verb that aligns with "Tammy Hunter", the subject of the sentence. D properly creates the phrase "Tammy Hunter . . . found", while A and C both create fragments and B creates a comma splice.

QUESTION 13.

Choice A is correct. For this question, find a phrase involving a DIRECT reference to Hunter's personal life: "a meal with her children" would refer directly to Hunter's life outside of work. B refers to the phone calls Hunter received, C indicates how Hunter balanced her obligations, and D refers to other professions: none of these directly describe what Hunter was doing outside of work.

QUESTION 14.

Choice C is correct. The passage as a whole is about flex time, and the remainder of this paragraph talks about the different by-the-hour arrangements that flex time allows. This information, which defines flex time, does not occur elsewhere (since the author shifts to considering positives and negatives later, eliminating A) and in fact EXPLAINS some of Hunter's problems (eliminating B). Here, the author is presenting facts, not an argument: eliminate D for attributing the wrong function to the underlined content.

QUESTION 15.

Choice B is correct. The sentence should involve a contrast between "Some employees" and "others" for the best possible parallelism: eliminate singular choices A and C. While D assumes a similarity with "and", B properly introduces a contrast with "while" and is thus the best answer.

QUESTION 16.

Choice B is correct. The underlined verb should be in parallel with "leaves", since it describes a second thing that Hunter does. B, "makes" is thus the best answer: A is an -ing form and C and D are both past tense forms that are not as clearly in parallel as the present-tense "makes".

QUESTION 17.

Choice C is correct. The pronoun "They" should directly refer to the preceding noun "government agencies", which are "employers" that must deal with "their employees" as described in the sentence containing the underlined portion. C is an effective choice, while A and D are both singular (creating disagreement with the pronoun "their") and B is illogical, since employees would not be likely to have their own employees in context.

QUESTION 18.

Choice A is correct. In the original, a semicolon is properly used to combine two independent clauses ("That is", "a . . . study found"), while B introduces a comma splice. Both C (condition or hypothetical) and D (contrast) introduce sentence relationships that do not fit the content, since the author is simply EXPLAINING how the finding is "not a trifling matter".

QUESTION 19.

Choice B is correct. While previous paragraphs have discussed the apparent assets of flex scheduling, this paragraph calls attention to the limitations and "tension" that flex scheduling can involve: B effectively shifts to these negatives. A refers directly to Hunter, C to legal measures, and D to the Georgetown University study: these topics are addressed only, if at all, in previous paragraphs.

QUESTION 20.

Choice A is correct. As originally constructed, the subject "Having" takes the verb "creates", so that the sentence is grammatically correct. B needlessly introduces the pronoun "you" (which is not used elsewhere), C introduces an ambiguous "they", and D gives the sentence a plural subject, "Some positions with flextime options and some without", that cannot agree with "creates".

QUESTION 21.

Choice B is correct. The original phrasing in A inappropriately describes employers, since an "opportunist" is someone who takes easy or unfair advantage. While B is a more neutral phrasing that simply means "to utilize to one's benefit", C and D are both too colloquial or informal for the style of this passage.

QUESTION 22.

Choice D is correct. The underlined portion should involve a noun modified by an adjective, since this portion takes the verb "will diminish". A wrongly pairs an adverb with a noun, B does not contain a noun, and C indicates that "flextime" is "associating" or "socializing" and thus creates an illogical meaning. Only D fulfills all requirements for both logic and grammar.

QUESTION 23.

Choice C is correct. The underlined portion must describe the Apache, who "were on the warpath". A and B are both redundant (since it is already clear that the Apache appeared in "Wild west films"), while D involves defective parallelism. Only C properly reiterates the "were" construction introduced earlier.

QUESTION 24.

Choice A is correct. The underlined portion requires a second noun that is in parallel with "superiority": the singular "fact" is an excellent choice. B introduces a dependent clause, C introduces a plural noun, and D wrongly puts "superiority" in parallel with "defending", which can function as an adjective.

QUESTION 25.

Choice C is correct. In context, the author is describing a few different characters in movies: the underlined pronoun should refer to Flash Gordon, "he", as the nearest noun that fits the passage's meaning. A and B both introduce plurals rather than describing a single hero, while D, "one", cannot be used interchangeably with "he" even though both are singular.

QUESTION 26.

Choice D is correct. Throughout the passage, the author praises heroes such as Nyoka who opposed powerful forces to defend justice: the underlined portion offers detail explaining how Zorro acted similarly. This phrase should thus be kept. The author never claims that Zorro and Flash Gordon are indistinguishable (only similar, eliminating A), never outlines the reader's own possible knowledge (eliminating B), and only discusses Zorro in this paragraph (eliminating C).

QUESTION 27.

Choice A is correct. In this paragraph, the author is describing how a "local cinema offered a program for children": the program's contents should be described in the same past tense. A rightly involves a simple past tense, while B and C are appropriate only for action that continues into the present (which the program apparently does not, since it was from the author's youth), while D introduces a future tense.

QUESTION 28.

Choice A is correct. The underlined portion should indicate that relief was "soon to happen" or "accessible": "at hand" is a common English phrase that takes these meanings. Both B and C are words that mean PHYSICALLY nearby or related in REASONING (respectively), while D is too wordy and informal for the passage.

QUESTION 29.

Choice C is correct. Because the author has already established Nyoka as a female character and later describes how she starred in her own film series, eliminate A and B as redundant. While D simply registers the author's uncertainty, C indicates that the author was more drawn to Nyoka than to Tarzan and thus returns to one of the passage's most important ideas (how closely the author related to different characters).

QUESTION 30.

Choice B is correct. Coordinate both grammar and punctuation for this question. While both C and D introduce comma splices, A wrongly uses a single comma to divide the subject "problem" from the verb "discouraged". B is thus the most effective answer since it employs proper colon and comma placement.

QUESTION 31.

Choice D is correct. The underlined pronoun must be replaced by a noun that involves "storylines": while people (A, C) and "values" (B) would not be appropriate choices, narrative "films" such as those discussed earlier would involve storylines. D is thus the best answer.

QUESTION 32.

Choice C is correct. In context, the author is describing two complementary obstacles: the lake covered in burning oil would be located "before" or in front, while the hordes would be "behind". A is incorrect because the obstacles are presented as simultaneous, NOT in sequence; B and D both set up contrasts, NOT two aspects of a single scene.

QUESTION 33.

Choice C is correct. While paragraph 2 describes the "climax of the morning's entertainment", paragraph 3 introduces the early stages of the film program. Thus, paragraph 2 should be removed from this incorrect position (eliminating A) and placed directly after paragraph 3, or before paragraph 4. While B would place the paragraph too early, explaining the events of the film showcase before setting the context, D would place the discussion of the early features even FARTHER after the discussion of the climax.

Passage 4, Vacation, Without the Travel

QUESTION 34.

Choice B is correct. The relevant sentence should describe two past actions: first, the writer "had just checked" in, then "was making" his way to his room. Such "had" forms are appropriate for the earlier of two past actions. A (a "have" form) wrongly indicates an action that continues into the present, B indicates a possibility (not a completed action), and D is in present tense.

QUESTION 35.

Choice A is correct. In the first sentence of this paragraph, the author mentions the "strange sight" in the hotel. Because the underlined sentence simply re-phrases the idea that the sight is "strange", this sentence is redundant and should be eliminated. The sentence refers only to the writer's basic impression: it does not explain WHY the author has this impression (eliminating B), sum up the main idea about close-to-home vacations (eliminating C), or allude to other, later "attractions" (which are mostly American, eliminating D).

QUESTION 36.

Choice B is correct. In the later portions of the paragraph, the author explains why the Russians arranged their hotels in a particular way or outlines their "reasons": B anticipates this discussion effectively. While A ("things") and C ("lots of ideas") are more colloquial and imprecise, D uses needlessly elevated diction and refers to "musings" (or loose thoughts) rather than solid reasons.

QUESTION 37.

Choice A is correct. The writer is here describing how people acted in earlier "Russian society", so that A is the best answer in the context of the paragraph as a whole. B only refers to a few Russians, not to the broad category of "Russians of that era" that interests the writer, while C and D both wrongly refer to present-day individuals.

QUESTION 38.

Choice D is correct. For this question, check for idiomatic errors: the writer is explaining how people have disregarded certain attractions in the hotel, or do not have much "use for" them. While A is an English usage for things that would be used ALONGSIDE one another, B and C are not standard idioms.

QUESTION 39.

Choice C is correct. The writer is describing a tactic that has been used to address the "reality" of "Time consuming-travel", so that C properly coordinates the content of the passage. While A is wrongly negative towards the "companies" (which the author later describes as effective in their tactics), B assumes that tourism to Russia (not Russian leisure TACTICS) is the primary interest of these companies. D eliminates a needed transition and thus creates a comma splice.

QUESTION 40.

Choice A is correct. The original construction properly uses to adjectives, "growing" and "prospering", to describe the "communities". A is thus the best answer: C and D wrongly refer directly to the "communities" using adjectives, while B is an awkward phrasing that both distorts the meaning of the sentence and places an adverb directly before a noun.

QUESTION 41.

Choice B is correct. The underlined pronoun should refer to "people", so that "who" is the only appropriate choice. A refers to a thing, B refers to a place, and D introduces an illogical cause and effect, since the inability to travel does not CAUSE the numbers of people to be large.

QUESTION 42.

Choice A is correct. The portion between dashes must be coordinated so that the sentence makes sense even if this portion is removed. A, "and seasonal attractions . . . all under one roof", both preserves the parallelism with the earlier nouns and follows this sentence structure rule. C ("and seasonal . . . all") and D ("and . . . such as") both break the parallelism with the earlier nouns when the portion between dashes is removed; B results in the grammatically incorrect phrase "such as . . . all under one roof") when the portion between dashes is removed.

QUESTION 43.

Choice B is correct. The relevant sentence should place three verbs, which all take the subject "you", in parallel: B yields parallelism involving "find", "drop", and "settle", while A needlessly repeats "you" at the end of the sentence. C wrongly introduces a past tense, while D wrongly introduces an -ing form that can function as an adjective.

QUESTION 44.

Choice D is correct. The prompt for this question calls for a description of the "relative ease" of visiting the "Great Wolf Lodge": pointing out that only "a short car-ride" is necessary for such a vacation would fulfill this requirement. A is negative in tone (and involves a speculation, not a fact), B is also negative and deals mostly with travel by plane, and C addresses the reader without addressing or suggesting anything about the ease of visiting a Great Wolf Lodge.

Section 3: Math Test - No Calculator

QUESTION 1.

Choice C is correct. Substituting 5 for h yields $3 + 5(x-4) = 33$. Subtracting 3 from both sides yields $5(x-4) = 30$ and dividing by 5 gives $x - 4 = 6$, or $x = 10$.

Choice A is incorrect and may result from distributing the 5, combining like terms, and subtracting 17 from both sides rather than adding 17 to both sides. Choice B is incorrect and may result from errors in applying the distributive property appropriately. Choice D is incorrect and may result from solving for $5x$ rather than x.

QUESTION 2.

Choice A is correct. If Manny can ride his bicycle 5 miles in h hours and Manny rides h hours each day, then by substituting 5 miles for h hours, one knows that Manny rides 5 miles each day. So, if Manny rode his bicycle for d days at 5 miles per day, than Manny rode a total of $5d$ miles.

Choice B is incorrect and may result from incorrectly interpreting that Manny travels at a rate of 5 miles per hour and h represents the number of hours that Manny rides per day. Choices C and D are incorrect and may result from errors in calculating Manny's total mileage.

QUESTION 3.

Choice C is correct. Factoring $5x$ out of the expression $5x^2 - 20xy$ yields $5x(x-4y)$. Factoring $3y$ out of the expression $3xy - 12y^2$ yields $3y(x-4y)$. Substituting

$5x(x-4y)$ for $5x^2 - 20xy$ and $3y(x-4y)$ for $3xy - 12y^2$ in the expression $\dfrac{5x^2 - 20xy}{3xy - 12y^2}$

yields $\dfrac{5x(x-4y)}{3y(x-4y)}$, or simply $\dfrac{5x}{3y}$.

Choices A, B, and D are incorrect and may result from errors in properly factoring and simplifying the original expression.

QUESTION 4.

Choice B is correct. Expanding the expression $(-1+i)(-3+2i)$ yields $(-1)(-3) + (-1)(2i) + (i)(-3) + (i)(2i)$ which simplifies to $3 + -2i - 3i + 2i^2$, or $3 - 5i + 2i^2$. Substituting $\sqrt{-1}$ for i in the expression $2i^2$ yields $3 - 5i + 2(\sqrt{-1})^2$ which simplifies to $3 - 5i - 2$, or simply $1 - 5i$.

Choices A, C, and D are incorrect and may result from errors in expanding the expression $(-1+i)(-3+2i)$. For example, Choice A is incorrect because $(-1)(2i) + (i)(-3)$ was accidentally combined as $-1i$.

QUESTION 5.

Choice D is correct. The equation $B = 5{,}500(1.01)^t$ is an exponential growth model in the form $y = a(1+r)^t$, where a is the initial value and r is the percent growth in decimal form. Rewriting the equation $B = 5{,}500(1.01)^t$ in the form $B = 5{,}500(1+.01)^t$ reveals the percent of growth as .01, or 1%. Therefore, the constant 1.01 in the equation $B = 5{,}500(1.01)^t$ implies that the account balance will grow by 1% per year.

Choice A is incorrect because the account balance will never decrease for $t > 0$. Choices B and C are incorrect and may result from computational errors when converting to a percentage from decimal form.

QUESTION 6.

Choice A is correct. If the gamer were to use the equation to estimate total points, p, from the number of competitions entered, c, the equation should be solved for p in terms of c. Adding $9c$ to both sides of the equation $3p - 9c = 120$ yields $3p = 9c + 120$ and dividing both sides of this equation by 3 yields the the equation $p = 3c + 40$. In this form, it is apparent that the increase in the total of number of points per competition is equivalent to the slope, or the coefficient attached to the number of competitions entered, c. Therefore the increase in total points per competition is 3.

Choices A, B, and C are incorrect and may result from errors in converting the equation $3p - 9c = 120$ into an equivalent form where the change in total points per competition, or the slope, is present as a coefficient in the equation.

QUESTION 7.

Choice B is correct. Dividing both sides of $b = \dfrac{a}{5}$ by a yields $\dfrac{b}{a} = \dfrac{1}{5}$. Substituting $\dfrac{1}{5}$ for $\dfrac{b}{a}$ in the expression $\dfrac{25b}{a}$ yields $25(\dfrac{1}{5})$, or 5.

Choices A, C, and D are incorrect and may result from substitution errors when substituting for $\dfrac{b}{a}$. For example, Choice D is incorrect because 5 was substituted for $\dfrac{b}{a}$ instead of $\dfrac{1}{5}$ which yields $25(5) = 125$.

QUESTION 8.

Choice D is correct. Since $f(x) = \dfrac{b}{2}x^2$, it follows that $f(8) = \dfrac{b}{2}(8)^2$ being that 8 is in the place of x. Substituting 96 for $f(8)$ as defined by the question yields $96 = \dfrac{b}{2}(8)^2$. Multiplying both sides of the equation by 2 and squaring the 8 yields $192 = 64b$, or $b = 3$. This yields the equation $f(x) = \dfrac{3}{2}x^2$. Substituting 2 for x gives $f(2) = \dfrac{3}{2}(2)^2 = 6$.

Choices A, B, and C are incorrect and may result from substitution errors and/or calculation errors.

QUESTION 9.

Choice B is correct. If line k is perpendicular to the line with the equation $y = -\frac{1}{2}x + 7$, it has an equation with an opposite reciprocal slope, or a slope of 2. The equation of line k follows the form $y = 2x + b$. Substituting the point $(4,0)$ into this form of the equation for line k yields $(0) = 2(4) + b$, or $b = -8$. Therefore, the equation for line k is $y = 2x - 8$. Substituting the point $(2,-4)$ yields $(-4) = 2(2) - 8$, which is a true statement. Therefore the point $(2,-4)$ lies on line k.

Choices A, C, and D are incorrect because none of the coordinate points lie on the line with the equation $y = 2x - 8$.

QUESTION 10.

Choice C is correct. In the equation $S = \dfrac{(\frac{320}{h})(h-8)}{64B} - MPh$, making $x = (\frac{320}{h})(h-8)$

and $y = MPh$ yields a much more basic equation, $S = \dfrac{x}{64B} - y$. Adding y to both

sides gives $S + y = \dfrac{x}{64B}$ and multiplying each side by $64B$ yields $64B(S + y) = x$.

Dividing both sides of $64B(S + y) = x$ by $64(S + y)$ yields $B = \dfrac{x}{64(S + y)}$.

Substituting $x = (\frac{320}{h})(h-8)$ and $y = MPh$ back into this form of the equation yields

$B = \dfrac{(\frac{320}{h})(h-8)}{64(S + MPh)}$.

Choices A, B, and D are incorrect and may result from errors in correctly applying the order of operations when solving for B.

QUESTION 11.

Choice D is correct. If the system of equations $\begin{array}{l} 12x - 2y = 21 \\ -4x + Ay = -7 \end{array}$ is true for all values

of x and y, the two linear equations are the same and have infinitely many solutions.

Multiplying the second equation by -3 yields $12x - 3Ay = 21$. Looking at the system in

elimination form, $\begin{array}{l} 12x - 2y = 21 \\ 12x - 3Ay = 21 \end{array}$, it is apparent that -2 must be equivalent to $-3A$ in

order to have infinitely many solutions. Solving $-2 = -3A$ for A yields $A = \dfrac{2}{3}$.

Choices A, B, and C are incorrect and may result from errors in simplifying the system and calculating the correct value for A. For example, Choice A is incorrect because the

coefficients in the second equation are $-\dfrac{1}{3}$ times the coefficients in the first equation, but

$-\dfrac{1}{3}$ is the multiplier, not the value of A. $-\dfrac{1}{3}(-2) = \dfrac{2}{3}$, which is the correct value of A.

QUESTION 12.

Choice A is correct. The first phone service provider's long-distance billing can be represented by the equation $C = 1 + .03(m - 2)$, where C is the total cost of a long-distance call in dollars and m is overall call length in minutes. The second service provider's long-distance billing can be represented by the equation $C = .05m$, where C is the total cost of a long-distance call in dollars and m is the overall call length in minutes. Setting the two equations equal to each other yields $1 + .03(m - 2) = .05m$. Distributing .03 yields $1 + .03m - .06 = .05m$, or $.94 + .03m = .05m$. Subtracting $.03m$ from either side yields $.94 = .02m$, or simply $m = 47$ minutes. Substituting 47 back into the equation $C = .05m$ yields $C = .05(47) = 2.35$, or a call that costs \$2.35.

Choice B is incorrect and may result from calculating the incorrect call length by adding .06 to 1 instead of subtracting .06 from 1 when solving for m. Choice C is incorrect because 47 is the length of the phone call in minutes, not the cost of the phone call in dollars. Choice D is incorrect because 53 would be the length of the phone call in minutes if one were to add .06 to 1 instead of subtracting .06 from 1 when solving for m.

QUESTION 13.

Choice B is correct. Converting every part of the expression $\dfrac{16^x \bullet 4^y}{2}$ to a base of 2 yields $\dfrac{2^{4x} \bullet 2^{2y}}{2^1}$. The laws of exponents state that when one multiplies two powers with the same base one can add the exponents. Therefore, $\dfrac{2^{4x} \bullet 2^{2y}}{2^1}$ can be rewritten as $\dfrac{2^{4x+2y}}{2^1}$. The laws of exponents also state that when one divides powers with the same base one can subtract the exponents. Therefore, $\dfrac{2^{4x} \bullet 2^{2y}}{2^1}$ can be rewritten as $2^{4x+2y-1}$. Given that $4x + 2y - 1 = 5$, substituting 5 for $4x + 2y - 1$ yields 2^5, or 32.

Choices A, C, and D are incorrect and may result from errors in converting to the correct base. For example, D is incorrect because 1,024 is 4^5, not 2^5.

QUESTION 14.

Choice A is correct. In the equation $m(x^2 - b^2) = (2x - 1)(2x + 1)$, distributing m on the left and expanding the right hand side yields $mx^2 - mb^2 = 4x^2 - 1$. Looking at the symmetry of the equation, one can see that $mx^2 = 4x^2$, in which m clearly equals 4. By the same symmetry, $-mb^2 = -1$ and substituting 4 for m yields $-4b^2 = -1$. Dividing both sides of the equation by -4 yields $b^2 = \dfrac{1}{4}$ and after taking the square root of both sides, $b = \pm\dfrac{1}{2}$. Since the question states that $b < 0$, $-\dfrac{1}{2}$ is the correct value for b.

Choice B is incorrect and may result from an error in squaring instead of square rooting when solving the equation $b^2 = \dfrac{1}{4}$. Choices C and D are incorrect because they are positive solutions and the question states $b < 0$.

QUESTION 15.

Choice A is correct. In order to simplify the expression $\dfrac{\frac{1}{x-1}+\frac{1}{x-2}}{4x-6}$, one must create a common denominator in order to add the fractions in the numerator. Multiplying $\dfrac{1}{x-1}$ by $\dfrac{x-2}{x-2}$ and multiplying $\dfrac{1}{x-2}$ by $\dfrac{x-1}{x-1}$ yields $\dfrac{\frac{1}{x-1}\bullet\frac{x-2}{x-2}+\frac{1}{x-2}\bullet\frac{x-1}{x-1}}{4x-6}$. This expression simplifies to $\dfrac{\frac{x-2}{(x-1)(x-2)}+\frac{x-1}{(x-1)(x-2)}}{4x-6}$, and after adding the fractions in the numerator, the expression becomes $\dfrac{\frac{2x-3}{(x-1)(x-2)}}{4x-6}$. Since dividing by $4x-6$ is the same as multiplying by $\dfrac{1}{4x-6}$, the expression $\dfrac{\frac{2x-3}{(x-1)(x-2)}}{4x-6}$ can be rewritten as $\dfrac{2x-3}{(x-1)(x-2)}\bullet\dfrac{1}{4x-6}$. Factoring a 2 out of $4x-6$ yields $\dfrac{2x-3}{(x-1)(x-2)}\bullet\dfrac{1}{2(2x-3)}$ which allows one to cancel the expression $2x-3$ from the numerator and the denominator, which yields $\dfrac{1}{(x-1)(x-2)}\bullet\dfrac{1}{2}$. Finally, multiplying and expanding the denominator yields the correct expression, $\dfrac{1}{2x^2-6x+4}$.

Choices B, C, and D are incorrect and may result from errors in simplifying a rational expression and/or errors in applying the rules of division to fractions.

QUESTION 16.

The correct answer is 3. Factoring the left hand side of the equation $2x^2-9x+4<0$ yields $(2x-1)(x-4)<0$. The factors $2x-1$ and $x-4$ yield the roots $\dfrac{1}{2}$ and 4. Since the quadratic equation $y=2x^2-9x+4$ is concave up, or opens upward, all values of x between $\dfrac{1}{2}$ and 4 will yield a negative result that will make the statement $2x^2-9x+4<0$ true. The values 1, 2, and 3 fall between $\dfrac{1}{2}$ and 4. Therefore, there are 3 integer values of x that satisfy the inequality $2x^2-9x+4<0$.

QUESTION 17.

The correct answer is .25 or $\dfrac{1}{4}$. Setting the equations equal to each other yields $x^2-2x+1=-2x+\dfrac{13}{4}$ and adding $2x$ to both sides gives $x^2+1=\dfrac{13}{4}$. Subtracting 1 from both sides yields $x^2 = \dfrac{9}{4}$ and taking the square root of both sides gives $x = \pm\dfrac{3}{2}$.

Since $x_1 > 0$, substituting $\dfrac{3}{2}$ for x back into the equation $y = -2x + \dfrac{13}{4}$ yields

$y = -2(\dfrac{3}{2}) + \dfrac{13}{4} = -3 + \dfrac{13}{4} = \dfrac{1}{4}$. Therefore, if (x_1, y_1) is the solution to the system of

equations where $x_1 > 0$, then $y_1 = \dfrac{1}{4}$.

QUESTION 18.

The correct answer is 2.4 or $\dfrac{12}{5}$. If $\sin x° = \dfrac{5}{13}$, then the right triangle has one leg
that measures 5 and a hypotenuse that measures 13. As per the Pythagorean Theorem,
it follows that $(5)^2 + b^2 = (13)^2$. Squaring the 5 and the 13 yields $25 + b^2 = 169$. Then,
after subtracting 25 from both sides, the equation simplifies to $b^2 = 144$, which after
square rooting both sides yields $b = 12$. Given that this side length of 12 sits opposite the
other acute angle in the right triangle, the one that measures $y°$, the tangent of $y°$, or
the side opposite the angle that measures $y°$ divided by the side tangent to the angle that
measures $y°$, would be $\dfrac{12}{5}$.

Alternatively, one can recognize that a right triangle with one leg that measures 5 and a
hypotenuse that measures 13 is a part of the special right triangle with sides of length 5,
12, and 13. Then, the tangent of the angle opposite the side that measures 12, the angle
that measures $y°$, would be $\dfrac{12}{5}$.

QUESTION 19.

The correct answer is 1. Being that the given equation, $y = -a(x-h)^2 + 1$, follows the
vertex form of a quadratic, $y = a(x-h)^2 + k$ where (h,k) is the vertex, we know that the
vertex of the function in question occurs at the point $(h,1)$. Since the function crosses
the x-axis at the points 2 and 4, the x-coordinate of the vertex must occur at 3 given the
symmetry of the graph of a quadratic function in the xy-plane. This makes h equivalent
to 3 and yields the equation $y = -a(x-3)^2 + 1$. Substituting the coordinates of one of
the x-intercepts, in this case $(2,0)$, yields $(0) = -a(2-3)^2 + 1$. Simplifying the equation
gives $0 = -a + 1$, or $a = 1$.

QUESTION 20.

The correct answer is 19.5 or $\dfrac{39}{2}$. The similar triangle must have two sides that
measure 3 and 13. The area of a triangle is calculated using the formula $A_\triangle = \dfrac{1}{2}bh$,
where b is the length of the base and h is the height of the triangle. If one were to make
the base of the triangle 3, the heighest height the triangle could have would be 13. This
would occur if the side that measured 13 was perpendicular to the side that measured
3. If the two met at any other angle, the absolute height of the triangle would be lower,
thus making $\dfrac{1}{2}bh$ lower. Therefore, the greatest possible area for the smaller triangle is

$A_\triangle = \dfrac{1}{2}(3)(13) = \dfrac{39}{2}$.

Section 4: Math Test - Calculator

QUESTION 1.

Choice B is correct. Substituting 12 for y and 60 for x in the equation $\frac{y}{x} = k$

yields $\frac{12}{60} = k$. Therefore, $k = \frac{1}{5}$. Substituting 35 for x and $\frac{1}{5}$ for k yields $\frac{y}{35} = \frac{1}{5}$.

Multiplying both sides by 35 yields $y = 7$.

Choices A, C, and D are incorrect and may result from errors in substitution and calculation. For example, choice D is incorrect because if one accidentally substituted 35 for y instead of x in the equation $\frac{y}{x} = k$, the equation would become $\frac{35}{x} = \frac{1}{5}$ and when cross-multiplied, x would equal 175.

QUESTION 2.

Choice A is correct. The phrase "Three less than half of a number is twelve more than the number" can be written as $\frac{1}{2}x - 3 = x + 12$. Subtracting $\frac{1}{2}x$ from both sides of the equation yields $-3 = \frac{1}{2}x + 12$, and subtracting 12 from both sides yields $-15 = \frac{1}{2}x$.

Finally, multiplying both sides of the equation by 2 yields the solution, $x = -30$.

Choice B is incorrect and may result from neglecting to completely finish solving for x once the equation has reached $-15 = \frac{1}{2}x$. Choice C is incorrect and may result from multiplying both sides of the equation by $\frac{1}{2}$ in the last step of solving rather an multiplying by 2. Choice D is incorrect and may result from misplacing a negative during the process of solving.

QUESTION 3.

Choice C is correct. If 128 ounces is equivalent to one gallon then 64 ounces is equivalent to one-half gallon. Therefore, three half gallon containers of orange juice would hold $64 \times 3 = 192$ ounces. Dividing 192 ounces by 16 ounces yields $192 \div 16 = 12$. The three containers would fill 12 glasses.

Choice A, B, and D are incorrect and may result from calculation errors or errors in comprehension. For example, Choice D is incorrect and may result from calculating the result for three gallon containers of orange juice, not three half gallon containers.

QUESTION 4.

Choice A is correct. Subtracting 16 from both sides of $x^2 + 16 \leq 7$ yields $x^2 \leq -9$. Since the square of any integer is positive, one can look at the equation $x^2 \leq -9$ and see that there are no integer values of x that satisfy the inequality. The answer is 0.

Choices B, C, and D are incorrect and may result from calculation errors. For example, choice D is incorrect and may result from calculating the square root of -9 as -3, which results in the inequality $x \leq -3$, an inequality to which there are infinitely many integer solutions.

QUESTION 5.

Choice A is correct. Looking at the line graph, there are three different line segments that have three distinct slopes. Using the slope formula $m = \dfrac{y_2 - y_1}{x_2 - x_1}$, the slope from 0-2 hours is approximately equivalent to $\dfrac{18-0}{2-0}$ or 9, the slope from 2-4 hours is approximately equivalent to $\dfrac{58-18}{4-2}$ or 20, and the slope from 4-5 hours is approximately equivalent to $\dfrac{62-58}{5-4}$ or 4. Since Tom cycles faster than he runs and runs faster than he swims, his slope while running will be in the middle. Therefore, Tom could be running from 0-2 hours.

Choices B, C, and D are incorrect and may result from misreading the question and misinterpreting the relationship involving Tom's speed at which he cycles, runs, and swims.

QUESTION 6.

Choice C is correct. Since $\angle 1$ is twice the measure of $\angle 3$ and the two angles are supplementary, setting $\angle 3$ equivalent to x and $\angle 1$ equivalent to $2x$ yields the equation $x + 2x = 180$. Combining like terms and dividing by 3 yields $x = 60°$ and $2x = 120°$. Therefore, $\angle 1$ is equivalent to $120°$. Since line k and line m are parallel, $\angle 5$ is equivalent to $\angle 1$ because they are corresponding angles. Additionally, $\angle 5$ is also equivalent to $\angle 8$ because they are vertical angles. Therefore, $\angle 5 + \angle 8$ is equivalent to $120° + 120°$, or $240°$.

Choices A and D are incorrect and may result from calculation errors. Choice B is incorrect and may result from a substitution error when comparing $\angle 1$ and $\angle 3$.

QUESTION 7.

Choice C is correct. Since the 24 points in the scatterplot closely resemble a line with few to no outliers, the spread of the points is minimal, which makes the association strong and linear. Since the slope of the line of best fit is negative, the association is negative. Therefore, there is a strong negative linear association between the variables x and y.

Choices A and B are incorrect because they imply a positive association and the negative slope of the line of best fit implies a negative association. Choice D is incorrect because a weak association would be related to points that are more scattered.

QUESTION 8.

Choice A is correct. One can see by looking at the bar graph that the cumulative revenue in 2006 is .5 higher than the cumulative revenue in 2005. Since the company earned a revenue of $500,000 in 2005, it stands that the vertical scale is given in millions of dollars since $500,000 is equivalent to .5 million dollars. Further, since this change of $500,000 is present in the bar graphed for 2006 as compared to the bar graphed for 2005, instead of the bar graphed for 2005 as compared to the bar graphed for 2004, the cumulative revenue must be reported at the beginning of the year.

Choices B and D are incorrect because $500,000 is half of one million dollars, not half of one thousand dollars. Choice C is incorrect because if the cumulative revenue were reported at the end of the year, the $500,000 change from 2005 to 2006 would have been earned in 2006, not 2005.

QUESTION 9.

Choice D is correct. If b is equivalent to 7, then $7c$ would have to equal 30. Dividing 30 by 7 yields $\dfrac{30}{7}$, which is not an integer value.

Choice A is incorrect and may result from a student assuming that 2 is not a prime number. Choices B and C are incorrect because $3 \times 10 = 30$ which makes c equivalent to the integer 10 and $5 \times 6 = 30$ which makes c equivalent to the integer 6.

QUESTION 10.

Choice B is correct. The average of 11 consecutive numbers being equal to 9 can be expressed through the average formula as $\dfrac{Sum}{11} = 9$. Therefore, the sum of the 11 consecutive numbers is equivalent to $9 \times 11 = 99$. If the largest number were increased by 55, the sum would increase by 55 as well, $Sum = 99 + 55 = 154$. Dividing 154 by 11 yields a new average of $\dfrac{154}{11} = 14$. Therefore, the average increased by 5.

Alternatively, one can just divide 55 by 11 since 55 is the increase in the sum that will occur and the number of numbers in the average has not changed. Therefore, $\dfrac{55}{11} = 5$.

Choices A and C are incorrect and may result from calculation errors. Choice D is incorrect because 14 is the new average, not the increase in the average.

QUESTION 11.

Choice B is correct. In order to calculate the most appropriate line of best fit, one must first visually attempt to approximate the slope of the line that best represents the data points. This can be done by sketching a line through the center of the trend in the scatterplot. Looking at the scatterplot from left to right, at the lowest number of treatments, 5, the center of the trend appears to be at a diastolic blood pressure of approximately 110. Further to the right, when the number of treatments reaches 20, the center of the trend appears to be at a diastolic blood pressure of approximately 75.

Calculating the slope as the change in diastolic blood pressure over the change in the number of treatments, one can substitute the points $(5, 110)$ and $(20, 75)$ into the slope formula, $m = \dfrac{y_2 - y_1}{x_2 - x_1}$. This substitution yeilds $m = \dfrac{110 - 75}{5 - 20} = \dfrac{35}{-15} \approx -2.3$.

Substituting one of the approximated points used to find the slope, $(5, 110)$, into the equation $D = -2.3t + b$ yields $(110) = -2.3(5) + b$, or $110 = -11.5 + b$. Adding 11.5 to both sides yields $b = 121.5$ which makes the estimated equation for the line of best fit $D = -2.3t + 121.5$. The most similar equation for the line of best fit to this estimation is $D = -2.3t + 122$.

Choice A is incorrect and may result from assuming that the y-intercept was 110 and missing the fact that the scale on the x-axis starts at 5. Choices C and D are incorrect because the slopes of the lines of best fit are too steep to match the trend that is present in the scatterplot.

QUESTION 12.

Choice B is correct. For the patient who reported 10 treatments, the observed diastolic blood pressure was approximately 105 mm Hg. If one were to utilize the model $D = -2.3t + 122$ to estimate the diastolic blood pressure, D, for a person who had 10 treatments, substituting 10 for t would yield $D = -2.3(10) + 122$, or $D = 99$. Therefore, the difference between observed and estimated is $105 - 99 = 6$.

Choice A is incorrect and may result from a calculation error. Choices C and D are incorrect and may result from using the incorrect best fit model to estimate the diastolic blood pressure for a person who has had 10 treatments.

QUESTION 13.

Choice D is correct. In the original table, the longest time is 5:25 and the shortest time is 4:30, making the range 55 seconds. If Geraldine's time were to be changed to 4:25, the longest time would be 5:05 and the shortest time would be 4:25, making the range 40 seconds. Therefore, the range changes. In the original table, if the times are placed in order from fastest to slowest, the list would read: 4:30, 4:45, 4:50, 5:05, 5:05, and 5:25. The median is the average of 4:50 and 5:05, or approximately 4:58. If Geraldine's time were to be changed to 4:25, the new order from fastest to slowest would read: 4:25, 4:30, 4:45, 4:50, 5:05, and 5:05. The new median would be the average of 4:45 and 4:50, or approximately 4:48. Therefore, the median changes as well. Given that the times are given in minutes and seconds, finding the actual mean of the original list of times and the adjusted list of times is a time consuming task because one must first convert all of the times to just minutes or just seconds. Instead, it is easier to see that if Geraldine's time gets reduced, the sum of all of the times gets reduced, thus reducing the mean as well. Therefore, the range, the median, and the mean all change.

Choices A, B, and C are incorrect and may result from incorrect calculations of the range, median, and mean after Geraldine's time has been adjusted.

QUESTION 14.

Choice A is correct. Since $f(x) = 3x^2 - 6x + 2$ is quadratic equation with a positive coefficient attached to the x^2, the function has a minimum value at its vertex. Using the expression $-\dfrac{b}{2a}$ to determine the x-value of the vertex by substituting 3 for a and -6 for b yields $-\dfrac{(-6)}{2(3)}$, or 1. Substituting 1 for x in the original equation yields $f(1) = 3(1)^2 - 6(1) + 2$, or $f(1) = -1$.

Choices B, C, and D are incorrect and may result from calculation errors or a conceptual misunderstanding of quadratic equations and their graphs.

QUESTION 15.

Choice C is correct. The point $(0, 125)$ is the y-intercept of the graph. It is the amount of money that must be paid if 0 hours of labor take place. Since the line graph is showing the cost of labor only, the initial cost of \$125 must account for some form of labor that has taken place before the actual billed labor starts. At an autobody shop this initial charge would be considered the cost for the labor involved in diagnosing the estimated labor hours or repair issues.

Choice A is incorrect because the line graph shows cost versus time. The number of laborers is not a variable. Choice B is incorrect because the line graph is entitled "Labor Costs at an Autobody Shop." The cost for parts is not included in a graph that charts the cost for labor. Choice D is incorrect because it implies total cost involving labor and repairs where the graph only accounts for the cost of labor, and labor cost clearly rises with time.

QUESTION 16.

Choice A is correct. Labor cost per hour is the same as the change in cost divided by the change in time. This would be considered the slope of the two line segments in the graph. From 0 hours to 4 hours, the cost increases from \$125 to \$325. The change in cost divided by the change in time would be $\dfrac{325 - 125}{4 - 0}$, or \$50 per hour. From 4 hours to 10 hours, the cost changes from \$325 to \$475. This change in cost over change in time would be $\dfrac{475 - 325}{10 - 4}$, or \$25 per hour. Therefore, the difference in additional cost of labor per hour is $\$50 - \$25$, or \$25 per hour.

Choices B, C, and D are incorrect and may result from calculating the incorrect rate of change requested by the problem. For example, choice B is incorrect because \$35 per hour is the rate of change for the cost of labor for the entire 10 hour time period and choice C is incorrect because \$50 per hour is just the rate of change for the cost of labor from the 4th hour to the 10th hour.

QUESTION 17.

Choice A is correct. There are 27 graduate students studying business. Therefore, 27 of the 63 total students sampled are graduate students studying business. $\frac{27}{63}$ is equivalent to $\frac{3}{7}$, or approximately 43%.

Choices B, C, and D are incorrect because none of these categories account for approximately 43% of the sample.

QUESTION 18.

Choice A is correct. When the question states, "If a student studying business were to be selected at random...", a conditional probability is being defined. The total population is not the entire sample anymore. The total population now is the 45 students that are studying business. The probability of randomly selecting a student that is an undergraduate *given* that they are studying business, is $\frac{18}{45}$, which can be reduced to $\frac{2}{5}$.

Choices B, C, and D are incorrect and may result from errors in correctly applying conditions to the population. For example, Choice C is incorrect and may be the result of randomly selecting a student who is studying business *given* that the student is an undergraduate, as opposed to randomly selecting a student who is an undergraduate *given* that the student is studying business.

QUESTION 19.

Choice B is correct. Substituting a for the number of tickets sold in advance and d for the number of tickets sold the day of the performance, one can create a system of equations including one equation for the total number of ticket sales ($a + d = 200$) and one equation for the total amount of money raised ($5a + 7d = 1,150$). Multiplying the equation $a + d = 200$ by 5 yields $5a + 5d = 1,000$. Subtracting $5a + 5d = 1,000$ from $5a + 7d = 1,150$ yields $2d = 150$, or $d = 75$ tickets.

Choices A and D are incorrect and may result from errors in creating or solving the correct system of equations. Choice C is incorrect because 125 tickets in the number of tickets sold in advance, not on the day of the performance.

QUESTION 20.

Choice C is correct. Substituting 1 for x in both equations and s for y in both equations yields the system of linear equations $\begin{matrix} s = 2(1) + a \\ s = a(1) + 2 \end{matrix}$. Both equations simplify to the same equation, $s = a + 2$. Therefore, the statement $a + 2 = s$ is true.

Choices A, B, and C are incorrect because none of the expressions are equivalent to the expression $s = a + 2$.

QUESTION 21.

Choice D is correct. When the equation of a circle is written in the form $(x-a)^2 + (y-b)^2 = r^2$, the center is the point (a,b). In order to write the equation $x^2 + y^2 - 2y = 3$ in this form, one must complete the square for the expression $y^2 - 2y$. Adding 1 to both sides of the equation $x^2 + y^2 - 2y = 3$ yields $x^2 + y^2 - 2y + 1 = 3 + 1$. Factoring the expression $y^2 - 2y + 1$ yields $(y-1)^2$. Substituting $(y-1)^2$ for $y^2 - 2y + 1$ in $x^2 + y^2 - 2y + 1 = 4$ yields $x^2 + (y-1)^2 = 4$. Substituting $(x-0)^2$ for x^2 and 2^2 for 4 yields $(x-0)^2 + (y-1)^2 = 2^2$. In this form, one can see that the center of the circle is at the point $(0,1)$.

Choices A, B, and C are incorrect and may result from an error in understanding the form of a circle equation.

QUESTION 22.

Choice D is correct. A 35% discount implies that Helina is paying for $1 - .35$, or 65% of the purse. A sales tax of 6% means that after that discount, Helina is paying for $1 + .06$, or 106% of that discounted price. After setting the original selling price of the purse equal to x, if Helina's receipt said that she paid d dollars, then $x(0.65)(1.06) = d$. Solving for x, the original selling price of the purse, by dividing both sides of the

equation by $(0.65)(1.06)$ yields $x = \dfrac{d}{(0.65)(1.06)}$.

Choice A is incorrect and may result from incorrectly assuming that d is the original selling price of the purse and neglecting to subtract the 35% discount from 100% of the purse's selling price. Choice B is incorrect and may result from assuming that d is the original selling price of the purse rather than the price after discount and tax. Choice C is incorrect and may result from assuming that sales tax had not yet been applied to the price on the bill, d.

QUESTION 23.

Choice C is correct. Using S to represent the enrollment in Introductory Statistics and I to represent the enrollment in Intro to Statistics for Business, if S is 30% than I, then S is equivalent to 70% of I, or $S = .7I$. Substituting 210 for S yields $210 = .7I$ and dividing both sides by .7 makes $I = 300$.

Choice A is incorrect because 63 is 30% of 210 instead of 30% *more than* 210. Choice B is incorrect because 147 is 70% of 210 which is 30% *less than* 210, not 30% *more than* 210. Choice D is incorrect because 840 is 300% *more than* 210, rather than 30%.

QUESTION 24.

Choice B is correct. Setting h equal to 21 and solving for t in the equation $h = 22t - t^2$ will yield the time when the tennis ball first reaches the height of the top of the building and the second time it reaches the top of the building upon its descent. Setting h equal to 21 yields $21 = 22t - t^2$. Subtracting $22t$ and adding t^2 to both sides of the equation yields $t^2 - 22t + 21 = 0$. Factoring the left hand side of the equation yields $(t-1)(t-21) = 0$. The roots at 1 and 21 mean that the tennis ball reaches a height of 21 feet 1 second after it is released and again at 21 seconds. Therefore, the kids sitting on the roof can see the tennis ball for $21 - 1 = 20$ seconds.

Choices A, C, and D are incorrect and may result from substitution errors and/or factoring errors.

QUESTION 25.

Choice B is correct. A linear equation of the form $y = b$ where b is a positive constant is a horizontal line with a slope of 0. A horizontal line would best represent an income stream that has little to no change over time; an income stream that seems to hover around the same net profit each year. Therefore, book sales would be the income stream best represented by a line of the form $y = b$.

Choice A is incorrect because classes would best be represented by a line, but one with a positive slope of the form $y = mx + b$ where m and b are positive constants. Choice C is incorrect because equipment sales would best be represented by an exponential function of the form $y = ab^x$ where a and b are positive constants. Choice D is incorrect because book sales can be represented by a line of the form $y = b$.

QUESTION 26.

Choice D is correct. In 2010, the net profit from the sale of classes was $35,000. In 2014, the net profit from the sale of classes was $55,000. Calculating the change in net profit from the sale of classes divided by the number of years that have passed yields $\frac{55,000 - 35,000}{2014 - 2010}$, which simplifies to $\frac{20,000}{4}$, or $5,000 per year.

Choice A is incorrect and may result from overlooking the fact that the table is in thousands of dollars and from dividing by 5 years because there are 5 years listed in the table rather than the change which was only 4 years. Choice B is incorrect and may result from overlooking the fact that the table is in thousands of dollars. Choice C is incorrect and may result from dividing by 5 years because there are 5 years listed in the table rather than the change which was only 4 years.

QUESTION 27.

Choice D is correct. Converting both equations in the system of linear inequalities

$\begin{matrix} x+y < -1 \\ x-2y \ge 2 \end{matrix}$ to $y = mx+b$ form yields $\begin{matrix} y < -x-1 \\ y \le \frac{1}{2}x - 1 \end{matrix}$. Being that the two lines intersect at

the same y-intercept, $(0, -1)$, and that y must be less than or less than or equal to this point, it follows that y must be strictly less than -1 in order to satisfy both inequalities. Therefore, $y < -1$.

Choices A, B, and C are incorrect because there are coordinate points (x, y) that satisfy all three answers that are, however, not solutions to the system of linear inequalities.

QUESTION 28.

Choice A is correct. If a polynomial $f(x)$ were divided by the binomial $x-4$ and there were no remainder, 4 would be a root of the polynomial. In other words, if you substituted 4 for x in the polynomial, the output, $f(4)$, would be equivalent to 0, or $f(4) = 0$. However, when the polynomial is divided by $x-4$, there is a remainder of $\dfrac{5}{x-4}$. This implies that if $f(x)$ is divided by $x-4$, there is 5 left over. Therefore, $f(4) = 0+5$, or more simply $f(4) = 5$.
.

Choices B, C, and D are incorrect because none of the pairs of inputs and outputs are necessarily solutions to the polynomial $f(x)$. For example, choice D is incorrect because if $f(4) = 0$, there would be no remainder.

QUESTION 29.

Choice C is correct. If 6 students each played 50 mind games, the total number of games played by the 6 students is $6 \times 50 = 300$ games. Suming up all of the Gold Awards won by the 6 students yields $5+8+2+4+1+10 = 30$ gold awards. So, for every 300 games played, a student can reasonably expect 30 gold awards. So, if the website boasts that it has 45,000 games available, then one could solve the proportion $\dfrac{30}{300} = \dfrac{x}{45,000}$ for x, the number of gold awards to be expected if all 45,000 games are played. Cross-multiplying yields $30(45,000) = 300x$, or $x = \dfrac{30(45,000)}{300} = 4,500$.

Choices A, B, and D are incorrect and may result from calculation errors or errors in calculating a proportional estimate.

QUESTION 30.

Choice C is correct. A second quadratic equation with the same x- and y-intercepts and a vertex with an opposite y-value as the equation $y = -x^2 + 6x - 5$ would be the inversion of the equation, $y = x^2 - 6x + 5$. The vertex form of the equation $y = x^2 - 6x + 5$ would have the coordinates of the vertex, $(a, -b)$, as coefficients in the equation. In order to convert $y = x^2 - 6x + 5$ to vertex form, a form in which $y = a(x-h)^2 + k$ where the coordinate point (h, k) is the vertex of the equation, one must complete the square of the expression $x^2 - 6x$. By dividing –6 by 2 and squaring the outcome, the resulting outcome is 9. With this value, one can re-express $y = x^2 - 6x + 5$ as the equivalent equation $y = (x^2 - 6x + 9) + 5 - 9$ and, after factoring the expression $x^2 - 6x + 9$, the equivalent vertex form of the equation remains: $y = (x-3)^2 - 4$. In this form, the coordinates of the vertex, $(3, -4)$, appear as coefficients in the equation.

Choices A and B are incorrect because they are not in vertex form, the form in which the coordinates of the vertex appear as constants in the equation. Choice D is incorrect and may result from converting the original, non-inverted equation to vertex form.

QUESTION 31.

The correct answer is 16. Subtracting 3 from the 28 allowable pounds yields 25 available pounds to be accounted for by the candles. Since each candle weighs 1.5 pounds, dividing 25 by 1.5 yields $\frac{25}{1.5} = 16.333...$ Therefore, 16c andles is the maximum number of candles that can be shipped before Justine is charged for additional shipping.

QUESTION 32.

The correct answer is 110. If Filipe owns two warehouses that each contain 17,600 cubic feet of rental space, Filipe has a total of $17,600 \times 2 = 35,200$ cubic feet of rental space available. If each self-storage space that Filipe rents is 320 cubic feet, dividing 35,200 by 320 yields $\frac{35,200}{320} = 110$ available self-storage rental spaces.

QUESTION 33.

The correct answer is 12.5 < x < 17.5. If Daniella ran a total of 14 miles in 2 hours on the day of her fastest pace run, dividing 28 by 4 yields $\frac{14}{2} = 7$ miles per hour. If Daniella ran at her slowest pace of 5 mph for 2 and a half hours, multiplying yields $5 \times 2.5 = 12.5$ miles. If Daniella ran at her slowest pace of 7 mph for 2 and a half hours, multiplying yields $7 \times 2.5 = 17.5$ miles. Daniella could have run anywhere from 12.5 to 17.5 miles.

QUESTION 34.

The correct answer is 25. According to the line graph, the radiation reading in June was 1,000 uSV and the radiation reading in April was 800 uSV. If June has a higher radiation reading than April, multiplying the radiation reading in April by a growth factor of $(1+r)$, where r is the growth rate in decimal form, will yield the radiation reading in June. So, $800(1+r) = 1,000$. Dividing both sides of the equation by 800 yields

$$1 + r = \frac{1,000}{800}, \text{ or } 1 + r = 1.25.$$ Subtracting 1 from both sides of the equation yields

$r = 0.25$, or 25%.

QUESTION 35.

The correct answer is 200. Taking the square root of the area of the square yields 4, the side length of the square. Using the side length relationship of an isosceles right triangle, $x, x,$ and $x\sqrt{2}$, yields the length of the diagonal of the square, $4\sqrt{2}$. This diagonal happens to be the diameter of the circle which, when divided by 2, makes the circle's radius $2\sqrt{2}$. Using the formula for the area of a circle, $A = \pi r^2$, yields $A = \pi(2\sqrt{2})^2$, or $A = 8\pi$. The area of the square divided by the area of the circle is $\frac{16}{8\pi}$. Multiplying

$\frac{16}{8\pi}$ by 100 yields $\frac{1600}{8\pi}\%$, or $\frac{200}{\pi}\%$. If the area of the square is $\frac{a}{\pi}\%$ of the area of the circle and the area of the square is $\frac{200}{\pi}\%$, $a = 200$.

QUESTION 36.

The correct answer is 3. The function $g(x)$ is undefined for any value of x that creates a zero in the denominator. Factoring an x out of the denominator of the function

$g(x) = \dfrac{x-2}{x^3 - \frac{5}{2}x^2 + x}$ yields $g(x) = \dfrac{x-2}{x(x^2 - \frac{5}{2}x + 1)}$. Factoring the expression $x^2 - \frac{5}{2}x + 1$

yields $(x-2)(x-\frac{1}{2})$, revealing roots at 2 and $\frac{1}{2}$. Therefore, since an x was factored out of the denominator, which implies that the function is undefined at 0, and because 2 and $\frac{1}{2}$ are also roots of the function $y = x^3 - \frac{5}{2}x^2 + x$, there are three total values of x where $g(x)$ is undefined.

QUESTION 37.

The correct answer is 3. Substituting 24 for m in the expression

$\$2,100(1 + \dfrac{r}{100})^{\frac{m}{12}}$ and setting the expression equal to $\$2,227.89$ yields the equation

$\$2,100(1 + \dfrac{r}{100})^{\frac{24}{12}} = \$2,227.89$. Dividing both sides of the equation by $\$2,100$ yields

$(1 + \dfrac{r}{100})^2 = 1.0609$ and then taking the square root of both sides yields $1 + \dfrac{r}{100} = 1.03$.

After subtracting 1 from both sides $\dfrac{r}{100} = .03$ and multiplying by 100 leaves r equivalent to 3.

QUESTION 38.

The correct answer is 3.09. Substituting half of the amount of time, 12, for m in the

expression $\$2,100(1 + \dfrac{r}{100})^{\frac{m}{12}}$ and setting the expression equal to $\$2,227.89$ yields the

equation $\$2,100(1 + \dfrac{r}{100})^{\frac{12}{12}} = \$2,227.89$. Dividing both sides of the equation by $\$2,100$

yields $1 + \dfrac{r}{100} = 1.0609$. After subtracting 1 from both sides $\dfrac{r}{100} = .0609$ and multiplying

by 100 leaves r equivalent to 6.09. Given the answer explanation to question 37, in order for the account value to rise to $\$2,227.89$ after 24 months have passed, r must be equivalent to 3. In order for the account value to rise to $\$2,227.89$ in half of the amount of time, 12 months, r must be equivalent to 6.09. Therefore, r must be increased by 3.09.

TEST 4

Reading Test

65 MINUTES, 52 QUESTIONS

Turn to Section 1 of your answer sheet to answer the questions in this section.

Questions 1-10 are based on the following passage.

This passage is taken from a novel that appeared in 2013. In the scene that follows, two colleagues, Catherine and Edmond, are driving through the French countryside.

The road passed through the forest, now tinged with the russet shades of autumn; Catherine watched the afternoon shadows sway back and forth while Edmond, though familiar
Line with the road, stared conscientiously ahead. For the most
5 part, the trees crowded the roadside, yet every now and then there was a small open space, rather rutted in the places where drivers had stopped for recreation. In some of these clearings, there were stacks of logs from felled trees.

"The French are so cheeky!" Catherine exclaimed.
10 "Imagine churning up the forest like that. Look at those women over there: they just stopped their car in the middle of the glade and went to pick mushrooms. Anywhere else, those women would be prosecuted for Trespassing and Theft. I wonder what the owner would say."

15 "Nothing, I should think," remarked Edmond. "Actually, I am one of the owners."

Catherine shot him a surprised glance. Edmond explained, his English as balanced and careful as ever: "The national forests belong to the people of France. It is the right of every
20 French citizen to forage in the forests and gather food and kindling from the forest floor. Of course, the state attempts to look after the forest: thus the tree-felling and the protection of forest animals when hunting is no longer in season. Otherwise, we can do anything we like there."

25 "Even hunting, like English hunting? With hounds and horses?" Catherine was suddenly impassioned. "I hate hunting. It should be banned outright. There is no excuse for allowing a cruel and disgusting sport indulged in by the idle rich— unspeakable activities in pursuit of uneatable animals."

30 "There speaks the modern Englishwoman, who thinks that her food, perfectly shaped and washed and packaged,

appears miraculously at the supermarket, ready to go into the microwave. We French know that good food is food taken straight from the earth and not frozen and given a sell-by
35 date. We take food seriously. Our forests are full of edible produce: truffles, mushrooms, herbs, and of course deer and wild boar."

"So, you believe that hunting is acceptable?"

"Certainly, if the aim is to hunt food for the table. The
40 English don't believe that. They hunt for sport, for the thrill of the chase."

"No, hunting in any form is wrong. Chasing terrified animals with hounds ready to rip their prey to pieces—it's barbaric."

45 Edmond shrugged his shoulders. "I agree. No Frenchman would touch venison brought down in that way. Here, hunting an animal is not akin to murder. In France, the hounds chase the deer because the deer are agile runners— it is what makes their meat so lean and healthy—and the
50 dogs' role is to direct the deer to where it can be brought down by the huntsman, with one clean shot, so that it will be acceptable for eating."

"That is no way to treat any wild animal."

"All animals were originally wild. You think that
55 because some animals are reared on farms, those animals they are somehow house-trained; that's why you call them 'domestic' animals. Little calves and piglets are so sweet."

"Well, so they are."

"Oh, yes, sweet for three months, and then you take
60 them to the slaughterhouse. How else would you get your ham and veal?"

Catherine's face flushed. She felt confused, and wished she could answer Edmond in a French as flawless as his English.

65 There was silence in the car for the next few kilometers, then Edmond said, "I would like to turn off into the next Aire, if you do not mind."

"What's an 'Aire'?" Catherine asked crossly. "You mean a parking area?"

CONTINUE

70   "Yes, a parking area," he answered gently.
      The car bumped over a grass verge and into a small clearing. Edmond switched off the engine. The stillness now seemed tremendous, universal. Catherine gazed out the window. A red squirrel darted across the grass and scampered
75 up the gnarled trunk of an ancient oak. Then, once again, silence settled all around.
      Catherine leaned back in her seat. "It is beautiful." she said at last. "Your forest is so beautiful."

1

Which choice best describes the developmental pattern of the passage?

A) A record of an often tense conversation
B) A response to a nationwide controversy
C) A description of a compromise
D) A depiction of contemporary society

2

It can be inferred from the passage that Edmond is

A) of English descent and familiar with several other cultures.
B) of English descent but educated primarily in France.
C) of French descent and speaks English without difficulty.
D) of French descent but has relocated to the English countryside.

3

As used in line 39, "aim" most nearly means

A) line of sight.
B) positioning of a weapon.
C) direction.
D) objective.

4

In the passage, Edmond responds to Catherine's remarks by

A) accusing Catherine of actively supporting English hunting practices.
B) paraphrasing the line of reasoning that he assumes she is following.
C) forcefully persuading her to accept a moderate position.
D) distracting her with an entirely new proposal.

5

Which choice provides the best evidence for the answer to the previous question?

A) Lines 18-21 ("The national . . . floor")
B) Lines 30-33 ("There speaks . . . microwave")
C) Lines 45-47 ("No Frenchman . . . murder")
D) Lines 71-73 ("The car . . . universal")

6

In lines 45-52 ("Edmond . . . eating"), Edmond explains his stance on hunting by

A) comparing hunting to other environmental problems.
B) explaining a source of hostility between two countries.
C) describing some of his own experiences as a hunter.
D) presenting generalizations about his compatriots.

7

As used in line 51, "clean" most nearly means

A) ethical.
B) precise.
C) sanitized.
D) smooth.

8

Why does Catherine ask Edmond what an "Aire" is in lines 68-69?

A) She is frustrated with her imperfect French.
B) Her anger towards Edmond has abated completely.
C) She wishes to irritate Edmond further.
D) She has no idea where Edmond intends to drive next.

9

Catherine responds to the French attitude toward nature in a manner that is best described as

A) completely uninformed.
B) grudgingly tolerant.
C) sharply condemnatory.
D) entirely puzzled.

CONTINUE

10

Which choice provides the best evidence for the answer to the previous question?

A) Lines 9-10 ("The French . . . like that")

B) Lines 25-26 ("Even hunting . . . horses?")

C) Lines 62-64 ("Catherine's face . . . English")

D) Lines 68-69 ("What's an . . . area?")

Questions 11-21 are based on the following passage and supplementary material.

Adapted from Danielle Barkley, "International Sporting and the Economics of Enjoyment."

When the Olympic Games were originally held in Ancient Greece, these athletic contests acted as both a religious ritual and an opportunity to celebrate the feats of the human body.

Line In the present day, the latter motivation remains and a new
5 one has been added: much of the rhetoric surrounding the Games involves economic advantages to be gained by the country and city hosting the Games. As recent budgets for hosting the Games have ballooned, so has the insistence that spending money will make money for the host destination.
10 The financial benefits are seen as playing out in three major ways. First, tourism will increase for the duration of the Games, creating additional revenue. Second, the required investments in infrastructure completed prior to the Games will create economic opportunities. Third, though most nebulous, media
15 attention will open an opportunity to attract long-term business investment; in this final sense, the Games send a signal that the host country is a viable player in the world economy.

All of this sounds admirable in theory: what country wouldn't want to both draw in global prestige and economic
20 profit? The problem is that for most host cities there are few, if any, well-documented short-term economic rewards to hosting the Games. Building the necessary stadiums and competition sites costs millions of dollars, and very few hosts have been able to meaningfully repurpose these structures once the Games
25 wrap up. Moreover, these construction projects occupy real estate that often could have been used for more lucrative or strategic projects.

Simply put, Olympics infrastructure is a bad investment, and Olympics tourism may not be much better of a prospect.
30 While hosting the Games inarguably results in increased tourism, visitors who come to see the Games tend to do little else, so that traditionally popular and profitable tourist attractions will actually see a decline in business. In a city that would draw visitors with or without the Games, tourism
35 may actually decrease as prospective visitors indifferent to the Olympics seek to avoid the crowds and chaos. When London hosted the Summer Olympics in August 2012, the number of foreign tourists visiting Britain was actually 5% lower than in August 2011. Attractions such as the British Museum and
40 a number of popular London theaters experienced significant drop-offs in visitor volume.

Although the Olympics can easily backfire as a short-term investment, the findings surrounding the long-term payoff of hosting are more complex. A 2009 study investigating
45 the impact of hosting did find that countries that hosted the Olympics unequivocally experienced increased international

CONTINUE

trade in subsequent years. However, in an interesting twist, countries that made bids to host the Olympics but then failed to secure the hosting opportunity experienced the same upsurge
50 in trade. And, because these apparent "losers" didn't have to spend billions of dollars actually hosting the Games, they saw a far greater increase in overall economic benefit. There may be a link between the Olympics and a global perception of having a stable economy, yet having the confidence to simply
55 bid on the Games is all a country needs to play the Games to its advantage.

Philip Porter, an economist who specializes in the impact of sporting events, has concluded that "the bottom line is, every time we've looked—dozens of scholars, dozens of
60 times—we find no real change in economic activity." There is a growing belief among these scholars that the only way to make the Olympics palatable to citizens is to promise long-term economic benefits, whether or not those gains will ever be realized. Moreover, the same studies that Porter and others
65 have used to argue against tangible economic benefits do show significant increases in national pride and public satisfaction when a country hosts the Games. At least in that sense, the Olympics may be a wise investment after all.

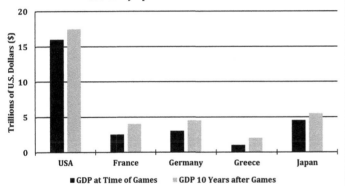

GDP of Olympic Games Host Countries

■ GDP at Time of Games   ▪ GDP 10 Years after Games

11

Over the course of the first paragraph (lines 1-17) the focus shifts from

A) a recounting of particular Olympic Games in an impoverished country to a discussion of the effects of the Games on its economy.

B) a synopsis of the creation and history of the Olympic Games to a brief description of the different host cities over the past century.

C) a summary of the historical motivations behind the Olympic Games to a list of supposed advantages of hosting the Games.

D) an explanation of the process behind the selection of a host country for the Olympics to an anecdote from a diplomat representing a host country.

12

The author implies that the Olympic Games

A) are usually hosted in cities popular with tourists.

B) ensure fame and success for a host city.

C) are no longer as profitable as they once were.

D) no longer exist to serve a spiritual purpose.

13

Which choice provides the best evidence for the answer to the previous question?

A) Lines 2-4 ("these athletic . . . remains")

B) Lines 7-9 ("As . . . destination")

C) Lines 14-16 ("media . . . investment")

D) Lines 20-22 ("The problem . . . Games")

14

As used in line 24, "meaningfully" most nearly means

A) expressively.

B) seriously.

C) usefully.

D) thoughtfully.

15

The author indicates that during the Olympics, a host city

A) receives both short-term and long-term benefits since the Games give the city media exposure that it would not receive otherwise.

B) that is already a popular tourist destination loses visitors as people seek to evade the crowds that flock to the city primarily for the Olympics.

C) gradually loses its culture as increased tourism and publicity make the city a target for commercialization.

D) eventually increases in population because media attention and prolonged tourism from the Games cause visitors to settle nearby.

16

Which choice provides the best evidence for the answer to the previous question?

A) Lines 18-20 ("what . . . profit")

B) Lines 33-36 ("In a city . . . chaos")

C) Lines 52-56 ("There may . . . advantage")

D) Lines 61-63 ("the only . . . benefits")

CONTINUE

17

As used in line 64, "realized" most nearly means

A) comprehended.

B) understood.

C) noticed.

D) fulfilled.

18

The "scholars" mentioned in the final paragraph (lines 57-68) would likely react to the "2009 study" (line 44) with

A) wholehearted enthusiasm.

B) restrained optimism.

C) utter indignation.

D) complete disagreement.

19

According to the passage, a positive effect of a country hosting the Olympics is that

A) citizens are more satisfied with the country and show increased patriotism.

B) growing tourism causes small businesses to flourish and industry to thrive.

C) foreigners become more educated and aware of the country's culture.

D) social issues prevalent in the country are exposed by the media.

20

Based on the graph, the GDP of countries that had hosted the Olympic Games generally

A) increased exponentially.

B) decreased after the Games.

C) stayed the same since the Games.

D) increased in modest amounts.

21

The author of the passage would most likely respond to the information in the graph with

A) agreement that hosting an Olympic Game guarantees a country an increase in tourism and a spike in economic activity.

B) doubt that the Olympic Games could cause economic progress and an increase in trade in countries that did not have stable markets before the Games.

C) the assertion that countries who had made bids to host the games but did not receive the opportunity had obtained the same long-term economic benefits.

D) the argument that a country hosting the Olympic Games receives no economic, cultural, or social advantages whatsoever.

CONTINUE

Questions 22-32 are based on the following passage and supplementary material.

Adapted from Nancy Hoffman, "Killing Leukemia Naturally: A New Approach Re-Deploys the Body's Own Defenses."

Leukemia is a cancer that targets and afflicts blood cells, which are formed in the bone marrow and, when mature, travel to all parts of the body through the blood vessels. There are
Line many types of leukemia, each of which can affect a different
5 element of human blood; most often the white blood cells are affected but bone marrow, red blood cells, and platelets can also become cancerous. Traditional treatments such as chemotherapy, radiation, and bone marrow transplants can be useful, but the success of such measures depends on many
10 factors, including how early the cancer is detected and the cancer's speed of progression.

Some of the newer cancer treatments focus on using the body's natural defensive mechanisms to destroy leukemia. For example, researchers have located genes called tumor
15 suppressor genes, which, like all genes, can be either activated or deactivated. A group led by Dr. Ross Dickins of the Walter and Eliza Hall Institute recently demonstrated that turning off a gene called Pax5 causes normal cells to become leukemia cells, and vice versa. Dr. Dickins suggests that this research will lead
20 scientists to "begin to look at ways of developing drugs that could have the same effect as restoring Pax5 function." Despite the promise of these findings, genes are not simple one-function switches; this experimental treatment improved patients' disease prognoses while also causing a variety of negative side
25 effects. Yet if further research is undertaken, it may be found that tumor suppressor genes could hold the key to treating many cancers.

Another new approach that uses the body's own defenses involves the immune system, which is sharply affected in
30 leukemia patients. In Acute Myeloid Leukemia (AML), the myeloid cells that fight bacterial infections, assail parasites, and stop the spread of tissue damage become cancerous and proliferate until they reach dangerous volumes. AML spreads quickly and is the most common form of leukemia in adults,
35 so that effective treatments are valuable. A team at the Scripps Research Institute, convinced that "a major goal in cancer research is to discover agents that transform malignant cells into benign cells," has discovered a mechanism that accomplishes just this goal and then goes one step further: the
40 team has found a way to convert the cancerous myeloid cells into a particular type of benign immune cell, the natural killer cell. These fearsome-sounding cells are a key part of how the body ensures good health, since they quickly destroy virally-infected cells and even tumors before an antibody response
45 (which tends to be somewhat slower) can trigger the activity of other types of immune cells, which destroy infected or malignant cells. Natural killer cells are normally highly adaptive and therefore are potentially useful to this type of cancer research.
50 When the Scripps team began its investigation, the team members were mainly looking for ways to get under-active bone marrow to produce more white blood cells, which could help people with immunodeficiency diseases. To do this, they used antibodies to trigger
55 growth in immature bone marrow cells so that these cells would mature. They were successful in this goal, but also intrigued to discover that some of the matured cells were of a completely different type and had turned into dendritic cells, the so-called messenger cells between
60 antibodies and white blood cells. After the dendritic cells matured further, they turned into natural killer cells.

The most astonishing result of this research was that, when scientists added the growth antibody to a sample of AML cells, the AML cells that turned into natural killer
65 cells only killed malignant AML cells: within one day, the converted natural killer cells had destroyed 15% of the AML cells. Because these cells only seem to kill cells of their former type, the researchers are referring to this treatment tactic as "fratricidal therapy," and are hopeful
70 that this specialized method will effectively combat many types of cancer.

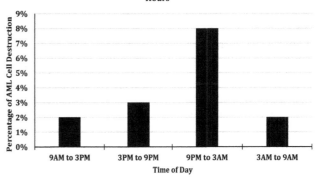

Destruction of AML Cells by Natural Killer Cells Within 24 Hours

22

The purpose of the first paragraph is to

A) explain an ailment and introduce a few methods that have been used to address it in the past.

B) indicate that Leukemia is becoming more prevalent and urge researchers to abandon past approaches.

C) introduce a speculation that will be substantiated later in the passage.

D) outline an argument that will be contradicted later in the passage.

CONTINUE

23

The author characterizes the research involving "tumor suppressor genes" (lines 14-15) as

A) superior to all other existing leukemia treatments.
B) inferior to more traditional leukemia treatments.
C) potentially valuable yet currently problematic.
D) fascinating in theory but still not tested experimentally.

24

Which choice provides the best evidence for the answer to the previous question?

A) Lines 7-11 ("Traditional . . . progression")
B) Lines 16-19 ("A group . . . versa")
C) Lines 21-25 ("Despite . . . effects")
D) Lines 28-30 ("Another . . . patients")

25

As used in line 31, "assail" most nearly means

A) combat.
B) mistreat.
C) vilify.
D) encounter.

26

It can be inferred from the passage that natural killer cells

A) are widely believed to be destructive and cancerous cells.
B) are being investigated by researchers interested in diseases other than cancer.
C) are not easily cultivated in laboratory settings.
D) are already instrumental in helping healthy individuals fight disease.

27

As used in line 45, "trigger" most nearly means

A) inflame.
B) initiate.
C) persuade.
D) agitate.

28

As described in the passage, the research project undertaken at the Scripps Research Institute involved

A) an insurmountable obstacle.
B) an unforeseen result.
C) an ongoing dispute.
D) a humanitarian agenda.

29

Which choice provides the best evidence for the answer to the previous question?

A) Lines 39-42 ("the team . . . killer cell")
B) Lines 50-54 ("When the Scripps . . . diseases")
C) Lines 56-60 ("They were . . . blood cells")
D) Lines 67-71 ("Because these . . . cancer")

30

It can be inferred from the passage that the Scripps researchers hope that their findings will

A) be applicable to ailments other than leukemia.
B) bolster the reputation of the Scripps Research Institute.
C) supersede the research undertaken by Dr. Ross Dickins.
D) help scientists to better understand the function of dendritic cells.

31

Data in the graph indicate that the greatest percentage of AML cell destruction occurred at which time?

A) 9AM to 3PM
B) 3PM to 9PM
C) 9PM to 3AM
D) 3AM to 9AM

32

Based on the graph and the passage, it can be reasonably inferred that the maturation of dendritic cells most likely occurred

A) before 9AM, but after 3AM.
B) before 3PM, but after 9AM.
C) before 9PM, but after 3PM.
D) before 3AM, but after 9PM.

Questions 33-42 are based on the following passage.

The following passage is an excerpt from a speech on the topic of modern American journalism, delivered by vice president Spiro Agnew on November 13, 1969.

At least 40 million Americans every night, it's estimated, watch the network news. Seven million of them view A.B.C., the remainder being divided between N.B.C. and C.B.S.
Line According to Harris polls and other studies, for millions of
5 Americans the networks are the sole source of national and world news. In Will Rogers' observation, what you knew was what you read in the newspaper. Today for growing millions of Americans, it's what they see and hear on their television sets.
   Now how is this network news determined? A small group
10 of men, numbering perhaps no more than a dozen anchormen, commentators, and executive producers, settle upon the 20 minutes or so of film and commentary that's to reach the public.
   This selection is made from the 90 to 180 minutes that may be available. Their powers of choice are broad. They
15 decide what 40 to 50 million Americans will learn of the day's events in the nation and in the world. We cannot measure this power and influence by the traditional democratic standards, for these men can create national issues overnight. They can make or break by their coverage and commentary a moratorium
20 on the war. They can elevate men from obscurity to national prominence within a week. They can reward some politicians with national exposure and ignore others. For millions of Americans the network reporter who covers a continuing issue—like the ABM or civil rights—becomes, in effect, the
25 presiding judge in a national trial by jury.
   It must be recognized that the networks have made important contributions to the national knowledge—through news, documentaries, and specials. They have often used their power constructively and creatively to awaken the public
30 conscience to critical problems. The networks made hunger and black lung disease national issues overnight. The TV networks have done what no other medium could have done in terms of dramatizing the horrors of war. The networks have tackled our most difficult social problems with a directness and
35 an immediacy that's the gift of their medium. They focus the nation's attention on its environmental abuses—on pollution in the Great Lakes and the threatened ecology of the Everglades. But it was also the networks that elevated George Lincoln Rockwell, founder of the American Nazi Party, from obscurity
40 to national prominence.
   Nor is their power confined to the substantive. A raised eyebrow, an inflection of the voice, a caustic remark dropped in the middle of a broadcast can raise doubts in a million minds about the veracity of a public official or the wisdom
45 of a Government policy. One Federal Communications Commissioner considers the powers of the networks equal

to that of local, state, and Federal Governments all combined. Certainly it represents a concentration of power over American public opinion unknown in history.
50   Now what do Americans know of the men who wield this power? Of the men who produce and direct the network news, the nation knows practically nothing. Of the commentators, most Americans know little other than that they reflect an urbane and assured presence,
55 seemingly well-informed on every important matter. We do know that to a man these commentators and producers live and work in the geographical and intellectual confines of Washington, D.C., or New York City, the latter of which James Reston terms "the most unrepresentative
60 community in the entire United States."
   Both communities bask in their own provincialism, their own parochialism. We can deduce that these men read the same newspapers. They draw their political and social views from the same sources. Worse, they talk
65 constantly to one another, thereby providing artificial reinforcement to their shared viewpoints. Do they allow their biases to influence the selection and presentation of the news? David Brinkley states, "objectivity is impossible" to normal human behavior. Rather, he says,
70 we should strive for "fairness."

33

The main purpose of the passage is to
A) emphasize the need for political transparency.
B) highlight the severity of media distortion.
C) differentiate local and national news.
D) question the influence of an elite group.

34

The central problem that Agnew describes in the passage is that the news has been
A) restricted by the influence of only a few.
B) limited by the availability of topics.
C) confined by staunch political correctness.
D) dominated by overwhelming medical coverage.

35

Which choice provides the best evidence for the answer to the previous question?
A) Lines 1-2 ("At . . . news")
B) Lines 9-12 ("A small . . . the public")
C) Lines 28-30 ("They . . . problems")
D) Lines 30-31 ("The . . . overnight")

CONTINUE

36

Agnew claims that which of the following was a relatively recent development?

A) The exposure of dishonest politicians

B) The decline in newspaper distribution

C) The increasing concern for the environment

D) The popularity of network news

37

As used in line 14, "broad" most nearly means

A) fortified.

B) general.

C) extensive.

D) liberal.

38

What function does the fourth paragraph (lines 26-40) primarily serve in the passage as a whole?

A) It acknowledges how the potential benefits of influential news programs can be also be detrimental.

B) It illustrates with several examples the favorable aspects of the news.

C) It provides a counterargument to those in support of the network news.

D) It endorses a practice that the author later proves to be problematic.

39

Which choice provides the best evidence for the answer to the previous question?

A) Lines 22-25 ("For . . . jury")

B) Lines 33-35 ("The networks . . . their medium")

C) Lines 38-40 ("But . . . prominence")

D) Line 41 ("Nor . . . substantive")

40

Agnew contends that the "communities" (line 61) are problematic because

A) they are of a distinct social class.

B) they lack varied viewpoints.

C) they are highly influenced by global news.

D) they remain disconnected from politics.

41

As used in line 63, "draw" most nearly means

A) depict.

B) derive.

C) persuade.

D) lure.

42

It can be reasonably inferred that Agnew believes which of the following about network news?

A) Its pervasive influence is fueled by corporate greed.

B) It ultimately betrays its intended purpose.

C) Its presentation and choice of information are distressingly subjective.

D) It unfortunately neglects to highlight actual societal problems.

CONTINUE

Questions 43-52 are based on the following passages.

The following two readings consider recent research in cell and molecular biology.

Passage 1

Are viruses alive? Among the criteria for life is the requirement that an organism be able to reproduce; most organisms do so without the help of other species. For example,
Line bacteria use binary fission, in which they replicate their genes
5 and then split into two new cells. More complex organisms, such as humans, combine genes from two parents in order to produce offspring.

With these biology fundamentals in mind, some scientists argue that viruses are not alive because they require hosts in
10 order to reproduce. In other words, viruses do not possess autonomous genetic material, and instead need to infect a host so that the host cells will generate and transmit infected genes. According to Paul Berg, a Nobel Prize winner in chemistry, scientists at Oak Ridge National Laboratory "discovered that
15 the virus 'turns off' the cell's machinery for making its own proteins and 'instructs' the cell's machinery to make proteins characteristic of the virus" instead.

However, many parasitic organisms require hosts in order to reproduce. For example, experiments performed by Ronald
20 Ross showed that *Plasmodium* (the malaria parasite) is injected into human blood when an infected female *Anopheles* mosquito bites a human. The parasite multiplies and develops in the human host and then circulates in the host's blood. When a mosquito bites the infected human, the parasites are swallowed
25 by the mosquito. They then migrate to the mosquito's salivary glands. When the infected mosquito bites another human, the parasite's life cycle begins again.

Despite the fact that *Plasmodium* would not be able to reproduce without infecting both mosquitoes and humans,
30 *Plasmodium* is classified as an organism. Thus, the fact that viruses require host infection in order to reproduce should not exclude them from the category of living things.

Passage 2

At least in their own minds, many researchers have settled the question of whether viruses are organisms or not. "A rock
35 is not alive. A metabolically active sack, devoid of genetic material and the potential for propagation [i.e. a virus], is also not alive. A bacterium, though, is alive," declared Luis P. Villarreal in the 2008 *Scientific American* article "Are Viruses Alive?" Of course, Villarreal could have shut down the
40 discussion then and there—but he didn't. Instead, he spent the remainder of his feature article explaining that the question of how to classify viruses is important because "how scientists regard this question influences their thinking about the mechanisms of evolution."

45 Despite their inability to propagate without taking control of a host, viruses possess other rudiments of life: Villarreal and other researchers, such as Philip Bell of Macquarrie University, have argued that cell nuclei are "of viral origin." But the evolutionary mechanism of "survival
50 of the fittest" is also closely associated with viruses. Some of this, of course, is pop culture hype: thanks to Michael Crichton's science fiction novel *The Andromeda Strain*, readers all over the world have been presented with the spectacle of hostile viruses from outer space, the
55 microscopic kin of bigger, bloodier Hollywood aliens. Some of this, however, is sound science: the struggle for dominance that plays out on a viral level can perhaps help us understand the struggles that play out across ecosystems.

60 Nor are viruses the only host-dependent life-forms or quasi-life-forms that illuminate the larger mechanisms of survival in the natural world. While debates over the status of viruses are settling down, a new discussion has sprung up over another source of biological affliction: tumors.
65 In 2010, Mark Vincent of the London Regional Cancer Program argued that tumor appearances are "speciation events," each of which involves the generation of a "cancer genome." Similar ideas were set forth one year later by researchers from the University of California,
70 Berkeley, who argued that a body cell that mutates into a cancer cell becomes "a cell with totally new traits—that is, a new phenotype." It now becomes possible to ask a radical new question: if tumors are essentially parasitic life forms struggling for survival, might viruses be similar yet
75 more rudimentary forms, struggling to attain the structures and advantages of autonomous life?

43

The main purpose of each passage is to

A) introduce and analyze perspectives in a scientific debate that surrounds viruses.

B) systematically argue in favor of the idea that viruses are living organisms.

C) explain why the question "are viruses alive?" cannot be answered in any definitive way.

D) suggest that viruses are similar to tumors.

44

As used in lines 15 and 16, "machinery" most nearly means

A) artificial creations.

B) specific technology.

C) social arrangements.

D) vital functions.

45

Like Luis P. Villarreal in Passage 2, the author of Passage 1 would agree that

A) viruses should not under any circumstance be classified as life forms.

B) viruses may plausibly be classified as life forms.

C) viruses do not contain their own independent genes.

D) viruses and bacteria have several common traits.

46

Which choice provides the best evidence for the answer to the previous question?

A) Lines 3-5 ("For example . . . cells")

B) Lines 10-12 ("In other . . . genes")

C) Lines 18-19 ("However, many . . . reproduce")

D) Lines 30-32 ("Thus, the fact . . . things")

47

The phrase "biology fundamentals" in line 8 of Passage 1 refers to

A) facts about how organisms create offspring.

B) questions about whether viruses are alive.

C) processes unique to single-cell organisms such as bacteria.

D) information about how viruses take over host cells.

48

The author of Passage 1 discusses *Plasmodium* (line 20) in order to show that

A) the ideas of Ronald Ross are gaining popularity.

B) both viruses and bacteria can cause disease epidemics.

C) viruses commonly infect large hosts by entering their blood cells.

D) viruses share important characteristics with recognized life forms.

49

The author of Passage 2 argues that current ideas about viruses have been

A) definitively summarized by Luis P. Villarreal.

B) impacted by works of the imagination.

C) held up to doubt as researchers learn more about tumors.

D) wrongly neglected by cell biologists.

50

Which choice provides the best evidence for the answer to the previous question?

A) Lines 39-40 ("Of course . . . didn't")

B) Lines 45-46 ("Despite their . . . life")

C) Lines 51-54 ("thanks to . . . space")

D) Lines 68-72 ("Similar ideas . . . phenotype")

51

As used in line 67, "generation" most nearly means

A) creation.

B) inspiration.

C) age group.

D) subdivision.

52

According to the author of Passage 2, tumors and viruses are similar in that both are

A) detrimental to fully-formed organisms.

B) rudimentary organic forms that can become independent organisms.

C) capable of "speciation events."

D) studied by scientists who seek to understand the origins of cell nuclei.

STOP

If you finish before time is called, you may check your work on this section only.
Do not turn to any other section.

Writing Test
35 MINUTES, 44 QUESTIONS

Turn to Section 2 of your answer sheet to answer the questions in this section.

DIRECTIONS

Each passage below is accompanied by a number of questions. For some questions, you will consider how the passage might be revised to improve the expression of ideas. For other questions, you will consider how the passage might be edited to correct errors in sentence structure, usage, or punctuation. A passage or a question may be accompanied by one or more graphics (such as a table or graph) that you will consider as you make revising and editing decisions.

Some questions will direct you to an underlined portion of a passage. Other questions will direct you to a location in a passage or ask you to think about the passage as a whole.

After reading each passage, choose the answer to each question that most effectively improves the quality of writing in the passage or that makes the passage conform to the conventions of standard written English. Many questions include a "NO CHANGE" option. Choose that option if you think the best choice is to leave the relevant portion of the passage as it is.

Questions 1-11 are based on the following passage and supplementary material.

Marine Biology: Combining Industry, Ecology, and Nutrition

For many marine biologists, careers in education and research **1** may be very appealing. Other marine biologists may gravitate to the numerous opportunities for industry and applied science careers after earning a Bachelor's or a Master's degree in marine biology— **2** believe it or not, in the aquaculture industry, which has had an 8.3% annual rate of growth worldwide since the mid-1980s and is currently the fastest-growing food production industry.

1

A) NO CHANGE.
B) are intrinsic to self-actualization.
C) are undeniably great things to have.
D) may appeal in truly massive ways.

2

A) NO CHANGE
B) astonishingly,
C) for instance,
D) in contrast,

CONTINUE

American demand for seafood [3] have risen in recent years, partly due to growing awareness of the health benefits of fish; the 2010 USDA Dietary Guidelines recommend that Americans eat eight ounces of fish per week for the beneficial omega-3 fatty acids. However, the majority of the farmed seafood that Americans consume is produced in foreign countries and imported to the U.S., which [4] produces five times less seafood than it once did.

[3]
A) NO CHANGE
B) has risen
C) have rose
D) has rose

[4]
Which choice offers the most accurate and relevant interpretation of the data in the table?
A) NO CHANGE
B) purchases most of its seafood from China.
C) produces five times less seafood than China.
D) is only the fifth largest-producer in the world.

Country	Global Rank	Million Metric Tons Produced Annually
China	1	44
Indonesia	2	5.8
India	3	4.9
Japan	4	4.73
United States	5	4.48

CONTINUE

In the United States, two-thirds of the marine aquaculture industry is shellfish production: oysters, clams, [5] and production of mussels. Marine shellfish are farmed in coastal areas, which makes these farms easily accessible but also limits the potential locations for these operations. Yet for a marine biologist looking to work in aquaculture, such a location can be the [6] cite of a promising career.

Some shellfish farms consist of floating cages or nets, to which shellfish like oysters and mussels [7] are attached. These organisms are exposed to the natural fluctuations in their environment. Other farms consist of enclosed tanks, [8] which have never been a source of controversy among animal rights groups. It is important for marine biologists to monitor these factors in the waters around shellfish farms in order to ensure that conditions remain optimal for the health and growth of the shellfish. Marine biologists can also research and provide novel solutions [9] with problems in shellfish production. For example, farmers can accelerate oyster growth by agitating the oysters in a tumbler. When tumbled, an oyster opens and closes its shell, resulting in a stronger core muscle and ultimately a bigger oyster, once it is harvested.

[5]
A) and production of mussels.
B) and that of mussels.
C) and mussels are produced.
D) and mussels.

[6]
A) NO CHANGE
B) sight
C) site
D) sighting

[7]
A) NO CHANGE
B) were attached
C) being attached
D) which are attached

[8]
The author wishes to provide information that explains the practical benefits of the enclosed tanks. Which choice best accomplishes the author's purpose?
A) NO CHANGE
B) which are growing more popular despite their high maintenance costs.
C) which utilize technologies first developed for agriculture.
D) which permit the farmer to control variables like temperature and salinity.

[9]
A) NO CHANGE
B) as problems
C) to problems
D) from problems

While not all aquaculture development is beneficial to the local environment, shellfish production can have a positive effect on local waters due to the way that oysters and mussels filter water as they feed. One oyster filters approximately 1-4 liters of water per hour. When the particles that the oyster consumes are contaminated with pollutants, the oyster consumes these pollutants and excretes them to the bottom of the waterway, where seaweed grows and captures the pollutants in **10** their cells. Marine biologists who have a thorough understanding of local ecology can ensure that a region's aquaculture is not only economically productive in the **11** short term; also sustainable in the long term.

10
A) NO CHANGE
B) there
C) its
D) its'

11
A) NO CHANGE
B) short term, it is also
C) short term, although also
D) short term but also

CONTINUE

Questions 12-22 are based on the following passage.

Furnishing Your Room with Mushrooms

The fields of home decoration and architectural design [12] has often taken inspiration from forms found in the natural world. But what happens when designers directly incorporate the natural world, instead of simply imitating or approximating the shapes of trees, fungi, and other organic material? In some respects, this question has been answered by Phil Ross, the founder of MycoWorks and [13] pioneering in mushroom-based home decoration.

[1] According to its web site, MycoWorks creates "inventions that use nature's systems to solve human challenges." [2] Ross calls the practice of creating mycelium shapes and designs "mycotecture." [3] While it is yet to be seen whether mycelium can become the basis of actual, full-scale architecture, [14] Ross's mycotecture has yielded a few promising constructions. [4] Mycelium can be shaped into individual bricks, and Ross [15] unveiled arches and also revealed wall segments made of such bricks in 2009 at the Dusseldorf Art Museum. [5] The most important of these inventions is the company's namesake, mycelium, a versatile fungus compound that is lightweight, biodegradable, and easily molded into different shapes. [16]

12
A) NO CHANGE
B) have often taken
C) which often takes
D) which often take

13
A) NO CHANGE
B) pioneering with
C) a pioneer in
D) a pioneer with

14
A) NO CHANGE
B) although Ross's mycotecture has yielded
C) if Ross's mycotecture yields
D) Ross's mycotecture yielding

15
A) NO CHANGE
B) unveiled arches and he revealed
C) unveiled both arches and
D) unveiled arches, revealing

16
To make the paragraph most logical, sentence 5 should be placed
A) where it is now.
B) after sentence 1.
C) after sentence 2.
D) after sentence 3.

Ross and his team have also unveiled a group of chairs and end tables called the Yamanakita series: these creations were "inspired by the fashion designer Alexander McQueen" and [17] collaborate textured, gold-tinted mycelium with elegant touches (such as smooth chair legs of solid walnut wood) that McQueen would have envied.

Mycelium [18] has indeed shown its promise as a design element. But perhaps more importantly for the environment-conscious executives and employees of MycoWorks, mycelium has revealed itself as an environment-friendly substance. The mycelium used in the Yamanaka furniture, for example, was grown [19] in large batches over several months. (If not disposed of properly, such by-products can become a source of pollution.) [20] Another innovation is the series of shapes called the "polyominoes." These oddly-angled bricks can hold traditional building elements, such as wooden beams, firmly in place. However, the polyominoes also bind to one another naturally, without any need for industrial or toxic adhesives, due to the cohesive action of the mycelium cells.

17
A) NO CHANGE
B) corroborate
C) confuse
D) combine

18
A) NO CHANGE
B) has however shown
C) in contrast shows
D) shockingly shows

19
Which choice most effectively supports the author's claims about the appeal of mycelium?
A) NO CHANGE
B) using a process known only to MycoWorks.
C) in the most inexpensive manner possible.
D) by recycling a few different agricultural by-products.

20
Which choice most effectively combines the underlined sentences?
A) Another innovation is the series of shapes called the "polyominoes," traditional building elements, such as wooden beams, being held firmly in place by oddly-angled bricks.
B) Another innovation is the series of shapes called the "polyominoes," oddly-angled bricks that can firmly hold in place traditional building elements, such as wooden beams.
C) Another innovation, called the "polyominoes," are a series of shapes and they are oddly-angled bricks that can hold more traditional elements, such as wooden beams, firmly in place.
D) Another innovation, called the "polyominoes," is a series of shapes and oddly angled bricks, it can hold more traditional building elements, such as wooden beams, firmly in place.

CONTINUE

But will Ross's mycelium ever be widely used, in home decoration or any other field? [21] At present, the Yamanakita tables sell for $300 each, the chairs for $3000. There is a sense that Ross's entire endeavor is something of an eccentric passion project, though, to be fair, Ross himself seems to sense this: he recently appeared in Scientific American wearing an impractically huge mycelium hat. The MycoWorks team nonetheless [22] soldiers on, and continues to find new believers. As the Scientific American reporter who covered MycoWorks declared, "the mushroom chairs might be beacons to the dream of a mushroom future. At the very least, they alerted me that such a dream existed."

[21]

The writer is considering deleting the underlined sentence. Should the writer do so?

A) Yes, because the author does not discuss the price of mycelium at any other point in the passage.

B) Yes, because it is inconsistent with the thoroughly positive tone taken by the author when discussing mycelium.

C) No, because it provides an example that leads into the discussion of differing perceptions of mycelium.

D) No, because it is consistent with the harshly critical tone taken by the author when discussing mycelium.

[22]

A) NO CHANGE
B) soldier
C) will soldier
D) had soldiered

Questions 23-33 are based on the following passage.

A Late Start, and a Better Start

"Early to bed, early to rise" has been a mantra for many generations. However, it may not be accurate for high school students. Humans have circadian rhythms, more commonly known as biological **23** clocks. These rhythms dictate when we would naturally be awake and asleep, as well as when we are most alert. When those rhythms are **24** disputed, students feel more tired, do not learn as effectively, **25** yet suffer from increased susceptibility to emotional problems, particularly depression.

According to a study published in *Learning, Media and Technology*, adolescents require nine hours of sleep per night, more **26** than other ages require. In addition, teens exhibit optimal mental and emotional functioning when they sleep later. The researchers in charge of the study noted the common belief among adults "that adolescents are tired, irritable and uncooperative because they choose to stay up too late or **27** are difficult to wake in the morning because they are lazy." In reality, teens' biological clocks simply run on a later timetable.

23

Which choice best combines the two sentences at the underlined portion?
A) clocks, even though they
B) clocks, when they
C) clocks, and
D) clocks, which

24

A) NO CHANGE
B) distressed
C) disrupted
D) demolished

25

A) NO CHANGE
B) and suffer
C) although they
D) suffering

26

A) NO CHANGE
B) then other ages
C) than people of other ages
D) then people of other ages

27

A) NO CHANGE
B) had been
C) have been
D) were

CONTINUE

The researchers also noted the unfortunate difference between "social time" (the time of day in which teens are expected to attend school, do homework, and participate in after-school activities) [28] to "biological time" (the time during which teenagers are most alert and receptive to new information). The latter time is not a matter of choice; rather, it is dictated by adolescents' biological clocks. [29] Many high schools start classes between 7:00 and 8:00 a.m., so that students are required to wake up around 5:00 or 6:00 a.m. Teenage circadian rhythms, however, suggest that teens should wake up around 9:00 or 9:30, and so a school start time of 11:00 or 11:30 a.m. would be optimal.

28

A) NO CHANGE
B) from
C) and
D) or

29

Which choice best supports the author's argument that school schedules are not coordinated to follow the biological clocks of high school students?

A) NO CHANGE
B) School administrators have attempted to keep their students energetic by providing healthy breakfast choices.
C) When teenagers get out of school, they often have reserves of excess energy that should be harnessed for homework and extracurricular pursuits.
D) Many teenagers would prefer to do their homework between 8:00 and 10:00 at night, yet parents with traditional views insist that hours immediately after school (3:00 to 6:00) are optimal.

[1] Even though 8:40 am is probably still too early for high school students to function at their best, data indicate that the results of the change were promising. [2] After becoming aware that teens might benefit from later school start times, the Minneapolis school district performed an [30] experiment involving the temporary adoption of a later start time for its high schools: 8:40 am instead of the traditional 7:15 am. [3] In a study of 50,000 Minneapolis students, student achievement and satisfaction rose with the later start time, and most parents reported that their teens were "easier to live with." [4] It is thus not surprising that approximately 90% of the Minneapolis parents surveyed were in favor of the later start time. [31]

[32] These positive results along with other scientific data, suggest that adolescents would benefit not only academically but also emotionally from start times that align with their circadian rhythms. As a result of having happier and more successful children, [33] later high school start times would reap benefits for parents too.

[30]
A) NO CHANGE
B) experiment; involving
C) experiment, it involved
D) experiment, this involves

[31]
To make the order of ideas in the paragraph most logical, sentence 1 should be placed
A) where it is now.
B) after sentence 2.
C) after sentence 3.
D) after sentence 4

[32]
A) NO CHANGE
B) These positive results, along with other scientific data
C) These positive results along, with other scientific data,
D) These positive results, along with other scientific data,

[33]
A) NO CHANGE
B) benefits too would be reaped for parents by later high school start times.
C) parents too would reap benefits from later high school start times.
D) high schools that have later start times would reap benefits for parents too.

CONTINUE

Questions 34-44 are based on the following passage.

Richard Brinsley Sheridan: A Man for All Comedies

— 1 —

"Comedy of Manners" is the classification that literary critics use for these plays. Wycherley and Congreve were the major seventeenth-century innovators, but this mode of writing has continued through to the present day; [34] they claim that the popular *Carry On* films are examples of this persistent yet frequently tedious form of comedy. The two main concerns of the genre seem to be wealth and romance. While no one would deny [35] when the pursuit of love and money occupies a great deal of energy and time, the treatment of these themes under Comedy of Manners conventions was, [36] unfortunately, often superficial.

— 2 —

Thirty years after the death of Shakespeare, the performance of plays was [37] forbid by order of British head of state Oliver Cromwell. This ban was not lifted until the return of the Stuart monarchy in 1660, when a new, very different brand of theater was instituted. The recently-returned king, the "Merry Monarch" Charles II, [38] had been sent into exile by politicians who viewed Cromwell favorably and was ready to give encouragement to all the delights of the new theaters. Many of the new plays presented were comedies, and comedies moreover that derived their humor from mocking the manners and foibles of their fashionable audiences.

34

Which of the following is the best replacement for the underlined portion?
A) critics
B) plays
C) Wycherley and Congreve
D) wealth and romance

35

A) NO CHANGE
B) because the pursuit
C) if the pursuit
D) that the pursuit

36

A) NO CHANGE
B) surprisingly,
C) consequently,
D) for example,

37

A) NO CHANGE
B) forbidding
C) forbidden
D) being forbid

38

Which of the following most effectively offers background explaining why Charles would promote the delights of the new theaters and the comedies they presented?
A) NO CHANGE
B) had enjoyed years of revelry in the more frivolous France
C) was well known for his merry temperament
D) knew much about the theaters from Shakespeare's time

— 3 —

Luckily, there is at least one Comedy of Manners writer who allows **39** one to see how laughter can lead us beyond the artificiality of witty dialogue, who enables us to glimpse the true depths of the human condition. That man was Richard Brinsley Sheridan. Sheridan was born in Ireland in 1751, moved to England with his theatrically-inclined parents, eloped with a young heiress, and **40** eventually became the owner of the Royal Theatre in London. He went on to write several comedies, all of them successful in their time. Sheridan loved the wit and depth of language, not only what words reveal in their day-to-day usage but also what they can reveal of character in their rhythm and sound. He gave his characters names that indeed **41** don't make any sense at first, but in fact reveal specific personalities and psychologies: Mr. Snake, Mrs. Candour, Sir Benjamin Backbite, Lady Teazle.

39
A) NO CHANGE
B) you to see
C) us to see
D) DELETE the underlined portion

40
A) NO CHANGE
B) eventually he became the owner
C) became eventual the owner
D) he became the owner eventual

41
A) NO CHANGE
B) are really weird
C) seem rather superficial
D) nobody in the real world has

CONTINUE

— 4 —

A playwright of multi-faceted intelligence, **[42]** humor and misfortune can go hand-in-hand, as Sheridan also knew. When his own theater caught fire and burned to the ground, Sheridan was ruined financially. **[43]** Although the theater was destroyed, a friend found him in a coffee house across the road, a glass of wine in his hand. Sheridan looked up and said gently, "A man may surely be allowed to take a glass of wine by his own fireside."

— 5 —

Now, *that* is Comedy of Manners.

Question [44] asks about the previous passage as a whole.

[42]

A) NO CHANGE
B) humor and misfortune can go hand-in-hand, as Sheridan has also known.
C) Sheridan also knew that humor and misfortune can go hand-in-hand.
D) Sheridan has also known that humor and misfortune can go hand-in-hand.

[43]

A) NO CHANGE
B) On the night of the fire,
C) In the vicinity of the theater,
D) Moreover,

Think about the previous passage as a whole as you answer question 44.

[44]

To make the passage most logical, paragraph 1 should be placed

A) where it is now.
B) after paragraph 2.
C) after paragraph 3.
D) after paragraph 4.

STOP
If you finish before time is called, you may check your work on this section only.
Do not turn to any other section.

Math Test - No Calculator

25 MINUTES, 20 QUESTIONS

DIRECTIONS

For each question from 1-15, choose the best answer choice provided in the multiple choice bank and fill in the appropriate circle in the provided answer key. Alternatively, for questions **16-20,** answer the problem and enter your answer in the grid-in section of the answer key. Refer to the directions given before question 16 as to how to enter your answers for the grid-in questions. You may complete scratch work in any empty space in your test booklet.

NOTES

A. Calculator usage **is not allowed** in this section.
B. Variables, constants, and coefficients used represent real numbers unless indicated otherwise.
C. All figures are created to appropriate scale unless the question states otherwise.
D. All figures are two-dimensional unless the question states otherwise.
E. The domain of any given function is all real numbers x for which the function, $f(x)$, is a real number unless the question states otherwise.

REFERENCE

$A = \pi r^2$
$C = 2\pi r$

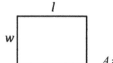
$A = lw$

$A = \frac{1}{2}bh$

$c^2 = a^2 + b^2$

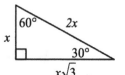
Special Right Triangle

Special Right Triangle

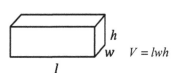
$V = lwh$

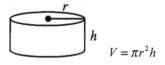
$V = \pi r^2 h$

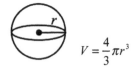
$V = \frac{4}{3}\pi r^3$

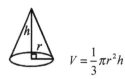
$V = \frac{1}{3}\pi r^2 h$

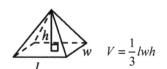
$V = \frac{1}{3}lwh$

There are $360°$ in a circle.
There are 2π radians in a circle.
There are $180°$ in a triangle.

CONTINUE ➡

1

Resha and Kiley wrote a total of 842 text messages in the last month. If Resha wrote 4 less than twice the number of text messages that Kiley wrote, which of the following equations could be solved to find x, the number of text messages written by Kiley?

A) $2x - 4 = 842$

B) $3x - 4 = 842$

C) $4 - 2x = 842$

D) $4 - x = 842$

2

$$b\sqrt{b}$$

The expression above is *not* equivalent to which of the following expressions?

A) $\sqrt{b^3}$

B) $b^{\frac{3}{2}}$

C) $\dfrac{b^3}{b^2}$

D) $\sqrt{\dfrac{b^5}{b^2}}$

3

If $4x^2 - 17 = 11$, what is the value of $16x^2$?

A) -24

B) 7

C) 56

D) 112

4

$$4x + 9y = 12$$
$$5x + 3y = 12$$

What is the value of $3x + 4y$ given that the coordinate pair (x, y) is a solution to the system of equations above?

A) 6

B) 8

C) 12

D) 24

CONTINUE

5

$$\frac{a-2}{2} = \frac{3a}{a+8}$$

If the equation above is true, what is the value of a^2 ?

A) −4

B) 4

C) 16

D) 256

6

A professional steam cleaning service charges its clients by using the expression $CLh + f$, where C is the number of cleaning machines, L is the number of laborers, h is the number of hours, and f is the square footage of the area to be cleaned. If the carpets at a certain location are stained much deeper than expected, which of the following values would be affected the most?

A) C

B) L

C) f

D) CLh

7

Line m is perpendicular to a line with the equation $y = -Kx + t$. If line m goes through the point $(4,3)$ and has a y-intercept at the point $(0,b)$, which of the following is equivalent to b?

A) $b = 4 - \dfrac{3}{K}$

B) $b = 3 - \dfrac{4}{K}$

C) $b = 4 + 3K$

D) $b = 3 + 4K$

8

$$2x + y = 15$$
$$kx - 4y = 100$$

If the system of equations above has one solution at the point $(1, y)$, what is the value of k?

A) 13

B) 48

C) 152

D) 168

CONTINUE

9

The quadratic function $y = -(x-2)^2 + 4$ intercepts the origin. If the absolute maximum of the function occurs at point A, what is the distance between point A and the origin?

A) $2\sqrt{3}$

B) $2\sqrt{5}$

C) 5

D) $4\sqrt{3}$

10

In the polynomial $g(x)$, if $g(2) = 1$, which of the following must be true?

A) $x-2$ is a factor of $g(x)$.

B) $x-1$ is a factor of $g(x)$.

C) $x+2$ is a factor of $g(x)$.

D) The remainder when $g(x)$ is divided by $x-2$ is 1.

11

The quadratic function $y = x^2 - 12x + 20$ intercepts another quadratic function $y = -x^2 + 12x - 34$ at the points A and B. What is the length of $\overline{AB}$?

A) 3

B) 4

C) 6

D) 9

12

If the expression $2x^2 - 7x + M$ is divided by the binomial $2x + 5$, the remainder is $\dfrac{4M}{2x+5}$. What is the value of M?

A) 6

B) 10

C) 36

D) 100

CONTINUE

13

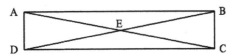

In the figure above, quadrilateral ABCD is a rectangle. If the measure of $\angle DAE$ is four times the measure of $\angle BAE$, what is the measure of $\angle AED + \angle BEC$ in degrees?

A) 18

B) 36

C) 72

D) 144

14

For integers a and b, if $|a-b| = 2a$ and $a+b = 0$, which of the following must be true?

I. $a^2 = b^2$
II. $a - b < 0$
III. $ab < 0$

A) I only

B) I and III only

C) II and III only

D) I , II, and III

15

The coordinate pairs $(\frac{-1+\sqrt{13}}{3}, 0)$ and $(\frac{-1-\sqrt{13}}{3}, 0)$ are solutions to which of the following equations?

A) $y = 3x^2 + 2x - 4$

B) $y = \frac{3}{2}x^2 + 2x - 8$

C) $y = x^2 - 16x + 39$

D) $y = 3x^2 - 40x + 13$

CONTINUE

DIRECTIONS

For each question from 16-20, solve and enter your answer in the grid-in section of your answer sheet as described below.

A. Write out your answers in the boxes at the top of each column in order to help you fill in the circles accurately. Remember, you will only receive credit for the circles that are filled in correctly, not for the written answer at the top of the columns.

B. Mark only a single circle in each column.

C. There are no negative answers.

D. If the problem has more than one correct answer, grid only one of the correct answers.

E. When your answer is a **mixed number**, such as $1\frac{1}{2}$, it should be entered as 1.5 or $3/2$. You cannot enter a mixed number because there is no room to fill in a circle that represents a space.

F. If you enter a **decimal answer** with more digits then the grid can handle, the answer may be rounded or truncated, but it absolutely must fill the entire grid.

Answer: $\frac{8}{21}$

Answer: 6.4

Answer: 102 - both positions are correct

REMEMBER:
You can begin writing your answers in any column as long as there is enough space. Leave unused columns blank.

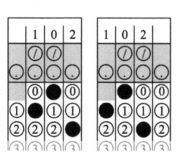

The ways to correctly grid $\frac{7}{9}$ are:

CONTINUE

©Integrated Educational Services, 2016 **www.ies2400.com** | Unauthorized copying or reuse of any part of this page is illegal.

16

$$2 + \frac{3}{7}\left(x - \frac{1}{3}\right) = \frac{5}{2}$$

What value of x makes the equation above true?

17

For what value of x, where $x > 0$, is the equation $255 = (x^2 + 1)(x^2 - 1)$ true?

18

In a recent gymnastics competition, Team A scored 30 points less than four times the number of points that Team B scored. Team C scored 61 points more than half of the number of points that Team B scored. If Team A and Team C shared in the victory, having earned the same number of points, how many more points did each team have than Team B?

19

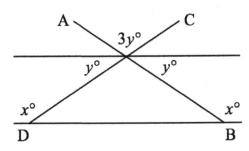

If $\overline{AB}$ intersects $\overline{CD}$ as shown in the figure above, what is the value of x?

CONTINUE

20

A 26 foot bridge crosses a stream at an incline. If one bank of the river is 2 feet above the height of the water and the other bank is 12 feet above water level, what is the tangent of the angle that the bridge makes with the surface of the water?

STOP

If you finish before time is called, you may check your work on this section only.

Do not turn to any other section.

Math Test - Calculator

55 MINUTES, 38 QUESTIONS

$A = \pi r^2$
$C = 2\pi r$

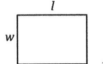

$A = lw$

$A = \frac{1}{2}bh$

$c^2 = a^2 + b^2$

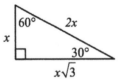

Special Right Triangle

Special Right Triangle

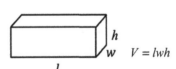

$V = lwh$

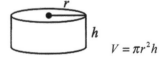

$V = \pi r^2 h$

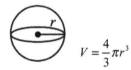

$V = \frac{4}{3}\pi r^3$

$V = \frac{1}{3}\pi r^2 h$

$V = \frac{1}{3}lwh$

There are $360°$ in a circle.
There are 2π radians in a circle.
There are $180°$ in a triangle.

CONTINUE

1

$$(12x^2 + 5x + 1) - (10x^2 - 5x - 1)$$

The difference of the polynomials shown above is equivalent to which of the following expressions?

A) $2x^2 + 10x + 2$

B) $2x^2 + 10x$

C) $2x^2 + 2$

D) $2x^2$

2

x	y
-3	5
0	7
6	11
9	13

Which of the following linear equations is displayed in the *xy*-table above?

A) $y = \dfrac{2}{3}x + 7$

B) $y = \dfrac{2}{3}x + 5$

C) $y = 2x + 7$

D) $y = 3x + 5$

3

Distribution of Actuarial Students

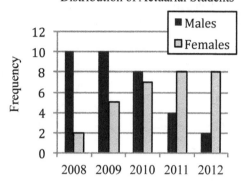

If one actuarial student were to be selected at random from all of the actuarial students from 2008 to 2012, what is the probability that the student is a female from either 2011 or 2012?

A) $\dfrac{3}{32}$

B) $\dfrac{1}{8}$

C) $\dfrac{1}{4}$

D) $\dfrac{11}{32}$

4

Approximately 22% of the students at Lakesedge High School are sophomores and 40% of the sophomores took the class Contemporary American Issues. If there are 1670 students in Lakesedge High School, approximately how many sophomores took Contemporary American Issues?

A) 135

B) 150

C) 370

D) 670

CONTINUE

5

Sales for a Computer Wholesale Company from 1994 to 1999

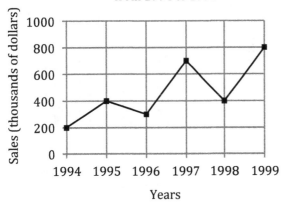

The graph above shows the total sales in thousands of dollars each year from 1994 to 1999 for a computer wholesale company. Which of the following best describes the trend in sales from 1994 to 1999?

A) The sales steadily increased each year.

B) The sales increased and then decreased.

C) The sales increased on average by approximately $100 each year.

D) The sales increased on average by approximately $100,000 each year.

6

If $\dfrac{7}{2}a = \dfrac{5}{b}$ and $a = 5$, what is the value of b?

A) $\dfrac{2}{7}$

B) $\dfrac{7}{2}$

C) $\dfrac{50}{7}$

D) 14

7

Madeline can drink 13 bottles of water in 5 minutes. Approximately how many seconds would it take Madeline to drink 3 bottles of water?

A) 1.2

B) 15

C) 23

D) 69

8

The enrollment for a training seminar for construction foremen on how to employ tablets as a means of updating progress at construction sites has increased by 18 people since the seminar's inception six years ago. If the current enrollment is 42 construction foremen, which of the following linear equations could be used to estimate the enrollment, y, based on the number of years, x, that have passed since the first year the seminar was held?

A) $y = 18x + 42$

B) $y = 18x + 24$

C) $y = 3x + 42$

D) $y = 3x + 24$

CONTINUE

9

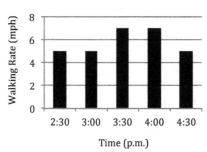

Average Walking Rate During an
Afternoon Hike

Hernando was hiking one afternoon and he would record
his walking rate in miles per hour every half an hour until
his hike was over. At one point during his hike, Hernando
switched from walking uphill to walking downhill. If
Hernando walks at a constant rate uphill and a constant
rate downhill, Hernando most likely transitioned from
walking uphill to walking downhill during which of the
following time frames?

A) 2:30 to 3:00

B) 3:00 to 3:30

C) 3:30 to 4:00

D) 4:00 to 4:30

10

$$y = a(x-h)^2 + k$$

The quadratic equation above is the vertex form of a
quadratic function where a, h, and k are constants and
(h,k) is the vertex of the function's graph. Which of the
following equations gives the x-coordinate of the vertex in
terms or y, a, x, and k, where $x > 0$?

A) $h = \dfrac{y-k}{a} - x$

B) $h = x - \dfrac{y-k}{a}$

C) $h = \sqrt{\dfrac{y-k}{a}} - x$

D) $h = x - \sqrt{\dfrac{y-k}{a}}$

Questions 11 and 12 refer to the following information.

Name of Tree	Growth Rate (Feet per year)	Years to Maturity
Empress	15	3.33
Lombardy Poplar	10	6
Eucalyptus	8	5
Quaking Aspen	5	10
Cleveland Pear	4	7.5

The chart above shows the names, growth rates, and years to
maturity of 5 of the fastest growing trees in the world. A tree's
maturity is defined as the point at which a tree's future growth
is negligable and the tree has reached its highest height.

11

Which of the following pairs of trees will be of the same
approximate height when they have reached maturity?

A) Empress and Lombardy Poplar

B) Eucalyptus and Cleveland Pear

C) Empress and Quaking Aspen

D) Lombardy Poplar and Quaking Aspen

12

The tree with the greatest height at maturity is what
percent taller than the tree with the lowest height at
maturity?

A) 50

B) 66

C) 100

D) 200

CONTINUE

13

At an arcade, a machine dispenses 4 tokens for every dollar placed in the machine. If a boy uses his tokens at a steady rate and puts a ten dollar bill in the machine every 20 minutes, which of the following equations represents t, the total number of tokens dispensed by the machine in m total minutes of time?

A) $t = 20(4)m$

B) $t = 20(10)(4)m$

C) $t = \dfrac{4m}{20}$

D) $t = \dfrac{10(4)m}{20}$

14

Name	Time (seconds)
Andrew	12
Brenda	9
Larissa	14
Mandeep	8
Roger	13
Shobitha	6
Willamina	12
Xavier	8

As a fun project to get her students interacting with each other, a kindergarten teacher decided to have every student tie both of his or her shoes and she recorded the time that it took each student to complete the task. She recorded the data in the table above. What is the median time it takes one of the students to tie his or her shoes?

A) 9

B) 10.5

C) 11.5

D) 12

15

A student conducting an experiment would like to test the theory that temperature affects the elasticity before breaking of a rubber band. The student takes a random sample of 20 rubber bands from Company A and places them in the freezer for 15 minutes. The student also takes a random sample of 20 of the same sized rubber bands from Company B and places them on a warming tray for 15 minutes. After the 15 minutes have passed, the student tests all 40 rubber bands. All of the rubber bands from the freezer snapped at under 10 inches of stretch length and all of the rubber bands from the warming tray broke at over 10 inches of stretch length. Which of the following conclusions can be drawn by the student?

A) Frozen rubber bands have less elasticity before breaking than rubber bands that have not been frozen.

B) Frozen rubber bands have less elasticity before breaking than rubber bands that have been warmed.

C) Frozen rubber bands from Company A have less elasticity before breaking than frozen rubber bands from Company B.

D) The student cannot draw a conclusion because he does not know whether the frozen rubber bands have less elasticity before breaking because they were frozen or because they were made by a different company.

16

Osmium is the densest of all metals. A single liter of osmium weighs 50 pounds. If there are 3.88 liters in every gallon, how many gallons of osmium would weigh 582 pounds?

A) 2

B) 2.65

C) 3

D) 11.64

CONTINUE

▼

Questions 17 and 18 refer to the following information.

$$y = 10 + 62x$$

$$y = 10(2)^x$$

Two stock market analysts have generated models for the growth of a stock that recently became publicly traded. The models predict the trading price of the stock, y, based on x, the number of years that have passed from the stock's opening trading date. Both analysts believe that the stock is going to be extremely successful over its first few years. However, one analyst believes that the stock will follow a linear growth model and the other analyst believes that the stock will see exponential growth.

17

By how much more does the analyst who generated the exponential model feel that the stock is going to increase from its 3rd to 4th year, than the analyst who predicts linear growth?

A) 18

B) 22

C) 40

D) 80

18

The linear growth model places the stock at its greatest advantage over the exponential model after approximately how many years have passed?

A) 2

B) 3

C) 4

D) 5

19

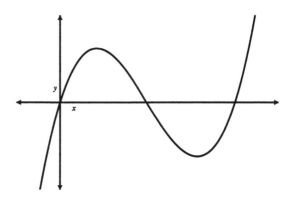

The function $g(x)$ is graphed in the xy-plane above. Which of the following could be the equation for $g(x)$?

A) $y = -x^2 + 2x$

B) $y = (x-3)^3$

C) $y = x^3 - 6x^2 + 8x$

D) $y = x^3 + 6x^2 + 8x$

20

The sum of four numbers is 84. If one of the numbers is equivalent to the sum of the other three numbers, what is the average of the other 3 numbers?

A) 7

B) 14

C) 21

D) 42

CONTINUE

21

On halloween, Mrs. Darcy had enough candy to give each person who came by her house 2 pieces of candy, and she then had 24 pieces of candy left over. If Mrs. Darcy had given each trick-or-treater 5 pieces of candy, she would have needed twice as much candy to give an equal amount to everyone that came by her house. How many trick-or-treaters came by Mrs. Darcy's house?

A) 48

B) 60

C) 96

D) 120

22

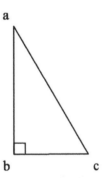

If the measure of $\angle acb$ is equivalent to $7x+4$ degrees and the measure of $\angle cab$ is equivalent to $4x-2$ degrees, what is the tangent of $\angle acb$?

A) $\dfrac{1}{2}$

B) $\dfrac{1}{\sqrt{3}}$

C) $\sqrt{3}$

D) 2

23

A cylindrical container of salt stands 6 inches tall and has a diameter of 3 inches. If all of the salt in the container is poured into another cylindrical container that has 3 times the diameter of the first container, how tall must the second container be, in inches, in order to hold the same amount of salt?

A) $\dfrac{1}{3}$

B) $\dfrac{2}{3}$

C) $\dfrac{4}{3}$

D) 2

24

$$H(x) = 2.1x + 48$$

The equation above is a best fit line that is used to predict the height of a person in inches, $H(x)$, given the person's shoe size, x, for shoe sizes where $6 < x < 13$. In a scatterplot, the residual of a data point is defined as the difference between an observed data point and a predicted data point, or *observed − predicted* . If the residual for a particular person who had a size 10 shoe was -3, what was the observed height in inches of the person?

A) 66

B) 69

C) 72

D) 75

CONTINUE

25

By what percent must each side of a cube with a volume of 8 cubic inches be increased in order to attain a volume of 27 cubic inches?

A) 25%

B) 50%

C) 67%

D) 150%

26

Which of the following *does not* detail an account balance that grows exponentially?

A) At the end of each month, an account grows by 5% of the total value of the account.

B) At the end of each month, an account increases by one tenth of its current value.

C) At the end of each month, an account increases by 10% more than $100.

D) At the end of each month, an account increases by 99% less than its current value.

27

Two different lines with two different slopes are both satisfied by the coordinate pairs $(5, 24)$ and $(15, h^2)$, where h happens to be the value of each of their respective slopes. What is the sum of the two slopes?

A) −10

B) −2

C) 10

D) 14

28

$$a = 2b + 3$$
$$4c = 5d + 6$$

In the system of linear relationships above, if a is equivalent to $3c$, which of the following expressions is equivalent in value to d?

A) $\dfrac{8b-6}{15}$

B) $\dfrac{8b+6}{5}$

C) $\dfrac{8b-3}{15}$

D) $\dfrac{2b-3}{5}$

CONTINUE

29

A radioactive isotope has decayed to a size of 202 kilograms over the last 20 years. If the isotope has a half-life of 40 years, which of the following is equivalent to I, the initial mass of the isotope 20 years prior?

A) $I = 202(\frac{1}{2})^2$

B) $I = 101(\frac{1}{2})^2$

C) $I = 101\sqrt{2}$

D) $I = 202\sqrt{2}$

30

In a group of 250 men and women, some are doctors and some are lawyers. There are 50 more women than men and there are 100 fewer doctors than lawyers. If there are 30 male doctors and a woman is to be selected at random, what is the probability that the woman is a lawyer?

A) $\dfrac{3}{10}$

B) $\dfrac{2}{5}$

C) $\dfrac{3}{5}$

D) $\dfrac{7}{10}$

CONTINUE

DIRECTIONS

For each question from 31-38, solve and enter your answer in the grid-in section of your answer sheet as described below.

A. Write out your answers in the boxes at the top of each column in order to help you fill in the circles accurately. Remember, you will only receive credit for the circles that are filled in correctly, not for the written answer at the top of the columns.

B. Mark only a single circle in each column.

C. There are no negative answers.

D. If the problem has more than one correct answer, grid only one of the correct answers.

E. When your answer is a **mixed number**, such as $1\frac{1}{2}$, it should be entered as 1.5 or 3/2. You cannot enter a mixed number because there is no room to fill in a circle that represents a space.

F. If you enter a **decimal answer** with more digits then the grid can handle, the answer may be rounded or truncated, but it absolutely must fill the entire grid.

Answer: $\frac{8}{21}$

Answer: 6.4

Written answer →
Decimal → point
← Fraction line

The ways to correctly grid $\frac{7}{9}$ are:

Answer: 102 - both positions are correct

REMEMBER:
You can begin writing your answers in any column as long as there is enough space. Leave unused columns blank.

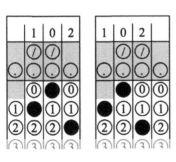

CONTINUE

31

If the function $g(x)$ is created by adding the expression $-x^2 + 22$ to the expression $2x^2 + 7x - 52$, what is the absolute value of the sum of the roots of $g(x)$?

32

Jefferson has at least one ten-dollar bill, one five-dollar bill, and one one-dollar bill in his wallet. If Jefferson has $30 in his wallet, what is one possible number of one-dollar bills he can have in his wallet?

33

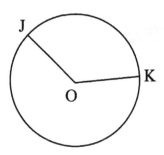

If the measure of arc $\overset{\frown}{JK}$ is 7 and the area of circle O is 16π, what is the measure of $\angle JOK$ in radians?

34

If $x > -2$ and $y \geq \dfrac{13}{2}x + 20$, what is the least integer value of y that satisfies the system of linear inequalities?

CONTINUE

35

The sum of 8 different positive integers is 124. If at least 3 of the integers are greater than 10, what is the greatest possible value that one of the integers can have?

36

$$f(x) = x^2 + abx + bc$$

In the function above, a, b, and c are positive integer constants. If $f(x)$ has only one root at the point $(-4, 0)$ and $b < a < c$, what is one possible value for the product abc?

CONTINUE

Questions 37-38 refer to the following information.

$$w = mg$$

The weight of an object, measured in Newtons, N, is the force of gravity acting on the object It can be calculated by multiplying the mass of an object, in kilograms, or kg, by gravitational acceleration in meters per second squared, or m/s^2 . The gravitational acceleration on Earth is 9.8 m/s^2 and the gravitational acceleration on Mars 3.75 m/s^2 .

37

If one Newton of force is equivalent to approximately 0.225 pounds of force and a 200-pound man were to stand on a standard scale on the surface of Mars, what would the scale read in pounds? *(Round the answer to the nearest tenth of a pound.)*

38

If the same man were to stand on the scale on a mysterious planet and the scale read 1,000 pounds, the planet would have to have a gravitational acceleration that was how many times as large as the gravitational acceleration on Mars? *(Round the answer to the nearest whole number.)*

STOP

If you finish before time is called, you may check your work on this section only.
Do not turn to any other section.

Answer Key: TEST 4

SAT

SECTION 1—READING

1.	A	11.	C	22.	A	33.	D	43.	A
2.	C	12.	D	23.	C	34.	A	44.	D
3.	D	13.	A	24.	C	35.	B	45.	C
4.	B	14.	C	25.	A	36.	D	46.	B
5.	B	15.	B	26.	D	37.	C	47.	A
6.	D	16.	B	27.	B	38.	B	48.	D
7.	B	17.	D	28.	B	39.	B	49.	B
8.	A	18.	D	29.	C	40.	B	50.	C
9.	C	19.	A	30.	A	41.	B	51.	A
10.	A	20.	D	31.	C	42.	C	52.	A
		21.	C	32.	C				

SECTION 2—WRITING

1.	A	12.	B	23.	D	34.	A
2.	C	13.	C	24.	C	35.	D
3.	B	14.	A	25.	B	36.	A
4.	D	15.	C	26.	C	37.	C
5.	D	16.	B	27.	A	38.	B
6.	C	17.	D	28.	C	39.	C
7.	A	18.	A	29.	A	40.	A
8.	D	19.	D	30.	A	41.	C
9.	C	20.	B	31.	B	42.	C
10.	C	21.	C	32.	D	43.	B
11.	D	22.	A	33.	C	44.	B

SECTION 3—MATH

1.	B
2.	C
3.	D
4.	B
5.	C
6.	D
7.	B
8.	C
9.	B
10.	D
11.	C
12.	B
13.	C
14.	A
15.	A

Fill-Ins:

16.	3/2 or 1.5
17.	4
18.	48
19.	144
20.	5/12, .416, or .417

SECTION 4—MATH

1.	A	13.	D	24.	A
2.	A	14.	B	25.	B
3.	C	15.	D	26.	C
4.	B	16.	C	27.	C
5.	D	17.	A	28.	A
6.	A	18.	B	29.	D
7.	D	19.	C	30.	D
8.	D	20.	B		
9.	B	21.	A		
10.	D	22.	C		
11.	C	23.	B		
12.	C				

Fill-Ins:

31.	7
32.	5, 10, or 15
33.	7/4 or 1.75
34.	8
35.	86
36.	64 or 128
37.	76.5
38.	13

Answer Explanations

SAT Practice Test #4

Section 1: Reading

QUESTION 1.

Choice A is correct. The passage depicts a conversation between Catherine, who becomes "impassioned" (line 26) when the topic of hunting is raised, and Edmond, who often challenges her views. The abundant quotations and descriptions of tones and gestures support A, while B ("nationwide") and D ("contemporary society") both raise topics that are much too broad for the content. C wrongly describes a "compromise": Catherine and Edmond simply terminate their dispute with "silence" (line 65), not with negotiation or mutual understanding.

QUESTION 2.

Choice C is correct. Although Edmond identifies himself as one of "We French" (line 33), he also speaks "flawless" (line 63) English. This information supports C and can be used to quickly eliminate A and B, which misidentify Edmond as an individual of ENGLISH descent. D rightly notes Edmond's country of origin, but makes a faulty assumption about his place of residence: it is not clear where exactly he lives, and, if anything, throughout the passage he voices familiarity with the FRENCH countryside.

QUESTION 3.

Choice D is correct. The word "aim" refers to hunting "food for the table" (line 39) and should thus be taken as a description of a purpose, goal, or "objective". A and B both refer to literal or physical "aiming", while C is out of context: people have the GOAL of hunting food, but are not necessarily ORDERED to hunt food or given a "direction" by others.

QUESTION 4.

Choice B is correct. In lines 30-33, Edmond raises a viewpoint on hunting and food that is attributed to Catherine as a "modern Englishwoman". This information supports B: A is too extreme (since Edmond learns in lines 25-29 that Catherine opposes English hunting) and C is too balanced (since Edmond does bluntly point out what he sees as flaws in Catherine's reasoning, and does NOT succeed in making her change her views). D involves a misreading of lines 65-67: the argument has ENDED by this point, so the new proposal cannot rightly be described as a distraction.

QUESTION 5.

Choice B is correct. See above for the explanation of the correct answer. A explains the ownership of the French national forests, C explains the view taken by the French, and D describes a period of relative calm AFTER the discussion between Catherine and Edmond. Keep in mind that A and C offer general factual statements, not strong attitudes towards Catherine.

QUESTION 6.

Choice D is correct. The line reference begins with an allusion to the "way" (line 46) hunting is performed in England, then goes on to describe hunting practices "In France" (line 47). This information supports D and eliminates A, since the comparison ONLY involves the practices surrounding hunting. B is out of scope, since Edmond cites a difference but not a form of conflict; C is also out of scope, since it is not clear that Edmond's information, which he could have gotten indirectly, is based on personal experience.

QUESTION 7.

Choice B is correct. The word "clean" refers to a "shot" that quickly and efficiently kills wildlife, in a manner that is NOT "barbaric" (line 44) or "akin to murder" (line 47). B is the best answer; A refers to morality and D refers to appearance (while the context primarily involves EFFECTIVENESS or ACCURACY). C means "free of infection" or "free of unpleasantness" and highlights the wrong priority. The animals are still killed, but quickly.

QUESTION 8.

Choice B is correct. The author explains that Catherine's French is not "as flawless" as Edmond's English (lines 63-64); Catherine would thus be cross (lines 68-69) because Edmond is using an unfamiliar French word in the wake of their argument. This information supports A and eliminates B (since Catherine is cross) and C (since Catherine is HERSELF irritated and displays no motive for irritating Edmond). D is out of scope: the author does not explain Catherine and Edmond's destinations, which may well be known to Catherine.

QUESTION 9.

Choice C is correct. In lines 9-10, Catherine criticizes French women who are foraging in the forest; later, she criticizes the presence of hunting in France. This information supports C and eliminates B (because Catherine is outspoken in her criticisms) and D (because Catherine does formulate strong, decisive opinions). A is a trap answer: although Catherine does not seem fully informed about French forestry and hunting practices, she may be informed about OTHER elements of the French attitude towards nature that are not mentioned.

QUESTION 10.

Choice A is correct. See above for the explanation of the correct answer. B captures momentary confusion and raises the topic of English hunting, C notes differences in Catherine's and Edmond's language aptitudes, and D indicates a flaw in Catherine's French. Make sure not to wrongly take B as a justification for Question 9 A or D.

QUESTION 11.

Choice C is correct. The paragraph begins by explaining why the Olympic Games were "originally held" (line 1), goes on to explain "recent budgets" (line 7) and recent motives, and concludes with three reasons (lines 11-17) that would justify hosting the games. This information supports C. A is too broad (since the Games in general, not "particular Olympic Games", are considered), B introduces a faulty specific (since "different host cities" are never named), and D introduces a faulty source (since only the author's voice is presented and a "diplomat" is never quoted or cited).

QUESTION 12.

Choice D is correct. In lines 2-4, the author explains that the Olympics originally acted as both "a religious ritual" and a celebration of the "feats of the human body": now, only the "latter motivation" remains, so that the Olympics have lost their spiritual motivation. This information supports D, while other answers distort the actual arguments of the passage. The Olympics are seen as a strategy for luring tourists (but are not determined by existing tourist numbers, eliminating A), but can actually hurt tourism (eliminating B). Moreover, the author does not consider DECLINES in profits for the Olympics, only PROBLEMS faced by host cities: thus, eliminate D as out of scope.

QUESTION 13.

Choice A is correct. See above for the explanation of the correct answer. B indicates that the Olympics budget has increased, C indicates that host cities are seen as economically viable, and D indicates that there are few short-term economic rewards to hosting the Olympic games. None of these answers aligns with an answer to the previous question, though make sure not to falsely align B with Question 12 B, C with Question 12 A, or D with Question 12 C.

QUESTION 14.

Choice C is correct. The word "meaningfully" refers to the ability to "repurpose" (line 24) Olympic Games structures, or to successfully find new uses. C is thus on topic, while A, B, and D all refer to how PEOPLE act or think, not to the process of changing the use of a STRUCTURE.

QUESTION 15.

Choice B is correct. In lines 33-36, the author explains that Olympics host cities can drive away tourism, since prospective visitors would attempt to "avoid the crowds and chaos". This information supports B: A and D both present positive outcomes that clash with the author's overall, negative thesis, while C raises issues (culture and commercialization) that are tangential to the author's focus on economics and profits.

QUESTION 16.

Choice B is correct. See above for the explanation of the correct answer. A presents an assumption about the benefits of hosting the Olympics, C indicates that a country does not actually need to host the Olympics in order to benefit from a hosting bid, and D indicates that only long-term economic benefits will make an attempt to host the Olympics acceptable to residents of a host country. Although some of these answers raise topics not discussed in the previous question, be careful of falsely aligning D with Question 15 A, which also discusses long-term benefits.

QUESTION 17.

Choice D is correct. The word "realized" refers to "gains", which may or may not materialize or "be fulfilled". D is the only acceptable answer, while A, B, and C all refer to processes that involve THOUGHT or PERCEPTION rather than FINANCES.

QUESTION 18.

Choice D is correct. The "scholars" are not convinced that the Olympics are economically beneficial, even though long-term economic gains and psychological benefits have been cited. For its part, the "study" describes an increase in trade, indicating that the Olympics may have tangible economic benefits. The scholars would react to this study in a clearly negative manner, so that D is an effective answer and A and B must both be eliminated as too positive. While negative, C is incorrect because there is no clear indication that the scholars would be indignant about or be OFFENDED by a conclusion that they would not accept: they would be more likely to clearly and strongly disagree.

QUESTION 19.

Choice A is correct. While the author voices many doubts about the true benefits of hosting the Olympics, one clear benefit is an increase in "national pride and public satisfaction" (line 66). This information supports A. The author would be skeptical of a purely economic benefit such as that described in B, while C (information among foreigners) and D (social issues and the media) both raise topics that are unrelated to the passage's focus on economics.

QUESTION 20.

Choice D is correct. According to the graph, each Olympic host country exhibited an increase in GDP ten years after hosting the games: eliminate B and C, which do not indicate increases. However, an "exponential" increase would require the initial GDP to increase several times, not by a small margin or increment as shown for each country: eliminate A and choose D as the best answer.

QUESTION 21.

Choice C is correct. While the graph records increased GDP for Olympics host countries, the author argues that countries that bid on the games but did not actually host saw "a far greater increase in overall economic benefit" (lines 50-52). This information supports C. Keep in mind that the author is SKEPTICAL of the benefits of hosting the Olympics: thus, eliminate the extreme positive answer A and the extreme negative answer D. B considers the whether Olympic host countries have "stable markets", an issue of little interest to the author: eliminate this answer as out of scope.

QUESTION 22.

Choice A is correct. In the first paragraph, the author explains that Leukemia "is a cancer that targets and afflicts blood cells" (line 1), then goes on to discuss existing treatments such as "chemotherapy, radiation, and bone marrow transplants" (line 8). This content supports A. The author simply states FACTS about Leukemia at this stage, rather than urging a new approach (eliminating B), offering a "speculation" (eliminating C), or presenting an "argument" (eliminating D).

QUESTION 23.

Choice C is correct. In lines 21-25, the author refers to the research introduced earlier, arguing that the utilization of tumor suppressor genes offers both "promise" and "negative side effects". This awareness of both positives and negatives supports C and eliminates A (entirely positive) and B (entirely negative). D must be eliminated because the author is describing a tested "treatment" (line 23) not a theoretical approach that has not been "tested experimentally".

QUESTION 24.

Choice C is correct. See above for the explanation of the correct answer. A describes earlier research approaches, B simply explains the use of tumor suppressor genes, and D introduces a new approach. While neither A nor D refer to the "tumor suppressor genes" research, B offers a mostly neutral description that does not fit any of the answers to the previous question.

QUESTION 25.

Choice A is correct. The word "assail" refers to "myeloid cells" that keep the body healthy by attacking negative influences, and is moreover aligned with the words "fight" (line 31) and "stop" (line 32). A, "combat", is thus the best answer: B and C both refer to acts undertaken only by PEOPLE, while D does not introduce an appropriately negative tone.

QUESTION 26.

Choice D is correct. In lines 42-43, the author describes natural killer cells as "a key part of how the body ensures good health" outside the context of leukemia experiments. This information supports D and contradicts the negative answer A. B is out of scope, since the author of the passage is interested entirely in leukemia and other forms of cancer; C is problematic because the researchers in the passage have cultivated the adaptive natural killer cells and find them "potentially useful" (line 48).

QUESTION 27.

Choice B is correct. The word "trigger" explains how the activity of "immune cells" is caused or initiated, making B the best answer. While A and D are typically negative in meaning, C can only refer to an action that involves talking and reasoning, not to a biological process.

QUESTION 28.

Choice B is correct. In lines 56-60, the author explains that the researchers were "intrigued" by a new transformation observed in "matured cells". This new and "unforeseen" result justifies B as the best answer. Although the leukemia research described in the article is broadly applicable and went through a few different phases, the author does not specify any un-removed obstacles, disputes, or humanitarian applications: thus, do not assume that these topics are relevant, and eliminate A, C, and D.

QUESTION 29.

Choice C is correct. See above for the explanation of the correct answer. A describes the basic nature of the research undertaken by the team, B describes the objective of the Scripps team, and D describes a possible new avenue for research. None of these answers are negative, and thus Question 28 A and Question 28 C should be readily eliminated.

QUESTION 30.

Choice A is correct. In lines 69-70, the author indicates that the Scripps researchers hope that their "specialized method" for treating leukemia could help to combat "other types of cancer". This information supports A, while B refers to an objective that (even if true) is nowhere mentioned in the passage. C refers to an objective that is never named and that might in fact have been accomplished (since the author focuses on the problems with Dickins's research). D wrongly shifts the emphasis from fighting cancer to dendritic cells, a topic incidental to the Scripps team's research.

QUESTION 31.

Choice C is correct. According to the graph, 2% of AML cells were destroyed during the first time interval (A), 3% during the second (B), 8% during the third (C), and 2% during the fourth (D). C is thus the best answer: even if the first and second time intervals decrease the overall AML cell count, the decrease is so INSIGNIFICANT that 8% of a slightly smaller number would still be the largest decrease recorded.

QUESTION 32.

Choice C is correct. The author of the passage notes that "dendritic cells" (line 59) mature further into the natural killer cells that target AML cells. It can be reasonably inferred that dendritic cells were present in the stages immediately BEFORE the highest rate of AML cell destruction: C, the timeframe between 3PM and 9PM, is situated at exactly this stage. A places the dendritic cell generation AFTER the creation of natural killer cells, B places this stage much too early, and D wrongly assumes that the stage of highest natural killer cell activity is ALSO the stage of highest dendritic cell activity.

QUESTION 33.

Choice D is correct. In the passage, Agnew notes that the media is dominated by "A small group of men" (lines 9-10) and, despite mentioning a few of the media's valuable purposes, criticizes the media elite for "provincialism" and "parochialism" (lines 61-62) that render its authority problematic. This evidence supports D. A misstates the focus of Agnew's critique (the media, not politics), B mistakes a tactic discussed in the passage ("media distortion") for the main target of Agnew's discussion (the elite behind the media), and C does not capture the passage's negative tone.

QUESTION 34.

Choice A is correct. In lines 9-12, Agnew explains that "a small group of men" dictate the few minutes of news that will reach the public, thus omitting a large amount of information. This information supports A and contradicts B (since topics are available, but omitted) and D (since the coverage is restrictive, not overwhelming). The "political correctness" mentioned in C is not a concern of the passage: if anything, the networks may not be "politically correct" because they approach "difficult social problems" (line 34) in a dramatic way.

QUESTION 35.

Choice B is correct. See above for the explanation of the correct answer. A records the number of Americans who watch the news, and C and D both describe the functions of the networks. However, none of these answers describes a "problem": A is neutral and C and D are positive in their assessments.

QUESTION 36.

Choice D is correct. In lines 6-8, Agnew contrasts an earlier situation (the prominence of newspapers) with the new reality that Americans are guided by "what they see and hear on their television sets". This information supports D. A and C both refer to capabilities of network news that Agnew cites in lines 13-40, yet that he does not designate as NEW or RECENT developments. B relies on a faulty inference: while Agnew notes that the network news has grown more popular, he never argues that newspapers have grown LESS popular in consequence.

QUESTION 37.

Choice C is correct. The word "broad" refers to the "powers" (line 14) of the men who determine what network news Americans will encounter: these men thus have enormous or "extensive" power in shaping public opinion. C is the best answer: A refers to physical powers or military buildup, B is inaccurate (because Agnew explains EXACTLY how the powers work), and D describes a temperament or a political affiliation, not the extent of an ability.

QUESTION 38.

Choice B is correct. In lines 33-35, Agnew explains that news networks have called attention to "our most difficult social problems": much of the rest of the paragraph describes problems in public health, war, and the environment that have been highlighted by the news. B thus best captures the mostly positive tone and function of this paragraph, which only changes in the final few lines. While A and C both wrongly assume that the paragraph is PRIMARILY negative, D misstates the logic of the passage: Agnew indeed endorses how the news networks approach social problems, but finds a different aspect of the news (the limited nature of the network leadership) problematic.

QUESTION 39.

Choice B is correct. See above for the explanation of the correct answer. A describes how reporters can be influential (but primarily addresses problems not considered in the fourth paragraph), C highlights a negative aspect of the news, and D transitions away from the discussion in the fourth paragraph. None of these answers capture the positive tone of the fourth paragraph (and allude to the issues that it considers at length) in the manner of B.

QUESTION 40.

Choice B is correct. Agnew establishes that the "communities" rely on "intellectual confines" (line 58), "provincialism" (line 61), and "parochialism" (line 62). This information supports B and eliminates C, which wrongly indicates that the "communities" are in fact broad-minded and take a global approach. A misconstrues Agnew's critique: the "communities" are geographically and intellectually distinct, but social class is never explicitly mentioned. D is a misinterpretation of the passage: the "communities" are AWARE of politics, but DISTORT political news in a way that Agnew dislikes.

QUESTION 41.

Choice B is correct. The word "draw" is used to explain the "sources" of political and social views: a view would naturally be obtained or "derived" from such a source. B is the best answer, while A is out of scope (since Agnew is referencing the sources of views, not the FINAL depiction of views on the news) and C and D both refer to ways of winning others over, not to the basic process of how a view originates.

QUESTION 42.

Choice C is correct. In the passage, Agnew explains that network news involves a problematic "concentration of power over American public opinion" (lines 48-49) because a relatively small group decides what news will be prioritized and presented. This information supports C. A mentions the wrong problem (since Agnew criticizes the isolation of the media elite, not its links to business), and B and D are contradicted by the fact that Agnew IS positive about how the news can "constructively and creatively" (line 29) address social problems.

QUESTION 43.

Choice A is correct. Passage 1 raises the question "Are viruses alive?" (line 1) and goes on to explain the stances of experts such as Paul Berg and Ronald Ross; Passage 2 begins by referencing "the question of whether viruses are organisms or not" (line 34) and then explains the stances of experts such as Luis P. Villarreal and Mark Vincent. This information supports A. Only Passage 1 argues strongly that viruses could be organisms (eliminating B), while only Passage 2 raises the topic of tumors (eliminating D). Neither passage indicates that the question "are viruses alive?" cannot be answered, only that perhaps it HAS NOT been answered definitively so far: thus, eliminate C as a misreading of the content.

QUESTION 44.

Choice D is correct. The word "machinery" refers to life structures that can be found within a cell and that are influenced strongly by a virus: "vital functions" is an appropriate choice. A, B, and C all refer to topics that involve human activity and initiative, NOT to the operations of a cell, and must all be deleted as irrelevant.

QUESTION 45.

Choice C is correct. In lines 10-12, the author of Passage 2 points out that viruses do not "possess autonomous genetic material"; similarly, Villarreal notes that a virus is "devoid of genetic material" (lines 35-36). This information supports C. Keep in mind that the author of Passage 1 is open to the idea that viruses may be classified as life forms, while Villarreal is not: A is only applicable to Villarreal, while B and D would only be remotely applicable to the author of Passage 1 (and in any event over-state the author's claims).

QUESTION 46.

Choice B is correct. See above for the explanation of the correct answer. A explains how bacteria reproduce, C explains that many parasitic organisms require hosts for reproduction, and D indicates that the author of Passage 1 is not convinced that viruses are non-living. Only D mentions viruses directly, and CONTRADICTS Villarreal's stance.

QUESTION 47.

Choice A is correct. The first paragraph of Passage 1 describes how organisms "reproduce" (line 2); the second paragraph begins with a direct reference to this topic, so that the "biology fundamentals" in question are facts about reproduction. While the author's general topic is whether viruses are alive, the SPECIFIC reference deals with reproduction, a topic that sets up this broader discussion: eliminate B and D as misdirected. Eliminate C ("single-cell organisms") as too narrow, since the author also discusses human reproduction in the first paragraph.

QUESTION 48.

Choice D is correct. The author of Passage 1 presents Plasmodium as an example of an organism that requires a host "in order to reproduce" (lines 18-19) just as a virus does, but that is nonetheless "classified as an organism" (line 30), much unlike a virus. This information supports D. Although Plasmodium is a malaria parasite that enters human blood, the author of Passage 1 never EXPLICITLY links both viruses and Plasmodium to either blood or epidemics. Eliminate B and C, but also eliminate A, since only the particulars of Ross's research (not the overall status of the research) are discussed.

QUESTION 49.

Choice B is correct. In lines 51-54, the author of Passage 2 explains that "pop culture hype", particularly a "science fiction novel" by Michael Crichton, has shaped perceptions of viruses and their role in evolution. This information supports B, while A is contradicted by the passage: the author in fact argues BEYOND Villarreal's ideas to link viruses to tumors. C is out of scope, since viruses and tumors are simply COMPARED and debates about the status of viruses are "settling down" (line 63); D is a distortion of the passage, because researchers such as Philip Bell (line 47) have in fact linked viruses and living cells.

QUESTION 50.

Choice C is correct. See above for the explanation of the correct answer. A indicates that Villarreal continued to discuss viruses after delivering a strong assessment, B indicates that viruses do resemble life forms in some respects, and D sets forward an idea about how tumors are generated. Make sure not to mistake A as evidence for Question 49 A or B as evidence for Question 49 D.

QUESTION 51.

Choice A is correct. The word "generation" describes the cancer genome that appears during a speciation event: such a genome is thus "created". A is an effective choice, while B refers to human emotions or motives and C and D both refer to PEOPLE or OBJECTS, not to a PROCESS of generation.

QUESTION 52.

Choice A is correct. The author of Passage 2 associates viruses with the "struggle for dominance" (lines 56-57) in the natural world, but also notes that tumors struggle "for survival" (line 74) to the detriment of their hosts. This information supports A, while neither tumors nor viruses are definitively described as capable of independence (eliminating B), only tumors appear to be capable of "speciation events" (eliminating C), and only viruses are directly related to cell nuclei (eliminating D).

Section 2: Writing
Passage 1, Marine Biology: Combining Industry, Ecology, and Nutrition

QUESTION 1.

Choice A is correct. The paragraph as a whole points out the kinds of careers that attract marine biologists: the underlined portion should thus be a concise and logical phrase that captures how "careers in education and research" appeal to marine biologists. A fits such requirements, while B is needlessly elevated in diction and C and D are both awkward and too colloquial or informal for the tone of the passage.

QUESTION 2.

Choice C is correct. As a whole, the sentence calls attention to "industry and applied science careers" for marine biologists. One example would be work in the "aquaculture industry", making C, which sets up an example, an appropriate transition. A and B both indicate surprise, yet there is no context to show WHY the writer's information would be surprising: D wrongly assumes that the author is establishing a difference, not expanding upon a point.

QUESTION 3.

Choice B is correct. The subject of the underlined verb is the singular "demand": eliminate plural answers A and C. Because the proper past participle form of "to rise" is "risen", eliminate the faulty wording in D and choose B as the only grammatically correct answer.

QUESTION 4.

Choice D is correct. The table lists five seafood-producing countries by rank according to metric tons produced: the United States is ranked fifth of all countries, so that D is the best answer. A (past seafood production) and B (purchases from abroad) both deal with factors addressed nowhere in the table, while C understates a difference in seafood production: the United States produces roughly ten times less seafood than China does.

QUESTION 5.

Choice D is correct. For effective parallelism at the underlined portion, provide another noun that is in series with "oysters" and "clams": "and mussels" is a concise and effective choice. A introduces the noun "production" rather than designating another type of shellfish, B introduces the ambiguous pronoun "that", and C introduces the phrase "are produced", which is redundant because "production" has been mentioned earlier in the sentence.

QUESTION 6.

Choice C is correct. The underlined word should refer to a "location", as required by the sentence: "site" is the only choice that does so, since all the other choices introduce diction errors. A refers to the act of referencing (or citation), while B and D both refer to vision.

QUESTION 7.

Choice A is correct. The underlined portion should be in present tense (eliminating A), since the "shellfish farms" are described earlier in present tense. In addition, the underlined portion should provide a verb for the subject "shellfish" to create a full subject-verb clause after the linking phrase "to which": C creates a fragment and D distorts the grammar with a second "which". Only B provides a concise, effective verb phrase as needed.

QUESTION 8.

Choice D is correct. The question requires a reference to a "practical benefit" of the tanks: D indicates that the tanks give farmers a considerable degree of "control" and are useful in this way. While B provides a drawback and C indicates a timeline (NOT a benefit), A is a trap answer: how CONTROVERSIAL the tanks are and how USEFUL they are should be understood as two different issues. Controversial methods, in fact, could have enormous practical benefits.

QUESTION 9.

Choice C is correct. For this sentence, provide the correct idiomatic phrase to describe "solutions" that are provided: "solutions to" is the accepted usage. A should not be confused for the idiomatic phrase "problems with", B wrongly compares problems and solutions, and D, which at first seems to indicate that the solutions proceed "from problems", is not a standard English idiom.

QUESTION 10.

Choice C is correct. The underlined possessive should refer to "seaweed", which "grows" and is thus singular. Eliminate A and choose C: B only refers to placement or situation and is not a possessive, while D does not exist in English.

QUESTION 11.

Choice D is correct. This sentence should pair the descriptions "productive" and "sustainable" with the standard phrase "not only . . . but also". D does so, while A places a fragment after a semicolon, B creates a comma splice, and C distorts the standard phrase with "although also".

Passage 2, Furnishing Your Room with Mushrooms

QUESTION 12.

Choice B is correct. The underlined verb should be paired with the subject "fields", since "of home decoration and architectural design" is an interrupting descriptive phrase that must be factored out. B uses the correct plural form: A is singular, while C and D both create sentence fragments by introducing the needless transitional pronoun "which".

QUESTION 13.

Choice C is correct. The underlined portion of the sentence should be in parallel with the noun "founder", which describes Phil Ross: A and B introduce adjectives and must be eliminated. Idiomatically, the correct phrase for someone who is a pioneer in a specific pursuit is "pioneer in": D would wrongly indicate that Ross is "with" or ACCOMPANIES "mushroom-based home decoration". C is thus the best answer.

QUESTION 14.

Choice A is correct. While the author has begun the sentence with a subordinate clause (introduced by "While"), the underlined portion requires a full subject-verb combination: A, "mycotecture has yielded", is the best choice. B ("although") and C ("if") both create fragments by introducing new, needless transitions, while D creates a fragment by providing an -ing form rather than a proper verb form for the sentence's subject.

QUESTION 15.

Choice C is correct. In A, B, and D, different forms of the words "unveil" and "reveal" appear: because these words are interchangeable, all of these answers are redundant. C rightly uses only "unveiled", and also makes effective use of the standard phrase "both . . . and" when describing two items.

QUESTION 16.

Choice B is correct. Sentence 5 explains "mycelium" and its properties at length: however, sentences 2 and 3 both explain APPLICATIONS of mycelium and thus assume that the reader already possesses the knowledge provided in sentence 5. Thus, sentence 5 should occur after sentence 1 and introduce sentence 2: C interrupts the description of mycelium applications while A and D place the information in sentence 5 much too late in the paragraph.

QUESTION 17.

Choice D is correct. The underlined verb should refer to "creations" that are made of "mycelium" and feature "elegant touches", or "combine" these traits. The other answer choices introduce diction errors: A refers to working together, B refers to supporting a position, and C is an inappropriate negative.

QUESTION 18.

Choice A is correct. In the previous paragraph, the author describes a mycelium-based furniture project: this evidence would SUPPORT the idea that mycelium is a design element, so that the positive relationship in A ("indeed") is correct. B and C both wrongly introduce contrasts, while D wrongly assumes that the writer or readers would see the use of mycelium as shocking. If anything, the writer indicates that mycelium is APPROPRIATE to design projects.

QUESTION 19.

Choice D is correct. Earlier in the paragraph, the author points out that mycelium is "an environment friendly substance": the use of recycled material, as described in D, would support a claim about mycelium's environment-friendly "appeal". Nowhere does the author describe the mycelium production process as part of the material's "appeal", and the use of mycelium in high-end design indicates that the substance may in fact be expensive. Together, this information can be used to eliminate A, B, and C, which are concerned primarily with such factors.

QUESTION 20.

Choice B is correct. Assess the structure and grammar of each answer choice: A involves a misplaced modifier (since the "polyominoes" are wrongly described as "traditional building elements"), C involves subject-verb disagreement ("innovation . . . are"), and D involves a comma splice. Only B avoids such grammatical problems while properly describing the "polyominoes" as "oddly-angled bricks".

QUESTION 21.

Choice C is correct. The paragraph indicates that the appeal of mycelium MAY be limited: while B is too positive and D is too negative for the author's discussion, C rightly indicates that the cost of mycelium objects could be a drawback and leads into the discussion of other "perceptions". A introduces incorrect reasoning: even if the price has not been mentioned, there is no reason why this specific evidence cannot be used to strengthen the author's argument.

QUESTION 22.

Choice A is correct. The underlined verb should agree with the singular noun "team", so choose A and eliminate the plural B. Because the underlined verb should ALSO be in parallel with "continues", eliminate the future-tense C and the past-tense D.

Passage 3, A Late Start, and a Better Start

QUESTION 23.

Choice D is correct. The original sentences explain that "biological clocks" are "rhythms", so that the phrase "These rhythms" should refer back to "biological clocks and can be replaced by "which". A wrongly introduces a contrast, B refers to clocks (things) as though they are events ("when"), and D distorts the use of the verb "dictate". The "clocks" dictate: "Humans" do NOT "have circadian rhythms . . . and dictate".

QUESTION 24.

Choice C is correct. The sentence indicates that negative effects will result if the systems are changed, or "disrupted". The other answers introduce diction errors: A refers to argumentation, B refers to human emotion, and D refers to a PHYSICAL thing that cannot be restored, not to a rhythm that may return.

QUESTION 25.

Choice B is correct. The underlined portion should be in parallel with the earlier verbs "feel" and "do . . . learn" and must describe a further negative effect: while A and C both wrongly introduce CONTRASTS, D breaks parallelism. B both adds a new present tense verb and shows that the sentence relationship involves addition or simultaneity.

QUESTION 26.

Choice C is correct. This sentence creates a comparison between "adolescents" and the underlined portion: use "than" as the standard comparison phrasing (not "then", which indicates time) and eliminate B and D. The "adolescents" must also be compared to other "people", not to "ages": eliminate A and choose C as the best answer.

QUESTION 27.

Choice A is correct. At this point, the passage describes the tendencies of adolescents using a series of present-tense verbs: for the best possible verb agreement, eliminate past-tense answers B, C, and D and choose the present-tense answer A.

QUESTION 28.

Choice C is correct. The sentence that contains the underlined portion pairs off "school time" and "biological" time using the standard phrase "between . . . and". C is the only answer that correctly implements this standard phrase: make sure to temporarily disregard the information in parentheses in order to see the expected construction and quickly eliminate A, B, and D.

QUESTION 29.

Choice A is correct. The final sentence of the paragraph lists the optimal wake-up and school-start times for teens: on the basis of the times listed in A, the start times for "Many high schools" and the corresponding wake-up times for teens are several hours earlier. This information supports the author's argument about "schedules", while B focuses on diet choices, C indicates that teenagers are energetic but avoids the issue of school scheduling, and D lists PREFERENCES, rather than DRAWBACKS as demanded by the prompt.

QUESTION 30.

Choice A is correct. Check the answers for sentence structure errors: B wrongly introduces a fragment after a semicolon while C and D both introduce comma splices. Only A creates an effective transition ("involving") into the discussion of the details of the experiment.

QUESTION 31.

Choice B is correct. Sentence 1 refers to the "promising" results of changing a specific school time to 8:40: sentence 2 introduces an "experiment" that involved exactly this time change. Because the experiment should be introduced BEFORE its results are described, eliminate A and choose B. Both C and D would both wrongly place the initial reference to "promising" results after the description of WHY the results were promising.

QUESTION 32.

Choice D is correct. Use the commas to properly coordinate ideas: in D, two commas properly offset the phrase "along with other scientific data" from the subject-verb combination "results . . . suggest". While A and B both wrongly interrupt the subject and verb with only a single comma, C wrongly splits the proposition "along" from the noun to which it refers, "data".

QUESTION 33.

Choice C is correct. The underlined portion must begin by mentioning a group that would have "happier and more successful children" in order to avoid a misplaced modifier. The best choice is C, "parents": "start times" (A), "benefits" (B), and "high schools" (D) would not logically have children of their own.

Passage 4, Richard Brinsley Sheridan: A Man for All Comedies

QUESTION 34.

Choice A is correct. The underlined pronoun must be replaced by a reference to people who would "claim" in the "present day". While B and D both refer to things or qualities, C refers to two playwrights who lived centuries ago. Only A, critics, properly fits the meaning of the sentence.

QUESTION 35.

Choice D is correct. Idiomatically, the underlined portion must refer to the act of denying a specific idea: to "deny that" is the best English usage. A uses the wrong transition, B indicates cause and effect (not an assertion), and C indicates a hypothetical condition (not a statement).

QUESTION 36.

Choice A is correct. The writer is here pointing out a negative characteristic of Comedy of Manners plays, their superficiality: A properly registers the negative tone of the sentence. Although the writer never indicates that this negative quality is unexpected (eliminating B), the writer does not provide the reasoning behind or specific examples of superficial Comedy of Manners plays: thus, eliminate C and D, respectively.

QUESTION 37.

Choice C is correct. "To forbid" is an irregular verb that takes the past tense form "was forbidden" as in answer C. While A wrongly repeats the present tense "forbid", B and D both create wordy constructions that appear to be present-tense -ing uses: avoid these since the paragraph is describing seventeenth-century British history.

QUESTION 38.

Choice B is correct. Find an answer that addresses the "delights of the new theaters" and "comedies" in relation to King Charles: A deals with Charles's exile, C is redundant (since Charles is already described as the "Merry Monarch"), and D deals with earlier Shakespearean theaters, NOT the "new theaters". B calls attention to the "revelry" Charles enjoyed in a "more frivolous" country, and thus explains why he would have a temperament suited to delightful and comic theater.

QUESTION 39.

Choice C is correct. Throughout this sentence, the writer uses the pronoun "us" to describe the effect of Sheridan's Comedy of Manners writings: C preserves this usage, while A ("one") and B ("you") disrupt it. D results in the phrase "allows how laughter can lead us", which is disjointed in phrasing and disrupts the meaning of the original sentence.

QUESTION 40.

Choice A is correct. The underlined portion should be in parallel with the other past-tense verbs that occur in this sentence: "became" on its own keeps parallelism, while "he became" adds a needless pronoun. Eliminate B and D, and then eliminate C, since "eventual" should be the adverb "eventually", which describes HOW or WHEN Sheridan "became". A is thus the best answer.

QUESTION 41.

Choice C is correct. This sentence should present a contrast between how the names seem at first and the important information that they ultimately "reveal": pointing out that the names "seem rather superficial" creates exactly such a contrast. A, B, and D all indicate that the names are STRANGE, not that they seem SIMPLISTIC as demanded by the contrast contained in the sentence. Some of these answers can also be eliminated as too informal or imprecise for the style of the essay.

QUESTION 42.

Choice C is correct. The underlined portion must begin with a noun designating "A playwright of multi-faceted intelligence": "Sheridan" is an acceptable choice. Eliminate A and B, which create misplaced modifiers. D must be eliminated because it employs the wrong verb tense: "has . . . known" indicates that the action is continuing into the present, yet Sheridan lived and died centuries ago. C, which simply indicates that Sheridan "knew", is thus the best answer.

QUESTION 43.

Choice B is correct. Create an effective transition that avoids redundancy: while B helpfully indicates EXACTLY when the action is taking place, A simply repeats the fact that the theater "burned to the ground" and C repeats the fact that Sheridan is "across the road" from the theater. D should only be used when presenting two linked or complementary IDEAS, not when coordinating a description of TIME and EVENTS.

QUESTION 44.

Choice B is correct. While paragraph 2 describes the new "comedies" that originated under Charles II and that mock "manners and foibles", paragraph 1 explains the reception of "Comedy of Manners" after Charles's time. Paragraph 2 should thus be placed immediately BEFORE paragraph 1, since paragraph 2 explains the origins of Comedy of Manners. Eliminate A, but also eliminate C and D, since these placements would interrupt the passage's later focus on a single playwright, Richard Brinsley Sheridan.

Section 3: Math Test - No Calculator

QUESTION 1.

Choice B is correct. If x is the total number of text messages that Kiley wrote, then since Resha sent 4 less than twice the number of text messages Kiley sent, Resha sent $2x - 4$ text messages. Since Resha and Kiley sent a total of 842 text messages together, then $x + 2x - 4$ must be equivalent to 842, or $3x - 4 = 842$.

Choice A is incorrect and may result from neglecting Kiley's text messages as a part of the total. Choices C and D are incorrect and may result from errors in translating the context to mathematical equations.

QUESTION 2.

Choice C is correct. The expression $b\sqrt{b}$ can be rewritten as $b^1 \bullet b^{\frac{1}{2}}$. Exponent rules state that when one is multiplying powers, the exponents are added together. Therefore, $b^1 \bullet b^{\frac{1}{2}} = b^{\frac{3}{2}}$. The division rule for exponents states that when dividing powers, one subtracts the exponents. Therefore, the expression $\dfrac{b^3}{b^2}$ can be rewritten as b^1 and since $b^{\frac{3}{2}}$ is not equivalent to b^1, choice C is the correct answer.

Choice A is incorrect because $\sqrt{b^3}$ can be rewritten as $b^{\frac{3}{2}}$, which is equivalent to $b\sqrt{b}$. Choice B is incorrect because $b^{\frac{3}{2}}$ is equivalent to $b\sqrt{b}$. Choice D is incorrect because $\sqrt{\dfrac{b^5}{b^2}}$ can be rewritten as $\sqrt{b^3}$, which can be rewritten as $b^{\frac{3}{2}}$, which is equivalent to $b\sqrt{b}$.

QUESTION 3.

Choice D is correct. Adding 17 to both sides of $4x^2 - 17 = 11$ yields $4x^2 = 28$. Multiplying both sides by 4 yields $16x^2 = 112$.

Choice A is incorrect and may result from subtracting 17 from 11, yielding $4x^2 = -6$, which after multiplying by 4 on both sides becomes $16x^2 = -24$. Choice B is incorrect and may result from solving for x^2 rather than $16x^2$. Choice C is incorrect and may result from calculation errors.

QUESTION 4.

Choice B is correct. Taking the sum of $4x + 9y = 12$ and $5x + 3y = 12$ yields $9x + 12y = 24$. Dividing both sides of the equation by 3 yields $3x + 4y = 8$.

Choices A, C, and D are incorrect and may result from calculation errors while adding or subtracting the equations, or from calculation errors while attempting to solve for x and y individually.

QUESTION 5.

Choice C is correct. In the equation $\dfrac{a-2}{2}=\dfrac{3a}{a+8}$, cross-multiplying yields $(a-2)(a+8)=6a$. Expanding the left-hand side of the equation yields $a^2+6a-16=6a$ and after subtracting $6a$ from either side one can see that $a^2-16=0$, or $a^2=16$.

Choices A and B are incorrect and may result from solving for a instead of a^2. Choice D is incorrect and may result from calculation errors.

QUESTION 6.

Choice D is correct. If the carpets were stained much deeper than expected, it would take a longer time to get the stains out with the same number of machines and laborers. Therefore, h, the number of hours, would be the variable that would change the most with deeply stained carpets. The only expression that includes h is CLh.

Choices A, B, and C are incorrect because they do not include h, which is the only variable that gets affected by extended time.

QUESTION 7.

Choice B is correct. A line that is perpendicular to a line with the equation $y=-Kx+t$ will have an opposite reciprocal slope. Therefore, the equation of this line in slope-intercept form would be $y=\dfrac{1}{K}x+b$. If the line goes through the point $(4,3)$, substituting 4 for x and 3 for y yields $3=\dfrac{1}{K}4+b$. Subtracting $\dfrac{4}{K}$ from both sides reveals that $b=3-\dfrac{4}{K}$.

Choice A is incorrect and may result from incorrectly substituting 3 for x and 4 for y. Choice C is incorrect and may result from giving the line a parallel, or the same, slope and substituting 3 for x and 4 for y. Choice D is incorrect and may result from giving the line a parallel, or the same, slope.

QUESTION 8.

Choice C is correct. Since the point $(1,y)$ is the only solution to the system of linear equations, one can substitute 1 for x in the equation $2x+y=15$, which yields $2(1)+y=15$, or simply $y=13$. Substituting 1 for x and 13 for y in the other equation, $kx-4y=100$, yields $k(1)-4(13)=100$ or $k-52=100$, which simplifies to $k=152$.

Alternately, one can multiply the first equation, $2x + y = 15$, by 4 on both sides, which yields $8x + 4y = 60$. Adding this new equation to $kx - 4y = 100$ yields $(k+8)x = 160$. Substituting 1 for x yields $k + 8 = 160$, or simply $k = 152$.

Choices A, B, and D are incorrect and may result from basic substitution and/or calculation errors. For example, choice D is incorrect and results from adding 8 to 160, rather than subtracting 8.

QUESTION 9.

Choice B is correct. Since the quadratic function $y = -(x-2)^2 + 4$ is in vertex form, the form given by $y = a(x-h)^2 + k$ where (h, k) is the coordinate of the vertex, one can see that the vertex of the quadratic function in question is $(2, 4)$. Substituting the points $(2, 4)$ and $(0, 0)$ into the distance formula, $D = \sqrt{(x_2 - x_1)^2 + (y_2 - y_1)^2}$ yields $D = \sqrt{(2-0)^2 + (4-0)^2}$, which simplifies to $D = \sqrt{4 + 16} = \sqrt{20}$. Therefore, after simplifying the radical, $D = 2\sqrt{5}$.

Choices A, C, and D are incorrect and may result from a misunderstanding of the vertex form of a quadratic function or an incorrect application of the distance formula.

QUESTION 10.

Choice D is correct. If $g(2)$ were equivalent to 0, $(2, 0)$ would be an x-intercept of the function $g(x)$ and $x - 2$ would be a factor of $g(x)$. However, $g(2)$ does not equal 0, but instead, $g(2) = 1$. Looking at it another way, one can see that $g(2) = 0 + 1$. Therefore, if the function $g(x)$ were divided by the factor $x - 2$, there would be a remainder of 1.

Choices A, B, and C are incorrect because the question does not state that $g(2) = 0$, $g(1) = 0$, or $g(-2) = 0$, the conditions that would make $x - 2$, $x - 1$, and $x + 2$ factors of the function $g(x)$, respectively.

QUESTION 11.

Choice C is correct. Setting the equation $y = x^2 - 12x + 20$ equivalent to $y = -x^2 + 12x - 34$ yields $x^2 - 12x + 20 = -x^2 + 12x - 34$. Moving all terms in the equation to the left hand side by adding $x^2 - 12x + 34$ to both sides yields $2x^2 - 24x + 54 = 0$. Factoring out a 2 yields $2(x^2 - 12x + 27) = 0$, and factoring the expression $x^2 - 12x + 27$ yields $2(x - 9)(x - 3) = 0$. This makes the two solutions to the equation, 9 and 3. Substituting 3 for x in the equation $y = x^2 - 12x + 20$ yields $y = (3)^2 - 12(3) + 20$, or $y = -7$. Substituting 9 for x in the same equation yields $y = (9)^2 - 12(9) + 20$, or $y = -7$. Since the y-values of each point are the same, one can calculate the straight line distance between 9 and 3. The straight line distance between 9 and 3 is $9 - 3 = 6$.

Choices A and D are incorrect and may result from calculating the *x*-value of the points of intersection not the distance between them. Choice B is incorrect and may result from a calculation error.

QUESTION 12.

Choice B is correct. Dividing the expression $2x^2 - 7x + M$ by the binomial $2x + 5$ yields the following:

$$
\begin{array}{r}
x - 6 \\
2x+5 \overline{) 2x^2 - 7x + M} \\
-(2x^2 + 5x) \\
\hline
-12x + M \\
-(-12x - 30) \\
\hline
M + 30
\end{array}
$$

Therefore, the remainder is $\dfrac{M+30}{2x+5}$. If the remainder is given in the form $\dfrac{4M}{2x+5}$, it follows that $M + 30 = 4M$. Subtracting M from both sides yields $30 = 3M$, or $M = 10$.

Choices A, C, and D are incorrect and may result from calculation errors in performing polynomial long division or synthetic division.

QUESTION 13.

Choice C is correct. $\angle DAE$ and $\angle BAE$ are complementary angles whose sum is $90°$. If $\angle BAE$ was equivalent to *x*, it follows that $\angle DAE$ is equivalent to $4x$. Then, solving the equation $x + 4x = 90$ yields $x = 18$. Therefore, $\angle DAE$ is equivalent to $4(18) = 72°$. Due to the symmetry of a rectangle, $\angle ADE$ is equivalent to $\angle DAE$ making $\triangle AED$ isosceles. Subtracting $2(72)$ from 180 yields the measure of $\angle AED$ which is $36°$. Since $\angle DAE$ and $\angle BEC$ are vertical angles, $\angle BEC$ also measures $36°$. Therefore, $\angle AED + \angle BEC$ is equivalent to $36° + 36°$, or $72°$.

Choices A, B, and D are incorrect and may result from errors in understanding complementary angles and/or neglecting to account for the sum of two angles.

QUESTION 14.

Choice A is correct. If $|a - b| = 2a$ then *a* must be non-negative since absolute values can only produce non-negative outcomes. Since $a + b = 0$, then *b* must be equivalent to $-a$ in order to make both statements true. If $b = -a$, then the equation $a^2 = b^2$ would be equivalent to $a^2 = (-a)^2$, which is true. In the equation $a - b < 0$, if $b = -a$ then $a - (-a) < 0$, which is *not* true. Finally, in the equation $ab < 0$, if $b = -a$ then $a(-a) < 0$, which is true. However, if $a = 0$ the equation would not be true and the question never states that *a* cannot be the same as *b*, nor that *a* cannot be equal to 0.

Choice B is incorrect because if a is equivalent to 0, ab is *not* less than 0. Choices C and D are incorrect because if $b = -a$ then $a - (-a)$ is *not* less than 0 and if a is equivalent to 0, ab is *not* less than 0.

QUESTION 15.

Choice A is correct. If one were to apply the quadratic formula, $\dfrac{-b \pm \sqrt{b^2 - 4ac}}{2a}$,

to the equation $0 = 3x^2 + 2x - 4$, where $a = 3$, $b = 2$, and $c = -4$, the result would

be $\dfrac{-(2) \pm \sqrt{(2)^2 - 4(3)(-4)}}{2(3)}$. Simplifying yields $\dfrac{-2 \pm \sqrt{52}}{6}$ which can be rewritten as

$\dfrac{-2 \pm 2\sqrt{13}}{6}$, or $\dfrac{-1 \pm \sqrt{13}}{3}$.

Choices B, C, and D are incorrect because they do not have roots with x-values

equivalent to $\dfrac{-1 + \sqrt{13}}{3}$ and $\dfrac{-1 - \sqrt{13}}{3}$.

QUESTION 16.

The correct answer is 1.5 or $\dfrac{3}{2}$. Subtracting 2 from both sides of the equation

$2 + \dfrac{3}{7}(x - \dfrac{1}{3}) = \dfrac{5}{2}$ yields $\dfrac{3}{7}(x - \dfrac{1}{3}) = \dfrac{1}{2}$. Multiplying each side by $\dfrac{7}{3}$ yields $x - \dfrac{1}{3} = \dfrac{7}{6}$,

and adding $\dfrac{1}{3}$ to both sides gives $x = \dfrac{9}{6}$. After simplifying, $x = \dfrac{3}{2}$.

QUESTION 17.

The correct answer is 4. Multiplying the binomial $x^2 + 1$ by the binomial $x^2 - 1$ in the equation $255 = (x^2 + 1)(x^2 - 1)$ yields $255 = x^4 - 1$. Adding 1 to both sides of the equation gives $256 = x^4$ and the 4th root of 256 is equivalent to ± 4. Since x must be greater than 0, the answer is 4.

QUESTION 18.

The correct answer is 48. If Team A scored 30 points less than four times the number of points that Team B scored, using a for Team A's score and b for Team B's score yields $a = 4b - 30$. If Team C scored 61 points more than half of the number of points that

Team B scored, using c for Team C's score and b for Team B's score yields $c = \dfrac{1}{2}b + 61$.

If Team A and Team C shared in the victory then $a = c$. Therefore, $4b - 30 = \dfrac{1}{2}b + 61$.

Subtracting $\dfrac{1}{2}b$ and adding 30 to both sides of the equation yields $\dfrac{7}{2}b = 91$. Multiplying

both sides by $\dfrac{2}{7}$ yields $b = \dfrac{182}{7}$, or $b = 26$. Substituting 26 for b in either equation,

$a = 4b - 30$ for example, yields $a = 4(26) - 30 = 74$. Therefore, Team A and Team C scored $74 - 26 = 48$ more points than Team B.

QUESTION 19.

The correct answer is 144. Given that $\overline{AB}$ intersects $\overline{CD}$, the angle below the angle that measures $3y°$ also measures $3y°$ because they are vertical angles. Therefore, $y° + 3y° + y° = 180°$ because the angles form a straight line. Combining like terms yields $5y° = 180°$ and dividing by 5 gives $y° = 36°$. Since on both sides of the triangle the exterior angles on the top measure $y°$ and the exterior angles on the bottom measure $x°$, we know that the two horizontal lines in the diagram are parallel. Therefore, using the rule that the interior angles on the same side of a transversal are supplementary, it follows that $x° + y° = 180°$. Substituting 36 for y yields $x° + 36° = 180°$ and after subtracting 36° from both sides, $x° = 144°$.

QUESTION 20.

The correct answer is .416, .417, or $\dfrac{5}{12}$. If the height of the bridge is 2 feet above the level of the water on one side and 12 feet above the level of the water on the other side, the actual height increase is 10 feet from one side of the river to the next. Looking at the distance straight across the river as one leg of a right triangle measuring x feet, the increase in the height of the river bank from one side to the other as the other leg which measures 10 feet, and the bridge's length of 26 feet as the hypotenuse, the Pythagorean Theorem, $a^2 + b^2 = c^2$, states that $x^2 + (10)^2 = (26)^2$. Simplifying yields the equation $x^2 + (10)^2 = (26)^2$ which is equivalent to $x^2 + 100 = 676$. Subtracting 100 from both sides yields $x^2 = 576$, or $x = 24$ feet. Alternatively, one could recognize the special right triangle side length relationship 5-12-13 which, when doubled, would yield 10-24-26. The tangent of the angle that the bridge makes with the surface of the water would be opposite over adjacent, which is the height change of the bank over the deistance straight across the river, or $\dfrac{10}{24} = \dfrac{5}{12}$.

Section 4: Math Test - Calculator

QUESTION 1.

Choice A is correct. Distributing the negative sign to the second half of the expression $(12x^2 + 5x + 1) - (10x^2 - 5x - 1)$ yields $12x^2 + 5x + 1 - 10x^2 + 5x + 1$. Combining like terms yields $2x^2 + 10x + 2$.

Choice B is incorrect and may result from neglecting to distribute the negative sign to the -1 at the end of the expression. Choice C is incorrect and may result from neglecting to distribute the negative sign to the $-5x$ near the end of the expression. Choice D is incorrect and may result from neglecting to distribute the negative sign to both the $-5x$ and the -1 at the end of the expression.

QUESTION 2.

Choice A is correct. In order to calculate the slope of the line that represents the points in the table, one can use the points $(-3,5)$ and $(0,7)$, as well as the formula for finding slope, $m = \dfrac{y_2 - y_1}{x_2 - x_1}$. Substituting 7 for y_2, 5 for y_1, 0 for x_2, and -3 for x_1 yields $m = \dfrac{(7)-(5)}{(0)-(-3)} = \dfrac{2}{3}$. Being that $m = \dfrac{2}{3}$ and the y-intercept, b, is 7, as given by the point $(0,7)$, the equation of the line that represents the data in the table in the form $y = mx + b$ is $y = \dfrac{2}{3}x + 7$.

Choices B and D are incorrect because their y-intercepts would indicate that the point $(0,5)$ should be in the table, which it is not. Choice C is incorrect because the slope of the line, 2, does not match the change in y in relation to the change in x that is present in the table.

QUESTION 3.

Choice C is correct. In order to calculate the total number of actuarial students from 2008 through 2012, one must count every male and female from 2008 through 2012. This yields the sum $(10+2)+(10+5)+(8+7)+(4+8)+(2+8)$, which is equivalent to 64. The number of female students in 2011 was 8 and the number of female students in 2012 was also 8, which makes the total number of female students from 2011 and 2012 equivalent to 16. Therefore, the probability of randomly selecting a female actuarial student from 2011 or 2012 from all of the actuarial students from 2008 to 2012 is $\dfrac{16}{64}$, or $\dfrac{1}{4}$.

Choice A is incorrect and may result from calculating the probability of selecting a male from 2011 and 2012 instead of a female. Choice B is incorrect and may result from calculating the probability of selecting a female from only 2011 or from only 2012, but not from either/or. Choice D is incorrect and may result from calculating the probability of selecting any actuarial student from 2011 or 2012, not females only.

QUESTION 4.

Choice B is correct. If there are 1670 students in Lakesedge High School and approximately 22% of the students are sophomores, there are approximately $1670(.22) \approx 367$ sophomores. If approximately 40% of the sophomores take Contemporary American Issues, then approximately $367(.40) \approx 147$ students take the course. Therefore, approximately 150 sophomores take Contemporary American Issues.

Choices A, C, and D are incorrect and may result from percentage calculation errors.

QUESTION 5.

Choice D is correct. In 1994 the computer wholesale company had \$200,000 in sales. Over the next 5 years, the annual sales increased and decreased but generally rose to \$800,000 in sales in 1999. The increase in sales over the change in years is equivalent to $\dfrac{\$800,000 - \$200,000}{1999 - 1994} = \$120,000$ per year. This approximately represents a \$100,000 per year increase in sales, on average, from 1994 to 1999.

Choice A is incorrect because the sales do not steadily increase. The sales increase and decrease year after year. Choice B is incorrect because the sales did not increase then decrease from 1994 to 1999. The sales increased and decreased year after year. Choice C is incorrect and may result from misinterpreting the scale of the y-axis of the graph.

QUESTION 6.

Choice A is correct. Substituting 5 for a in the equation $\dfrac{7}{2}a = \dfrac{5}{b}$ yields $\dfrac{7}{2}(5) = \dfrac{5}{b}$, or $\dfrac{35}{2} = \dfrac{5}{b}$. Cross-multiplying yields $35b = 10$ and after dividing both sides of the equation by 35, the equation yields $b = \dfrac{10}{35} = \dfrac{2}{7}$.

Choices B, C, and D are incorrect and may result from calculation errors while solving for b.

QUESTION 7.

Choice D is correct. If Madeline can drink 13 bottles of water in 5 minutes, she can drink 13 bottles of water in $5(60) = 300$ seconds. If Madeline can drink 13 bottles of water in 300 seconds, then she can drink 3 bottles of water in x seconds One can solve the proportion $\dfrac{13}{300} = \dfrac{3}{x}$ in order to find x, the number of seconds it takes Madeline to drink 3 bottles of water. Cross-multiplying yields $13x = 900$ and dividing both sides by 13 yields $x \approx 69$ seconds.

Choice A is incorrect and may result from calculating the approximate number of minutes it takes Madeline to drink 3 bottles of water instead of the approximate number of seconds. Choice B is incorrect and may result from a calculation error. Choice C is incorrect and may result from solving for approximately how long it takes Madeline to drink 1 bottle of water instead of 3 bottles of water.

QUESTION 8.

Choice D is correct. If the current enrollment for the training seminar for construction foremen is 42 and 6 years have passed since the seminar's inception, the point $(6, 42)$ would be a solution to the linear model that represents the enrollment in the seminar. Further, if enrollment has increased by 18 over 6 years, the slope of the linear model that represents the current enrollment would be $\dfrac{18}{6} = 3$ foremen per year. Substituting 3 for

m in the linear form $y = mx + b$ and substituting the point $(6,42)$ for x and y yields $(42) = (3)(6) + b$, or $42 = 18 + b$. Subtracting 18 from both sides of the equation gives $b = 24$, which leads to the linear model $y = 3x + 24$.

Choices A and B are incorrect because a slope of 18 implies that the seminar's enrollment grew by 18 foremen per year, when in fact it grew by 18 foremen over the course of 6 years. Choice C is incorrect because the y-intercept of 42 is actually the current enrollment, not the initial enrollment that the y-intercept should represent.

QUESTION 9.

Choice B is correct. If Hernando were walking downhill his walking rate in miles per hour would be faster than his walking rate while walking uphill. At 3:00, Hernando recorded that he was walking at a rate of 5 miles per hour. At 3:30, Hernando reported that he was walking at a rate of 7 miles per hour. At some point in time between 3:00 and 3:30, Hernando switched from moving at a rate of 5 miles per hour to a rate of 7 miles per hour. Therefore, this implies that between 3:00 and 3:30, Hernando switched from walking uphill to walking downhill.

Choices A and C are incorrect because the walking rate does not change from 2:30 to 3:00, nor does it change from 3:30 to 4:00, which implies that during these times Hernando was walking uphill or downhill, but did not switch from one to the other. Choice D is incorrect because from 4:00 to 4:30 Hernando's walking rate drops, which would imply switching from walking downhill to walking uphill, not the opposite.

QUESTION 10.

Choice D is correct. Isolating the x-coordinate of the vertex, h, in the vertex form of a quadratic equation, $y = a(x-h)^2 + k$, first involves subtracting k from either side of the equation which yields $y - k = a(x-h)^2$. Dividing both sides of the equation by a yields $\dfrac{y-k}{a} = (x-h)^2$ and taking the square root of both sides of the equation yields $\sqrt{\dfrac{y-k}{a}} = x - h$. Adding h to both sides and subtracting $\sqrt{\dfrac{y-k}{a}}$ from both sides gives h in terms of y, a, x, and k, $h = x - \sqrt{\dfrac{y-k}{a}}$.

Choices A, B, and C are incorrect and may result from errors in correctly applying the order of operations in order to isolate the variable h.

QUESTION 11.

Choice C is correct. An Empress tree grows at a rate of 15 feet per year and reaches maturity after 3.33 years. Therefore, the height of a mature Empress tree is $15(3.33) \approx 50$ feet. The Quaking Aspen tree grows at a rate of 5 feet per year and reaches maturity after 10 years. Therefore, the height of a mature Quaking Aspen is $5(10) = 50$ feet. At maturity, the Empress tree and the Quaking Aspen are approximately the same height.

Choices A, B, and D are incorrect because none of these pairs of trees are the same height when they have reached maturity.

QUESTION 12.

Choice C is correct. The Lombardy Poplar tree grows at a rate of 10 feet per year and reaches maturity after 6 years. Its height at maturity is $10(6) = 60$ feet, representing the tallest tree at maturity in the table. The Cleveland Pear tree grows at a rate of 4 feet per year and reaches maturity after 7.5 years, making its height at maturity $4(7.5) = 30$ feet, representing the shortest tree at maturity in the table. Multiplying the height of the shortest tree at maturity by the growth factor $(1+r)$ and setting the expression equal to the height of the tallest tree at maturity will allow one to solve for r, the percentage increase in the height of the shortest tree compared to the height of the tallest tree. Therefore, $30(1+r) = 60$. Dividing both sides of the equation by 30 yields $1+r = 2$ and subtracting 1 from both sides makes $r = 1$, or 100%. Therefore, the height of the tallest tree at maturity in the table, the Lombardy Poplar tree, is 100% taller than the height of the shortest tree in the table, the Cleveland Pear tree.

Choice A is incorrect because 50% is how much shorter the shortest tree is at maturity than the highest tree at maturity. Choice B is incorrect and may result from a calculation error. Choice D is incorrect and may result from calculating what percent the tallest tree at maturity is compared to the height of the shortest tree at maturity rather than what percent *larger* the tallest tree at maturity is than the shortest tree at maturity.

QUESTION 13.

Choice D is correct. If the boy approaches the token dispensing machine once every 20 minutes for a total of m minutes, taking m and dividing it by 20 yields $\frac{m}{20}$, the total number of times the boy uses the token dispensing machine. If every time the boy uses the machine he uses a ten-dollar bill and the machine dispenses 4 tokens for every dollar it receives, then multiplying 10 by 4 yields $10(4)$, the number of tokens the boy receives every time he uses the token machine. If the boy visits the machine $\frac{m}{20}$ times and receives $10(4)$ tokens every time he uses the machine, then multiplying the two expressions together yields t, the total number of tokens the machine dispenses to the boy in m minutes. Therefore, $t = \frac{10(4)m}{20}$.

Choices A, B, and C are incorrect because they do not equal the correct number of total tokens, t, dispensed by the machine over the course of m minutes.

QUESTION 14.

Choice B is correct. By definition, the median is the middle number in a list of ordered numbers. If there is an even number of numbers in the list, the median is the average of the middle two numbers. In this case, placing the students' times in order from least to greatest yields: 6, 8, 8, 9, 12, 12, 13, and 14. The two middle times are 9 seconds and 12 seconds. The average of 9 and 12 is $\dfrac{9+12}{2}=10.5$ seconds.

Choices A and D are incorrect and may result from selecting one of the 2 middle numbers when all of times are in order, rather than taking the average of the two middle numbers. Choice C is incorrect and may result from a calculation error.

QUESTION 15.

Choice D is correct. The student's experiment is an example of poor experimental design. The student places rubber bands of one type in a colder environment and rubber bands of another type in a warmer environment. In the end the results are clear that the rubber bands from Company A that were placed in the freezer for 15 minutes are less elastic before breaking than the rubber bands from Company B that were placed on the warming tray for 15 minutes. The issue is that the initial experiment as to whether or not temperature affects the elasticity before breaking of rubber bands is not clearly answered. The rubber bands from Company A that were in the freezer for 15 minutes definitely snapped at a shorter stretch distance. However, the student does not know whether or not the rubber bands snapped at a shorter stretch distance because they were colder in temperature, or because they were made by a different company. The fact of the matter is that according to this student's experimental design, it is possible that temperature has no effect on elasticity before breaking. Company A may just make a less elastic rubber band. Therefore, temperature is confounded with rubber band manufacturer and the student cannot make a legitimate inference about temperature and elasticity of rubber bands.

Choices A, B, and C are incorrect because none of the statements can be proven because of a poor experimental design due to confounding variables.

QUESTION 16.

Choice C is correct. If a single liter of Osmium is equivalent to 50 pounds, then 582 pounds of Osmium would be equivalent to $\dfrac{582}{50}=11.64$ liters of Osmium. If there are 3.88 liters in a gallon, then 11.64 liters of Osmium would be equivalent to $\dfrac{11.64}{3.88}=3$ gallons of Osmium.

Choices A, B, and D are incorrect and may result from calculation errors and/or errors in correctly applying unit conversions.

QUESTION 17.

Choice A is correct. Using the exponential model for the stock's growth, $y=10(2)^x$, yields a price of $y=10(2)^3=\$80$ after 3 years have passed and a price of $y=10(2)^4=\$160$ after 4 years have passed. Therefore, the analyst who predicts exponential growth for the stock predicts that the stock will rise by $\$160-\$80=\$80$ from the third year to the fourth year. Looking at the linear model for the stock's growth, $y=10+62x$, one can see that the slope, or change in price per year, is 62. Therefore, the analyst who predicts linear growth for the stock predicts that the stock will rise by $62 from the third year to the fourth year. Therefore, since $80 − $62 = $18, the analyst who predicts exponential growth believes that the stock will grow by $18 more from the third to fourth year than the analyst who predicts linear growth.

Choices B, C, and D are incorrect and may result from substitution and calculation errors while using the linear and exponential growth models.

QUESTION 18.

Choice B is correct. Building a table for the value of the stock, y, predicted by both the linear model and the exponential model at x, the times of 0, 1, 2, 3, 4, and 5 years after the stock's opening trading date yields the following:

$x =$	0	1	2	3	4	5
$y = 10 + 62x$	10	72	134	196	258	320
$y = 10(2)^x$	10	20	40	80	160	320

Three years after the stock's opening date, the linear model predicts the stock's price to be $196 whereas the exponential model predicts the stock's price to be $80. This is a difference of $196 − $80 = $116, which is the largest advantage the linear model ever has over the exponential model.

Choices A, C, and D are incorrect because the difference between the linear model's prediction for the stock's price and the exponential model's prediction for the stock's price is not as high as year 3 in any of these years.

QUESTION 19.

Choice C is correct. Looking at the graph of $G(x)$ in the xy-plane, one can see that the function has 3 x-intercepts, or roots, one of which is at 0 and the other two of which have positive x-values. Therefore, one of the factors of the function $G(x)$ will be x and the other two factors will be in the form $(x − a)$ and $(x − b)$, where a and b represent the positive values of the two x-intercepts. Factoring the x out of the right-hand side of the function $y = x^3 − 6x^2 + 8x$ yields $y = x(x^2 − 6x + 8)$ and further factoring the expression $x^2 − 6x + 8$ yields $y = x(x − 2)(x − 4)$. Therefore, the function $y = x^3 − 6x^2 + 8x$ has two positive roots and one root at zero, the characteristics present in the graph of $G(x)$.

Choice A is incorrect because it is a polynomial of degree two and only has two roots, whereas the graph of $G(x)$ has three distinct roots. Choice B is incorrect because even though it is a cubic function, it only has one root at $x = 3$. Choice D is incorrect because in its factored form, $y = x(x + 2)(x + 4)$, it is clear there is a root at 0, but there are also two negative roots which are not present in the graph of $G(x)$.

QUESTION 20.

Choice B is correct. Suppose that the four numbers are a, b, c, and d. Then, $a+b+c+d=84$. Further, if a is equivalent to $b+c+d$, then via substitution $(b+c+d)+b+c+d=84$. Combining like terms yields $2b+2c+2d=84$ and dividing both sides of the equation by 2 yields $b+c+d=42$. Since the average of the other three numbers, b, c, and d, is equivalent to $\dfrac{b+c+d}{3}$, dividing both sides of the equation $b+c+d=42$ by 3 yields $\dfrac{b+c+d}{3}=\dfrac{42}{3}=14$.

Choices A, C, and D are incorrect and may be the result of not correctly applying the average formula or misinterpreting the target of the question. For example, choice D is incorrect because 42 is the sum of the other three numbers, not the average of the other three numbers.

QUESTION 21.

Choice A is correct. Making c the total number of candies that Mrs. Darcy had and t the number of trick-or-treaters that came to the house, if Mrs. Darcy had enough pieces of candy to give each trick-or-treater 2 pieces with 24 pieces left over, then $c=2t+24$. Further, if Mrs. Darcy only had enough money to give half of the trick-or-treaters 5 pieces of candy, then $c=5(\frac{1}{2}t)$. Setting the two equations equal to each other yields $2t+24=5(\frac{1}{2}t)$. Subtracting $2t$ from both sides of the equation yields $24=\frac{1}{2}t$ and after multiplying both sides by 2, t is equivalent to 48 trick-or-treaters.

Choices B, C, and D are incorrect and may result from calculation errors when solving for the number of trick-or-treaters or errors in creating the appropriate equations to represent Mrs. Darcy's total candy count.

QUESTION 22.

Choice C is correct. Since $\angle acb$ and $\angle cab$ are complementary angles, the sum of $7x+4$ and $4x-2$ must be equivalent to 90. Combining like terms in the equation $7x+4+4x-2=90$ yields $11x+2=90$. Subtracting 2 from both sides of the equation yields $11x=88$ and then dividing by 11 yields $x=8$. Substituting 8 for x in the expression $7x+4$ yields $7(8)+4=60$ and substituting 8 for x in the expression $4x-2$ yields $4(8)-2=30$. Being that $\triangle abc$ is a 30-60-90 right triangle, the ratio of $\overline{ab}$ to $\overline{bc}$ is equivalent to $\sqrt{3}$ to 1. Therefore, the tangent of $\angle acb$ is equivalent to $\dfrac{\sqrt{3}}{1}$, or just $\sqrt{3}$.

Choice A is incorrect because $\dfrac{1}{2}$ is the cosine of $\angle acb$. Choice B is incorrect because $\dfrac{1}{\sqrt{3}}$ is the tangent of $\angle cab$, not $\angle acb$. Choice D is incorrect because 2 is the cosecant of angle $\angle acb$.

QUESTION 23.

Choice B is correct. A cylindrical container with a height of 6 inches and a diameter of 3 inches has a radius of 1.5 inches. Substituting 6 for h and 1.5 for r into the formula for the volume of a cylinder, $V = \pi r^2 h$, yields $V = \pi(1.5)^2(6) = 13.5\pi$ cubic inches. The other cylindrical container with a diameter that is three times the diameter of the first cylindrical container will have a radius that is three times the original radius which would be $3 \times 1.5 = 4.5$ inches. A cylindrical equation with a radius of 4.5 inches would have a volume of $V = \pi(4.5)^2 h$ cubic inches. Setting $\pi(4.5)^2 h$ equal to 13.5π yields $\pi(4.5)^2 h = 13.5\pi$. Dividing both sides by π yields $(4.5)^2 h = 13.5$ and squaring 4.5 yields $20.25h = 13.5$. Then, dividing both sides by 20.25 gives $h = 0.66...$ or $\dfrac{2}{3}$.

Choice A is incorrect because a container with a diameter of 9 and a height of $\dfrac{1}{3}$ would not have enough volume to hold all of the salt. Choices C and D are incorrect because containers with diameters of 9 and heights of $\dfrac{4}{3}$ inches and 2 inches, respectively, would hold more salt than 13.5π cubic inches.

QUESTION 24.

Choice A is correct. Substituting 10 for x in the equation $H(x) = 2.1x + 48$ yields $H(10) = 2.1(10) + 48$, which makes $H(10)$ equivalent to 69 inches. If a residual is defined as an observed data point minus a predicted data point, a residual of -3 would be equivalent to $Observed - 69$. If $Observed - 69 = -3$, adding 69 to both sides of the equation yields $Observed = 66$ inches. Therefore, the actual height of the person, or the observed height, is equivalent to 66 inches.

Choice B is incorrect because if the person's actual height were 69 inches, there would be a residual of 0. Choice C is incorrect and may result from accidentally flipping observed and expected in the defined equation for a residual. Choice D is incorrect and may result from a calculation error.

QUESTION 25.

Choice B is correct. A cube with a volume of 8 cubic inches has sides of length 2 because $\sqrt[3]{8} = 2$. A cube with a volume of 27 cubic inches has sides of length 3 because $\sqrt[3]{27} = 3$. If each side length is increased from 2 to 3, multiplying 2 by $(1+r)$ and setting the expression equal to 3 will reveal r, the percent increase in decimal form. Dividing both sides of $2(1+r) = 3$ by 2 yields $1 + r = 1.5$ and after subtracting 1 from both sides $r = .5$, or 50%.

Choices A and C are incorrect and may result from calculation errors while solving for the percent increase in side length. Choice D is incorrect because 150% represents the percent that the side length of the cube with a volume of 27 is of the side length of the cube with a volume of 8, not how much *larger* the side length is comparatively.

QUESTION 26.

Choice C is correct. If at the end of each month an account increased by 10% more than $100, then the account would increase by $100(1.10) = $110 each month. Increasing by $110 each month represents linear growth, not exponential growth.

Choices A, B, and D are incorrect because all three answers describe an account that increases by a fixed percent each month, thus representing exponential growth.

QUESTION 27.

Choice C is correct. The slope of each line, h, is equivalent to m in the equation $m = \frac{y_2 - y_1}{x_2 - x_1}$. Substituting h for m and the points $(5, 24)$ and $(15, h^2)$ into the equation $m = \frac{y_2 - y_1}{x_2 - x_1}$ yields $h = \frac{(h^2) - (24)}{(15) - (5)}$. Simplifying gives $h = \frac{h^2 - 24}{10}$ and multiplying both sides by 10 yields $10h = h^2 - 24$. Subtracting $10h$ from both sides yields $0 = h^2 - 10h - 24$ and factoring the right-hand side gives $0 = (h - 12)(h + 2)$, which reveals the roots of 12 and -2. Therefore, the sum of the roots is $12 + (-2) = 10$.

Choices A, B, and D are incorrect and may result from miscalculating the signs of one or both of the roots.

QUESTION 28.

Choice A is correct. Substituting $3c$ for a in the equation $a = 2b + 3$ yields $3c = 2b + 3$ and dividing each side of the equation by 3 yields $c = \frac{2}{3}b + 1$. Then, substituting $\frac{2}{3}b + 1$ for c in the equation $4c = 5d + 6$ yields $4(\frac{2}{3}b + 1) = 5d + 6$. Distributing the 4 on the left-hand side yields $\frac{8}{3}b + 4 = 5d + 6$ and subtracting 6 from both sides gives $\frac{8}{3}b - 2 = 5d$. Dividing both sides of the equation by 5 reveals that $d = \frac{8}{15}b - \frac{2}{5}$, or $d = \frac{8b - 6}{15}$.

Choices B, C, and D are incorrect and may result from substitution and/or calculation errors while attempting to solve for d.

QUESTION 29.

Choice D is correct. The decay of a radioactive isotope can be represented by an exponential decay model of the form $y = I(r)^{\frac{t}{a}}$, where y represents the mass of an isotope after t years have passed, with an initial mass of I, a decay factor of r, and a time of a years that it takes the isotope to complete one cycle of the decay factor. Substituting 202 for y, 20 for t, $\frac{1}{2}$ for r, and 40 for a yields $202 = I(\frac{1}{2})^{\frac{20}{40}}$. Raising $\frac{1}{2}$

335

to the power of $\frac{1}{2}$, or taking the square root of $\frac{1}{2}$, on the left hand side of the equation

yields $202 = I\sqrt{\frac{1}{2}}$. Since $\sqrt{\frac{1}{2}}$ can be rewritten as $\frac{\sqrt{2}}{2}$, the equation $202 = I\sqrt{\frac{1}{2}}$

can be rewritten as $202 = \frac{\sqrt{2}I}{2}$. Multiplying both sides of the equation by $\sqrt{2}$ yields

$I = 202\sqrt{2}$.

Choices A, B, and C are incorrect and may result from an error in setting up the appropriate exponential decay equation involving I. For example, choice A is incorrect because I and 202 were incorrectly swapped when their substitution took place.

QUESTION 30.

Choice D is correct. In a group of 250 men and women, if there are 50 more women than men, one can use x for men and $x + 50$ for women to develop the equation $x + x + 50 = 250$ which simplifies to $2x + 50 = 250$. Subtracting 50 from both sides of the equation yields $2x = 200$ and dividing by 2 makes $x = 100$. Therefore, there are 100 men and 150 women. Similarly, if there are 100 fewer doctors than lawyers, one can use x for lawyers and $x - 100$ for doctors to develop the equation $x + x - 100 = 250$ which simplifies to $2x - 100 = 250$. Adding 100 to both sides of the equation yields $2x = 350$ and dividing by 2 makes $x = 175$. Therefore, there are 175 lawyers and 75 doctors. If there are 30 male doctors, the remaining 45 doctors must be female. If there are a total of 150 women and 45 of them are doctors, the remaining 105 women are lawyers. If a woman is to be selected at random, the probability of selecting a lawyer is $\frac{105}{150}$, or $\frac{7}{10}$.

Choice A is incorrect because $\frac{3}{10}$ is the probability of selecting a doctor if a woman is to be selected at random. Choice B is incorrect because $\frac{2}{5}$ is the probability of selecting a man if a lawyer is selected at random. Choice C is incorrect because $\frac{3}{5}$ is the probability of selecting a woman if a lawyer is selected at random.

QUESTION 31.

The correct answer is 7. Adding $-x^2 + 22$ to $2x^2 + 7x - 52$ makes $g(x)$ equivalent to $x^2 + 7x - 30$. Factoring the right-hand side of the function $g(x) = x^2 + 7x - 30$ yields $g(x) = (x + 10)(x - 3)$. This form shows that the roots of the function $g(x)$ are -10 and 3. Therefore, the absolute value of the sum the roots is equivalent to $|-10 + 3| = 7$.

QUESTION 32.

The correct answer is 5, 10, or 15. Jefferson could have the following sets of bills in his wallet to sum to a total of $30:

1-$10 bill,	1-$5 bill,	and 15-$1 bills.
1-$10 bill,	2-$5 bills,	and 10-$1 bills.
1-$10 bill,	3-$5 bills,	and 5-$1 bills.
2-$10 bills,	1-$5 bill,	and 5-$1 bills.

Any other configuration of $10, $5, and $1 bills that summed to $30 would not have at least one of each bill. Therefore, the only possible number of $1 bills Jefferson could have in his wallet would be 5, 10, or 15 one-dollar bills.

QUESTION 33.

The correct answer is 1.75 or $\frac{7}{4}$. If the area of circle O is 16π, setting 16π equal to πr^2 yields $\pi r^2 = 16\pi$. Dividing both sides by π yields $r^2 = 16$ and taking the square root of both sides of the equation reveals that the radius is 4. Given that the length of an arc is equivalent to the radius of the circle multiplied by the measure of the arc's central angle in radians, one can say that $7 = 4(\theta)$, where θ is the measure of the central angle that defines the arc in radians. Dividing both sides of the equation by 4 yields $\theta = \frac{7}{4}$, or 1.75 radians.

QUESTION 34.

The correct answer is 8. Solving the inequality $y \geq \frac{13}{2}x + 20$ as an equality,

$y = \frac{13}{2}x + 20$, for x, yields $y - 20 = \frac{13}{2}x$ and after multiplying both sides of the equation by $\frac{2}{13}$ the equation reveals x as $x = \frac{2}{13}(y - 20)$. Distributing $\frac{2}{13}$ and combining like terms yields $x = \frac{2y - 40}{13}$. Substituting $\frac{2y - 40}{13}$ for x in the inequality $x > -2$ yields $\frac{2y - 40}{13} > -2$. Multiplying both sides of the inequality by 13 yields $2y - 40 > -26$ and adding 40 to both sides gives $2y > 14$. Finally, dividing both sides by 2 yields $y > 7$. Therefore, the least integer value of y that satisfies the system of inequalities is 8.

QUESTION 35.

The correct answer is 86. If the sum of 8 different integers is 124 and at least three of them are greater than 10, the greatest possible value for one of the integers can be found by minimizing the other 7 integers. Since 5 of the integers are at most 10, the least possible values for these 5 integers would be 1, 2, 3, 4, and 5. Further, since the other two integers must be greater than 10, the least possible values for these two integers would be 11 and 12. Using x to represent the value of the largest possible integer in the set of 8 numbers yields the equation $1 + 2 + 3 + 4 + 5 + 11 + 12 + x = 124$. Simplifying yields $38 + x = 124$, or $x = 86$.

QUESTION 36.

The correct answers are 64 or 128. If the function has only one root at the point $(-4,0)$, the only factor of the function is $x+4$. In order to create the function, the only factor $x+4$ must be squared to create $(x+4)^2 = x^2+8x+16$. Therefore, if $x^2+8x+16$ is equivalent to the function $x^2+abx+bc$, one can see that ab is equivalent to 8 and bc is equivalent to 16. The following set of values for a, b, and c satisfy both conditions:

1. $a=1$ $b=8$ $c=2$
2. $a=2$ $b=4$ $c=4$
3. $a=4$ $b=2$ $c=8$
4. $a=8$ $b=1$ $c=16$

Since the question states that $b < a < c$, then cases 3 and 4 are the only two combinations of a, b, and c that work. Therefore, $(4)(2)(8)=64$ or $(8)(1)(16)=128$.

QUESTION 37.

The correct answer is 76.5. If one newton of force is equivalent to approximately 0.225 pounds of force, then dividing 200 pounds by 0.225 pounds would yield the man's weight as approximately equivalent to 888.89 newtons. Substituting 888.89 for w and 9.8 (the gravitational acceleration on Earth) for g in the equation $w=mg$ yields $(888.89)=m(9.8)$. Dividing both sides of the equation by 9.8 reveals the man's mass, $m \approx 90.7$ kilograms. Substituting 90.7 for m and 3.75 (the gravitational acceleration on Mars) for g in the equation $w=mg$ yields $w=(90.7)(3.75)$, or $w=340.125$ newtons. Multiplying 340.125 by 0.225 reveals the man's weight on Mars, $340.125 \times 0.225 \approx 76.5$ pounds.

Alternatively, since the man's mass of approximately 90.7 kilograms never changes, then the man's weight in pounds is directly proportional to the gravitational acceleration of the planet on which his weight is being calculated. So, weight in pounds on Earth divided by 9.8 m/s^2 is equivalent to weight in pounds on Mars divided by 3.75 m/s^2. Cross-multiplying in the proportion $\dfrac{200}{9.8} = \dfrac{x}{3.75}$ yields $200(3.75)=9.8x$. Dividing both sides by 9.8 yields $x = \dfrac{200(3.75)}{9.8} \approx 76.5$ pounds.

QUESTION 38.

The correct answer is 13. Since the scale on the mysterious planet reads 1,000 pounds, or 5 times his current weight on Earth of 200 pounds, then the gravitational acceleration on the planet would have to be 5 times the gravitational acceleration on Earth due to the fact that the man's mass, $m \approx 90.7$ kilograms as calculated in the answer explanation for Question 37, never changes. Therefore, the gravitational acceleration on the mysterious planet would be $5 \times 9.8 = 49$ m/s^2. Dividing 49 by 3.75 yields approximately 13.067. Therefore, the gravitational acceleration on the mysterious planet is approximately 13 times the gravitational acceleration of 3.75 m/s^2 on Mars.

TEST 5

Reading Test

65 MINUTES, 52 QUESTIONS

Turn to Section 1 of your answer sheet to answer the questions in this section.

DIRECTIONS

Each passage or pair of passages below is followed by a number of questions. After reading each passage or pair, choose the best answer to each question based on what is stated or implied in the passage or passages and in any accompanying graphics (such as a table or graph).

Questions 1-10 are based on the following passage.

This passage is adapted from Joseph Conrad's novel *Lord Jim*, originally published in 1900.

He was an inch, perhaps two, under six feet, powerfully built, and he advanced straight at you with a slight stoop of the shoulders, head forward, and a fixed from-under stare which
Line made you think of a charging bull. His voice was deep, loud,
5 and his manner displayed a kind of dogged self-assertion which had nothing aggressive in it. It seemed a necessity, and it was directed apparently as much at himself as at anybody else. He was spotlessly neat, apparelled in immaculate white from shoes to hat, and in the various Eastern ports where he got his living
10 as ship-chandler's water-clerk he was very popular.

A water-clerk need not pass an examination in anything under the sun, but he must have Ability in the abstract and demonstrate it practically. His work consists in racing under sail, steam, or oars against other water-clerks for any ship about
15 to anchor, greeting her captain cheerily, forcing upon him a card—the business card of the ship-chandler—and on his first visit on shore piloting him firmly but without ostentation to a vast, cavern-like shop which is full of things that are eaten and drunk on board ship; where you can get everything to make
20 her seaworthy and beautiful, from a set of chain-hooks for her cable to a book of gold-leaf for the carvings of her stern; and where her commander is received like a brother by a ship-chandler he has never seen before. There is a cool parlour, easy-chairs, bottles, cigars, writing implements, a copy of harbour
25 regulations, and a warmth of welcome that melts the salt of a three months' passage out of a seaman's heart. The connection thus begun is kept up, as long as the ship remains in harbour, by the daily visits of the water-clerk. To the captain he is faithful like a friend and attentive like a son, with the patience of Job,

30 the unselfish devotion of a woman, and the jollity of a boon companion. Later on the bill is sent in. It is a beautiful and humane occupation. Therefore good water-clerks are scarce. When a water-clerk who possesses Ability in the abstract has also the advantage of having been brought up to the sea, he is
35 worth to his employer a lot of money and some humouring. Jim had always good wages and as much humouring as would have bought the fidelity of a fiend. Nevertheless, with black ingratitude he would throw up the job suddenly and depart. To his employers the reasons he gave were obviously inadequate.
40 They said "Confounded fool!" as soon as his back was turned. This was their criticism on his exquisite sensibility.

To the white men in the waterside business and to the captains of ships he was just Jim—nothing more. He had, of course, another name, but he was anxious that it should not
45 be pronounced. His incognito, which had as many holes as a sieve, was not meant to hide a personality but a fact. When the fact broke through the incognito he would leave suddenly the seaport where he happened to be at the time and go to another—generally farther east. He kept to seaports because
50 he was a seaman in exile from the sea, and had Ability in the abstract, which is good for no other work but that of a water-clerk. He retreated in good order towards the rising sun, and the fact followed him casually but inevitably. Thus in the course of years he was known successively in Bombay, in
55 Calcutta, in Rangoon, in Penang, in Batavia—and in each of these halting-places was just Jim the water-clerk. Afterwards, when his keen perception of the Intolerable drove him away for good from seaports and white men, even into the virgin forest, the Malays of the jungle village, where he had
60 elected to conceal his deplorable faculty, added a word to the monosyllable of his incognito. They called him Tuan Jim: as one might say—Lord Jim.

CONTINUE ➡

1

Over the course of the first two paragraphs (lines 1-41) the focus of the passage shifts from

A) a humorous anecdote about a character's typical day at work to a more serious recounting of his personal background.

B) an account of the responsibilities and tasks a water-clerk takes on to a narration of a particular voyage the author was on.

C) a synopsis of the history of a prestigious and esteemed profession to an illustration of a man who was successful in the field.

D) a physical depiction of an interesting character to a detailed description of the duties and requirements of the character's occupation.

2

As used in line 2, "slight" most nearly means

A) superficial.

B) minor.

C) delicate.

D) meaningless.

3

In the second paragraph, the use of the word "her" mainly serves to

A) imply that a water-clerk is usually female.

B) personify the captain's ship.

C) compare a water-clerk's ship to a woman.

D) characterize a water-clerk's tasks as feminine.

4

The author mentions the "patience of Job, the unselfish devotion of a woman, and the jollity of a boon companion" (lines 29-31) primarily in order to

A) cite evidence for the author's claim that the duties of a water-clerk require rigorous preparation.

B) indicate the qualities that a ship-chandler must possess in order to be successful.

C) illustrate the way that an effective water-clerk behaves towards the captain of the ship.

D) point out qualities Lord Jim had that were unique to him alone and caused his ship-chandler to hire him.

5

According to the passage, the main goal of the water-clerk is to

A) make the captain of a ship feel comfortable and welcome so that he is more willing to purchase food, drinks, and decorations for his ship.

B) promote the shop of the ship-chandler he works for by distributing his business card and delivering his goods to different ships.

C) travel to ports in various countries and sell items necessary for the operation of a ship to captains and sailors.

D) make and distribute advertisements for a ship-chandler's shop and circulate them around the city he lives in.

6

As used in line 22, "received" most nearly means

A) greeted.

B) collected.

C) assimilated.

D) secured.

7

The passage indicates that Lord Jim would leave for new ports because

A) he had lost the abilities that had initially made him so successful as a water-clerk.

B) he was unsatisfied with the way he was treated at his previous occupation by his superiors.

C) he possessed a secret about himself that had been revealed at his then-current location.

D) he had become too famous where he previously worked and changed locations to maintain privacy.

8

Which choice provides the best evidence for the answer to the previous question?

A) Lines 11-13 ("A water-clerk . . . practically")

B) Lines 37-39 ("Nevertheless . . . inadequate")

C) Lines 46-49 ("When . . . another")

D) Lines 56-61 ("Afterwards, when . . . incognito")

CONTINUE

9

The author indicates that the qualifications of a water-clerk

A) are extremely difficult to meet, making water-clerks in low supply.

B) are unique to the occupation and cannot be applied to any other job.

C) are so abstract in nature as to be unquantifiable.

D) are not innate and so can be taught successfully to most people.

10

Which choice provides the best evidence for the answer to the previous question?

A) Lines 26-28 ("The connection . . . water-clerk")

B) Lines 33-35 ("When a . . . humouring")

C) Lines 49-52 ("He kept . . . water-clerk")

D) Lines 53-55 ("Thus . . . Batavia")

Questions 11-21 are based on the following passage and supplementary material.

Adapted from Patrick Kennedy, "What's Bad for the Economy Can Be Good for You."

If "everybody wins" situations are impossible in modern economics, at least "everybody loses" situations are equally impossible. Among the industries that can weather even the
Line worst economic climates are tax service companies, waste
5 disposal services, and (morbid though it sounds) elder care facilities and funeral homes. After all, businesses such as these provide necessities so basic—remember the old saying about "death and taxes" being life's only two certainties?—that no sensible economy can do without them. Entertainment
10 companies are widely, though not entirely accurately, believed to fare well in periods of economic misfortune for a complementary reason: why not forget death, taxes, unemployment, and all the rest with an afternoon at the movies?

But while some companies simply endure and outlast a
15 recession or a crisis, others thrive. Such "win while everyone else is losing" businesses aren't doing anything out of the ordinary—certainly nothing on the order of the money managers profiled in Michael Lewis's book *The Big Short*, men who risked millions betting that the U.S. economy would
20 crash and reaped millions of dollars in profit when, in 2008, it in fact did. Instead, there are some businesses that are naturally structured to do well in tough times. Economic trickery has nothing to do with how they operate.

In many cases, the businesses in question are only a bit
25 more glamorous than the tax service companies and elder care facilities I mentioned above. Dollar stores and other deep discounters, candy manufacturers, and soft drink companies are but a few of the companies that can do well when most of the economic news is bad. The first group—low-cost stores and
30 retailers—benefits from some of the same logic that explains why a funeral home won't fold in even the worst of times: simple necessity. Consumers can't cut back too much on home essentials during poor economies, but they can certainly hunt around for essentials at cheaper prices. A $7 bag of frozen
35 vegetables from Whole Foods is suddenly replaced by a similar, $2 bag of frozen vegetables from Dollar Tree, and the rest of the shopping list follows suit.

And when these cash-strapped consumers are done shopping, they may nonetheless pick up a bag of chips or a can
40 of Coke on the way out. Web journalist Andrew Beattie has argued that "the desire for comforts doesn't leave, it simply scales down"—leading to small purchases such as "a nightly glass of wine, a pack of cigarettes, or a chocolate bar." In fact, the candy bar industry prospered during the Great Depression,
45 while candy makers such as Cadbury and Nestle saw their profits grow even in the face of the Financial Crisis of 2008. It

342

CONTINUE

seems that inexpensive tiny-luxury food in general has a good track record in bad economies: McDonald's, after all, was one of the few economic success stories of the 1970s.

50   I should warn you, though, that none of this amounts to a comprehensive theory of how to get rich in a bad economy. There are simply too many variables and incongruities: luxury handbag manufacturers are good at resisting economic downturns while casinos aren't. There is also an ever-shifting

55 economic future, one that presents the possibility of radically reinvented models of consumer behavior: I have no idea how good Amazon.com would be at weathering a series of recessions simply because there has never been a part low-price retail, part online infrastructure, part think tank business quite

60 like Amazon.com. What I can recommend, though, is adding a few of these bad-economy-resistant businesses to your stock portfolio. When the economy dips again—and it will—you'll find that your nearest Dollar Tree is good for something other than super-cheap groceries.

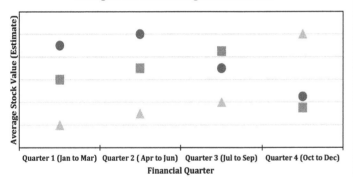

Average Stock Value During 2008 Fiscal Year

● S&P 500   ▲ Dollar Tree   ■ Amazon

The S&P 500 is a stock market index that charts an aggregate value for the stock values of a large number of businesses.

11

The main purpose of the passage is to

A) encourage consumers to spend less on luxuries on account of a predicted economic decline.

B) outline the management tactics that are becoming more popular among low-cost retailers.

C) consider how a few different types of businesses will fare in a bad economy.

D) refute misconceptions about how candy and soft-drink companies operate.

12

As used in line 4, "climates" most nearly means

A) areas.

B) temperatures.

C) conditions.

D) biases.

13

The main purpose of the passage is to provide

A) practical advice about how to benefit during an economic downturn.

B) a model of behavior that explains all aspects of how a bad economy functions.

C) an ethical argument that redeems often-vilified businesses.

D) a classification system that differentiates local and national businesses.

14

Which choice provides the best evidence for the answer to the previous question?

A) Lines 21-23 ("Instead, there . . . operate")

B) Lines 29-32 ("The first . . . necessity")

C) Lines 50-51 ("I should warn . . . economy")

D) Lines 60-62 ("What I can . . . portfolio")

15

The author's argument about consumer spending habits relies on which of the following assumptions?

A) Earlier attempts to explain the dynamics of poor economies have been mostly unsuccessful.

B) Clever marketing can lead consumers to make fundamentally unwise choices.

C) Businesses that succeed in bad economies receive little publicity.

D) Many of the goods available at high-cost stores are comparable to the goods available at low-cost stores.

16

Which choice provides the best evidence for the answer to the previous question?

A) Lines 9-11 ("Entertainment . . . misfortune")

B) Lines 34-37 ("A $7 bag . . . follows suit")

C) Lines 38-40 ("And when . . . way out")

D) Lines 48-49 ("McDonald's . . . 1970s")

CONTINUE

17

As used in line 53, "resisting" most nearly means

A) arguing against.

B) prospering despite.

C) turning away from.

D) stubbornly ignoring.

18

The author refers to *The Big Short* by Michael Lewis (line 18) in order to

A) introduce an approach to economic problems that differs from the approach emphasized elsewhere in the passage.

B) explain why focusing on long-term economic growth is a more advisable strategy than prioritizing short term profits.

C) commemorate a small group of visionary economic scholars.

D) criticize the materialism of those who make foolish stock market investments.

19

Based on the data in the graph, in which quarter did the average Dollar Tree stock rise above the others in 2008?

A) Quarter 1

B) Quarter 2

C) Quarter 3

D) Quarter 4

20

Which statement about the effect of the Financial Crisis of 2008 is best supported by the graph?

A) At least one company did not experience a significant decrease in average stock value.

B) Only one company experienced a significant decrease in average stock value.

C) All of the companies achieved an increase in average stock value.

D) The company with the highest average stock value in Quarter 1 had the lowest average stock value in Quarter 4.

21

The author would most likely attribute Dollar Tree's average stock value in Quarter 4 as represented in the graph to

A) "Economic trickery" (line 22)

B) "simple necessity" (line 32)

C) "tiny-luxury food" (line 47)

D) "reinvented models" (line 56)

CONTINUE

Questions 22-31 are based on the following passages.

These two passages consider recent developments in zoological research.

Passage 1

Thanks to technological advances, we can better understand aspects of the world that cannot effectively be inspected by the naked eye: atoms, molecules, microbes,
Line and—believe it or not—certain species of birds. Consider the
5 peregrine falcon, which is regarded by many as the world's fastest flier. An adult peregrine falcon can reach speeds of up to 220 miles per hour: ornithologists are well aware of this stunning figure, but how, exactly, does it feel to move at more than five times the speed limit on many roadways? This is one
10 of the questions that was addressed by researchers Suzanne Amador Kane and Marjon Zamani, who used portable video cameras to capture a falcon's-eye view of the world. Kane and Zamani's findings, which were published in the *Journal of Experimental Biology*, rely on the kind of mounted camera
15 technology popularized by GoPro, which sells devices that allow human athletes and hobbyists to record their feats. Scaled-down, GoPro-like cameras were strapped to the heads of the falcons that Kane and Zamani monitored. While the results of this research will allow behavioral biologists to more
20 precisely comprehend how falcons operate in the wild—how falcons determine the best angle of approach when attacking prey, and how they make use of those astonishing speeds—the findings may also facilitate further technological advances. As Kane and Zamani note, the falcon footage could speed along
25 "the development of computer models of predation and the integration of sensory and locomotion systems in biomimetic robots."

Unfortunately for more traditional researchers, the dives during which falcons reach their absolute top speeds have only
30 seldom been observed in the wild. Yet here again, technology is a boon to avian research. Rather than waiting to see falcons attain those stunning 240 miles per hour again and again, a group of Germany-based scientists led by Benjamin Ponitz used observations of falcon anatomy, wind tunnel analysis,
35 and computer modeling to determine exactly how falcons dive. Ponitz's 2014 study offers the most accurate depiction to date of falcon "body shape and wing contour": diving falcons configure their bodies in a spade-like shape, wings held straight to the side and hunched slightly forward.

Passage 2

40 The peregrine falcon is arguably the fastest creature that flies, depending on how vigorously one will argue semantics: can diving truly be called flying? The dive itself makes no use of this falcon's extraordinary wingspan, nor does the attack. Flight must involve the wings: flapping, soaring, or somehow
45 using the wings to propel the bird. A falcon doesn't use its wings until after the dive is completed, deploying them as air brakes. The bird doesn't "fly." It falls. Is the fastest man alive the one who can run the fastest, or the man who skydives?
50 Today, some scientists contend that the White-Throated Needletail, a large variety of swift, is the fastest bird in the animal kingdom, reaching speeds of 105 miles per hour by flapping its wings. This seems a much more realistic way of determining which animal is the fastest
55 flier.

These birds are so fast that the only real threat to their well-being is their own speed. Many die by crashing head-first into windows, reflective surfaces, wires, lighthouses, and other man-made structures. The
60 Needletail is also virtually uncatchable: scientists aiming to study it have to rely heavily on luck, either finding a Needletail nest by chance, or finding a younger bird while it sleeps. The bird is simply too fast to apprehend otherwise. Females hunting to find food for their young
65 have been known to travel hundreds of miles just to find a specific breed of locust or beetle. Even the location of the nest can elude a researcher; most are built in hollow trunks of extremely tall trees, or on small rocky outcrops on the faces of sheer cliffs. The bird fashions a cement
70 of twigs, leaves, feathers, and saliva that adhere to a rock face, making its nest look like nothing more than a bump protruding just a few inches. The rare snake or mink might find its way to a nest, but most predators pose no threat to a White-Throated Needletail. Not even man.

22

As used in line 3, "naked" most nearly means

A) blatant.

B) unembellished.

C) unaided.

D) vulnerable.

23

Both passages contain references to

A) new technologies that have aided bird research.

B) the methods that researchers use to study certain bird species.

C) a scientific debate that has become a source of controversy.

D) published research papers on the peregrine falcon.

CONTINUE

24

Unlike the author of Passage 2, the author of Passage 1

A) does not discuss any bird species other than the peregrine falcon.

B) offers a strong opinion about which living bird species is the fastest.

C) describes how a peregrine falcon attains high speeds in flight.

D) questions the validity of a widely-accepted criterion.

25

As described in Passage 1, the research project devised by Suzanne Amador Kane and Marjon Zamani is noteworthy because

A) it settled a longstanding dispute about the top speeds reached by peregrine falcons.

B) it helped increase the popularity of GoPro cameras.

C) it inspired the research undertaken by Benjamin Ponitz.

D) it could inspire the creation of new technology.

26

Which choice provides the best evidence for the answer to the previous question?

A) Lines 9-12 ("This is one . . . the world")

B) Lines 17-18 ("Scaled down . . . monitored")

C) Lines 23-27 ("As Kane . . . robots")

D) Lines 31-35 ("Rather than . . . dive")

27

As used in line 69, "fashions" most nearly means

A) designs.

B) mixes.

C) formulates.

D) gathers.

28

The author of Passage 2 responds to the idea that the peregrine falcon is "the fastest creature that flies" (lines 40-41) by

A) raising a counterargument that is ultimately rejected.

B) dismissing this description as vague and inconsequential.

C) surveying expert opinion and listing several examples of fieldwork.

D) examining a concept and offering an alternative choice.

29

As described in these passages, the peregrine falcon and the White-Throated Needletail are similar in that both of these birds

A) attain their top speeds by diving.

B) attain their top speeds by flapping their wings.

C) have been studied using computer imaging.

D) can be difficult to study in the wild.

30

The author of Passage 2 indicates that an appreciable threat to the White-Throated Needletail is

A) the peregrine falcon.

B) human hunting and poaching.

C) collision with buildings.

D) diminishing food sources.

31

Which choice provides the best evidence for the answer to the previous question?

A) Lines 40-43 ("The peregrine . . . attack")

B) Lines 57-59 ("Many die . . . structures")

C) Lines 64-66 ("Females hunting . . . beetle")

D) Lines 69-72 ("The bird . . . inches")

CONTINUE

Questions 32-41 are based on the following passage.

This reading is adapted from the 2010 "Remarks at Human Rights Town Hall Day" delivered by Secretary of State Hillary Rodham Clinton. The acronym "NGO" stands for "Non-Governmental Organization."

Those of us in this great Dean Acheson Hall who lived through the civil rights movement, the fall of the Soviet Union, the end of apartheid, and so much else know that these singular
Line achievements are by no means the work of governments
5 alone. In fact, it took civil society pushing governments, and sometimes pulling them against their natural inclination, to just protect the status quo. It took groups of citizens in shipyards and lunch counters and even prisons to keep prodding the conscience of governments and the rest of us.
10 So for the United States, supporting civil society around the globe is a crucial priority. I made that clear in a speech I gave last summer at the Community of Democracies in Krakow, where we laid out an agenda of support for civil society, because we think it's not only a matter of good global
15 citizenship, but it's a key to advancing so many of our national security priorities.
So we intend to make engagement with civil society a defining feature of our diplomacy. We've asked our embassies and missions around the world to develop strategies to elevate
20 support for and protection of civil society. Next year, I will launch the new strategic dialogue with civil society to bring together representatives from government and civic groups for regular consultation, just as we do in our strategic dialogues with other countries.
25 We have seen increased efforts by governments to restrict civic space, whether in Cuba or China's efforts to somehow divert the world's attention from the Nobel Peace Prize Ceremony today. We really know that we have our work cut out for us. And in Krakow, I called on the UN Human Rights
30 Council to do more to protect civil society and announced the creation of a new fund for embattled NGOs . . .
Now, just last week, I was in Central Asia, a place where civil society faces severe challenges. And we worked hard to give civil society a voice at the OSCE summit in
35 Astana, Kazakhstan. And in each country, from Kazakhstan to Kyrgyzstan to Uzbekistan, I met with the brave men and women who are committed to improving the lives of their fellow citizens, often at significant personal risk. These meetings, as they always are for me, were inspiring and
40 deepened my appreciation for the difficult work that you and many others on the front lines of human rights and civil rights actually face every day.
As mentioned earlier today, I presented the Eleanor Roosevelt Award for Human Rights to outstanding individuals:
45 Sarah Cleto Rial, an activist who sought refuge in the United

States from Sudan; Wade Henderson, with whom I have worked over many years; and Louis and Alice Henkin, who together helped to promote and protect human rights in international law. And so we're working to lead by
50 example and hold ourselves accountable. And actually, we're trying to live up to Eleanor Roosevelt's challenge that America should be the best possible mirror of democracy that she can be.
So this year's State Department Human Trafficking
55 Report, for the first time, graded our own efforts as well as others. Last month, we presented our own human rights record as part of the UN's Universal Periodic Review. And just as we ask other governments to work with civil society groups, we also held a special event
60 to allow NGOs from around the world to speak directly with officials from 12 different federal agencies, and we webcast the proceedings.
We're doing that and a lot more, but we need your advice, your support, your recommendations, your
65 constructive criticism, because we want to help. Human Rights Day is a celebration of you and of what you are doing, and it is also a reminder and a challenge about how much more we all have to do.

32

Which of the following best describes the developmental pattern of the passage?

A) A listing of achievements of civil society and civic groups to an impassioned appeal for more legislative action.

B) A serious synopsis of events about protesting the oppression of democracy to a more optimistic prediction of the social change to come.

C) A description of the advances made by civil society groups and organizations to a statement that there is still more progress to be made.

D) A report of current events around the world and influential decisions to an explanation of the events' significance.

33

As used in line 7, "protect" most nearly means

A) maintain.

B) defend.

C) save.

D) shelter.

CONTINUE

34

In the first paragraph, Clinton mentions "shipyards," "lunch counters," and "prisons" primarily to

A) reveal the previously unknown fact that the government actually had very little to do with influencing legislation regarding civil rights.

B) emphasize that the fight for civil rights is not over by citing examples of places where people are still being oppressed.

C) support her argument that social change is largely influenced by the actions of citizens not working in government.

D) argue that protest by ordinary citizens is the catalyst for social change and the only thing keeping government from becoming too powerful.

35

The passage indicates that Clinton

A) had begun to meet routinely with the leaders of many developing countries about civil society.

B) had expressed her appreciation for and encouragement of civil society in the past.

C) had attempted to repress civil society in her initial years as a politician.

D) has been working on a program that advances economic reform in impoverished countries.

36

Which choice provides the best evidence for the answer to the previous question?

A) Lines 10-12 ("So . . . Democracies")

B) Lines 20-22 ("Next . . . groups")

C) Lines 33-35 ("we . . . Kazakhstan")

D) Lines 50-53 ("And . . . be")

37

According to Clinton, the governments of some countries

A) had proposed to aid Clinton economically in her plans to promote civil society in non-democratic countries.

B) have asked Clinton for assistance in making their countries more democratic and egalitarian.

C) had worked with Clinton previously but have since rejected her offers to collaborate.

D) have attempted to prevent the spread of civil society in both overt and subtle ways.

38

Which choice provides the best evidence for the answer to the previous question?

A) Lines 17-20 ("So. . . society")

B) Lines 25-28 ("We . . . today")

C) Lines 32-35 ("Now . . . Kazakhstan")

D) Lines 54-58 ("So . . . Review")

39

Clinton argues that supporting civil society not only has social benefits for citizens but also

A) improves and benefits the national security of the United States.

B) strengthens the economy of the United States and other developed countries.

C) improves the reputation and approval rates of the United States.

D) reduces corruption in the governments of many developed countries.

40

As used in line 52, "mirror" most nearly means

A) illusion.

B) replication.

C) imitation.

D) representation.

41

Clinton uses the word "we" throughout the final paragraph (lines 63-68) mainly to

A) indicate that America as a nation must also make progress.

B) establish a sense of acceptance among a group of people.

C) reinforce the need for laws supporting social change.

D) suggest that the United States is less democratic than initially thought.

CONTINUE

Questions 42-52 are based on the following passage and supplementary material.

Adapted from Philip Kowalski, "An Unnatural History of the American Zoo."

The first American zoo was established in Philadelphia in 1874, and for most Americans today, zoos figure as positive impositions on the landscape. They preserve many species
Line threatened in their natural habitats by forces such as climate
5 change in the Arctic and the mercenary poaching in Africa—forces that might spell the potential extinction of polar bears and elephants, among others. But this conservatorship that zoos offer also reflects the values of a culture that still privileges a traditional human-centered and human-controlled view of the
10 natural world. As theorized by the American philosopher and intellectual historian A. O. Lovejoy in the 1930s, the so-called "Great Chain of Being" assumed that "man" ruled over the entire natural world and, like Adam in the Garden of Eden, was the caretaker of all living things.
15 During the latter half of the twentieth century and well into the twenty-first century, however, this totalizing belief of man's intellectual and physical superiority has been challenged by philosophers, most notably Peter Singer and Cary Wolfe, who argue that animals should enjoy equal status with human
20 beings. As a result, zoos—which have long been considered places of education and amusement, where both children and adults witness tigers in their seemingly "natural" lair, male lions as nominal heads of their prides, and elephants as friendly companions—are no longer viewed as innocent recreation.
25 Rather, this seemingly innocuous act of "just looking" at animals constitutes a transgression of the fundamental dignity of non-human species who have the right to roam and to make their own decisions regarding their survival, for better or for worse, just as all humans do.
30 As Mary Benbow explains, in late nineteenth-century and early twentieth-century America "zoos developed in close association with parks and created landscapes infused with middle-class ethos . . . and became civic symbols of city expansion" that "were therefore also engaged in social reform
35 intended to educate the working and immigrant classes." Educational goals aside, zoos conceived on this model express the principle that humanity controls all nature by ruling over, designating, categorizing and deciding where all living things belong and how they should subsequently behave.
40 According to Carol J. Adams, "zoos present a restricted, imperialistic, supremacist view of the natural world. Zoos are cruel. They inflict pain . . . Animal captivity therefore is harmful to the captive animal and to the human spectator." Despite these claims that animals are on par with humans,
45 most Americans still view animals in captivity as situated in a cozy environment where they are fed, taken care of, and not exposed to the dangers of the survival of the fittest in the natural world. But is supposed freedom from danger really the yardstick by which quality of life can be measured?
50 Granted, captive animals may in most cases fare better in these artificial conditions, but that doesn't necessarily imply that zoos figure as the most viable venues for continued survival. Zoo elephants, according to People for the Ethical Treatment of Animals (PETA), have been
55 subjected to a "lack of exercise and long hours standing on hard surfaces." Such conditions have contributed to "foot problems and arthritis," which are "the leading reasons why captive elephants are euthanized. Many die decades short of their expected lifespan."
60 The question of whether zoos are productive or destructive institutions is symptomatic of larger issues concerning the way human beings have historically treated the environment. Even after experiencing a growing number of natural catastrophes over the past several years,
65 much of the world has still not taken substantial measures to allay the problems with man's relation to nature. The series of droughts, floods, and forest fires, as well as the continuous strip-mining of the globe attest to the fact that "man" still confronts his environment with a kind
70 of hostile aggression. While many Americans balk at the thought that animals possess the self-determination of human beings, those who question the role and benefits of modern zoos suggest ways of thinking sympathetically about the natural world that can help the Earth to heal
75 itself.

CONTINUE

Figure 1

Primary Perspective of Americans Towards Zoos

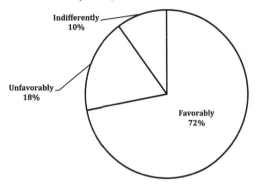

Indifferently
10%

Unfavorably
18%

Favorably
72%

Figure 2

Reason for Favorable Perspective Toward Zoos

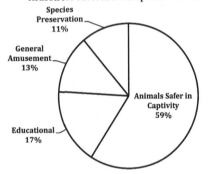

Species
Preservation
11%

General
Amusement
13%

Educational
17%

Animals Safer in
Captivity
59%

The above is adapted from a 2015 survey on zoo visitation.

42

In the first paragraph, the author does which of the following?

A) Concedes that zoos may have some ecological benefits

B) Explains why zoos have so often been criticized

C) Implies that zoos will only continue to grow in popularity

D) Cites a philosopher who wrote about the earliest American zoos

43

The function of the information provided in lines 10-14 ("As theorized . . . things") is to

A) introduce a historical figure whose ideas are no longer widely studied.

B) summarize an argument that zookeepers often use to defend their practices.

C) provide background for a belief that the author finds problematic.

D) imply that Lovejoy's theory has been interpreted inaccurately by subsequent scholars.

44

According to the author, Americans overwhelmingly view the act of keeping animals in zoos as

A) controversial.

B) harmless.

C) economically empowering.

D) philosophically questionable.

45

Which choice provides the best evidence for the answer to the previous question?

A) Lines 25-29 ("Rather, this . . . humans do")

B) Lines 30-33 ("As Mary . . . ethos")

C) Lines 44-48 ("Despite these . . . world")

D) Lines 70-75 ("While many . . . itself")

46

As used in line 3, "preserve" most nearly means

A) safeguard.

B) commemorate.

C) store.

D) make static.

CONTINUE

47

The author would most likely argue that debates surrounding zoos are important because

A) zoos can foster character traits such as sympathy and imagination.

B) organizations that oppose zoo-keeping practices are growing in popularity.

C) zoos are oblivious to the pain that zoo animals experience.

D) attitudes towards zoos are relevant to broader concerns.

48

Which choice provides the best evidence for the answer to the previous question?

A) Lines 20-24 ("As a result . . . recreation")

B) Lines 48-49 ("But is supposed . . . measured?")

C) Lines 53-56 ("Zoo elephants . . . surfaces")

D) Lines 60-63 ("The question . . . environment")

49

As used in line 56, "have contributed to" most nearly means

A) have collaborated with.

B) are responsible for.

C) deserve recognition for.

D) play a supporting role in.

50

The quotations from Mary Benbow and Carol J. Adams differ in that Benbow

A) explains the origins of a feature of American life, while Adams offers harsh criticisms of that same feature.

B) focuses on how zoos impact the animals that they house, while Adams focus on how zoos impact their human visitors.

C) indicates where zoos where originally most popular, while Adams explains why zoos are declining in popularity.

D) defends modern zoos from their critics, while Adams praises the efforts of these same critics.

51

Which choice is supported by the data in the first figure?

A) The number of Americans who view zoos favorably is greater than the number of those who view zoos unfavorably.

B) The number of Americans who view zoos unfavorably is greater than the number of those who view zoos favorably.

C) People who view zoos with indifference are less likely to visit zoos.

D) People who view zoos unfavorably are more likely to visit zoos.

52

Taken together, the two figures suggest that the greatest number of Americans view zoos

A) favorably, because of the entertainment value.

B) unfavorably, because of the lack in species preservation.

C) favorably, because animals are considered safer in captivity.

D) unfavorably, because the educational aspect has diminished over time.

STOP

If you finish before time is called, you may check your work on this section only.
Do not turn to any other section.

Writing Test
35 MINUTES, 44 QUESTIONS

Turn to Section 2 of your answer sheet to answer the questions in this section.

DIRECTIONS

Each passage below is accompanied by a number of questions. For some questions, you will consider how the passage might be revised to improve the expression of ideas. For other questions, you will consider how the passage might be edited to correct errors in sentence structure, usage, or punctuation. A passage or a question may be accompanied by one or more graphics (such as a table or graph) that you will consider as you make revising and editing decisions.

Some questions will direct you to an underlined portion of a passage. Other questions will direct you to a location in a passage or ask you to think about the passage as a whole.

After reading each passage, choose the answer to each question that most effectively improves the quality of writing in the passage or that makes the passage conform to the conventions of standard written English. Many questions include a "NO CHANGE" option. Choose that option if you think the best choice is to leave the relevant portion of the passage as it is.

Questions 1-11 are based on the following passage.

Mary, Queen of Scots: Making History Live

— 1 —

[1] As far as history is concerned, I am a romantic, not a scholar. [2] Dates and treaties and demographic studies are of little interest to me; however, the characters of the people who made history are spellbinding. [3] For instance, I have always been captivated by the character of Mary, Queen of Scots. [4] I can relate to her because of her resemblance

1 as people I know personally—people who, like Mary, have struggled with the tangled circumstances of their own lives. **2**

1
A) NO CHANGE
B) to people
C) with people
D) for people

2
To make the order of ideas in the paragraph most logical, sentence 3 should be placed
A) where it is now.
B) before sentence 1.
C) after sentence 1.
D) after sentence 4.

CONTINUE →

— 2 —

Born on December 8, 1542, [3] Mary's father James V of Scotland died when Mary became a queen six days later. In 1558 she was sent to France. Surrounded by the indulgence and intrigue of the French court, the naïve yet artistic teenage girl found her new life exotic and thrilling. At just sixteen, she was joined in marriage to a young man named Francis, [4] who became King of France the following year.

— 3 —

Yet Mary rapidly shifted from wife to widow: Francis died suddenly, and a year later Mary sailed to Scotland, ready to play a new role as Queen. She landed in an alien world. For the first time in her life, Mary was seen as a pawn in a grand political scheme [5] rather than as a lively, independent woman. The Scots insisted that she marry to the advantage of the country's future and they chose Henry Stuart, Earl of Darnley, as Mary's husband.

— 4 —

The union between Mary and Darnley was a disaster. Selfish, spoiled, and arrogant, Darnley treated Mary abominably: his only redeeming quality was his status as a potential heir to the English throne should Elizabeth, the English monarch, never marry, [6] a privilege which seemed increasingly likely. Mary ignored him as much as possible, [7] and the marriage did produce a son.

[3]
A) NO CHANGE
B) it was six days later when Mary's father, James V of Scotland, died and Mary became a queen.
C) James V of Scotland, Mary's father, died six days later when Mary became a queen.
D) Mary became a queen six days later when her father, James V of Scotland, died.

[4]
A) NO CHANGE
B) he became
C) becoming
D) then became

[5]
A) NO CHANGE
B) or as
C) and as
D) as

[6]
A) NO CHANGE
B) a possibility which
C) this
D) and it

[7]
A) NO CHANGE
B) because
C) however
D) although

— 5 —

For me, this is what history is about. Mary may have been flawed, but she [8] is determined to live her life to the fullest. Many of her contemporaries were glad to be rid of her, no doubt. Then again, most of them are forgotten, but Mary is not.

— 6 —

This unpleasant marriage ended abruptly in February of 1567, when Darnley was killed in an explosion. Mary's misadventures, however, only continued: she tried to flee Scotland with her [9] lover, the Earl of Bothwell only, to be foiled in this attempt by the Scots. When a second, more effectual flight led her to England, she was promptly imprisoned by [10] Queen Elizabeth and remained under strict watch for eighteen years. Eventually, Elizabeth decided to have Mary executed, yet the bold, showily-dressed Mary used the scene of her execution as one last opportunity to assert her strong personality.

Question [11] asks about the previous passage as a whole.

[8]
A) NO CHANGE
B) has determined
C) was determined
D) were determined

[9]
A) NO CHANGE
B) lover, the Earl, of Bothwell only, to be foiled
C) lover, the Earl of Bothwell only to be foiled
D) lover, the Earl of Bothwell, only to be foiled

[10]
A) NO CHANGE
B) Queen Elizabeth, who remained
C) Queen Elizabeth, she remained
D) Queen Elizabeth, they remained

Think about the previous passage as a whole as you answer question 11.

[11]
To make the passage most logical, paragraph 5 should be placed
A) where it is now.
B) after paragraph 1.
C) after paragraph 2.
D) after paragraph 6.

CONTINUE

Questions 12-22 are based on the following passage and supplementary material.

Africa and the Future of the World Economy

Depictions of the African economy are seldom positive. Western news outlets consistently focus on outbreaks of disease, instances of political corruption, and [12] <u>poverty and its intense scenes.</u> These are indeed realities for many individuals living in Africa, but there are also [13] <u>an indication</u> that Africa holds strong potential for economic growth and development in the upcoming decades.

Africa possesses a number of mostly [14] <u>untapped</u> economic assets. Between 2000 and 2010, six of the world's top ten fastest-growing countries were located in Africa. During that same time period, foreign investment grew to ten times what it had been before. Africa [15] <u>offers increasing</u> a viable site for manufacturing and commodity production. The continent provides access to key natural resources, possessing almost 10% of the world's crude oil and natural gas reserves. As the global population grows, adequate food production will become a major economic challenge, and [16] <u>Africa continues to import communications devices at a steady rate.</u>

[12]
A) NO CHANGE
B) scenes which feature intense poverty.
C) scenes of intense poverty.
D) poverty in intense scenes.

[13]
A) NO CHANGE
B) indications
C) that which indicates
D) indicating

[14]
A) NO CHANGE
B) unknown
C) impossible
D) unusual

[15]
A) NO CHANGE
B) increasingly offers
C) increasingly offering
D) offering to increase

[16]
Which choice best supports the author's argument in this paragraph?
A) NO CHANGE.
B) older African industries such as diamond mining have been abandoned.
C) negative stereotypes about Africa are now being more aggressively questioned by the media.
D) Africa has the potential to become a significant site of agricultural production.

A number of recent developments have facilitated the growth of the African economy. The expansion of technology  **[17]** (in 2011, the continent boasted 600 million mobile phone subscribers) has made business development possible. At the same time, as Africa becomes increasingly urbanized, the concentration of population in urban centers **[18]** far away from the countryside makes it easier for businesses to thrive. Demographics also play a role: Africa's youthful and growing population may one day serve as the foundation of a strong work force, and encourage investment in the region, particularly as population growth slows in regions such as Asia and Latin America. Economist Charles Robertson offers a **[19]** compulsive comparison: "If there's any continent that can do what China has done . . . in the last 30 years, it'll be Africa in the next 30."

[17]

Which choice provides the most accurate and relevant information from the graph?

A) NO CHANGE

B) (before 2013, few Africans were interested in buying electronic devices)

C) (even though foreign companies are now unwilling to set up stores in African communities)

D) (by 2017, the number of mobile phone subscribers in Africa is expected to reach more than 1.1 billion)

[18]

A) NO CHANGE

B) instead of rural settings

C) in contrast to earlier demographic patterns

D) DELETE the underlined portion.

[19]

A) NO CHANGE

B) complimentary

C) compelling

D) collaborative

Cell Phone Subscription Growth 2010-2017

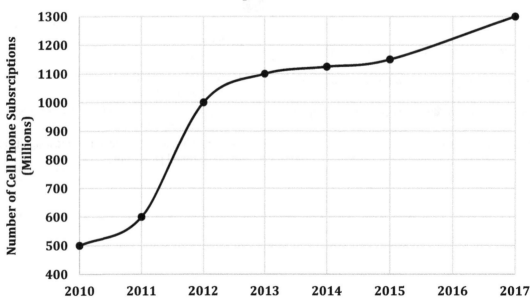

CONTINUE

[20] When Africa has the potential for sustainable economic growth, such growth is not entirely assured. The trend towards stable and democratic governments in African countries needs to be solidified; the presence of effective political leadership is a key determinant of investment, particularly investment by foreign companies. Such companies could be instrumental in providing a brighter future for African nations. The foreign policy of developed nations has tended to [21] focus, on providing aid, yet investment in ventures ranging from call centers to the financial industry stands a better chance of generating long-term economic prosperity. If global investors continue to see Africa as an unstable and high-risk region, Africa's growth could be curtailed and the volatility that investors fear [22] has only grown worse. If, on the other hand, the global community chooses to contribute to economic development by supporting industry and business expansion, there is a very real possibility that Africa can rapidly evolve into a significant economic force on the world stage.

20

A) NO CHANGE
B) While Africa
C) Because Africa
D) Africa

21

A) NO CHANGE
B) focus on providing, aid yet investment
C) focus on providing aid yet investment,
D) focus on providing aid, yet investment

22

A) NO CHANGE
B) could only grow worse.
C) growing worse.
D) worsening.

Questions 23-33 are based on the following passage.

Rate My Curator

To bring their exhibitions and scholarly publications to life, museums rely on the seasoned professionals known as curators. A curator, more or less, is to a museum showcase [23] what a director is: curators are responsible for the [24] momentary decisions involving theme, focus, and presentation, but must necessarily rely on others for the fine details. Many curators, of course, are masters of [25] detail themselves. They worked as assistant curators before attaining roles of final authority. But the most important role of a curator is often to show why a museum exhibition is relevant and meaningful, and this role often entails high visibility. A curator may contribute the leading essay in the catalog for a major traveling exhibition, for instance, or may make a speech thanking donors, benefactors, and resident scholars at an exhibition opening. [26] Few if any of these activities will interfere with a curator's personal life: in fact, many curators are able to set their own hours and work from home.

23
A) NO CHANGE
B) what a director of movies is
C) what a director is to a movie
D) what a director is to that of a movie

24
A) NO CHANGE
B) momentous
C) exaggerated
D) extreme

25
Which choice most effectively combines the two sentences at the underlined portion?
A) detail themselves, when they worked
B) detail themselves, having worked
C) detail themselves; working
D) detail themselves, however, they worked

26
The writer is considering deleting the underlined sentence. Should the writer make this deletion?
A) Yes, because it detracts from the paragraph's focus on the importance of curators to museums.
B) Yes, because the writer establishes earlier that curators have very demanding work schedules.
C) No, because it offers a further example of the responsibilities of curators.
D) No, because writer discusses the personal lives of museum curators later in the passage.

CONTINUE

Curators are essential to museums, but are they appreciated by the outside world? The truth is that some curators will organize exhibitions that are of interest primarily to specialists. It doesn't take much to extrapolate a broader stereotype of curators as little more than glorified art buffs, in theory interested in bringing art to the public [27] and in practice interested in getting lost in art history minutiae. Yet many curators themselves would [28] object, with good reason—to this description of their job.

For some curators, [29] a removed exhibition can become an opportunity to alter the course of art history itself. Consider Patricia Junker, curator at the Seattle Art Museum. In 2014, Junker staged *Modernism in the Pacific Northwest: The Mythic and the Mystical*. This exhibition called attention to innovative American artists such as Mark Tobey and Morris Graves, painters who are little known to the public (or at least the public beyond the Northwest) but who played a tremendous role in the creation of American abstract art. It was Junker's intention, in bringing these artists back into the spotlight, [30] to enlighten both museum-goers and "critics and scholars who will continue to work to construct the full, inclusive account of modern art in America."

[27]
A) NO CHANGE
B) and then practically
C) but in practice
D) but then practically

[28]
A) NO CHANGE
B) object—with good reason, to this description of their job.
C) object; with good reason to this description of their job.
D) object, with good reason, to this description of their job.

[29]
A) NO CHANGE
B) a lonely
C) an isolated
D) a single

[30]
A) NO CHANGE
B) by enlightening
C) as enlightened
D) enlightening

Other curators work with media that would not commonly be expected in museums. Klaus Biesenbach of the Museum of Modern Art is one curator **31** where he works almost entirely outside the traditional media of painting, drawing, and sculpture. Instead, he has recently organized exhibitions devoted to musicians such as Björk, **32** actresses such as Tilda Swinton, and headline-grabbing celebrities such as Yoko Ono. Biesenbach's endeavors are controversial: his 2015 Björk exhibition was greeted with the ArtNet News headline "MoMA Curator Klaus Biesenbach Should Be Fired Over Björk Show Debacle." However, such heated controversy may only prove how important curators—and the art they promote—truly **33** is to society today.

31

A) NO CHANGE
B) as he
C) which
D) who

32

The writer wishes to add specific information that supports the main idea of this paragraph. Which choice best accomplishes this goal?

A) NO CHANGE
B) although he has also offered input on showcases of major painters such as Sigmar Polke.
C) whose work is inspired by some of the same sources that have influenced contemporary video artists.
D) even though the Museum of Modern Art remains best known for exhibitions that focus on celebrated painters such as Pablo Picasso and Henri Matisse.

33

A) NO CHANGE
B) are
C) was
D) were

CONTINUE

Questions 34-44 are based on the following passage.

A Quantum of Physics

    Perhaps more than in any other scientific field, quantum physics—the study of extremely small particles and their interactions— [34] which presents a bewildering array of paradoxes. For example, from a quantum [35] prospective, light can act as both a particle and a wave, while a cat inside a box can be both alive and dead. Of course, when posed against everyday experiences of reality, these situations can seem absurd; a cat is either alive or dead, never both. [36] Do such possibilities ever occur to most people?

    The answer, according to quantum physicists, has to do with the idea of probability. Before the advent of quantum physics, it was assumed that the smallest units of matter, such as atoms and electrons, behaved like tiny clockwork mechanisms. As such, their behavior and their motion [37] was entirely predictable. According to quantum physics, however, we live in a probabilistic universe, in which the smallest units of matter do not behave according to any definite patterns. Instead, subatomic particles, such as electrons, are governed by [38] probability functions. These are equations that tell us the relative likelihood that they will behave in a certain way. Even odd, rare, and seemingly illogical likelihoods thus become possible.

34

A) NO CHANGE
B) it presents
C) presents
D) will present

35

A) NO CHANGE
B) prospectus
C) spectacle
D) perspective

36

Which choice offers the most effective transition to the paragraph that follows?
A) NO CHANGE
B) How can the situation be otherwise?
C) Are there other examples?
D) When did quantum paradoxes become popular?

37

A) NO CHANGE
B) were
C) is
D) are

38

Which choice best combines the two sentences at the underlined portion?
A) probability functions, which are
B) probability functions, those are
C) probability functions, from
D) probability functions, to

We still have not fully come to terms with the implications of this discovery—for, if [39] one is to accept it fully, one might find ourselves truly disheartened. After all, are not our bodies made up of nothing more than subatomic particles? And, [40] by extension, are not the discoveries of quantum physics also discoveries about our very selves? The prospects of a "quantum self," however, are nothing short of depressing. If individuals accept a strict version of quantum theory, then they must admit that they are little more than probability functions, and that their behavior, like [41] electrons, is unpredictable and random. As such, people cannot be accountable for their failures—nor can they take credit for any of their successes.

39
A) NO CHANGE
B) you are to accept it fully, you might
C) we are to accept it fully, we might
D) they are to accept it fully, they might

40
A) NO CHANGE
B) in contrast,
C) according to new research,
D) as is widely known,

41
A) NO CHANGE
B) with electrons
C) that of electrons
D) those of electrons

CONTINUE

This very prospect—that quantum physics seemed to [42] <u>nullify</u> any responsibility that we might have for our actions—infuriated even Einstein himself. Upon wrestling [43] <u>for such startled</u> unconventional perspectives, the exasperated Einstein famously shouted, "God does not play dice!" Like Einstein, I, too, cannot accept the fact that I am little more than a random number generator. [44] <u>Of course, I do not possess Einstein's expertise in multiple branches of theoretical physics and complex mathematics.</u> As much as quantum theory illuminates the mysteries of the subatomic world, it cannot explain away the most fascinating sides of human behavior.

42

A) NO CHANGE
B) upset
C) throw away
D) be done with

43

A) NO CHANGE
B) with such startled
C) for such startlingly
D) with such startlingly

44

The writer is considering deleting the underlined portion. Should the writer delete this sentence?

A) Yes, because it does not offer a meaningful statement about the nature of quantum physics.
B) Yes, because the writer's own viewpoint is not a focus of the passage.
C) No, because it helps the reader to understand why the writer of the passage is quoting Einstein.
D) No, because it establishes that the writer is a respected authority in the scientific community.

STOP

If you finish before time is called, you may check your work on this section only.
Do not turn to any other section.

Math Test - No Calculator

25 MINUTES, 20 QUESTIONS

DIRECTIONS

For each question from 1-15, choose the best answer choice provided in the multiple choice bank and fill in the appropriate circle in the provided answer key. Alternatively, for questions **16-20**, answer the problem and enter your answer in the grid-in section of the answer key. Refer to the directions given before question 16 as to how to enter your answers for the grid-in questions. You may complete scratch work in any empty space in your test booklet.

NOTES

A. Calculator usage **is not allowed** in this section.
B. Variables, constants, and coefficients used represent real numbers unless indicated otherwise.
C. All figures are created to appropriate scale unless the question states otherwise.
D. All figures are two-dimensional unless the question states otherwise.
E. The domain of any given function is all real numbers x for which the function, $f(x)$, is a real number unless the question states otherwise.

REFERENCE

$A = \pi r^2$
$C = 2\pi r$

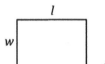
$A = lw$

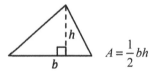
$A = \frac{1}{2}bh$

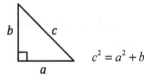
$c^2 = a^2 + b^2$

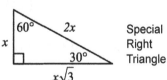
Special Right Triangle

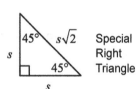
Special Right Triangle

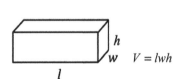
$V = lwh$

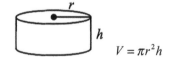
$V = \pi r^2 h$

$V = \frac{4}{3}\pi r^3$

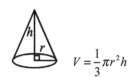
$V = \frac{1}{3}\pi r^2 h$

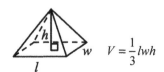
$V = \frac{1}{3}lwh$

There are $360°$ in a circle.
There are 2π radians in a circle.
There are $180°$ in a triangle.

CONTINUE ➡

1

$$103 = 8x + 9$$

Given the equation above, what is the value of $4x + 4$?

A) 12

B) 51

C) 52

D) 102

2

The coordinate point $(1, -1)$ is a solution to which of the following systems of linear inequalities?

A) $x + y \geq 0$
$x - y \leq 0$

B) $x - y \geq 0$
$x + y \leq 0$

C) $2x + 3y < 0$
$3x + 4y > 0$

D) $-x - 2y < 0$
$-x + 4y > 0$

3

Line r is perpendicular to line s in the xy-plane. If line r goes through the points $(-10, 0)$ and $(0, 5)$ and line s goes through the origin, at what value of x do the two lines intersect?

A) -2

B) -1

C) 2

D) 4

4

$$\sqrt{g} + 3 = x$$

If $g = 3x + 1$ and x must be greater than 1, what is the value of x?

A) 1

B) 3

C) 8

D) 9

CONTINUE

5

A kindergarten teacher's supply of crayons during the school year follows the linear model $N = 450 - 3c$, where N is the remaining supply of crayons and c is the number of classes that have passed. What does the value -3 most likely represent in this equation?

A) The number of crayons that the teacher distributes for use during class each day

B) The number of crayons that the teacher distributes for use to each student each day

C) The number of crayons that are used up or lost by each student each day of class

D) The number of crayons that are used up or lost by the entire class each day

6

Which of the following expressions is equivalent to the expression $4x^2 - 35$?

A) $(2x+6)(2x-6)+1$

B) $(2x+6)(2x-6)-1$

C) $(2x+3)(2x-3)+26$

D) $(2x+3)(2x-3)-16$

7

The measure of the length of an arc in degrees can be calculated using the expression $\dfrac{\theta \pi d}{360}$, where θ is the measure of the central angle that defines the arc in degrees and d is the diameter of the circle. What is the smallest integer diameter that a circle can have if the measure of the arc is π inches and $\theta < 120°$?

A) 2

B) 3

C) 4

D) 6

8

If $a^{x^2} \bullet a^{4x} \bullet a^4 = a^9$, $a > 0$, and $x > 0$, what is the value of x?

A) -5

B) 1

C) 3

D) 7

CONTINUE

9

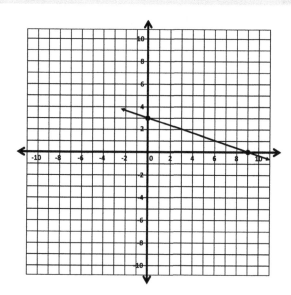

Line h is parallel to the line graphed in the xy-plane above. If line h goes through the point $(0, -\frac{4}{3})$, what is the x-value of the x-intercept of line h?

A) -4

B) -3

C) $-\frac{9}{4}$

D) $\frac{3}{4}$

10

Which of the following equations has a graph in the xy-plane where y is always less than or equal to 6?

A) $y = x^2 + 6$

B) $y = -x^2 + 36$

C) $y = |x - 6|$

D) $y = -|x| + 6$

11

A fallen tree branch in the woods has an initial mass of 125 kilograms and decays by 15% of its mass every year. Which of the following equations gives the current mass, M, of the fallen tree branch after x years have passed?

A) $M = .85(125)^x$

B) $M = .15(125)^x$

C) $M = 125(.85)^x$

D) $M = 125(.15)^x$

12

The function $f(t) = t^2 - 8t + 4$ crosses the x-axis twice at the coordinate points $(x_1, 0)$ and $(x_2, 0)$. What is the absolute distance between x_1 and x_2?

A) $8 + 4\sqrt{3}$

B) $8\sqrt{3}$

C) 8

D) $4\sqrt{3}$

CONTINUE

13

$$\frac{5-2i}{5+3i}$$

If the expression above is written in the form $a+bi$ where $i=\sqrt{-1}$, which of the following is the value of a?

A) $-\dfrac{25}{34}$

B) $-\dfrac{2}{3}$

C) $\dfrac{19}{34}$

D) 1

14

The equation $y=-\dfrac{x}{m}+b_2$ is the equation of a line that is perpendicular to the line with an equation of the form $y=mx+b_1$. Which of the following equations gives m in terms of y, x, and b_2?

A) $m=\dfrac{x}{b_2-y}$

B) $m=\dfrac{x}{y-b_2}$

C) $m=\dfrac{b_2-y}{x}$

D) $m=\dfrac{y-b_2}{x}$

15

If x does not equal $-\dfrac{1}{2}$, what is the average of the expressions $\dfrac{8x+1}{2x+1}$ and $4+\dfrac{3}{2x+1}$?

A) 4

B) $4+\dfrac{1}{2x+1}$

C) $4+\dfrac{3}{2x+1}$

D) 8

CONTINUE

DIRECTIONS

For each question from 16-20, solve and enter your answer in the grid-in section of your answer sheet as described below.

A. Write out your answers in the boxes at the top of each column in order to help you fill in the circles accurately. Remember, you will only receive credit for the circles that are filled in correctly, not for the written answer at the top of the columns.

B. Mark only a single circle in each column.

C. There are no negative answers.

D. If the problem has more than one correct answer, grid only one of the correct answers.

E. When your answer is a **mixed number**, such as $1\frac{1}{2}$, it should be entered as 1.5 or $3/2$. You cannot enter a mixed number because there is no room to fill in a circle that represents a space.

F. If you enter a **decimal answer** with more digits then the grid can handle, the answer may be rounded or truncated, but it absolutely must fill the entire grid.

Answer: $\frac{8}{21}$ Answer: 6.4

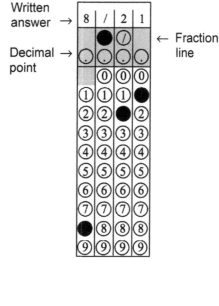

The ways to correctly grid $\frac{7}{9}$ are:

Answer: 102 - both positions are correct

REMEMBER:
You can begin writing your answers in any column as long as there is enough space. Leave unused columns blank.

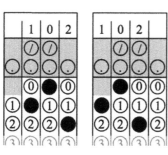

CONTINUE ➡

16

An isosceles right triangle has a hypotenuse that measures $50\sqrt{2}$. If a similar triangle has a longest side length of $5\sqrt{8}$, what is the sum of its shorter two sides?

17

Mr. Waterman has \$5, \$10, and \$25 gift certificates to a local ice cream parlor. He would like to give each of his nephews and nieces \$55 worth of gift certificates to the ice cream parlor. If he wants to make sure that each nephew and niece receives at least one of each type of gift certificate, what is the difference between the maximum number of \$5 gift certificates and minimum number of \$5 gift certificates that each child could receive?

18

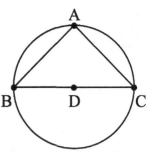

In the circle above, the measure of $\overline{AB}$ is equivalent to $5\sqrt{2}$ and the measure of $\overline{BC}$ is equivalent to 10. If the measure of $\angle ACB$ in radians is given by the expression $H\pi$, what is the value of H?

19

$$A^2x + 10y = 75$$
$$Ax + 2y = 15$$

For what positive value of A does the system of equations above have infinitely many solutions?

CONTINUE

20

$$(2a+B)^2 = Ma^2 + 8a + Q$$

If the equation above is true for all values of a and if B, M, and Q are all positive constants, what is the value of the product BMQ?

STOP

If you finish before time is called, you may check your work on this section only.

Do not turn to any other section.

Math Test - Calculator

55 MINUTES, 38 QUESTIONS

DIRECTIONS

For each question from 1-30, choose the best answer choice provided in the multiple choice bank and fill in the appropriate circle in the provided answer key. Alternatively, for questions **31-38**, answer the problem and enter your answer in the grid-in section of the answer key. Refer to the directions given before question 31 as to how to enter your answers for the grid-in questions. You may complete scratch work in any empty space in your test booklet.

NOTES

A. Calculator usage **is allowed**.
B. Variables, constants, and coefficients used represent real numbers unless indicated otherwise.
C. All figures are created to appropriate scale unless the question states otherwise.
D. All figures are two-dimensional unless the question states otherwise.
E. The domain of any given function is all real numbers x for which the function, $f(x)$, is a real number unless the question states otherwise.

REFERENCE

$A = \pi r^2$
$C = 2\pi r$

$A = lw$

$A = \frac{1}{2}bh$

$c^2 = a^2 + b^2$

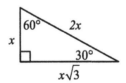

Special Right Triangle

Special Right Triangle

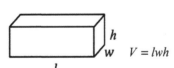

$V = lwh$

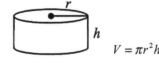

$V = \pi r^2 h$

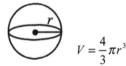

$V = \frac{4}{3}\pi r^3$

$V = \frac{1}{3}\pi r^2 h$

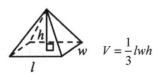

$V = \frac{1}{3}lwh$

There are $360°$ in a circle.
There are 2π radians in a circle.
There are $180°$ in a triangle.

CONTINUE

1

A cell phone vendor at a trade show makes $15 for every accessory that he sells and has to pay $35 per hour to rent the table at the trade show. If the vendor sells a accessories and rents the table for h hours, which of the following expressions is equivalent to the vendor's profit in dollars?

A) $15a - 35h$

B) $15a + 35h$

C) $35a - 15h$

D) $35a + 15h$

2

Janelle always gives away 24% of her jelly beans to friends at her lunch table. If Janelle has a bag with 75 jelly beans, how many will she eat?

A) 18

B) 24

C) 51

D) 57

3

Which of the following quadratic equations has the same x-intercepts as the equation $y = 2(x + 2)(x - 3)$?

A) $y = x^2 + x - 6$

B) $y = -x^2 + x + 6$

C) $y = 2x^2 - 10x - 12$

D) $y = 4x^2 + 20x + 24$

4

12 times a number is equivalent to 30 more than 6 times the number. What is the value of 30 less than 6 times the number?

A) 0

B) 15

C) 30

D) 45

CONTINUE

▼

Questions 5 and 6 refer to the following information.

The percentage of the night's profits that a restaurant owner pays out to his employees on any given night is inversely proportional to the number of patrons that visit the restaurant on that night. On a night when 50 people ate dinner at the restaurant, the owner paid out 80% of the profits to the employees. On a night when 125 people ate dinner at the restaurant, the owner paid out 32% of the profits to his employees.

5

What percentage of the night's profit would the restaurant owner pay out to his employees on a night when 250 patrons visited the restaurant?

A) 4

B) 8

C) 10

D) 16

6

One night the restaurant is charging every customer a $10 door charge to enter for an all you can eat buffet. If 160 customers eat at the buffet and the owner has 5 employees working that night, how much money, in dollars, will each employee take home?

A) 80

B) 320

C) 400

D) 1600

▲

7

The amount of remaining gas, G, in a car's gas tank can be calculated using the equation $G = 13 - \dfrac{1}{21}m$, where m represents the number of miles driven since the last time the gas tank was filled. If the gas tank has 11 gallons of gas remaining, how many miles has the car driven since its most recent fill-up?

A) 2

B) 11

C) 21

D) 42

8

Arielle has been collecting figurines since she was a child. Every year she receives one figurine from her parents and one from her grandmother on both her birthday and again during the holiday season. If Arielle currently has 56 figurines and had f figurines collected before she started receiving them as presents from her parents and grandmother 6 years ago, what is the value of f?

A) 32

B) 44

C) 50

D) 52

CONTINUE

9

Nadia is selling hardcover books for $2 each and paperback books for $1 each at a garage sale. Nadia would like to sell at least 40 books to make at least $60. Using h for the number of hardcover books and p for the number of paperback books, which of the following systems of linear inequalities accurately represents the number of book sales and the amount of money that Nadia would like to make?

A) $h + p \geq 60$
   $2h + p \geq 40$

B) $h + p \geq 40$
   $2h + p \geq 60$

C) $h + p \geq 60$
   $h + 2p \geq 40$

D) $h + p \geq 40$
   $h + 2p \geq 60$

10

A random sample of 85 adults leaving a local Mexican restaurant were asked to answer a quick one-question survey without giving their names. The survey revealed that 82% of the participants preferred to eat out on a regular basis as opposed to eating at home. The results of this survey are unreliable for gauging the dining preferences of adults in the population mainly due to which of the following?

A) Insufficient sample size

B) Inappropriate sample collection methods

C) Biased sampling location

D) All of the above

11

A ball is tossed upward from the ground and its height, $h(x)$, after x seconds have passed is given by the equation $h(x) = -4x^2 + 24x$. Which of the following inequalities represents all of the times, x, when the height of the ball, $h(x)$, is above 20 feet?

A) $20 \geq -4x^2 + 24x$

B) $20 \leq -4x^2 + 24x$

C) $0 > -4x^2 + 24x - 20$

D) $0 < -4x^2 + 24x - 20$

12

If $t(8) = 9$, $s(7) = 2t(8)$, and $r(x) = \sqrt{2x}$, what is the positive value of $r(s(7))$?

A) 3

B) 6

C) 81

D) 1,296

375

CONTINUE

13

	Miles Driven	Hours Driven
Monday	248	4
Tuesday	120	2
Wednesday	240	6
Thursday	256	4
Friday	136	4

The table above shows the number of miles driven and the number of hours that Mike spent on the road in the first week of his job. Which of the following is Mike's average speed, in miles per hour, for the week?

A) 40

B) 48

C) 50

D) 56

14

On average, Mrs. Teetertotter can grade 8 tests in an hour. If Mrs. Teetertotter gives 24 tests a year and has approximately 16 students in each of her 4 classes, how many full 24-hour days does Mrs. Teetertotter spend grading tests?

A) 4

B) 8

C) 192

D) 1,536

15

Number of Reported Incidents of Bullying

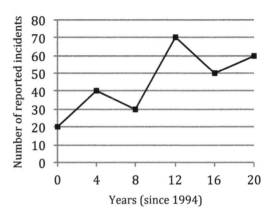

During which 4-year period did the greatest change in reported incidents of bullying take place?

A) 1994-1998

B) 2002-2006

C) 2006-2010

D) 2010-2014

16

Jessica's pottery class is 25% larger than Michelle's pottery class. Lauren's pottery class is 50% smaller than Michelle's pottery class. Jessica's pottery class is what percent larger than Lauren's pottery class?

A) 75

B) 150

C) 250

D) 300

376

CONTINUE

17

Breakfast Sales and Pancake Sales

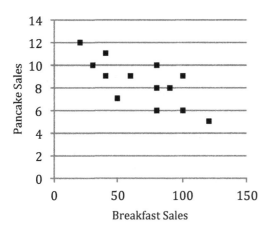

A local diner kept track of the total number of breakfast meals sold and the number of those meals that were pancake breakfasts on 13 separate days. If one of the days that the restaurant had 50 or more breakfast sales is chosen at random, what is the probability that there were more than 6 pancake meals sold?

A) $\dfrac{6}{13}$

B) $\dfrac{8}{13}$

C) $\dfrac{2}{3}$

D) $\dfrac{8}{9}$

18

A cereal manufacturer wants to keep the weight of its cereal boxes to 9.5 ounces at a minimum and 12.5 ounces at a maximum. Which of the following equations defines x, the weight of an acceptable cereal box?

A) $|x-11| \le 1.5$

B) $|x-1.5| \le 11$

C) $|x-12.5| \le 3$

D) $|x+9.5| \le 3$

▼

Questions 19 and 20 refer to the following information.

	A	B	C	D	F
Freshman	8	8	3	1	0
Sophomore	10	6	3	1	0
Junior	13	2	4	1	0
Senior	6	12	1	0	1

In a recent survey, a group of 50 students from each grade level in a local high school were asked how many A's, B's, C's, D's, and F's they received among the 20 marking period grades they received for the year. The average responses for each grade level were recorded in the table above.

19

Which of the following is the average number of B's that could be expected in a single school year for all of the students in the high school?

A) 1

B) 3

C) 7

D) 9

20

If there are a total of 428 freshman in the high school, which of the following is the best estimate for the total number of grades lower than B to be expected from the entire freshman class?

A) 30

B) 110

C) 1,700

D) 6,400

▲

CONTINUE

21

Data collected from the guidance counseling department of Jefferson High School stated that the most popular number of colleges applied to by graduating seniors was 4, the median number of colleges applied to was 4.5, and the mean number of colleges applied to was 2.5. Which of the following could explain the difference between the median and the mean number of colleges applied to?

A) Half of the students applied to 4 colleges or fewer.

B) A large majority of the students applied to 2 or 3 colleges.

C) A few students applied to more than 4 colleges.

D) A few students applied to no colleges at all.

22

$$x^2 + 8x + y^2 = 20$$

What is the area of the circle, in units squared, defined by the equation above?

A) 4π

B) 16π

C) 20π

D) 36π

Questions 23 and 24 refer to the following information.

$$F = k\frac{Q_1 Q_2}{r^2}$$

Coulomb's Law states that the force, in newtons, between two charges Q_1 and Q_2, measured in Coulombs, at a separation distance of r meters can be calculated using the equation above where k is a constant.

23

Which of the following represents the distance between the charges, r, in terms of the force between the two charges, the charges themsleves, and the constant k?

A) $r = \sqrt{\dfrac{kQ_1 Q_2}{F}}$

B) $r = \sqrt{\dfrac{FQ_1 Q_2}{k}}$

C) $r = \sqrt{\dfrac{F}{kQ_1 Q_2}}$

D) $r = k(\dfrac{Q_1 Q_2}{F})^2$

24

If the distance between the two charges is doubled, the force between the two charges will decrease by what percent?

A) 25

B) 50

C) 75

D) 100

CONTINUE

25

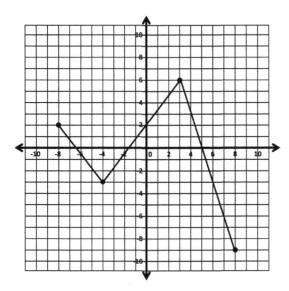

The entire function $g(x)$ is shown in the graph above. For how many values of x is $g(x)$ equivalent to $g(-8)$?

A) 0

B) 1

C) 2

D) 3

26

The line with the equation $y = 2x + 2$ and the line with the equation $y = 6$ intersect at the point A. The line defined by the equation $y = -x - 1$ intersects the line $y = \frac{1}{2}x - 4$ at the point B. Which of the following best defines the slope of the line that intersects point A and point B?

A) It equals 0.

B) It is undefined.

C) It is positive.

D) It is negative.

27

$$y = 2b + 1$$
$$y = x^3 + 8b$$

The system of equations above has one negative integer value for x that satisfies the system when b is equivalent to which of the following?

A) 1

B) $\dfrac{9}{2}$

C) $\dfrac{14}{3}$

D) 5

28

Two hundred forty kilograms of organic matter decay following the exponential decay model $R = 240(0.5)^x$, where R is the mass of the remaining organic matter in kilograms and x is the number of years that have passed. One hundred fifty-five kilograms of inorganic matter decay in a linear fashion following the model $R = -35x + 155$, where R is the mass of the remaining inorganic matter in kilograms and x is the number of years that have passed. For how many years is the mass of the organic matter lower than the mass of the inorganic matter?

A) 2

B) 3

C) 4

D) 5

CONTINUE

29

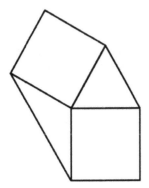

The figure above contains two squares of equal size, an equilateral triangle, and an isosceles triangle. If the area of the equilateral triangle is $13\sqrt{3}$ and the area of the isosceles triangle is $A\sqrt{3}$, what is the value of A?

A) $\dfrac{13}{2}$

B) 13

C) 26

D) 52

30

The equation of a line that goes through two non-adjacent vertices of a square is $y = -3x + 2$. Line r passes through the point $(3,5)$ and is parallel to the line that goes through the other non-adjacent vertices of the square. If the y-intercept of line r is $(0,b)$, what is the value of b?

A) 4

B) 8

C) 10

D) 14

CONTINUE

DIRECTIONS

For each question from 31-38, solve and enter your answer in the grid-in section of your answer sheet as described below.

A. Write out your answers in the boxes at the top of each column in order to help you fill in the circles accurately. Remember, you will only receive credit for the circles that are filled in correctly, not for the written answer at the top of the columns.

B. Mark only a single circle in each column.

C. There are no negative answers.

D. If the problem has more than one correct answer, grid only one of the correct answers.

E. When your answer is a **mixed number**, such as $1\frac{1}{2}$, it should be entered as 1.5 or $3/2$. You cannot enter a mixed number because there is no room to fill in a circle that represents a space.

F. If you enter a **decimal answer** with more digits then the grid can handle, the answer may be rounded or truncated, but it absolutely must fill the entire grid.

Answer: $\frac{8}{21}$

Written answer →

Decimal point →

← Fraction line

Answer: 6.4

The ways to correctly grid $\frac{7}{9}$ are:

Answer: 102 - both positions are correct

REMEMBER:
You can begin writing your answers in any column as long as there is enough space. Leave unused columns blank.

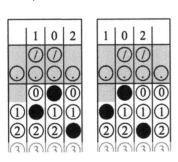

CONTINUE →

31

A beekeeper estimates that a population of bees will double every year for the foreseeable future. If the initial population of bees is 31,250 bees, how many years will pass before the population reaches one million bees?

32

A ladder measures exactly 12 feet 6 inches in length. If 1 inch is equivalent to 2.54 centimeters, what is the length of the ladder in centimeters?

33

$$C(x) = 125 + 50mh$$

A painting company uses the linear model above to calculate $C(x)$, the total estimated price of a job that requires m men to paint for h hours. If a job were to last 8 hours, what would be the client's estimated cost per additional man in dollars?

34

Angel and Sebastian logged a total of 136 hours combined at a woodworking residency in New Hampshire. If Sebastian logged 204 hours less than four times the number of hours that Angel logged, how many additional hours had Angel logged over Sebastian?

CONTINUE

35

$$y = ax^2 + 2ax + c$$

If the quadratic equation above contains the point $(-3, a)$ and $c = -\dfrac{1}{4}$, what is the value of a?

36

The points R and S lie on circle O. If the length of $\overset{\frown}{RS}$ is 4π and the area of circle O is 64π, what is the area of $\triangle RSO$?

CONTINUE

Questions 37-38 refer to the following information.

$$3, 9, 21, 33, \ldots$$

The sequence given above is defined by the equation $A_n = d(1 + n(n-1))$, where A_n is the value of the nth term of the sequence, d is a positive constant, and n is the number of the term in the sequence.

37

What value of the constant d makes the equation produce the given sequence?

38

The kth term of the sequence has a value of 1659. What is the value of k?

STOP

If you finish before time is called, you may check your work on this section only.
Do not turn to any other section.

Answer Key: TEST 5

SECTION 1—READING

1.	D	11.	C	22.	C	32.	C	42.	A
2.	B	12.	C	23.	B	33.	A	43.	C
3.	B	13.	A	24.	A	34.	C	44.	B
4.	C	14.	D	25.	D	35.	B	45.	C
5.	A	15.	D	26.	C	36.	A	46.	A
6.	A	16.	B	27.	B	37.	D	47.	D
7.	C	17.	B	28.	D	38.	B	48.	D
8.	C	18.	A	29.	D	39.	A	49.	B
9.	B	19.	D	30.	C	40.	D	50.	A
10.	C	20.	A	31.	B	41.	A	51.	A
		21.	B					52.	C

SECTION 2—WRITING

1.	B	12.	C	23.	C	34.	C
2.	A	13.	B	24.	B	35.	D
3.	D	14.	A	25.	B	36.	B
4.	A	15.	B	26.	A	37.	B
5.	A	16.	D	27.	C	38.	A
6.	B	17.	A	28.	D	39.	C
7.	D	18.	D	29.	D	40.	A
8.	C	19.	C	30.	A	41.	C
9.	D	20.	B	31.	D	42.	A
10.	A	21.	D	32.	A	43.	D
11.	D	22.	B	33.	B	44.	A

SECTION 3—MATH

1.	B	12.	D
2.	B	13.	C
3.	A	14.	A
4.	C	15.	A
5.	D		
6.	A	**Fill-Ins:**	
7.	C	16.	20
8.	B	17.	2
9.	A	18.	1/4 or .25
10.	D	19.	5
11.	C	20.	32

SECTION 4—MATH

1.	A	13.	C	24.	C	**Fill-Ins:**	
2.	D	14.	B	25.	D	31.	5
3.	B	15.	B	26.	B	32.	381
4.	A	16.	B	27.	C	33.	400
5.	D	17.	C	28.	B	34.	0
6.	A	18.	A	29.	B	35.	1/8 or .125
7.	D	19.	C	30.	A	36.	32
8.	A	20.	C			37.	3
9.	B	21.	D			38.	24
10.	C	22.	D				
11.	D	23.	A				
12.	B						

Answer Explanations

SAT Practice Test #5

Section 1: Reading

QUESTION 1.

Choice D is correct. While the first paragraph describes the appearance and demeanor of a single "powerfully built" (lines 1-2) and "popular" (line 10) character, the second paragraph explains the general working conditions of "A water clerk" (line 11), the occupation of the character described in the first paragraph. This information supports D. A wrongly locates humor in the factual and serious first paragraph, while both B and C reverse the actual structure of these paragraphs and indicate that the general discussion of water-clerks comes first.

QUESTION 2.

Choice B is correct. The word "slight" is applied to the "stoop of the shoulders" (lines 2-3) observable in an otherwise imposing and impressive character: this stoop would thus stand in "minor" contrast to his overall appearance. B is the best choice: A and D refer to the wrong qualities (how deep or thoughtful a person or idea is, not PHYSICAL details), while C is a positive that wrongly assumes that the "stoop" was delicate and desirable.

QUESTION 3.

Choice B is correct. The word "her" occurs in line 15 ("greeting her captain cheerily") and lines 19-20 ("to make her seaworthy and beautiful"). Because a ship would have a captain and could be made seaworthy, B is the best answer. A and D both refer to the working conditions of a water-clerk, and thus mistake the general topic for the direct reference to "her"; C rightly mentions a ship, but wrongly assumes that it is owned by the "water-clerk", not the captain.

QUESTION 4.

Choice C is correct. The qualities mentioned in the line reference explain how exactly a water-clerk acts "To a captain" (line 28) in a pleasant and effective business connection. This evidence supports C and can be used to eliminate B, since a "ship-chandler" (lines 22-23) is not the same as a water-clerk. A is faulty because the line reference refers to traits exhibited on the job and as a result of good personality, not to PREPARED requirements; D is faulty because the line reference describes general traits that make water-clerks effective and that may be found in water-clerks OTHER than Jim.

QUESTION 5.

Choice A is correct. The passage explains that successful water-clerks will have agreeable personalities and will direct captains to goods "that are eaten and drunk on board ship" (lines 18-19): such contact will continue as long as the captain's ship "remains in harbor" (line 27). This information supports A and eliminates C, since a water-clerk specializes in helping the ships in a SINGLE port. B and D both rightly state that a water-clerk serves a ship-chandler, but do not stress the importance of bonding with the captain and imparting a "warmth of welcome" (line 25) in the necessary manner.

QUESTION 6.

Choice A is correct. The word "received" refers to a captain, who is treated "like a brother" (line 22) by a ship-chandler and would naturally be greeted warmly. A rightly refers to pleasant personal contact, while B and D would normally refer to THINGS, not PEOPLE. C introduces a faulty meaning, since things that are "assimilated" are "made the same" or "incorporated" in a way that changes their nature or position.

QUESTION 7.

Choice C is correct. In lines 46-49, the author explains that Jim had an "incognito" (or identity used to maintain secrecy) and that when a "fact broke through" this incognito Jim would change location. This information supports C, while A, B, and D all wrongly assume that Jim was unhappy with his working conditions. In fact, the opposite is true, since he would work as "the water-clerk" (line 56) at each new location.

QUESTION 8.

Choice C is correct. See above for the explanation of the correct answer. A explains some of the general requirements for a water-clerk, B indicates that Jim would leave locations suddenly and without providing satisfactory reasons (but not WHY he would leave), and D indicates the extent of Jim's retreat from certain locations. While B and D refer to Jim's tendency to leave jobs behind, they do not explain the MOTIVES for his actions as demanded by the previous question.

QUESTION 9.

Choice B is correct. In lines 49-52, the author explains that Jim was confined to one profession because Jim's form of talent is "good for no other work but that of a water-clerk". This information supports B. While the author does note that a water-clerk must have specific interpersonal skills (eliminating C), the passage never explains WHETHER these skills are widespread or HOW they are attained: eliminate A and D, respectively, which assume that the passage raises these issues.

QUESTION 10.

Choice C is correct. See above for the explanation of the correct answer. A explains how a water-clerk creates a successful connection to a captain, B introduces a factor that may make a water-clerk especially valuable, and D records Jim's travels. Neither A nor B aligns with an answer to the previous question, while D does not effectively offer a general statement about "the qualifications of a water clerk".

QUESTION 11.

Choice C is correct. The passage begins with a reference to the industries that "can weather even the worst economic climates" (lines 3-4) and goes on to consider how dollar stores, candy manufacturers, and other specific businesses will react. This information supports C, while B (low-cost retailers) and D (candy and soft drink companies) refer to only a few of the businesses the author considers. A misstates the author's argument: the passage outlines behavior that could apply to ANY economic decline, rather than PREDICTING a new decline and advising consumers how to respond.

QUESTION 12.

Choice C is correct. The word "climates" is used in reference to economic situations that companies can "weather" or endure: C, "conditions", is an effective answer. While A and B both take "climates" in a literal or geographical sense, D is too narrow: the broad quantifiable conditions of a market, not simply the perceptions and opinions of consumers, are being considered.

QUESTION 13.

Choice A is correct. After describing the types of businesses that can do well during economic downturns, the author refers to a group of businesses (lines 60-62) and recommends adding a few of them to a "stock portfolio". This practical advice makes A the best answer, while the author's emphasis on only a few business sectors makes B ("all aspects") an overstatement. C introduces the wrong kind of recommendations (since economic viability, not ethics, interests the author), while D introduces the wrong system of classification (since the author is interested in how businesses REACT to a bad economy, not in matters of size or scope).

QUESTION 14.

Choice D is correct. See above for the explanation of the correct answer. A explains that some businesses can do well in bad economies without resorting to trickery, B explains how some businesses do well, and C explains that the author does NOT present a "comprehensive theory" in this passage. Disregarding the negative may make C seem like a justification for Question 13 D.

QUESTION 15.

Choice D is correct. In lines 34-37, the author provides an example of "similar" goods at noticeably different prices in order to illustrate why low-cost stores can do well in bad economies. This information supports D. The author never criticizes earlier economic studies (eliminating A) or consumers (eliminating B), and is mostly concerned with the RESULTS achieved by certain businesses, not with how well or how widely they are publicized (eliminating C).

QUESTION 16.

Choice B is correct. See above for the explanation of the correct answer. A introduces a possible misperception about entertainment companies, C explains that consumers will still indulge in small pleasures during tough times, and D explains that McDonald's was successful during the 1970s. Make sure not to take A as a justification for Question 15 C or C as a justification for Question 15 B.

QUESTION 17.

Choice B is correct. The word "resisting" describes how certain businesses effectively react to "economic downturns" (lines 53-54), or survive and do well despite negative events. B is an effective answer, while A refers to the wrong issue (argumentation) and C and D both indicate that the businesses are uninterested in the downturn, not that they continue to take positive action.

QUESTION 18.

Choice A is correct. In the relevant section of the passage, the author explains the risky strategy followed in *The Big Short*, then explains that some businesses, in contrast, can thrive in negative economies without such "Economic trickery" (line 22). This information supports A, while B offers a contrast (long-term versus short-term) that distorts the real contrast (risky versus accepted) that the author is emphasizing. C wrongly identifies the money managers in *The Big Short* as "scholars", while D wrongly applies a negative tone to *The Big Short*, since the strategy that this book describes was in fact profitable.

QUESTION 19.

Choice D is correct. For the first three quarters of 2008, the value of Dollar Tree was below the value of the S&P 500 (an index that represents aggregate stock values) and below the value of Amazon. Eliminate A, B, and C and choose D, since Dollar Tree surpassed both Amazon and the S&P 500 in value at the beginning of Quarter 4.

QUESTION 20.

Choice A is correct. According to the graph, even though there was a broad decrease in stock value (as recorded by the declining S&P 500), Dollar Tree stock increased in value. This information supports A, while B is out of scope (since companies other than Amazon most likely saw decreases, according to the S&P 500) and C is contradicted by the clear decrease in Amazon stock value. D is itself out of scope: although Amazon went from a high to a low stock value in the period designated, it is not in any way clear that Amazon had the highest average stock value of ANY company.

QUESTION 21.

Choice B is correct. In lines 24-37, the author explains how companies such as Dollar Tree can do well because they sell discounted essentials to consumers: this information supports B. A refers to the kind of risky strategy that, according to the author, Dollar Tree does NOT follow. C (which refers to different companies, such as snack and soft drink manufacturers) and D (which refers to changes associated with companies such as Amazon.com) refer to parts of the general economic situation that Dollar Tree faces, but not to Dollar Tree's overall business strategy.

QUESTION 22.

Choice C is correct. The word "naked" refers to the act of inspecting the world without the assistance of "technological advances" (line 1): such inspection is thus "unaided" by these advances. C is an effective answer, while A means obvious or direct, B means without decoration, and D means without protection. None of these choices properly describes an "eye" that inspects without technological aid.

QUESTION 23.

Choice B is correct. While Passage 1 explains how birds are being studied through the use of "mounted camera technology" (lines 14-15) and "computer modeling" (line 35), Passage 2 explains that scientists performing fieldwork must rely on "luck" (line 61) to study a particular bird species. This information on methods of study supports B: only Passage 1 deals with technology (eliminating A) or published research on the peregrine falcon (a bird that Passage 2 only mentions in passing, eliminating D). Neither of these passages describes a "controversy" (eliminating C), since both passages are factual and deal mostly with fieldwork. At most, Passage 2 alone contains references to the "debate" over the fastest bird.

QUESTION 24.

Choice A is correct. While the author of Passage 1 describes two methods of studying the peregrine falcon and avoids reference to any other bird, the author of Passage 2 considers both the peregrine falcon and the "White-Throated Needletail" (lines 50-51). This information supports A. Passage 2 raises the possibility that the Needletail is the fastest bird (eliminating B) and questions the use of diving speed as a criterion for determining the fastest bird (eliminating D) in lines 40-55. Passage 1 never discusses how the actual FLIGHT speeds of falcons are attained (eliminating C): in fact, both passages focus on how falcons "fall" or "dive".

QUESTION 25.

Choice D is correct. In lines 23-27 the author indicates that Kane and Zamani's research, which involves footage of falcons, could enable "the development of computer models". This information supports D. Although Kane and Zamani's research involved GoPro-like cameras attached to falcons flying at high speeds, the research did not necessarily settle a "dispute" about falcon speeds (eliminating A) or popularize the cameras (eliminating B). C also involves a faulty relationship: Ponitz himself investigated falcons, but was not necessarily inspired to do so by Kane and Zamani.

QUESTION 26.

Choice C is correct. See above for the explanation of the correct answer. A calls attention to how Kane and Zamani focused on the falcons' perspective, B describes the small cameras that Kane and Zamani employed, and D discusses the research undertaken by Ponitz, but does NOT relate it to the research of Kane and Zamani. Make sure not to take A as evidence for Question 25 A or B as evidence for Question 25 B.

QUESTION 27.

Choice B is correct. The word "fashions" refers to the "cement" that is formed from various materials to create a nest for a White-Throated Needletail. The Needletail thus "mixes" these materials, which have already been "gathered" (eliminating D). Both A and C refer to creative or analytic activities typically undertaken by humans, not to the less sophisticated activity of a bird mixing different materials.

QUESTION 28.

Choice D is correct. The author of Passage 2 explains that the peregrine falcon's activity is best described as "diving" (line 42), not as flying, and presents the "White-Throated Needletail" (lines 50-51) as a better candidate for the fastest-flying bird. This information supports D and can be used to eliminate A (since the author ultimately ACCEPTS an alternative to the peregrine falcon) and C (since fieldwork on only a single bird, the White-Throated Needletail, is presented). B uses flawed reasoning: the author dismisses the CRITERIA used to determine the fastest bird, but does not find the ideas of "flying" and "diving" themselves to be vague and inconsequential. **391**

QUESTION 29.

Choice D is correct. While the author of Passage 1 notes that peregrine falcons flying at top speeds "have only seldom been observed in the wild" (lines 29-30), the author of Passage 2 notes that White-Throated Needletails are difficult to study, since scientists must "rely heavily on luck" (line 61) to observe these birds. This information supports D, while other answers refer to only one bird or the other. The peregrine falcon attains its top speeds by diving (A) and has been studied using computer imaging (C), while the Needletail attains its top speed by flapping its wings (B).

QUESTION 30.

Choice C is correct. In lines 56-59, the author of Passage 2 explains that many White-Throated Needletails die through collision with "man-made structures". This information supports C: because the author of Passage 2 notes that the only real threat to White-Throated Needletails is "their own speed" (line 57), A, B, and D can be readily eliminated.

QUESTION 31.

Choice B is correct. See above for the explanation of the correct answer. A describes the peregrine falcon (NOT the White-Throated Needletail), C describes the efforts that Needletails will make to find food, and D describes Needletail nests. Do not wrongly assume that C is evidence for Question 30 B, which refers to food SCARCITY, not to the Needletail's PREFERENCES.

QUESTION 32.

Choice C is correct. While Clinton's first paragraph lists achievements that resulted from "civil society" (line 5) initiatives, Clinton spends later stages of her speech promoting a "new strategic dialogue" (line 21) and explaining "how much more we all have to do" (lines 67-68). This information best supports C. The other answers involve subtle inaccuracies: A wrongly assumes that Clinton is most focused on "legislative" action, B wrongly assumes that Clinton (who in fact points out challenges and problems) is overwhelmingly optimistic in her later remarks, and D wrongly assumes that Clinton returns to earlier events (when in fact she shifts her focus to new initiatives as the speech progresses).

QUESTION 33.

Choice A is correct. The word "protect" refers to the status quo that certain governments were interested in keeping from change, or that they wanted to "maintain". A is the best answer in context: B would refer to an argument or a physical position that is facing attack, and C and D both refer to actions that could be taken to help an actual person. B, C, and D are also all positive, making them inappropriate, since Clinton criticizes governments for protecting the status quo.

QUESTION 34.

Choice C is correct. The "shipyards", "lunch counters", and "prisons" that Clinton mentions are locations where people would meet to promote social change even when governments resisted such change. This information supports C and eliminates B, since Clinton is here focusing on PAST activities. Although Clinton criticizes governments, she does not indicate that such criticisms were previously "unknown" (eliminating A); although Clinton also praises citizens for their activities, she does not argue that small protests are the "only" way to prevent government abuses (eliminating D).

392

QUESTION 35.

Choice B is correct. In lines 10-12, Clinton explains that in a speech "last summer" she had expressed support for global initiatives focusing on civil society. This information supports B. Other answers are out of scope: Clinton has met with leaders (but never describes such meetings as routine, eliminating A), discusses her career (but never considers its early stages OR speaks negatively about civil society, eliminating C), and analyzes initiatives (but never actually focuses on economics, eliminating D).

QUESTION 36.

Choice A is correct. See above for the explanation of the correct answer. B presents a new initiative, C describes an initiative in which Clinton had been involved, and D indicates that Clinton is interested in adhering to humanitarian ideals set forward by Eleanor Roosevelt. None of these answers directly aligns with an answer to the previous question, even though the line references generally refer to Clinton's major topic, civil society.

QUESTION 37.

Choice D is correct. In lines 25-28, Clinton notes that governments oppose civil society both by restricting "civil space" and by attempting to divert "the world's attention". Both overt and subtle measures that hamper civil society are thus being utilized, so that D is the best answer. The other answers, which focus on Clinton's efforts, misrepresent the content of the passage: Clinton is not mainly concerned with economics (eliminating A), works mainly with organizations (eliminating B, which shifts the emphasis to countries), and has not faced clear rejection in her work (even though her work to promote civil society is challenging, eliminating C).

QUESTION 38.

Choice B is correct. See above for the explanation of the correct answer. A describes an initiative that Clinton hopes will be successful, C notes that civil society faces severe challenges in Central Asia, and D refers to records and measures that register progress in promoting civil society. None of these answers provide a characterization of the "governments of some countries" in a manner that aligns with an answer to the previous question.

QUESTION 39.

Choice A is correct. In lines 15-16, Clinton explains that advancing civil society is a key to advancing "national security priorities" in the United States. This information directly supports A. Clinton generally avoids discussion of economics (eliminating B) and refers to American responsibilities in lines 50-53, but not to America's measurable reputation (eliminating C). Although promoting civil society may in fact reduce corruption, Clinton does not focus on corruption at any clear point in the passage (eliminating D as lacking evidence).

QUESTION 40.

Choice D is correct. The word "mirror" refers to America's positive role as an example of democracy: America should thus be the "best possible" (line 52) "representation" of democracy. D is the best answer, while A and C both assume that America is not GENUINELY or DEEPLY democratic and B refers to the act of reproducing or doubling, not to the act of standing for a strong principle.

QUESTION 41.

Choice A is correct. In the final paragraph, the word "we" refers to a group that Clinton represents (most logically, Americans) and that needs assistance because there is "much more we all have to do" (line 68). Thus, the word "we" calls attention to Americans as a group and their potential to make progress: A is effective while D too strongly criticizes the United States. B is inaccurate because Clinton has used the word "we" much earlier to connect with her audience (line 17) and is not first establishing acceptance in the final paragraph; C is inaccurate because the topic of "laws" is not directly mentioned in Clinton's discussion of future progress.

QUESTION 42.

Choice A is correct. While much of the passage calls attention to the negative role of zoos, in the first paragraph the author notes that zoos preserve "many species threatened in their natural habitats" (lines 3-4). This information supports A, while B refers to frequent criticisms (which are only a major concern of later paragraphs) and C misstates the logic of the paragraph (since zoos ARE positive, but will not necessarily become INCREASINGLY popular as a result of good perceptions). D is also problematic: while philosopher A.O. Lovejoy is mentioned, Lovejoy wrote about the order of the natural world overall, NOT about zoos in particular.

QUESTION 43.

Choice C is correct. The information in the line reference further explains the "human-centered" (line 9) view of the world by introducing the ideas of A.O. Lovejoy: ultimately, the author rejects aspects of this view and argues that quality of life for animals must also be considered. This information supports C. Zookeepers are never directly mentioned at this stage (eliminating B), while Lovejoy's ideas are simply explained: he is neither characterized as unpopular (eliminating A) nor as misunderstood (eliminating D).

QUESTION 44.

Choice B is correct. In lines 44-48, the author explains that "most Americans" believe that zoo animals are kept in a "cozy" and safe environment. This information supports B and, on account of the consensus, eliminates A. For most Americans, keeping animals in zoos benefits the animals, not humans engaged in economic activities (eliminating C). Moreover, unlike many Americans, the author HIMSELF would argue that keeping animals in zoos is philosophically questionable (eliminating D).

QUESTION 45.

Choice C is correct. See above for the explanation of the correct answer. A records an idea that can be attributed to philosophers (not to "Americans" in general), B explains the development of zoos in an earlier time period, and D presents the author's own ideas. Make sure not to assume that the author's thesis is representative of American ideas about zoos: in fact, some of the author's ideas go entirely against popular opinion.

QUESTION 46.

Choice A is correct. The word "preserve" is used to describe how zoos protect or "safeguard" species that are "threatened in their natural habitats" (line 4). A is thus the best answer, while other choices would not effectively refer to species that face threats to survival. B means to honor or to commit to memory, C refers to items or supplies, and D wrongly assumes that the animals would cease to move.

QUESTION 47.

Choice D is correct. In lines 60-63, the author argues that ideas about zoos are "symptomatic of larger issues" that involve how humans relate to the environment. This information supports D. A is contradicted by the author's often negative or skeptical attitude towards the benefits of zoos, B is contradicted by the fact (noted in lines 44-48) that Americans view zoos positively, and C misstates the author's true criticisms of zoos, which cause humans to misunderstand or de-value animals but do not necessarily cause animals "pain".

QUESTION 48.

Choice D is correct. See above for the explanation of the correct answer. A indicates that zoos are a source of debate (but not WHY such debates are important), B refers to a problem with modern zookeeping practices, and C provides a fact about unpleasant conditions that elephants face in zoos. None of these answers directly addresses the author's main ideas about debates surrounding zoos as effectively as D does.

QUESTION 49.

Choice B is correct. The phrase "have contributed to" refers to conditions that have caused medical problems in "captive elephants" (line 58). These conditions are thus responsible for the problems that they have caused, so that B is the best answer. A and C both refer to the activities of HUMANS (and are both often used in positive contexts), while D neglects the fact that the conditions are a MAJOR factor in the problems elephants face, not a "supporting" factor.

QUESTION 50.

Choice A is correct. While Benbow explains how zoos "developed" (line 31) according to certain historical values, Adams criticizes zoos as "cruel" (line 42) institutions that harm both humans and animals. This information best supports A, which rightly indicates that Benbow is impartial and that Adams is highly negative. B is incorrect because Benbow focuses primarily on HUMANS and their motivations, C is incorrect because Adams never notes that zoos are becoming unpopular (even though she might WANT to see zoos decline in popularity), and D is incorrect because Benbow never takes a strong position for or against zoos.

QUESTION 51.

Choice A is correct. According to the first figure, 72% of Americans view zoos favorably while 18% of Americans view zoos unfavorably. This information supports A and can be used to eliminate B, which assumes the opposite relationship. C and D are both out of scope: the information is taken from a "survey on zoo visitation" and only lists preferences among people who have already visited zoos. The LIKELIHOOD of these people visiting zoos again is never considered.

QUESTION 52.

Choice C is correct. The first figure clearly indicates that the majority of Americans view zoos favorably, so that B and D can both be eliminated. While only 13% of Americans view zoos favorably because of the general amusement or entertainment value of zoos, 59% of Americans view zoos favorably because zoo animals are considered safer in captivity. Thus, eliminate A and choose C as the only accurate answer.

Section 2: Writing
Passage 1, Mary, Queen of Scots: Making History Live

QUESTION 1.

Choice B is correct. This question requires the idiomatic phrase "resemblance to" ("resemblance to a sibling", "resemblance to a historical figure"). Be careful of A, C, and D: there are English idioms that use the phrases "as people", "with people", and "for people", though none of these prepositional phrases can be paired with the word "resemblance.

QUESTION 2.

Choice A is correct. While sentences 1 and 2 deal with the author's general ideas about history, sentence 4 discusses Mary's life: because sentence 3 introduces Mary, it is an effective transition and should be kept in its current placement. B begins the passage with an idea ("For instance") that requires introduction, C interrupts the author's general ideas about history, and D wrongly places the introduction of Mary AFTER the brief analysis of her life.

QUESTION 3.

Choice D is correct. The paragraph as a whole describes Mary's early life. Thus, it can reasonably inferred that the date of birth is Mary's, so that D is the best answer. B ("it") creates a misplaced modifier, while A and C both wrongly attribute the date of birth to "James V" and wrongly indicate that James V died BECAUSE Mary became a queen, not that she became a queen because her father died.

QUESTION 4.

Choice A is correct. The underlined portion should refer directly to Francis, "who became" King of France. A is the best answer: B introduces a comma splice, while C and D both create sentence structures that refer back to Mary herself, NOT to Francis.

QUESTION 5.

Choice A is correct. The sentence as a whole should indicate a contrast: Mary was seen "as a pawn", not "as a lively, independent woman". A properly creates such a contrast, while B sets up comparable alternatives, C indicates a similarity, and D both skews the grammar of the sentence and creates a comparison.

QUESTION 6.

Choice B is correct. The author here is referring to the situation of Queen Elizabeth, or to the likely "possibility" that she would never marry. While B effectively sums up the content of the passage, A wrongly and without context attributes a highly positive tone to Elizabeth's situation, while C creates a comma splice and D uses an ambiguous pronoun. Since the "possibility" is never summed up using a single noun, a single pronoun cannot be used.

QUESTION 7.

Choice D is correct. The writer here describes how, even though Mary "ignored" her husband, Mary's marriage produced a son. The sentence as a whole must therefore set up a contrast: A indicates similarity, B indicates cause and effect, and C creates a comma splice. (It is not possible to link two independent clauses using "however" in the absence of a semicolon.) Only D establishes the right relationship using a grammatically correct transition.

QUESTION 8.

Choice C is correct. In the passage, the author establishes Mary as a figure from an earlier century and discusses her in the past tense. C properly continues this past tense usage: A and B both refer to Mary in the present, as though she were still alive, while D wrongly introduces the plural "were".

QUESTION 9.

Choice D is correct. Commas should be used to separate out the information that describes Mary's "lover", who was "the Earl of Bothwell". A wrongly uses a comma to divide "only" from the phrase "only to be", B splits up the reference to the Earl's position, and C creates a run-on sentence by only placing a single comma before "the Earl." Only D properly coordinates the subordinate, descriptive information about Mary's lover.

QUESTION 10.

Choice A is correct. The sentence describes the fate of Mary, who would naturally be "imprisoned" and then "watched" during this imprisonment. A rightly communicates this meaning, while B indicates that Queen Elizabeth HERSELF was watched (not that she had Mary watched) and C and D both introduce comma splices.

QUESTION 11.

Choice D is correct. Paragraph 5 offers an overall statement about the author's interest in Mary's life, and thus seems like a logical conclusion for the passage. Moreover, while paragraph 4 explains Mary's unpleasant marriage, paragraph 6 refers directly to "This unpleasant marriage". Link these paragraphs by eliminating A, but also eliminate B (because paragraph 5 makes some of the same points a that are made in paragraph 1, and would be redundant if placed so nearby) and eliminate C (since this placement would interrupt the author's description of Mary's life).

Passage 2, Africa and the Future of the World Economy

QUESTION 12.

Choice C is correct. The underlined portion requires a concise phrase that is in parallel with "outbreaks of disease" and "instances of political corruption". The phrase "scenes of intense poverty" uses the same structure and the same preposition: A and B are both wordier and out of parallel, while D is awkward and uses "in" instead of "of".

QUESTION 13.

Choice B is correct. The underlined portion is the subject of "are", since this sentence uses an inverted subject-verb combination. B, which yields "there are indications", is the correct usage: A, C ("that", which is singular), and D ("indicating", a singular noun like "walking") all create subject-verb disagreement.

QUESTION 14.

Choice A is correct. In this portion of the passage, the author is explaining Africa's "strong potential for economic growth and development": "untapped", or present but not yet utilized, would best describe the continent's "economic assets". While C and D are both negatives, B is an illogical choice. The assets ARE known to the author, but have not yet been utilized.

QUESTION 15.

Choice B is correct. The underlined portion must provide a verb for the subject "Africa": both C and D create sentence fragments, while A creates an illogical meaning, since the site offered by Africa is not ITSELF increasing or growing. Instead, Africa "increasingly offers" opportunities since its economic viability is being recognized.

QUESTION 16.

Choice D is correct. In this paragraph, the author is making note of Africa's potential for impressive economic growth: noting that Africa could be a "significant site of agricultural production" effectively fits the author's position. While A and B call attention to economic ACTIVITIES, they do not specifically outline ADVANTAGES. C refers to a topic raised in the first paragraph ("Depictions" of Africa), but does not provide the kind of economic arguments that would support the author's point in THIS paragraph.

QUESTION 17.

Choice A is correct. The sentence must describe technology expansion that has been completed and that "has made business development possible. A references the 2011 cell phone subscription figure from the graph, while B (interest in technology) and C (foreign countries) reference factors that the graph does not explicitly consider. D is a trap answer: this choice refers to growth that "is expected", not growth that HAS occurred.

QUESTION 18.

Choice D is correct. For this question, eliminate redundant false answers: by DEFINITION, urban centers are far from the countryside (A) and are not rural (B), while the author has already made it clear that "demographic patterns" related to urbanization are being discussed (C). Only D, which creates a grammatically correct sentence without such needless information, is an acceptable answer.

QUESTION 19.

Choice C is correct. The author is citing a "comparison" that is convincing and effective, or "compelling". Other choices create diction errors: A means unable to resist an urge or action, B means either free of charge or relating to polite compliments, and D means working together.

QUESTION 20.

Choice B is correct. The sentence involves a contrast between Africa's positive "potential" and the negative fact that economic growth is not "assured". B establishes the best sentence relationship, while A indicates simultaneity, C indicates cause and effect, and D introduces a comma splice.

QUESTION 21.

Choice D is correct. The commas should clarify the sentence structure: the "focus on providing aid" (one major idea) should be separated from the discussion of "investment" (second major idea) by a single comma and then a conjunction. D offers the proper arrangement, while A wrongly treats "on providing aid" as a qualifying phrase, B separates "providing" from the reference to the "aid" that is provided, and C wrongly pairs off "aid" and "investment".

QUESTION 22.

Choice B is correct. The sentence is describing hypothetical situations: B, which offers a hypothetical phrasing that is in parallel with "could be curtailed", is an effective choice. A treats something that is hypothetical ("investors fear") as something that "has" happened, while C and D both introduce -ing forms that break parallelism.

Passage 3, Rate My Curator

QUESTION 23.

Choice C is correct. The sentence must create an analogy between what a curator organizes (museum showcases) and what a director organizes (movies). C establishes this analogy while observing strong parallelism: false answers A and B both indicate, in context, that a director organizes "museum showcases", while D contains the ambiguous pronoun phrase "that of".

QUESTION 24.

Choice B is correct. A showcase, as explained in the sentence, will involve many decisions, and a curator will be involved in the important or "momentous" ones, since a curator is a figure of authority. Choose B and eliminate A (which means "not lasting long"), C (which takes an inappropriate negative tone), and D (which indicates that the decisions are radical or dramatic, an idea that is not supported by the passage).

QUESTION 25.

Choice B is correct. The underlined portion should create an effective transition, and should describe what curators do "before attaining roles of authority": the past tense "having worked" properly refers to the "curators". Trap answer A wrongly refers to the earlier nouns in the sentence using "when", even though no specific times are mentioned. C introduces a fragment after a semicolon, while D creates a comma splice. (In cases such as this, "however" must be preceded by a semicolon to effectively introduce a new clause.)

QUESTION 26.

Choice A is correct. While the author is primarily concerned with enumerating the job duties of curators, the underlined sentence distracts from this discussion by introducing the topics of "personal life" and work schedules. A correctly sums up this reasoning, while the reasoning in B calls attention to an irrelevant (though perhaps accurate) fact about the demands faced by curators. The author is listing scheduling conditions, not specific responsibilities (eliminating C) and never returns to the topic of the "personal lives" of curators (eliminating D).

QUESTION 27.

Choice C is correct. The underlined portion should contrast with "in theory" and should follow a parallel structure: "but in practice" is an effective choice. B and D break parallelism, while A indicates SIMILARITY ("and"), not contrast.

QUESTION 28.

Choice D is correct. The non-essential phrase "with good reason" should be offset with two identical units of punctuation. D effectively uses two commas, while A and B use faulty combinations involving one dash and one comma each. C places a sentence fragment after a semicolon and is thus grammatically incorrect.

QUESTION 29.

Choice D is correct. The paragraph as a whole calls attention to one exhibition staged at the Seattle Art Museum: thus, beginning this paragraph with a reference to "a single" exhibition is highly appropriate. In context, A, B, and C all indicate that the exhibition is detached from society or inaccessible and do not effectively capture the paragraph's emphasis on only one exhibition.

QUESTION 30.

Choice A is correct. This sentence requires the idiomatic phrase "intention . . . to", since the information between commas must be temporarily factored out. Watch for misreading: while B and D may seem to describe Junker's "enlightening" actions and C may seem to refer to museum-goers "as enlightened", none of these choices yield a grammatically and idiomatically correct sentence.

QUESTION 31.

Choice D is correct. The underlined portion should refer directly to "one curator" who "works", so that D is the best answer. A refers to a location, B sets up a comparison (not appropriate here), and C refers to a thing.

QUESTION 32.

Choice A is correct. The underlined portion should indicate that some curators work with unexpected "media", much as Biesenbach has pursued projects "outside the traditional media of painting, drawing, and sculpture": A refers to an actress and a celebrity and thus supports the main idea of the paragraph. B and D return to forms of traditional art rather than explaining Biesenbach's contrasting approach, while C explains an artist who interests Biesenbach, NOT the ideas of Biesenbach and other curators who prioritize unexpected media.

QUESTION 33.

Choice B is correct. The subject of the sentence is "curators", and the sentence itself describes curators who are active "today". Eliminate the singular A and the past-tense C and D and choose the plural, present-tense B as the best choice.

Passage 4, A Quantum of Physics

QUESTION 34.

Choice C is correct. The underlined verb should take the subject "quantum physics", which the author discusses in present tense in this paragraph. C is an effective answer, while A creates a sentence fragment, B introduces the needless pronoun "it", and D disrupts the author's present-tense discussion with a future tense.

QUESTION 35.

Choice D is correct. The writer is here describing scenarios that can be understood from the viewpoint of quantum physics, or a quantum "perspective". Other choices introduce diction errors: A and B both refer to possibilities while trap answer C indicates a THING that is viewed, not a WAY of viewing.

QUESTION 36.

Choice B is correct. In this paragraph, the writer has called attention to situations that "seem absurd": the question in B highlights the strangeness and seeming unlikelihood of the situations mentioned, though "probability" offers something of an explanation for such situations in the next paragraph. Other answers are genuinely open-ended questions that call attention to "most people" (A), "other examples" (C), and the popularity of "quantum paradoxes" (D), rather than anticipating the discussion of "probability" that follows.

QUESTION 37.

Choice B is correct. The underlined verb should take the plural subject "behavior and . . . motion": eliminate singular forms A and C. Because the author is describing pre-quantum physics beliefs about how matter "behaved", the past tense is required. Thus, eliminate D and choose B.

QUESTION 38.

Choice A is correct. At this point, the author is explaining that probability functions are "equations": referring back to "probability functions" using "which" creates an effective transition. While B creates a comma splice, C and D are awkward uses that indicate that the functions MOVE or PROCEED "to" or "from" the equations rather than that they ARE equations.

QUESTION 39.

Choice C is correct. This paragraph makes extended reference to "ourselves", so that the underlined portion (which refers to the same group) should use "us" or "we" for pronoun agreement. A, B, and C all use different pronouns that would be acceptable in other cases, but NOT in the context of a paragraph that has already utilized "ourselves" as this paragraph does.

QUESTION 40.

Choice A is correct. In this paragraph, the author is setting up two complementary ideas: because bodies are made up of subatomic particles, quantum physics (which explains those particles) can explain human behavior. The second idea is an "extension" of the first, justifying A and eliminating the contrast outlined in B. The author is here concerned with a line of logical argument, not new research or general knowledge: thus, eliminate C and D, respectively.

QUESTION 41.

Choice C is correct. This sentence compares the behavior of individuals ("their behavior") to the behavior of electrons: C properly uses the pronoun "that" to stand in for electron "behavior". A wrongly compares behavior to "electrons", B commits the same error and adds in an awkward second preposition, and D wrongly uses a plural pronoun ("those") for "behavior".

QUESTION 42.

Choice A is correct. The previous paragraph describes the things that people supposedly CANNOT do under quantum physics: quantum physics thus appears to "nullify" or cancel out responsibility and initiative. A is an effective choice, while B refers to an emotional reaction, C refers to a physical action, and D is too informal for the style of the essay.

QUESTION 43.

Choice D is correct. This sentence should involve the idiomatic phrase "wrestling with" (to deal with a challenge or obstacle): eliminate A and C, which would indicate that Einstein is literally wrestling "for" a team or a side. Then, eliminate the faulty description in B: "startled" is an adjective and refers to an emotional reaction, while "startlingly" in D is the adverb required to explain HOW unconventional the "perspectives" were.

QUESTION 44.

Choice A is correct. The underlined portion shifts emphasis from the author's ARGUMENT about quantum physics to the author's BACKGROUND. While the author does have a clear viewpoint (eliminating B), the author's motives for quoting Einstein are already apparent (since Einstein supports the author's argument, eliminating C) and the author's own status is a minor concern (eliminating D). Only A rightly eliminates the phrase and explains why it is a distraction.

Section 3: Math Test - No Calculator

QUESTION 1.

Choice B is correct. Subtracting 1 from both sides of the equation $103 = 8x + 9$ yields $102 = 8x + 8$. Dividing both sides by 2 yields $51 = 4x + 4$. Therefore, the expression $4x + 4$ is equivalent to 51.

Choice A is incorrect because 12 is the value of x, not $4x + 4$. Choices C and D are incorrect and may result from calculation errors from not completely solving for the target, $4x + 4$.

QUESTION 2.

Choice B is correct. Substituting the point $(1, -1)$ into the inequality $x - y \geq 0$ yields $(1) - (-1) \geq 0$, which simplifies to $2 \geq 0$, which is a true statement. Substituting $(1, -1)$ into the inequality $x + y \leq 0$ yields $(1) + (-1) \leq 0$, which simplifies to $0 \leq 0$, which is also a true statement. Therefore, the coordinate point $(1, -1)$ is a solution to the system of linear inequalities $\begin{array}{l} x - y \geq 0 \\ x + y \leq 0 \end{array}$.

Choices A, C, and D are incorrect because the coordinate point $(1, -1)$ is a solution to either one or none of the inequalities each system, but not both.

QUESTION 3.

Choice A is correct. If line r goes through the points $(-10, 0)$ and $(0, 5)$, substituting into the slope formula, $m = \dfrac{y_2 - y_1}{x_2 - x_1}$, yields $m = \dfrac{(5) - (0)}{(0) - (-10)} = \dfrac{5}{10} = \dfrac{1}{2}$. Therefore, if the slope of line r is $\dfrac{1}{2}$ and the y-intercept is 5, as defined by the point $(0, 5)$, then the equation of line r is $y = \dfrac{1}{2}x + 5$. Now, if line s is perpendicular to line r, then line s has an opposite reciprocal slope of -2, and since line s intercepts the origin, the y-intercept is 0, making the equation of line s equivalent to $y = -2x$. Setting the equations of line r and line s equal to each other yields $\dfrac{1}{2}x + 5 = -2x$. Multiplying both sides by 2 yields $x + 10 = -4x$ and further subtracting x from each side yields $10 = -5x$. Therefore, after dividing both sides by -5, $x = -2$.

Choices B and C are incorrect and may result from errors in calculating the appropriate equations for line r and line s, and/or substitution errors made once the equations have been identified. Choice D is incorrect because 4 is the y-value at the point where the two lines intersect, not the x-value.

403

QUESTION 4.

Choice C is correct. Substituting $3x+1$ for g in the equation $\sqrt{g}+3=x$ yields $\sqrt{3x+1}+3=x$. Subtracting 3 from both sides of the equation yields $\sqrt{3x+1}=x-3$. Squaring both sides yields $(\sqrt{3x+1})^2=(x-3)^2$, or $3x+1=x^2-6x+9$. Subtracting the expression $3x+1$ from both sides of the equation yields $0=x^2-9x+8$. Factoring the right-hand side of the equation gives $0=(x-8)(x-1)$ which reveals the roots at 8 and 1. Since x must be greater than 1, $x=8$.

Choice A is incorrect and may result from correctly solving the equation after $3x+1$ was substituted for g, but neglecting the fact that x must be greater than 1. Choices B and D are incorrect and may result from calculation and/or substitution errors.

QUESTION 5.

Choice D is correct. The equation $N=450-3c$ is a linear function of the form $y=b+mx$, where b is the y-intercept of the linear equation and m is the slope. Therefore, -3 is the slope, or rate of change of the remaining supply of crayons. Since -3 is being multiplied with c, which was defined in the question as the number of classes that have passed in a school year, a slope of -3 must imply that the overall stock of crayons is reduced by 3 for every class that passes. In other words, the entire class uses up or loses 3 crayons per class in total.

Choice A is incorrect because it is not clearly defined that the crayons distributed for use during class will not be returned at the end of each class. Choices B and C are incorrect because the answers imply that c is the number of students in class, where c is actually the number of classes that have passed.

QUESTION 6.

Choice A is correct. The expression $4x^2-35$ is equivalent to the expression $(4x^2-36)+1$. Factoring the difference of perfect squares $4x^2-36$ yields $(2x+6)(2x-6)$ and substituting back into the expression $(4x^2-36)+1$ yields $(2x+6)(2x-6)+1$.

Choice B is incorrect and may result from errors in manipulating the form of the initial expression $4x^2-35$. Choices C and D are incorrect and may result from errors in appropriately factoring the binomial in the expression after it has been modified.

QUESTION 7.

Choice C is correct. Setting the expression $\dfrac{\theta\pi d}{360}$ equivalent to a, the length of the arc, yields the equation $\dfrac{\theta\pi d}{360}=a$. Multiplying both sides by $\dfrac{360}{\theta\pi}$ yields $d=\dfrac{360a}{\theta\pi}$. Substituting π for a and 120 for θ yields $d=\dfrac{360\pi}{120\pi}=3$. However, since $\theta<120°$ and since θ is in the denominator of the expression $\dfrac{360a}{\theta\pi}$, d must be greater than 3. The smallest integer value that is greater than 3 is 4.

Choices A and B are incorrect because 2 and 3 are not greater than 3 and d must be strictly greater than 3. Choice D is incorrect because 4 and 5 are both smaller than 6, but strictly greater than 3.

QUESTION 8.

Choice B is correct. Exponent rules state that when multiplying powers, one must add the exponents. Therefore, the expression $a^{x^2} \bullet a^{4x} \bullet a^4$ simplifies to a^{x^2+4x+4} and substituting in the equation $a^{x^2} \bullet a^{4x} \bullet a^4 = a^9$ yields $a^{x^2+4x+4} = a^9$. Since the bases are the same, the exponents are equivalent, yielding the equation $x^2 + 4x + 4 = 9$. Subtracting 9 from both sides of the equation yields $x^2 + 4x - 5 = 0$. Factoring the left-hand side yields $(x+5)(x-1) = 0$. Therefore, the two values of x that are solutions to the equation are -5 and 1. Since x must be greater than 0, the answer is 1.

Choice A is incorrect because the question states that x must be greater than 0 and -5 is not greater than 0. Choices C and D are incorrect because neither answer is a solution that makes the equation $a^{x^2} \bullet a^{4x} \bullet a^4 = a^9$ true.

QUESTION 9.

Choice A is correct. The line graphed in the xy-plane intercepts the points $(0,3)$

and $(9,0)$. Substituting these points into the slope formula, $m = \dfrac{y_2 - y_1}{x_2 - x_1}$, yields

$m = \dfrac{(0)-(3)}{(9)-(0)} = -\dfrac{3}{9} = -\dfrac{1}{3}$. Therefore, the slope of line h is also $-\dfrac{1}{3}$ since line h is

parallel to the line graphed in the xy-plane. Given that the y-intercept of line h is $-\dfrac{4}{3}$,

as defined by the point $(0,-\dfrac{4}{3})$, the equation of line h in the form $y = mx + b$, is

$y = -\dfrac{1}{3}x - \dfrac{4}{3}$. In order to find the x-intercept of line h, one must substitute 0 for y which

yields $0 = -\dfrac{1}{3}x - \dfrac{4}{3}$. Adding $\dfrac{4}{3}$ to both sides of the equation yields $\dfrac{4}{3} = -\dfrac{1}{3}x$ and

multiplying both sides by -3 reveals the x-intercept, $x = -4$.

Choices B and C are incorrect and may result from calculation errors while developing the equation for line h. Choice D is incorrect because $\dfrac{3}{4}$ would be the x-intercept of line h if it were perpendicular to the line graphed in the xy-plane, not parallel to the line graphed in the xy-plane.

QUESTION 10.

Choice D is correct. An absolute value will always have a value of 0 or greater. Because of this, the expression $-|x|$ will always have a value of 0 or less. Therefore, the equation $y = -|x| + 6$ will have its maximum value of 6 when x is equal to 0 and the equation will be less than 6 for all other values of x.

Choices A, B, and C are incorrect because for all three equations there is a value of x that yields a y-value of greater than 6.

QUESTION 11.

Choice C is correct. Exponential growth and decay models are built off of the formula $y = a(1 \pm r)^x$, where a is the initial value and r is the growth or decay percentage in decimal form. Therefore, an initial mass of 125 kilograms would replace a in the formula and decaying by 15% would make r equivalent to $-.15$, making the equation $y = 125(1 - .15)^x$. Substituting M for y and simplifying yields $M = 125(.85)^x$.

Choice A is incorrect and may result from confusing the positions of the initial value and the decay factor in the formula of an exponential decay equation. Choice B is incorrect and may result from neglecting to subtract the decay rate from 1 and from confusing the positions of the initial value and the decay factor in the formula of an exponential decay equation. Choice D is incorrect and may result from neglecting to subtract the decay rate from 1.

QUESTION 12.

Choice D is correct. The quadratic equation $f(t) = t^2 - 8t + 4$ is written in standard form where $a = 1$, $b = -8$, and $c = 4$. Substituting these values into the quadratic formula, $\dfrac{-b \pm \sqrt{b^2 - 4ac}}{2a}$ yields $\dfrac{-(-8) \pm \sqrt{(-8)^2 - 4(1)(4)}}{2(1)}$, which simplifies to $\dfrac{8 \pm \sqrt{48}}{2}$. Further simplifying of the radical yields $\dfrac{8 \pm 4\sqrt{3}}{2}$ and dividing by 2 yields $4 \pm 2\sqrt{3}$. The absolute distance between $4 + 2\sqrt{3}$ and $4 - 2\sqrt{3}$ is equivalent to $\left|(4 + 2\sqrt{3}) - (4 - 2\sqrt{3})\right|$ which simplifies to $4\sqrt{3}$.

Choices A, B, and C are incorrect and may result from errors in applying the quadratic formula or errors in calculating the absolute distance between two radical points.

QUESTION 13.

Choice C is correct. Multiplying the expression $\dfrac{5 - 2i}{5 + 3i}$ by $\dfrac{5 - 3i}{5 - 3i}$ yields $\dfrac{5 - 2i}{5 + 3i} \bullet \dfrac{5 - 3i}{5 - 3i}$.

Multiplying the numerators together yields $(5-2i)(5-3i) = 25-25i+6i^2$. Substituting -1 for i yields $25-25i+6(-1) = 19-25i$. Multiplying the denominators together yields $(5+3i)(5-3i) = 25-9i^2$. Substituting -1 for i yields $25-9(-1) = 34$. The expression $\dfrac{5-2i}{5+3i} \bullet \dfrac{5-3i}{5-3i}$ can be rewritten as $\dfrac{19-25i}{34}$, or $\dfrac{19}{34} - \dfrac{25}{34}i$. Therefore, in the form $a+bi$, a is equivalent to $\dfrac{19}{34}$.

Choice A is incorrect because $-\dfrac{25}{34}$ is the value of b in the form $a+bi$, not a. Choices B and D are incorrect and may result from calculation errors while rationalizing the original expression $\dfrac{5-2i}{5+3i}$.

QUESTION 14.

Choice A is correct. Subtracting b_2 from both sides of the equation $y = -\dfrac{x}{m} + b_2$ yields $y - b_2 = -\dfrac{x}{m}$. Multiplying both sides of the equation by -1 yields $-y + b_2 = \dfrac{x}{m}$, or $b_2 - y = \dfrac{x}{m}$. Further, multiplying both sides of the equation by m yields $m(b_2 - y) = x$ and dividing both sides by the expression $b_2 - y$ yields $m = \dfrac{x}{b_2 - y}$.

Choices B, C, and D are incorrect because none of the equations are equivalent to the equation $y = -\dfrac{x}{m} + b_2$.

QUESTION 15.

Choice A is correct. Dividing $8x+1$ by $2x+1$ yields the following:

$$
\begin{array}{r}
4 \\
2x+1 \overline{)\,8x+1} \\
\underline{-(8x+4)} \\
-3
\end{array}
$$

So, $\dfrac{8x+1}{2x+1}$ is equivalent to the expression $4 - \dfrac{3}{2x+1}$. The average of $4 - \dfrac{3}{2x+1}$ and $4 + \dfrac{3}{2x+1}$ is equivalent to $\dfrac{(4 - \dfrac{3}{2x+1}) + (4 + \dfrac{3}{2x+1})}{2} = \dfrac{8}{2} = 4$.

Choices B, C, and D are incorrect and may result from errors in long division and/or applying the average formula to expressions.

QUESTION 16.

The correct answer is 20. The hypotenuse of the smaller isosceles right triangle that measures $5\sqrt{8}$ is equivalent to $10\sqrt{2}$, which is exactly $\frac{1}{5}$ of the size of the larger isosceles right triangle that has a hypotenuse with a measure of $50\sqrt{2}$. An isosceles right triangle is a 45-45-90 right triangle in which the hypotenuse is equivalent to the side length times $\sqrt{2}$. Therefore, the side length of the isosceles right triangle with a hypotenuse that measures $50\sqrt{2}$ is 50 and the sum of its shorter legs is $50+50=100$. If the smaller triangle has side lengths that are $\frac{1}{5}$ the length of the larger triangle, the sum of the shorter two legs of the smaller triangle is equivalent to $\frac{1}{5}(100)=20$.

QUESTION 17.

The correct answer is 2. If Mr. Waterman would like to give his nieces and nephews $55 worth of gift certificates to an ice cream parlor and each must receive at least one $5, one $10, and one $25 gift certificate, the possible combinations of gift certificates that he can give are as follows:

1 - $25, 1 - $10, and 4 - $5 which is equivalent to $55.
1 - $25, 2 - $10, and 2 - $5 which is equivalent to $55.

There are no other ways that Mr. Waterman can give each niece and nephew $55 worth of gift certificates and at least one of each type besides the two combinations above. Therefore, the difference between the greatest number of $5 gift certificates and the least number of $5 gift certificates he can give each niece and nephew is $4-2=2$.

QUESTION 18.

The correct answer is .25 or $\frac{1}{4}$. Since $\angle BAC$ intercepts an arc that measures $180°$ and point A lies on the circle, the measure of $\angle BAC$ is equivalent to $\frac{1}{2}(180°)=90°$. Since $\triangle BAC$ is a right triangle and the measure of one of its shorter legs, $5\sqrt{2}$, times $\sqrt{2}$ yields $5\sqrt{2}\bullet\sqrt{2}=10$, which happens to be the length of the triangle's hypotenuse, the triangle is an isosceles right triangle with angles that measure $45°$, $45°$, and $90°$. The measure of $\angle ACB$ in radians is equivalent to $45\bullet\frac{\pi}{180}=\frac{1}{4}\pi$. Therefore, if the measure of the angle in radians is given by the expression $H\pi$, H is equivalent to $\frac{1}{4}$.

QUESTION 19.

The correct answer is 5. In order for the system of equations $\begin{array}{c}A^2x+10y=75\\Ax+2y=15\end{array}$ to have infinitely many solutions the two equations must be exactly the same. Multiplying the second equation by 5 yields $\begin{array}{c}A^2x+10y=75\\5Ax+10y=75\end{array}$. Subtracting the second equation from the

the first equation yields $(A^2-5A)x=0$. Therefore, A^2-5A must be equivalent to 0. Setting A^2-5A equal to 0 yields $A^2-5A=0$ and after factoring the left-hand side, the equation is $A(A-5)=0$. The values of 0 and 5 make the equation true, and since A must be positive, the answer is 5.

QUESTION 20.

The correct answer is 32. Expanding the left-hand side of the equation $(2a+B)^2 = Ma^2 + 8a + Q$ yields $4a^2 + 4aB + B^2 = Ma^2 + 8a + Q$. Looking at the symmetery of the left and right sides of the equation, one can see that M is equivalent to 4, 8 is equivalent to $4B$, and Q is equivalent to B^2. Setting 8 equal to $4B$ yields $8=4B$ and dividing both sides by 4 yields $B=2$. Substituting 2 for B in the equation $Q=B^2$ yields $Q=(2)^2=4$. Since $B=2$, $M=4$, and $Q=4$, the product BMQ is equivalent to $(2)(4)(4)=32$.

Section 4: Math Test - Calculator

QUESTION 1.

Choice A is correct. If a cell phone vendor sells a accessories and makes \$15 for each accessory that he sells, the vendor makes $15a$ dollars. If the vendor rents a table for h hours and has to pay \$35 per hour for the table, the vendor has to pay $35h$ dollars for the table at the trade show. If the vendor makes $15a$ dollars and has to pay $35h$ dollars, his net profit is $15a-35h$ dollars.

Choice B is incorrect because the vendor would not make money from renting the table. So, the $35h$ should be $-35h$. Choices C and D are incorrect because each coefficient is attached to the incorrect variable.

QUESTION 2.

Choice D is correct. If Janelle gives away 24% of her jelly beans at lunch, then she will consume $100-24=76\%$ of them. 76% of 75 is $75(.76)=57$ jelly beans.

Choice A is incorrect because 18 jelly beans is 24% of 75, or the number of jelly beans Janelle is giving away, not consuming. Choices B and C are incorrect and may result from solving for the incorrect total and/or calculation errors.

QUESTION 3.

Choice B is correct. Factoring a -1 out of the equation $y=-x^2+x+6$ yields $y=-1(x^2-x-6)$ and factoring the expression x^2-x-6 yields $(x-3)(x+2)$ which makes the factor form of the original equation $y=-(x-3)(x+2)$. The x-intercepts of this equation are 3 and -2, which are the same x-intercepts as those of the equation $y=2(x+2)(x-3)$.

Choice A is incorrect because the signs of the x-intercepts are reversed, being -3 and 2. Choice C is incorrect because the x-intercepts occur at 6 and -1. Choice D is incorrect because the x-intercepts occur at -3 and -2.

QUESTION 4.

Choice A is correct. If 12 times a number is equivalent to 30 more than 6 times the number, then $12x = 6x + 30$. Subtracting $6x$ from both sides of the equation yields $6x = 30$. Further, subtracting 30 from both sides of the equation reveals the fact that $6x - 30 = 0$.

Choices B, C, and D are incorrect and may result from errors in developing the equations that match the context of the problem and/or calculation errors.

QUESTION 5.

Choice D is correct. If the restaurant owner pays out 80% of his profits on a night that 50 patrons visit the restaurant, then $80 \times 50 = 4,000$. Similarly, if the restaurant owner pays out 32% of his profits on a night that 125 patrons visit the restaurant, $32 \times 125 = 4,000$. Therefore, if 250 patrons visit the restaurant, $x\% \times 250 = 4,000$. Dividing both sides of the equation yields $x\% = 16\%$.

Choices A, B, and C are all incorrect because all three percentages would require a much larger number of patrons to match the inversely proportional relationship between number of patrons and the percent of profits paid to employees who are working.

QUESTION 6.

Choice A is correct. If the restaurant sees 160 patrons during the all you can eat buffet night, the owner will pay out $x\% \times 160 = 4,000$, or $x\% = 25\%$ of the night's profits to the employees working that night. If there are 160 patrons and each pays \$10, the total profits are $160 \times \$10 = \$1,600$. 25% of the \$1,600 in profits would be $\$1,600(0.25) = \$400$. If 5 employees were working that night, each employee would receive $\dfrac{\$400}{5} = \$80$.

Choice B is incorrect and may result from a calculation error while calculating the percentage of the profits that the owner would pay out to his employees. Choice C is incorrect because \$400 is the total amount of money that the owner will pay out to the employees who worked that evening. Choice D is incorrect because \$1,600 is the total amount of profits that the restaurant made from the buffet.

QUESTION 7.

Choice D is correct. Substituting 11 for G in the equation $G = 13 - \dfrac{1}{21}m$ yields $11 = 13 - \dfrac{1}{21}m$. Subtracting 13 from both sides of the equation yields $-2 = -\dfrac{1}{21}m$, and multiplying both sides by -21 reveals that $m = 42$ miles.

Choice A is incorrect because 2 represents the number of gallons of gas that have been used since the last fill-up. Choice B is incorrect because 11 is the number of gallons of gas that remain in the tank. Choice C is incorrect and may result from a calculation error.

QUESTION 8.

Choice A is correct. If Arielle has f figurines before her parents and grandmother started buying them for her 6 years ago, f represents Arielle's initial number of figurines. If Arielle's parents buy her a figurine and her grandmother buys her a figurine for her birthday and for the holiday season, Arielle receives 4 figurines per year. Therefore, if Arielle currently has 56 figurines, the equation $f + 4y = 56$ must hold true, where f is the initial number of figurines that Arielle had and y is the number of years that have passed. Substituting 6 for y yields $f + 4(6) = 56$, or $f + 24 = 56$. Subtracting 24 from both sides of the equation yields $f = 32$ figurines.

Choice B is incorrect and may result from calculating that Arielle only receives two figurines per year, rather than 4. Choice C is incorrect and may result from assuming that Arielle receives 1 figurine per year, rather than 4. Choice D is incorrect and may result from neglecting to account for the fact that Arielle received 4 figurines per year for 6 years, not just 1 year.

QUESTION 9.

Choice B is correct. Using h to represent the number of hardcover books and p to represent the number of paperback books, if Nadia wants to sell at least 40 books, then $h + p \geq 40$. If each hardcover book sells for \$2, then the expression $2h$ represents the total amount of money earned from selling h hardcover books. If each paperback book sells for \$1, then p not only represents the number of paperback books, but also the total amount of money earned from selling p paperback books. If Nadia would like to raise at least \$60 from the books, then $2h + p \geq 60$. Therefore, the system of equations

$h + p \geq 40$
$2h + p \geq 60$ accurately represents the number of book sales and the amount of money

that Nadia would like to make.

Choice A is incorrect and may result from confusing total book sales with total money earned. Choices C and D are incorrect because both systems of linear inequalities account for \$2 for each paperback book and \$1 for each hardcover book, which is reversed.

QUESTION 10.

Choice C is correct. Since the people being surveyed are leaving a Mexican restaurant, the population from which the people are being randomly selected is people who are already out at a restaurant. People who are already eating out at a restaurant would be more inclined to say that they prefer to dine out rather than dining at home. Therefore, the location of the survey creates an undesired bias.

Choice A is incorrect because a random sample of 85 people is sufficient in size. Choice B is incorrect because the people surveyed were randomly selected and the privacy of not having to give their names helps elicit a truthful response. Choice D is incorrect because Choices A and B were conducted appropriately.

QUESTION 11.

Choice D is correct. If $h(x) = -4x^2 + 24x$ represents the height of the ball, $h(x)$, after x seconds have passed. All of the times when the ball has a height greater than 20 feet would be all of the times where the expression $-4x^2 + 24x$ is greater than 20, or $-4x^2 + 24x > 20$. Subtracting 20 from both sides yields $-4x^2 + 24x - 20 > 0$, or $0 < -4x^2 + 24x - 20$.

Choices A and B are incorrect because both equations include the value of 20 as a solution whereas the question asked for values of x where the ball was at a height strictly greater than 20 feet. Choice C is incorrect because $0 > -4x^2 + 24x - 20$ represents all of the values of x where the height of the ball is *less than* 20 feet, not *greater than* 20 feet.

QUESTION 12.

Choice B is correct. If $t(8) = 9$, then $s(7) = 2(9) = 18$. If $s(7) = 18$ and $r(x) = \sqrt{2x}$, then $r(s(7)) = r(18) = \sqrt{2(18)}$. Since $\sqrt{2(18)} = \sqrt{36} = \pm 6$ and $r(s(7))$ must be positive, then $r(s(7)) = 6$.

Choices A, C, and D are incorrect and may result from substitution errors and/or calculation errors while solving. For example, Choice D is incorrect because 1,296 is $(36)^2$, not $\sqrt{36}$.

QUESTION 13.

Choice C is correct. Mike's average speed for the week would be his total miles traveled divided by his total driving time. Adding $248 + 120 + 240 + 256 + 136$ yields 1,000 total miles driven. Adding $4 + 2 + 6 + 4 + 4$ yields 20 total hours. Dividing 1,000 by 20 yields an average speed of 50 miles per hour.

Choices A, B, and D are incorrect and may result from a calculation error or a conceptual error involving the average formula.

QUESTION 14.

Choice B is correct. If Mrs. Tettertotter has approximately 16 students in each of her 4 classes, Mrs. Tettertotter has a total of $16(4) = 64$ students. If Mrs. Tettertotter gives 24 tests per year to each of these 64 students, Mrs. Tettertotter has to grade a total of $24(64) = 1,536$ tests. If she can grade 8 tests per hour, dividing 1,536 by 8 yields

$\dfrac{1,536}{8} = 192$ hours of grading, or $\dfrac{192}{24} = 8$ days.

Choices A, C, and D are incorrect and may result from incorrectly calculating for the inappropriate value. For example, choice C is incorrect because 192 is the total number of hours it would take Mrs. Tettertotter to grade the tests, not the total number of days.

QUESTION 15.

Choice B is correct. The greatest change in the number of reported instances of bullying occured from 8 years passed 1994 to 12 years passed 1994. This would be the years 2002 through 2006.

Choices A, C, and D are incorrect because none of these 4 year periods have a larger change than the years 2002 through 2006. The years 2006 through 2010 had the largest *decrease* in the number of reported incidents of bullying, but the question asked for the largest *change*, increase or decrease.

QUESTION 16.

Choice B is correct. If Jessica's pottery class is 25% larger than Michelle's pottery class, then, using J for Jessica and M for Michelle, $J = 1.25M$. If Lauren's pottery class is 50% smaller than Michelle's pottery class, then using L for Lauren and M for Michelle, $L = 0.50M$. Dividing both sides of $L = 0.50M$ by 0.50 yields $\frac{L}{0.50} = M$. Substituting $\frac{L}{0.50}$ for M in the equation $J = 1.25M$ yields $J = 1.25(\frac{L}{0.50})$, or $J = 2.50L$. If J were equivalent to $1L$, then J and L would be the same size. So, if $J = 2.50L$, or equivalently $J = (1 + 1.50)L$, then Jessica's pottery class is 150% *larger* than Lauren's class.

Choices A and D are incorrect and may result from calculation errors. Choice C is incorrect because 250% is what percent Jessica's pottery class *is of* Lauren's pottery class, not how much *larger*.

QUESTION 17.

Choice C is correct. Looking at the scatterplot from left to right, visualizing a vertical line at 50 breakfast sales, one can count the number of points on or to the right of that line, which is 9. There are 9 days on which the diner sold 50 or more breakfasts. Disregarding any other points besides these 9 points, one can visualize a horizontal line at 6 pancake meals and count the number of meals above this line, which is 6. Therefore, if a day is to be chosen at random from the days that the diner sold 50 or more breakfast meals, the probability that more than 6 pancake meals were sold on that day is 6 out of 9, or $\frac{2}{3}$.

Choice A is incorrect because $\frac{6}{13}$ is the probability that the diner sold 50 or more breakfast meals and more than 6 pancake meals given that a day is randomly selected from all of the days marked in the scatterplot. Choice B is incorrect because $\frac{8}{13}$ is the probability that the diner sold 50 or more breakfast meals and *at least* 6 pancake meals given that a day is randomly selected from all of the days marked in the scatterplot. Choice D is incorrect because $\frac{8}{9}$ is the probability of randomly selecting a day where *at least* 6 pancake meals were sold given that a day was randomly chosen from those days where 50 or more breakfast meals were sold.

QUESTION 18.

Choice A is correct. An absolute value measures the distance between to points regardless of direction. For example, $|4-7| = 3$. This tells us that the distance between 4 and 7 is 3. Therefore, if the cereal manufacturer wants to keep the weight of each cereal box between 9.5 and 12.5, the manufacturer wants to keep the weight of each box within 1.5 ounces of 11 ounces because $11-1.5 = 9.5$ and $11+1.5 = 12.5$. Therefore, since the distance between the weight of the box, x, and 11 ounces must be equal to 1.5 ounces, $|x-11| \leq 1.5$.

Choices B, C, and D are incorrect because all three absolute value equations have values of x that satisfy the equation that are not between 9.5 and 12.5.

QUESTION 19.

Choice C is correct. The formula of an average states that an average can be calculated by adding up the sum of all of the numbers in a set and dividing by how many numbers there are. In this case, adding up the average number of B's for the freshman, sophomore, junior, and senior respondents to the survey yields $8+6+2+12 = 28$. Dividing 28 by 4 yields $\frac{28}{4} = 7$. The average number of B's for the whole school is 7.

Choice A is incorrect because 1 is the approximate average number of D's to be expected from the whole school. Choice B is incorrect because 3 is the approximate average number of C's to be expected from the whole school. Choice D is incorrect because 9 is the approximate average number of A's to be expected from the whole school.

QUESTION 20.

Choice C is correct. Among the freshman respondents, the average number of C's is 3, the average number of D's is 1, and the average number of F's is 0. This is a total of $3+1+0 = 4$ total grades that are less than a B. If there are a total of 428 freshmen, the best estimate for the total number of grades lower than a B for the freshman class would be $428(4) = 1,712$, or approximately 1,700 grades below a B.

Choices A, B, and D are incorrect and may result from calculation errors.

QUESTION 21.

Choice D is correct. In a set of numbers, the mean is more strongly affected by outliers than the median. For example, in the set of numbers 2, 3, 4, 5, and 6, the median, or middle number, is 4. In addition, the mean, $\frac{2+3+4+5+6}{5}$, is also equivalent to 4. However, in the set of numbers 2, 3, 4, 5, and 16, the median stays the same, but the mean increases to $\frac{2+3+4+5+16}{5} = 6$. Therefore, if the mean is noticeably lower than the median, there must be a few numbers that are significantly lower than the rest of the numbers. So, most likely, there are a few students in the school who applied to 0 colleges.

Choices A, B, and C are incorrect. There is a chance that they could be true, yet they do not identify outliers that can explain why the mean is lower than the median.

QUESTION 22.

Choice D is correct. In order to find the area of the circle from the equation of the circle, one must first complete the square in the equation $x^2 + 8x + y^2 = 20$. Dividing the 8 by 2 and squaring the result yields 16, which must be added to the left-hand side of the equation and also subtracted from the left-hand side of the equation in order to have the equation remain the same. Therefore, adding 16 and subtracting 16 from the left-hand side of the equation yields $(x^2 + 8x + 16) + y^2 - 16 = 20$. Factoring the expression $x^2 + 8x + 16$ yields $(x+4)^2 + y^2 - 16 = 20$ and adding 16 to both sides yields $(x+4)^2 + y^2 = 36$. The formula for the equation of a circle is $(x-h)^2 + (y-k)^2 = r^2$, where (h,k) is the center of the circle and r is the radius of the circle. The equation $(x+4)^2 + y^2 = 36$ can be written in the form $(x+4)^2 + (y-0)^2 = 36$, where the 36 is equivalent to r^2. Therefore, being that the area of a circle is equivalent to πr^2, the area of the circle defined by the equation $x^2 + 8x + y^2 = 20$ is 36π.

Choices A, C, and D are incorrect and may result from errors in correctly completing the square and/or errors in calculating the radius of the circle. For example, Choice A is incorrect because if one were to incorrectly complete the square as $x^2 + 8x - 16$, one would then subtract 16 from both sides of the equation, thus yielding an area of 4π, not 36π.

QUESTION 23.

Choice A is correct. Multiplying both sides of the equation $F = k\dfrac{Q_1 Q_2}{r^2}$ by r^2 yields $Fr^2 = kQ_1 Q_2$. Dividing both sides by F yields $r^2 = \dfrac{kQ_1 Q_2}{F}$. Finally, taking the square root of both sides reveals the answer, $r = \sqrt{\dfrac{kQ_1 Q_2}{F}}$.

Choices B, C, and D are incorrect because when solved for F, none of the answers are equivalent to $F = k\dfrac{Q_1 Q_2}{r^2}$.

QUESTION 24.

Choice C is correct. If the distance between the two charges is doubled, then the radius is doubled to $2r$. Substituting $2r$ for r in the equation $F = k\dfrac{Q_1 Q_2}{r^2}$ yields $F = k\dfrac{Q_1 Q_2}{(2r)^2} = k\dfrac{Q_1 Q_2}{4r^2}$, or $F = \dfrac{1}{4}k\dfrac{Q_1 Q_2}{r^2}$. Therefore, doubling the charges' distance apart reduces the force to $\dfrac{1}{4}$ of its strength. Multiplying 1 by $(1-r)$, where r is the percent of decay in decimal form, should yield the new value of $\frac{1}{4}$. Solving the equation $1(1-r)=\frac{1}{4}$ for r yields 0.75, or 75%. Therefore, if the distance between two charges is doubled, the force between the two charges is reduced by 75%.

Choice A is incorrect because 25%, or 0.25 in decimal form, is the decay factor by which the force between two charges is multiplied if the distance between the charges is doubled. Choices B and D are incorrect and may result from calculation errors when solving for the decay percentage.

QUESTION 25.

Choice D is correct. Looking at the graph of $g(x)$, tracing up from -8 to a y-value of 2 reveals that the value of $g(-8)$ is 2. The number of values of x where $g(x)$ is equivalent $g(-8)$ is equivalent to the number of times that the graph of the function $g(x)$ intersects the horizontal line $y=2$. After visualizing or sketching the line $y=2$, one can see that the function $g(x)$ intersects this line at 3 distinct points.

Choices A, B, and C are incorrect and may result from a misunderstanding of finding x- and y-values in function notation.

QUESTION 26.

Choice B is correct. Setting $2x+2$ equal to 6 yields $2x+2=6$. Subtracting 2 from both sides of the equation yields $2x=4$ and dividing both sides by 2 yields $x=2$.

Setting $-x-1$ equal to $\frac{1}{2}x-4$ yields $-x-1=\frac{1}{2}x-4$. Adding x to both sides of the equation yields $-1=\frac{3}{2}x-4$ and adding 4 to both sides yields $3=\frac{3}{2}x$. Multiplying both sides of the equation by $\frac{2}{3}$ reveals that $x=2$. Any line that goes through two different points with the same x-value is a vertical line and all vertical lines have an infinite slope.

Therefore, the slope is undefined.

Choice A is incorrect because if the line that goes through the two points has a slope of zero, the two points would have a common y-value, not a common x-value. Choices C and D are incorrect because the two points have a common x-value and if there is no change in the x-value, there is no chance for a positive or negative slope.

QUESTION 27.

Choice C is correct. Setting $2b+1$ equal to x^3+8b yields $2b+1=x^3+8b$. Subtracting $8b$ from both sides yields $-6b+1=x^3$. Therefore, $-6b+1$ must be equivalent to a perfect cube. Substituting $\frac{14}{3}$ for b in the expression $-6b+1$ yields $-6(\frac{14}{3})+1$. Simplifying yields $-2(14)+1=-27$. Since -27 is a perfect cube, if b is equivalent to

416

$\dfrac{14}{3}$, then the system of equations has one solution.

Choices A, B, and D are incorrect because substituting any of these values for b in the system of equations yields a non-integer value of x.

QUESTION 28.

Choice B is correct. Substituting 1 for x in the equation $R = 240(0.5)^x$ yields $R = 240(0.5) = 120$ and substituting 1 for x in the equation $R = -35x + 155$ yields $R = -35 + 155 = 120$ as well. Substituting 4 for x in the equation $R = 240(0.5)^x$ yields $R = 240(0.5)^4 = 240(0.0625) = 15$ and substituting 4 for x in the equation $R = -35x + 155$ yields $R = -35(4) + 155 = -140 + 155 = 15$ as well. Therefore, the exponential decay model and the linear model have the same outcome after 1 year has passed and 4 years have passed. Substituting 2 for x in both equations yields $R = 240(0.5)^2 = 60$ for the exponential decay model and $R = -35(2) + 155 = 85$ for the linear decay model. Therefore, the exponential decay model, or model that the organic matter follows, is less than the linear model, or model the inorganic matter follows, between 1 and 4. Therefore, the mass of the organic matter is less than the mass of the inorganic matter for $4 - 1 = 3$ years.

Choices A, C, and D are incorrect and may result from calculation errors while substituting into both the exponential decay model and the linear decay model.

QUESTION 29.

Choice B is correct. If the measure of the largest angle in the isosceles triangle is x, then given the facts that all of the angles in an equilateral triangle measure 60 degrees and that all of the angles in a square measure 90 degrees, $x + 90 + 60 + 90 = 360$. Simplifying yields an x-value of 120 degrees. Cutting this isosceles triangle in half through the 120° angle yields two 30-60-90 triangles that have hypotenuses that have the same length as the side of the square. Repositioning the longest legs of these two 30-60-90 triangles adjacent to each other yields a single triangle with 3 sides that measure the same length as the side length of the squares. Since the original equilateral triangle has an area of $13\sqrt{3}$ and has sides that measure the same length as the sides of the squares, then the isosceles triangle must also have an area that measures $13\sqrt{3}$. Therefore, A is equivalent to 13.

Choices A, C, and D are incorrect and may result from errors in incorrectly assuming similarity or not fully understand the rules of special right triangles, mainly the 30-60-90 right triangle side length relationship. For example, Choice C is incorrect and may result from assuming that the area of the isosceles triangle is double that of the equilateral triangle since the equilateral triangle has angles that measure 60 degrees and the isosceles triangle has an angle that measures 120 degrees.

QUESTION 30.

Choice A is correct. If the line that goes through two non-adjacent vertices of a square has the equation $y = -3x + 2$, the line that goes through the other two non-adjacent vertices has a slope that is the negative reciprocal of -3, or $\frac{1}{3}$. Therefore, the slope of line r is $\frac{1}{3}$ and line r has the form $y = \frac{1}{3}x + b$. Substituting 3 for x and 5 for y yields $5 = \frac{1}{3}(3) + b$. Simplifying yields $5 = 1 + b$, or $b = 4$. Therefore, the y-intercept of Line r is 4.

Choice B, C, and D are incorrect and may result from a calculation error and/or a misunderstanding of the relationship between parallel and perpendicular lines as well as the relationship between the diagonals of a square.

QUESTION 31.

The correct answer is 5. One can use the exponential growth formula to create the inequality $31,250(2)^x = 1,000,000$. However, this equation requires logarithmic rules to solve. Since the number 31,250 is quite large to begin with, it may be easier for one to simply double the value of 31,250 as many times as it takes to reach 1,000,000:

1 - $31,250(2) = 62,500$
2 - $62,500(2) = 125,000$
3 - $125,000(2) = 250,000$
4 - $250,000(2) = 500,000$
5 - $500,000(2) = 1,000,000$

Therefore, five years will pass before the population of bees reaches 1,000,000.

QUESTION 32.

The correct answer is 381. If a ladder measures 12 feet 6 inches in length, multiplying 12 by 12 and adding 6 yields the ladder's length in inches, $12(12) + 6 = 150$ inches. If one inch is equivalent to 2.54 centimeters, then multiplying 150 by 2.54 yields the length of the ladder in centimeters, $150(2.54) = 381$ centimeters.

QUESTION 33.

The correct answer is 400. Substituting 8 for h in the equation $C(x) = 125 + 50mh$ yields $C(x) = 125 + 50m(8)$, or $C(x) = 125 + 400m$. The linear equation $C(x) = 125 + 400m$ has a slope of 400, which represents a positive change of \$400 for every additional man who works the job. Therefore, the client's estimated price per additional man is \$400.

QUESTION 34.

The correct answer is 0. Make x the number of hours that Angel logged at the woodworking residency. If Sebastian logged 204 hours less than four times the number of hours that Angel logged, then Sebastian logged $4x - 204$ hours at the woodworking residency. If the two men logged a total of 136 hours at the woodworking residency then $x + 4x - 204 = 136$. Combining like terms yields $5x - 204 = 136$ and adding 204 to both sides of the equation yields $5x = 340$. Dividing by 5 reveals the number of hours that Angel logged at the woodworking residency, $x = 68$ hours. Substituting 68 into the equation $4x - 204$ reveals Sebastians hours logged as $4(68) - 204 = 68$ hours. Therefore, the number of additional hours that Angel logged over Sebastian was $68 - 68 = 0$ hours.

QUESTION 35.

The correct answer is .125 or $\frac{1}{8}$. Substituting -3 for x, a for y, and $-\frac{1}{4}$ for c in the equation $y = ax^2 + 2ax + c$ yields $a = a(-3)^2 + 2a(-3) + (-\frac{1}{4})$. Simplifying yields $a = 9a - 6a - \frac{1}{4}$. Combining like terms yields $a = 3a - \frac{1}{4}$ and subtracting $3a$ from both sides yields $-2a = -\frac{1}{4}$. Finally, dividing both sides of the equation by -2 yields $a = \frac{1}{8}$.

QUESTION 36.

The correct answer is 32. Area is equivalent to πr^2 and if the area of circle O is 64π, then $r^2 = 64$, or $r = 8$. If the radius of circle O is 8, then the circumference, using the formula $2\pi r$, is equivalent to $2\pi(8) = 16\pi$. If the length of $\overset{\frown}{RS}$ is 4π and the circumference of circle O is 16π, then $\angle ROS$ is $\frac{1}{4}$ of $360°$, or $\frac{1}{4}(360°) = 90°$. Therefore, $\triangle RSO$ is an isosceles right triangle with two sides of the same length as the radius, 8. Using the formula for the area of a triangle, $\frac{1}{2}bh$, where the base and the height of the isosceles right triangle are both 8, yields $\frac{1}{2}(8)(8) = 32$.

QUESTION 37.

The correct answer is 3. If the first term of the sequence is equivalent to 3, substituting 1 for n and 3 for A_n in the equation $A_n = d(1 + n(n-1))$ yields $3 = d(1 + 1(1-1))$ which is equivalent to $3 = d(1 + 1(0))$, or $d = 3$.

QUESTION 38.

The correct answer is 24. Substituting k for n, 3 for d, and 1659 for A_n in the equation $A_n = d(1 + n(n-1))$ yields $1659 = 3(1 + k(k-1))$ and dividing both sides of the equation by 3 yields $553 = 1 + k(k-1)$. Subtracting 1 from both sides of the equation yields $552 = k(k-1)$ and expanding the expression $k(k-1)$ yields $552 = k^2 - k$. Subtracting 552 from both sides gives $0 = k^2 - k - 552$ and factoring the expression $k^2 - k + 552$ yields $0 = (k-24)(k+23)$ which reveals the roots, 24 and -23. Since k is the number of terms, k must be positive. Therefore, k is 24.